MICHAEL
GOLD

SUNY SERIES IN CONTEMPORARY JEWISH LITERATURE AND CULTURE

EZRA CAPPELL, EDITOR

Dan Shiffman, *College Bound:*
The Pursuit of Education in Jewish American Literature, 1896–1944

Eric J. Sundquist, editor, *Writing in Witness:*
A Holocaust Reader

Noam Pines, *The Infrahuman: Animality in Modern Jewish Literature*

Oded Nir, *Signatures of Struggle:*
The Figuration of Collectivity in Israeli Fiction

Zohar Weiman-Kelman, *Queer Expectations:*
A Genealogy of Jewish Women's Poetry

Richard J. Fein, translator, *The Full Pomegranate:*
Poems of Avrom Sutzkever

Victoria Aarons and Holli Levitsky, editors,
New Directions in Jewish American and
Holocaust Literatures: Reading and Teaching

Jennifer Cazenave, *An Archive of the Catastrophe:*
The Unused Footage of Claude Lanzmann's Shoah

Ruthie Abeliovich, *Possessed Voices:*
Aural Remains from Modernist Hebrew Theater

Victoria Nesfield and Philip Smith, editors,
The Struggle for Understanding: Elie Wiesel's Literary Works

Ezra Cappell and Jessica Lang, editors,
Off the Derech: Leaving Orthodox Judaism

Nancy E. Berg and Naomi B. Sokoloff, editors,
Since 1948: Israeli Literature in the Making

Patrick Chura, *Michael Gold: The People's Writer*

MICHAEL GOLD

The People's Writer

PATRICK CHURA

Cover image: Photograph of Michael Gold among a Large Group of Attendees after a Lecture, July 16, 1939. © Aaron Granich. *Source:* Granich family.

Published by State University of New York Press, Albany

For information, contact State University of New York Press, Albany, NY
www.sunypress.edu

Library of Congress Cataloging-in-Publication Data

Name: Chura, Patrick, 1964– author.
Title: Michael Gold : the people's writer / Patrick Chura.
Description: Albany : State University of New York Press, [2020] | Series: SUNY series in contemporary Jewish literature and culture | Includes bibliographical references and index.
Identifiers: LCCN 2020009142 | ISBN 9781438480978 (hardcover : alk. paper) | ISBN 9781438480985 (pbk. : alk. paper) | ISBN9781438480992 (ebook)
Subjects: LCSH: Gold, Michael, 1893–1967. | Authors, American—20th century—Biography.
Classification: LCC PS3513.O29 Z64 2020 | DDC 818/.5209 [B]—dc23
LC record available at https://lccn.loc.gov/2020009142

10 9 8 7 6 5 4 3 2 1

CONTENTS

ILLUSTRATIONS

ACKNOWLEDGMENTS

I would like to thank Nicholas and Carl Granich for sharing their personal recollections in multiple phone interviews. I owe double thanks to Nick Granich for welcoming me into his San Francisco home in June 2017, a visit I will always remember. I am also indebted to Aaron Granich and Reuben Granich for their friendly support and advice.

For immeasurable help including erudite advice and assistance, I would like to thank Alan Wald at the University of Michigan. For interviews, extended correspondence, and encouragement, I owe a debt of gratitude to Marcia Folsom.

Thanks go to Professors Robbie Lieberman and David Roessel for sharing their knowledge.

I am grateful also to the many who provided research assistance, including, most of all, Julie Herrada at the Labadie Special Collections Library at Michigan and Don Appleby with Caitlin Noussas at the University of Akron Bierce Library. My students at the University of Akron challenged my thinking and contributed many insights about Michael Gold. I would also like to thank production editor Jenn Bennett-Genthner and acquisitions editor Rafael Chaiken at SUNY Press.

Introduction

The People's Writer

As a novelist, essayist, playwright, poet, journalist, and editor, Michael Gold was the leading advocate of leftist, "proletarian" literature in the United States between the world wars. His acclaimed autobiographical novel of 1930, *Jews without Money*, is a vivid and historically important account of early-twentieth-century Jewish immigrant life in the tenements of Manhattan's Lower East Side. *Jews without Money* earned enthusiastic reviews and reached a wide audience, going through eleven printings in 1930 alone. In that year, Sinclair Lewis praised the novel in his Nobel Prize acceptance speech, crediting Gold with revealing "the new frontier of the Jewish East Side."[1]

During the 1930s Michael Gold became a national figure—the most famous Communist writer in America—as editor of the radical journal *New Masses* and columnist for the American Communist Party's *Daily Worker*. In a decade when many American artists explored poverty and took Marxist-influenced positions, Gold was the acknowledged leader among class-conscious writers. With his fiction, poems, and plays, along with hundreds of impassioned columns under the title *Change the World*, he staked a claim to being the originating force of the once-mighty movement for a workers' literature.

While the context of the "red decade" elevated Michael Gold, a second historical factor—the end of the Depression and the onset of World War II—had the opposite effect, marginalizing him as a cultural figure and destabilizing his career. After Stalin's murderous show trials of 1936–1938 and the Nazi-Soviet Nonaggression Pact of 1939, leftist writers and critics began to repudiate their Communist ties, but Gold remained firmly in the

1

Soviet camp, becoming by default a "critical hatchet man": the unofficial gatekeeper of the American Communist Party's rigid artistic standards.

The consequences of this role were apparent in *The Hollow Men*, a collection of *Daily Worker* columns that Gold expanded for publication in 1941. Never one to suppress his political passions, Gold excoriated the literary establishment and a cadre of famous writers who had once been his friends. Though these "literary renegades" had become critical of the Party and the USSR due to specific acts of Joseph Stalin, Gold equated their defection with a general abandonment of the exploited working classes.

Underneath it all, there was another factor that angered Gold. The proletarian spirit of the Depression decade, a spirit deeply infused with Marxism and impossible without it, was by 1940 being disparaged in literary circles. As major writers disavowed their allegiances, they rejected also the great people's culture of the 1930s, which Gold, arguably more than anyone, had helped create. In his view, the bourgeois apostates were denying democratic principles and preparing the way for fascism as World War II approached.

When McCarthyism took hold of the United States in 1950, Gold was living in France, where he had relocated in part because he foresaw the persecutions of the Cold War. But he returned to the United States in time to face the worst of the anti-Communist hysteria. With the Party under relentless attack, Gold was blacklisted, eventually losing even his low-paid newspaper work. Living on the brink of poverty, he took on menial jobs to support his family. Early in his career, the roster of Gold's professional allies had included Ernest Hemingway, John Dos Passos, and Eugene O'Neill, but in the McCarthy era he embraced and drew strength from a different circle, which included figures like Richard Wright, W. E. B. DuBois, Dorothy Day, Pete Seeger, and Paul Robeson. Everyone in the first group had abandoned the Left to the tune of Nobel Prizes or election to the American Academy of Arts and Letters. Everyone in the second group had remained radical and experienced arrest, blacklisting, exile, harassment, and in some cases indictment.

An unsuccessful national speaking tour in 1954 made it clear that the audience for Gold's work was dwindling, though he was now followed closely by J. Edgar Hoover's FBI. Through the 1950s he kept up correspondence with fellow dissidents, but the people's movement he'd once led was in disarray, clearly outstripped by the disasters of a reactionary time. Though Michael Gold had been "among the cultural luminaries of his generation,"[2] by midcentury he was an outcast, his life's work, and his politics, generally disregarded or disparaged.

This was the situation in 1966, when Michael Brewster Folsom, then a graduate student at the University of California–Berkeley, initiated a new and still relevant conversation about Gold's importance to US literary history. Folsom, reviewing for the *Nation* a mistake-plagued reprint edition of Gold's only novel, declared that "no literary achievement of the 1930s has suffered more from the obscurity and calumny which a frightened generation has heaped on that decade than Michael Gold's *Jews without Money*."[3] Folsom alleged that the novel had not been forgotten but "erased," and for a single, telling reason: its author remained a Communist (and a public figure) long after that ceased to be fashionable.

Bolstering this claim was the edition Folsom was reviewing, which, like a previous reprint issued in the McCarthy era, had omitted the novel's final paragraphs, a passage that describes the main character's conversion to socialism and constitutes the book's central argument. In Folsom's view, the textual corruption produced the exact opposite of Gold's intention, and did so in a way that symbolized the participation of the literary establishment in "the expurgation of radical opinion from American political life." The remedy Folsom proposed was not only to restore Gold's text and recognize the novel as a powerful work but to canonize it: "*Jews without Money* belongs in an undergraduate course in 20th-century American literature, for it is a work of literary art with an imagination and style of its own."[4]

Michael Folsom knew something about how radical literature could be systematically marginalized. Just after his enrollment in Berkeley's PhD program as a twenty-five-year-old in 1963, he proposed to write his dissertation on Michael Gold. Folsom's proposal was rejected by English Department chair Henry Nash Smith, a renowned scholar of culture studies and cofounder of the American Studies discipline, on the grounds that Gold was not a significant writer and "had not written enough of any consequence."[5]

To reach such conclusions, Smith had to either be unaware of the extent of Gold's work, or view that work as artistically inferior, or harbor a bias against it, or a combination of all three. It's likely that Smith quietly ascribed to views held generally in the academy that Communist art was crude and formulaic and that in promoting such art, Gold had once been the chief figure in a conspiracy against "real" literature. Professor Smith already had a reputation for rigidity; behind his back the doctoral students dubbed him "Henry Gnash Myths," a wry comment on his resistance to their ideas. Though Folsom argued his case, calling attention to Gold's achievements and alluding to the fact that the aging leftist author was living just across the Bay Bridge in San Francisco, the answer was still no.

After his intended topic was denied, a typical graduate student would have decided for practical reasons to forget about it for the duration of a rigorous doctoral program. But Folsom was deeply committed to the writer he'd later refer to as "the pariah of American letters." He ended up carrying a double burden of research toward an acceptable dissertation (he was allowed to write on Edward Bellamy, Upton Sinclair, and Jack London), while dedicating himself also to almost fanatical work on a full-scale Gold biography, becoming Gold's personal friend and recording long interviews with him in 1965–1966. That biography was never completed, and the dual focus imposed on Folsom delayed and nearly sank his dissertation project as well. Both circumstances were due in large part to the lack of imagination, tinged with elitism, of the Berkeley English Department.

Folsom's devotion to Gold endured for a decade, during which he produced scholarly articles and chapters, contributed an eloquent Gold obituary to the *National Guardian*, and even worked briefly to promote a film version of *Jews without Money* that never materialized. Finally, in 1972, he contracted with International Publishers (a Communist-affiliated press) to reissue a selection of Gold's writings under the title *Mike Gold: A Literary Anthology*. This sizable project, undertaken while Folsom was a newly hired assistant professor at Massachusetts Institute of Technology, was not enough to win him tenure there. Nevertheless Folsom was well satisfied with the book, seeing it as a valedictory tribute and culmination of his long recovery work, which came to a standstill soon afterward.

In the early 1980s, while teaching at Brandeis and pursuing a range of successful projects on New England history, Folsom's career was curtailed by serious health issues. In spite of this, he continued to respond with generous encouragement to scholars young and old who wrote to him for advice and assistance with research on the author of *Jews without Money*. Until he died in 1990 at age fifty-two, Michael Folsom did more than anyone to counteract and repair Mike Gold's elimination from twentieth-century literary history.

One of the researchers Folsom corresponded with in the 1970s was Alan Wald, a doctoral student and radical activist who shared Folsom's passionate interest in leftist history and a desire to revive awareness of Gold's important life. After Folsom's death, Wald communicated with his widow, Marcia, and with members of Mike Gold's family to arrange the permanent transfer of Folsom's research files and manuscripts to the Special Collections Library at the University of Michigan.

Wald, now a retired emeritus professor at Michigan, is at this writing the most knowledgeable expert on the history of the literary Left in North America. In 2002, he published the authoritative biographical chapter, "Inventing Mike Gold," in his ground-breaking study, *Exiles from a Future Time*. This chapter, which built on Folsom's work but was enhanced by meticulous archival research and new interviews, has been the best and most reliable starting point for all serious study of Mike Gold for almost twenty years. Any Gold biography, including this one, would be impossible without the previous efforts of Folsom and Wald.

The work of John Pyros is also worth mentioning. In the mid-1970s Pyros contracted with Twayne Publishers to produce a book on Gold for the Twayne's U.S. Authors series. He and the publisher had disagreements that delayed the project and the press eventually rescinded his contract, explaining that the Communist author did not warrant a biography. "Our policy is to assign studies on significant American writers who have established reputations," wrote the editors; "unfortunately, we do not believe that Gold has attracted sufficient critical or popular attention."[6] Pyros ended up self-publishing a manuscript, brave in its promotion of Gold, that is far from definitive but remains a valuable resource. The fact that until now there has been no real biography of Gold supports Wald's claim that his influence and reputation have yet to be fully assessed.

Though there has been a resurgence of interest in *Jews without Money* since the end of the Cold War, with more than thirty-five journal articles and book chapters published on various aspects of the novel since 1990, other phases of Gold's career await treatment, and one can still find signs that old animosities linger. Alfred Kazin's 1996 introduction to the most recent Carrol & Graf edition of *Jews without Money* insulted the author, calling Gold "a monumentally injured soul but clearly not very bright."[7] In this Kazin echoed Paul Berman's 1983 account of Gold's life in the *Village Voice*, which felt it necessary to remind readers in its first paragraph that Gold "was no genius."[8]

Equally puzzling and demonstrably inaccurate is the once widely held notion that Gold was unproductive as a writer. A famous novel, four full-length plays and several one-acts, two anthologies of journalism, two collections of short stories, and a book of literary commentary in themselves add up to a respectable published output. What is usually forgotten or discounted is that from 1914 to 1966 Gold also contributed over a thousand pieces—stories, poems, plays, reviews, and investigative reporting in addition to his regular column—to more than a dozen literary magazines and commercial newspapers. Defining Gold as insufficiently accomplished as a writer requires a willful dismissal of a vast body of work.

However much he wrote that is still of value, it's nevertheless true that Gold was never quite the artist he wished to be. This was because he forever served two masters: writing and social activism. He wanted to write more novels and plays, but helping strikes, protesting against war and fascism, working for the Unemployed Councils, walking in hunger marches and May Day parades, getting arrested for Sacco and Vanzetti, raising money for workers' cooperatives and to keep the *Daily Worker* alive, demonstrating for fair housing for Chicago blacks, for the Rosenbergs, for civil rights, and against the H-Bomb took time and other resources. And for fifty years, Gold's professional energies were given over to a poorly paid grind of daily politically charged journalism that won him an adoring national following and did, in fact, *change the world*, but also sapped his literary creativity.

When he died in 1967, Gold left behind a trove of literary false starts and unfinished manuscripts, including large sections of a memoir he'd been working on for more than a year. He also left a number of finished but unpublished manuscripts that have literary-historical value at this cultural moment. For example it would seem a good time to revisit and learn from *The Honorable Pete*, a drama about New York City Communist councilman Pete Cacchione. This never-performed play offers realistic treatments of the early 1930s hunger marches, the work of the Unemployment Councils, and the brutal 1932 attack by General Douglas Macarthur on the Bonus Marchers in the nation's capital. A second previously unknown play, *Song for Roosevelt*, depicts the rarely studied surge in hate crimes and anti-Semitic violence in 1940s New York while issuing guidelines and a call to collective action against fascism in the United States.

A definitive Gold biography is something that should have happened long ago. The handful of abortive attempts that have been made at such a book prompted one well-informed literary scholar, a Gold enthusiast, to half-jokingly warn that the subject was cursed. If this is true, it seems certain that the curse has been due in part to a difficulty faced by all biographers but perhaps unusually stark here: that of reconciling the subject's contradictions to reveal the person, in this case the first surviving child of Charles and Katie Granich, born Itzhok Isaak Granich. In his adult life Gold himself, despite his personal bravery, struggled mightily with questions of identity. Gold's children called him Mike Gold but kept the Granich last name, as did his wife, Elizabeth. The medical diabetes card he carried for the last twenty-five years of his life bore the name "Michael Granich." These clues are only symbolic of course, but as New Masses poet and critic Stanley Burnham once accurately deduced, Mike Gold "suffered from being a bundle of selves."[9]

In preparing this book I've searched for the right way of presenting a life of great activity by a public figure known for warmth, kindness and openness who could also be unpredictable, emotionally distant and self-involved and who was capable of displaying shocking lapses in empathy. Among the selves and moods Burnham alluded to, there were stunning inconsistencies. It is one thing for Gold to have attacked the "literary renegades" when they switched political sides, but he could show harshness also toward friends, lifelong Communists on his own side of the political divide, who had treated him with good will.

John Howard Lawson, for example, reacted with shock and near disbelief to a drama review in the April 10, 1934, New Masses, in which Gold stated that the "great hopes" for Lawson's career had "gone unfulfilled" because the playwright was full of "adolescent self-pity," had "learned nothing," and was "lost like Hamlet." Lawson's plays, Gold wrote, "projected his own confused mind on the screen of history."[10] Joseph Freeman and Albert Maltz endured similar stinging insults, and though Gold eventually apologized to these friends, it is unlikely that the harm was completely erased.

In this biography I do not ignore such episodes or the questions they raise, but my focus is generally elsewhere. My goal is to present a large amount of new biographical information in a clear and synthesized narrative while maintaining a balanced perspective on the subject's personal and literary life. A biography should work to uncover and convey something of the best spirit of its subject while not being blind to flaws.

The People's Writer is also not significantly a book about political or aesthetic theory, nor does it treat internal Communist Party politics or Gold's relationships with fellow Communists in depth. As I understand Gold, he was primarily a writer and reserved his deepest passions for that activist mission. It was widely known that he was uninterested in political minutiae, and his many deep friendships were not made at Party meetings.

Some Cold War–era historians and academics found it difficult to forgive Gold his views, much less understand them, and this was likely a factor inhibiting the publication of critical-biographical work dedicated to him. But much has changed in the nearly thirty years since the Cold War ended, perhaps making it somewhat easier to both distinguish Gold's personality from his politics and make fairer judgments about the type of activists US Communists really were. If we realize, as we should, that Gold was dead wrong about the exculpatory versions of Stalin's brutality he accepted and circulated, we should also recognize that American Communists were not guilty of such brutalities and were, in fact, collectively a peaceful, democratic, and consistently progressive force for good in US social history. Gold's legacy is a brilliant example, offering clear lessons about the means and methods of defeating racism, anti-Semitism, fascism and xenophobia, lessons that can help us survive these fearful times and break the cycle of terror and hate worldwide.

In consideration of these factors, this biography rests also on the premise that there is significance and inherent value *for today* in a book-length treatment of Gold's struggles as a radical writer. Having myself discovered the full range and impact of Gold's career fairly late, I vouch for the efficacy of internalizing his story, believing that there's much to learn from his oppositional life, lived so as to insistently question hierarchies while challenging tradition, the status quo, received assumptions, and the injustice they perpetuate.

A few words about the book's biographical content. In piecing together the facts of Gold's development, I've relied on the efforts of previous researchers supplemented by my own interviews and many hours of archival work. Some events are rendered using a level of detail that could prompt questions about how they were constructed. How do I know, for example, the exact steps of the process Gold and his brothers used to make suspender fasteners in 1903? How do I know that, while living in a chateau in rural France in summer 1948, Gold's sons fished from a surrounding moat by dropping a baited line out their bedroom window?

Much of the detail comes from phone and in-person discussions with Gold's sons Nick and Carl, now eighty-four and eighty years old, respectively, who generously shared memories of their family life during the 1940s and 1950s in New York and France. Concerning Gold's early childhood in the Lower East Side Jewish ghetto, I use new facts and anecdotes from a series of oral history interviews recorded by Gold's younger brother Manny in the early 1980s. These conversations were meant to become the basis of Manny's memoirs but remain unpublished. The transcript of the interview tapes, which runs to over 600 pages, is held in the Wagner Labor Archives of New York University's Tamiment Library.

Gold's own unpublished memoirs, consisting largely of monologues recorded in the last two years of his life and transcribed by Elizabeth Granich, were accessed in the Gold-Folsom Papers at Michigan and also helpful. Additionally, Gold's unfinished work manuscripts, scattered over several decades, contain many pages of personal writings that have yet to be fully organized and interpreted. Looking through these papers, one finds scribbled fragments of poetry, drafts of plays, and undated pages of descriptive prose about events like Gold's first trip to Russia or conditions he encountered while accompanying hunger marches in the early 1930s. The autobiographical notes that begin chapter 8 of this book exemplify my use of such fragmentary material, in this case to provide insight into Gold's domestic life under McCarthyism. There are more such artifacts in the fourteen boxes held in Ann Arbor at the University of Michigan Special Collections.

Another largely untapped source of information about Gold's life and habits lies in the hundreds of *Change the World* columns he wrote for the *Daily Worker* and later for the *San Francisco People's World*. A book much longer than this one could be stitched together from excerpts and passages in these columns. I have used the articles selectively for certain biographical anecdotes. Of special value are the 1959 *People's World* columns that were collected by Folsom under the title, *A Jewish Childhood in the New York Slums*, a series Gold referred to as a "sequel" to *Jews without Money*.

Gold's FBI surveillance file, a resource tapped also by Folsom and Alan Wald, occasionally offers insights that are unavailable elsewhere. The summary file compiled at the Washington, DC, headquarters of the FBI has long been available to scholars. In this biography, however, I also use newly declassified material not previously accessed. In particular I am grateful to John Perosio at the National Archives in College Park, Maryland, for declassifying, at my request, the Gold file compiled by the Detroit FBI Field Office from 1950 to 1956.

There is, of course, much more for future researchers to discover, but I hope these sources together make for an accurate and satisfying narration. In some passages I've felt confident enough to speculate about what Gold may have been thinking at certain moments. These interpretive liberties are based on my best conjecture after long study of Gold's world and work.

It's worth stating also that the writing of a scholarly book about Mike Gold comprises a challenge and a bit of a paradox. In 1914 Gold attended Harvard for a couple of months; ever afterward he was suspicious of the purists and professors, the "book-proud intellectuals" and smug arbiters of literary taste. He had a point. It was sometimes the academics who dismissed Gold and decided he was not a real artist. He missed few opportunities to push back against the ivory tower. "Literature is one of the products of civilization like steel or textiles," Gold wrote in 1929, "it is not any more mystic in its origin than a ham sandwich."[11] He exhorted young workers to "Write. Persist. Struggle," and advised them that the way to make literature was simply to tell about their lives in plain terms, "in the same language you use in writing a letter."[12] Clearly, a Gold biography written in a pedantic style would be wrong on many levels.

For related reasons it's fitting that one of the best portraits of Gold that I encountered in my work came from a professor of music and folklore studies who eventually gave up his academic job to become a social worker and union leader. Richard A. Reuss, author of the 2000 study *American Folk Music and Left-Wing Politics,* seems to have distilled Gold's character with understanding and precision. In chapter 6 I trace Gold's substantial role as a theorist of American leftist folk music, relying on Reuss among a handful of music scholars to tell the story. For now I want to close this introduction by sharing and enlarging on Reuss's insights to suggest or establish a few basic things about the personality of my subject.

"Michael Gold, a self-appointed critic of cultural affairs in the Communist movement for half a century, was a dynamic and controversial personality who stirred strong admiration or antipathy in those who came in contact with him."[13] The antipathy Reuss noted here was most often the direct product of Gold's firmly held leftist beliefs and the hostility he brought to bear against defectors or apostates. Even those who loved Gold knew that there could be no compromise about certain core convictions. As his lifelong friend Dorothy Day explained, he "would not hear" criticisms of the Soviet Union. Alan Wald has noted that Gold should be understood as a hard-core "campist." He unwaveringly chose the Soviet camp as fanatically as figures like Max Eastman and John Dos Passos eventually chose the "Western" (capitalist) camp. The Cold War exacerbated these long disputes, which left Gold isolated and largely silenced for most of his later career.

Reuss continues: "He became a radical in 1914, and from then until his death in 1967 devoted most of his energy to filling newspaper and magazine columns on nearly every phase of art and its place in society."[14] This is perceptive in two ways. First, where literary culture was concerned, Gold detested the notion of "art for art's sake." He rejected elitist or escapist works in favor of novels, stories, plays, and poetry that directly addressed contentious social issues. Second, Reuss refers to the question of how Gold spent his great but not limitless energy. Hemingway and O'Neill, who knew Gold well in the 1930s, bemoaned his activist writing, stating publicly their belief that he could be a major artist if he would sublimate his political aims, eschew propaganda, and give his best energy to questions of literary craft. Though there was never a chance of this happening, any valuation of Gold as a writer—favorable or unfavorable—hinges on one's notions about the role of art in society.

Labor reporter Art Shields, who was close to Gold for four decades, argued that literary elites were simply "blind to the quality" of his friend's newspaper work. Shields pointed out that "Journalism becomes an art—a literary art—in the hands of masters like John Reed and Mike Gold," and that "many of Mike's admirers"—especially working-class admirers, who decidedly lacked status as literary tastemakers—"think some of his best writing is found in his *Change the World* columns."[15] The process of researching this book has largely won me over to Shields's view.

Though Reuss seems bemused by the idea that "Gold's unorthodox ideas often horrified Communist Party leaders,"[16] this claim is accurate. For example in February 1932 the *Daily Worker* reported on a recently held debate between Gold and Heywood Broun on the question of "Socialism versus Communism." The article pointed out that Gold was unprepared and added a warning that the idea that he spoke for the Party was dangerous and harmful. Gold knew and understood that he was frequently off-message where the Marxist doctrine was concerned, but it didn't silence him or especially bother him. Eventually he and the Party reached a rapprochement that excused him from branch meetings and policy making while allowing him to represent the Party in the role of what First Secretary Earl Brower termed its (unofficial) "poet." Gold's strength, along with his value to the Communist movement, stemmed from his ability to bridge gaps between people and policies, between committee decisions and the aspirations of the masses.

As Reuss concludes his sketch of Gold's salient traits, he observes that the author "hated the capitalist system with a furious intensity. On its witting or unwitting supporters he unleashed some of the most vitriolic attacks in the annals of Communist literature. At the same time, he was sincerely devoted to the great masses of American men and women laborers and translated his affection into warm, often humorous accounts of their struggles and triumphs." As Shields remembered, his friend and colleague "never pretended to be a Leninist scholar," but "Mike's heart beat with the working class" in a role he always fearlessly embraced, a writer for the people.[17] Although, as Reuss acknowledged, "many intellectuals regarded him as a romantic visionary or a fool, . . . his popularity with rank and file sympathizers was enormous, and his journalism was among the most widely read in the movement."[18]

On a national speaking tour in 1954, Gold visited Minnesota, the home state of leftist-feminist writer Meridel LeSueur, who welcomed her visitor from New York, chaired the meeting at which he spoke, and introduced him to local progressives afterward. The thoughts Gold recorded about this visit for *Masses & Mainstream* showed how far his artistic priorities had traveled in the direction away from the *mainstream* toward the *masses*. Scanning the Minnesota countryside though a dirty bus window at the age of sixty-one, Gold thought first of the state's famous and canonized writers, F. Scott Fitzgerald and Sinclair Lewis. He then discarded these establishment artists because, as he realized in surveying the northern landscape, they "simply never saw or described the region." In Gold's view, "they were as far from the basic life of its masses as the first-class passenger on some ocean liner is from the reality of engine room and fo'cs'le." Then Gold considered LeSueur, a fellow ostracized writer largely unknown outside her community and the narrowing circle of progressives, and chose LeSueur's native-born activist persona as "an example of what a people's writer should be." LeSueur was an inspiration, Gold explained, because she was "involved in the freedom struggles of her people today."[19]

The national tour Gold was then completing occurred at a low and despairing moment in the history of the American Communist Party. Yet there was no pessimism in Gold about either the present or the future. Art Shields, Gold's friend for forty-five years, considered this trait important, once stating in print that "the cynic and Mike were at two opposite poles."[20] Reuss, the discerning professor cum union organizer, never met Gold but likewise understood: "All his life, he retained a passionate love for genuine working-class culture, which he professed to see proliferating at almost every turn down the road."[21]

Chapter One

Tributes

The high point of Mike Gold's career as a writer and cultural figure was March 2, 1941, the day of a mass celebration held in his honor in New York City. On a chilly Sunday afternoon in early spring, a crowd of thirty-five hundred packed the Manhattan Center on West Thirty-Fourth Street in order to, as the *Daily Worker* put it, "pay tribute to Gold's 25-year record of activity on behalf of the people, and honor the contributions of the famous revolutionary writer."[1]

Among the organizers of the Mike Gold Anniversary Meeting was a roster of leftist notables that included Elizabeth Gurley Flynn, Joseph North, Benjamin Davis, Shirley Graham and Richard Wright, all of whom spoke with passion about the quintessential proletarian writer. There were congratulatory telegrams: from Pennsylvania coal miners and Spanish Civil War veterans, Communist Party officials, and a group of New York clothing workers who assured Gold, "Keep it up, we will follow."[2] For entertainment, renowned baritone Mordecai Bauman sang works by J. S. Bach along with Yiddish folk ballads, and a troupe of student actors from Columbia University performed "Ex-Comrade X," a dramatic sketch by *Daily Worker* reporter Alan Max. Written especially for the anniversary, the skit parodied the many American writers who, unlike Michael Gold, had deserted the Communist cause in the wake of the 1939 Nazi-Soviet Nonaggression Pact.

Considering its subject matter, the skit was well timed. International Publishers was honoring the day by shipping dozens of weighty boxes to Manhattan Center: the first copies of Gold's latest book, *The Hollow Men*, a daring denunciation of what Gold termed the "literary renegades"—the same ex-comrades attacked in Max's play. At a moment of division and uncertainty in the American Communist movement, the anniversary celebration became a political rally that affirmed what loyal leftists still had in common: scorn for defectors and love for Gold. The enthusiastic crowd bought up 2,600 copies of *The Hollow Men*, then waited in line for the author's signature. Before and after the celebration, the *Daily Worker* declared that Mike Gold's career to date had been "an epoch of tremendous importance in the history of America."[3] The star power apparent that March Sunday showed that this was not an exaggeration.

Though it had actually been not twenty-five but twenty-seven years since his first publication in the *Masses*, Gold himself was not yet fifty, and photos from the celebration bespoke an athletic, still youngish persona. That the architect of proletarian literature and author of *Jews without Money* had physically changed little was significant; his *constancy* as a cultural and political touchstone was the very thing that accounted for his fame and, perhaps, the spiritual need of his followers to reaffirm him. A child of the Jewish ghetto who rose to popular success without denying his lowly origins, Gold embodied a familiar past and attested to a working-class future. Art Young's congratulatory note termed the proletarian hero "a natural boy of the people among those in poverty or fear of poverty, which is the vast majority of the human race."[4]

But tributes to careers inevitably imply endings of careers, a truth that must have somewhat diluted the meeting's festive mood. As they honored Gold, his acolytes could not have been unaware of an epochal shift, the evidence for which was all around. The Nazi-Soviet pact had shocked the world and prompted a mass exodus of American leftists who were appalled at Stalin's alliance with the fascist enemy. Another alliance, the once-broad Popular Front of antifascist liberals, progressives, and Soviet sympathizers, had unraveled, and new memberships in the Communist Party were down sharply. Since 1939, the House Un-American Activities Committee (HUAC), led by Texas Democrat Martin Dies, had been actively investigating the Communist International. In June 1940, Congress passed the Smith Act, which proscribed affiliations with revolutionary organizations in language crafted specifically to help the judicial branch indict Communists and deport labor leaders.

Since then, Franklin Roosevelt's deepening partnership with Great Britain clearly presaged eventual US participation in the European war, a factor that forced steadfastly peace-loving progressives to oppose a president they had once venerated. Gold's columns in the *Daily Worker*

Figure 1.1. Michael Gold with son Carl, c. 1942. *Source:* Granich family.

warned that "our leaders in Washington have no love for their people. They scheme and plot to thrust us into another war."[5] On the very morning of the anniversary tribute, newspapers announced FDR's latest draft call, the largest made to date, of 7,840 men from the New York district alone. Two of Gold's pacifist friends and political allies, Pete Seeger and Woody Guthrie, were singing anti-Roosevelt songs.

For the political Left, these were not even the most obvious warning signs. Heading the list of speakers at the Gold event was Communist Party general secretary Earl Browder, whose presence made for an unusual circumstance. At the time Browder delivered his encomium, he was a convict facing a jail term with a limited number of days to arrange his affairs. Three weeks before the meeting, the Supreme Court had upheld his four-year prison sentence on flimsy charges involving passport irregularities. And three weeks after the event, keynote speaker Browder would surrender himself to US marshals to be transported by rail to the Atlanta Federal Penitentiary.

Browder's taking time out to pay tribute to "one of America's most popular and best-loved writers" was therefore a paradoxical act. While it expressed extraordinary regard for Gold, it also introduced tensions. Probably no one doubted that the tribute, at which Secretary Browder spoke last and longest, doubled as a fierce protest meeting, and this was evident at the moment of Browder's arrival, which touched off a powerful "Free Earl Browder" demonstration that continued for a full five minutes. A fiery telegram sent by West Virginia coal miners bespoke these plural aims, naming Gold but also declaring, "On this occasion we pledge to carry forward the struggle to free Earl Browder."[6]

Another dual message was sent by Gold's new book, the content and argument of which were already known to his admirers. The publication blurb in the *Daily Worker* called *The Hollow Men* "the book that everybody has been watching and waiting for." This was accurate: *Daily Worker* readers had been pleading steadily for the text, which had initially been published serially under the title, "The Great Tradition, Can the Literary Renegades Destroy It?" But while Gold's readers and the Manhattan Center audience could indulge themselves in the book's ad hominem attacks on famous literary apostates without consequence, the author himself would pay dearly for the privilege.

As demonstrated even in Alan Max's skit, there was something unsavory and vindictive about the caricatures in *The Hollow Men*, which represented artists who had once admired Gold and embraced his world-view. The title of the piece came from a remark made by anarchist leader Prince Kropotkin. When one of Kropotkin's followers sadly reported a defection from the movement, saying, "Well, we have lost Comrade X," Kropotkin serenely replied, "Don't worry, we had the best of him, we had his youth."[7] The figures attacked in "Ex-Comrade X"—including Hemingway, Dos Passos, and Lewis Mumford—were treated less charitably, in cringe-worthy ways that were essentially in keeping with the tone of Gold's book, which maligned an array of artists and critics. For example Hemingway's moniker in the play—"Ernest Slummingway"—alluded to the best-selling author of *For Whom the Bell Tolls* as essentially a bourgeois tourist fond of slumming in the working-class world.

Over several decades, Gold would make this charge against other American authors, and in the main his accusations were not unjustified. In switching allegiances, the "renegades" had sent a signal that revealed the cultural and class loyalties they had held all along. The phenomenon of middle-class writers identifying with the causes of exploited workers, the poor and downtrodden, then abandoning that attachment when it became inexpedient, was not new or unusual. What was new was that they were being called out harshly by a proletarian artist and critic with a large following, one whose commitment to his class, and to the class struggle, was genuine and durable. In the process, Kropotkin's example of poise and equanimity went unheeded.

Responses to *The Hollow Men* were sharply divided along political lines, but the book certainly closed a lot of doors to Gold for the rest of his career as a writer. As Gold warned readers in his introduction, "One cannot avoid staining one's hand with the colors of one's material." If there seemed to be "a lack of love and hope" in certain sections of the book, it was because he was "concentrating on writers who have lost their own love and hope."[8] While his attacks on political deserters and dilettantes made him an outcast to the world of polite letters, those same attacks, interpreted as a measure of deep commitment to world socialism, endeared him forever to loyal Communists—a group that was in the process of being criminalized and divested of its civil rights.

A second tribute celebration for Mike Gold was held in 1950. This time the occasion was a "homecoming reception." Gold's family, including his French-born wife Elizabeth and their sons, thirteen-year-old Nick and ten-year-old Carl (they were named for "Nikolai" Lenin and Karl Marx), were returning to the United States after spending almost three years in France. They had left the country at an opportune moment, in May 1947, just after President Truman began targeting the current and past Communist Party affiliations of American citizens with an executive order mandating loyalty oaths for federal employees, a requirement that was quickly adopted in a large number of schools and private companies.

While Gold and his family were away, Cold War tensions had escalated. In 1949, the Soviet Union successfully tested an atomic bomb and the Foley Square trials of Communist leaders began. The first months of 1950 were defined by three related events in quick succession: Alger Hiss was convicted on perjury charges related to espionage, an emerging senator from Wisconsin brandished a list of 205 alleged members of the Communist Party working in the US State Department, and *Washington*

Post editorial cartoonist Herbert Block coined the term "McCarthyism." Leftists were being hounded by the FBI and the House Un-American Activities Committee with increasing intensity.

On March 9, when the writer and his family disembarked from the *Queen Elizabeth* at Pier 90, they were met by a group of friends including representatives from the *Daily Worker*, International Publishers, and the reorganized leftist journal *Masses & Mainstream*, media venues that were all being destabilized and driven underground by the ongoing attacks on the Communist Party. Posing for photos, a beaming Gold held forth about European political conditions, the wonders of French culture, and his participation as a delegate to peace conferences in Paris, Prague, Budapest, and Bucharest. Joseph North, covering the dockside event for the *Daily Worker*, called it "a happy reunion" of Gold with his fans.[9]

No doubt needing something to celebrate, those fans and other New York progressives with thick FBI files began organizing. Over the next several weeks they planned an event for the evening of Thursday, April 20, and ran announcements in the *Daily Worker*, which read, "America's leading working-class writer, Mike Gold will be greeted by his New York admirers at a reception in his honor at Manhattan Towers." The event sponsors—Howard Fast, John Gates, Shirley Graham, John Howard Lawson, Paul Robeson, and Samuel Sillen—hyped the "vivid articles" Gold had written on his travels, calling them "among the best in his career," and promised that Gold's talk at the reception would "describe his impressions and experiences in Europe."[10]

But a more urgent purpose for the April 20 celebration was to reinforce and revitalize ideas that were under assault during a reactionary time. "Many of those present," the notice read, "will be figures who came to the progressive world as a result of reading Gold throughout the Twenties and Thirties." To illustrate this influence, the organizers cited an essay Gold had published in November 1930 in the *New Republic*, explaining that the speakers "will recall such national cultural events as the time in the early Thirties Gold caused a literary furor by his celebrated critique of Thornton Wilder's *Bridge of San Luis Rey*."[11]

Touting a twenty-year-old book review as a means of energizing radicalism might seem dubious, but Gold's famous piece, which actually discussed several works by Wilder, had marked a historical turning point. Rejecting any and all art that comforted the status quo, lacked class consciousness, or did not do immediate cultural work, Gold set the tone for the 1930s by endorsing novels about starvation, breadlines, labor strikes, and factory work while insisting that literary art serve political purposes by reflecting and addressing the injustices of the capitalist system.

New Republic editor Edmund Wilson claimed that no essay he had ever published had aroused such controversy, and he openly took Gold's side in the debate it incited. The lesson Wilson took from Gold was that "nine-tenths of our writers would be much better off writing propaganda for Communism than doing what they are at present: that is, writing propaganda for capitalism under the impression that they are liberals or disinterested minds."[12]

In 1930, this message resonated and gained traction, but its demand that proletarian writers be allowed to participate in the central cultural conversation seemed extravagant by 1950, a time when all forms of radical speech were viewed as a clear and present danger. As a measure of further decline, perhaps no one at the McCarthy-era "welcome home" event dared hope for a second pyrotechnic discourse that would define the new decade. Probably what the organizers of the rally anticipated was a needed spiritual boost, provided by the rock upon which proletarian culture had been built. Though Gold could be counted on to help put the struggles of radicals in a global context and give purpose to the present, the essence of the evening, even more so than at the twenty-fifth anniversary meeting of nine years earlier, was nostalgia. Simply being there and being Mike Gold would be enough. "It will be a gala affair," observed the *Daily Worker*.

Looked at together, the 1941 and 1950 celebrations had much in common. On both occasions, honoring Gold was a pretext for rallying the Communist base at a moment of crisis. And when the second of the two ceremonies took place, Eugene Dennis, Earl Browder's successor as Party general secretary, was incarcerated. Along with ten other Communist leaders, Dennis had been convicted in 1949 for conspiring to advocate the violent overthrow of the US government (in other words, being a Communist), an offense for which he would eventually serve almost four years. As much as Gold's homecoming signified, it could not obliterate a reality in which the Smith Act trials were an existential threat, as Browder's pending incarceration had been at the 1941 anniversary.

At both tributes, Gold's presence was central but best described in terms of a surrogate role as designated champion of the embattled Party. In other words, he was the best available tool for bringing hope or clarity to a moment of uncertainty. "Mike is our poet," Browder said in 1941, "he may be lots of other things, too, but first and last, he's our poet—and we need poets." Gold would have acknowledged that being the author of

Jews without Money and hundreds of *Daily Worker* columns under the title *Change the World* carried linked and overlapping duties that tied him personally to the Left's fortunes. The nexus suggests the inseparability of the author's political purposes and literary commitments, an unstable trajectory that determined Gold's entire adult life. Another claim Browder made in 1941—that "Mike represents that section of cultural movement enlisted for the duration"—was prophetic.[13]

Finally, at both events, African Americans participated in significant ways. When Richard Wright helped organize the 1941 mass meeting, his blockbuster novel *Native Son* was still on the bestseller lists. Among that novel's many messages was one of condemnation for whites whose outreach to blacks reeked of social and racial condescension. The black author's relationship with Mike Gold was one of mutual admiration. In a speech that credited him, not only as a great Communist, but also as a model literary craftsman, Wright stated that Gold had helped him "solve the problem of relating what he had to say to the question of how to say it."[14] The event's chairman, Communist lawyer and future Harlem councilman Benjamin J. Davis, conveyed greetings and praise for Gold on behalf of New York's black community.

In 1950, world-renowned actor and singer Paul Robeson was the headliner among African American cultural figures. Black writer-activist Shirley Graham, later the wife of W. E. B. DuBois, was an organizer for both events. Throughout his life, Gold's activism transcended race in a way that some felt resembled the fierceness of antebellum white abolitionist John Brown, a comparison Gold would have encouraged. He worked tirelessly for civil rights causes and earned friendship and respect from a long list of black American leaders.

Their likenesses aside, the two tributes are also revealing as measures of Gold's narrowing cultural appeal in changed times. Gold's popularity in 1941 was remarked on even by his enemies, who took the opportunity to jealously mock the event by stating, "Though it may pain Mike, somebody made 'mon-yeh' on his exhibition" and referring to the many "rubles" that changed hands during its book-selling phase.[15] On that single Sunday in March 1941, probably no book in the United States sold more copies than *The Hollow Men,* a Communist work from a Communist publisher.

The 1950 effort to welcome Gold home from France was different; it was covered only by the *Daily Worker,* and if it elicited a form of mass participation, it was only among discreet, embattled remnants of radicalism. Less than a week after the return, the Lower East Side Women's

Peace Rally sponsored their own small "welcome home" rally and Gold speech. The week after that, the head of the Chinese American Theatre published a "Welcome Home" message in the *Daily Worker*, calling the returned author "Patron of Art and God-father in Our Striving."[16] Then in late April the Workmen's Circle held yet another homecoming party for "America's foremost proletarian writer, poet, and critic."[17]

A close look at the tributes also reveals basic changes in permissible political lexicon between 1941 and 1950. In the parlance of the *Daily Worker*, Mike Gold had always been a "revolutionary" or "Communist" writer. But by 1950, these terms were all but barred, and he became a "working-class writer" and a leader of the "progressive" movement. American political realities were censoring the allowable political vocabulary, forcing changes in the ways American citizens could be publicly identified in an altered context: a shift that eventually marginalized Mike Gold altogether as a cultural figure.

By 1954, a defining aspect of daily life for current or former US Communists was close observation by J. Edgar Hoover's Federal Bureau of Investigation. It's therefore both ironic and appropriate that the best way to piece together the details of a third Mike Gold tribute is to view the event as it was reported in his FBI file. On May 26, 1954, an FBI informant "of known reliability" attended an evening celebration of Gold's sixtieth birthday at the Rainbow Hall of the Rainbow Catering Company on Joy Road in Detroit. The gathering was part of a national tour that had formally begun with a reception at Steinway Hall in Midtown Manhattan on the actual date of Gold's birth, April 12. The highlight of that ceremony had been a speech by Elizabeth Gurley Flynn, a heroine of the left ever since she joined the Industrial Workers of the World (IWW) to lead strikes as a sixteen-year-old "rebel girl" in 1907. "This is a distinguished crowd," Flynn said in Gold's honor; "there are people here who have been in jail for their opinions, others who are about to go to jail, some who are threatened with deportation, others with denaturalization."[18]

Six weeks later in Detroit, Gold's eight-city, coast-to-coast sixtieth birthday tour was coming to an end. But while he had been traveling, much of the nation had been following the testimony of the Army-McCarthy hearings, which had begun to seriously undermine support for the Wisconsin senator's belligerent anti-Communist tactics. The hearings received unprecedented media attention, including gavel-to-gavel live coverage on national television beginning on April 22. The country's first sustained look at McCarthyism in action quickly exposed the brutality of the senator's overzealous attacks and raised basic questions about his integrity. By late May, it was clear that his charges against the US Army were not sticking and many in McCarthy's own party were turning against him.

With the nation riveted on the hearings in Washington, J. Edgar Hoover's far-flung network of agents and informers continued to do the work of gathering the information on which the persecutions were based. When the Michigan edition of the *Worker* ran announcements reading, "Greet Mike Gold on His Sixtieth Birthday," the Detroit FBI Field Office noticed. Gold's visit to Detroit created a buzz of activity in that office, a factor that produced an unusually detailed surveillance file that has remained largely unredacted because it was not declassified for release until 2018. The Detroit Field Office "Mike Gold" file helps us to see, hear, and experience the evening of May 26, 1954, with quoted passages from the tribute ceremony, overheard audience conversations, glimpses of actions taking place on the periphery while Gold spoke, and appended data about those in attendance.

Considered in context, the FBI's account of the tribute also enables a comparison of the tactics of Hoover and McCarthy as they intersected with the lives of cultural figures at the climax of the most virulently reactionary period of the Cold War, a moment when the gazes of the FBI and the American public were fixed in opposing directions and the national consensus was reaching a turning point. It seems worthwhile to examine what Mike Gold's message was at this time, while appreciating as well the unusual form of that message's preservation and its transmittal, carried out by J. Edgar Hoover's surveillance apparatus.

In reading the file, it is immediately clear that if McCarthy's fearmongering grip on the national consciousness was loosening, this process had not affected the praxis or priorities of the FBI. The unnamed informer in Detroit was careful to note that the guest of honor on May 26 was "very emphatic" in calling the people in attendance "fellow Communists" and that Gold "considered everybody in the hall to be Communists or people very close and friendly to them." The informer also reported that Carl Haessler (a longtime socialist-pacifist who had spent two years in prison for conscientious objection during World War I), was "chairman of the affair," and that the evening's program had begun with a piano concert by the Smith Trio, composed of Clarence, Honey, and Marva, "the children of HOPE SMITH, who rendered several musical selections."[19]

Chairman Haessler then read birthday congratulations sent to Gold from all over the world. Paul Robeson and William Z. Foster sent greetings.

The informant advised that there were five birthday messages from Moscow, one of which was from Vyacheslav Molotov, the Soviet minister of foreign affairs, who referred to Mike as his "good friend and comrade of the world." There were greetings from Belgium, Bulgaria, China, Czechoslovakia, East Germany, France, Korea, Poland, and Rumania. But the most personal and heartfelt may have been that of Harlem writer-activist Shirley Graham, who affirmed that, in her own battle against racial injustice, "Mike so perfectly symbolized the fact that I was not struggling alone. As long as there are people to fight for, Mike Gold will burn a light. Mike Gold will be there in the corner for us to gather round and know."[20]

The first speech of the evening was given by Abe Strauss, labor editor of the New York *Jewish Morning Freiheit*, who congratulated Gold as "the father of all working-class writers" and called attention to "the advancement of the progressive people since Gold has been writing, fighting, and letting the workers know the truth about world conditions." His message in introducing the guest of honor was that "the workers are uniting together" and that the movement was "on the increase against deplorable conditions in all types of industry."

As Gold took the podium for his talk, he remarked that "this was his first opportunity to return to Detroit in twenty years." (He was unaware that his presence in the city had been erroneously documented four years earlier by at least two FBI informers, including one in the audience that evening, who had confused him with Party official Mike Russo.) Gold then "stated that he was able to see a little of Detroit 'today' and related that it was not too far from the prisons of twenty years ago." The informant's report dutifully noted that by "prisons," Gold "was referring to the factories."

The speech then turned to the topic of conditions for industrial workers: "GOLD stated that he traveled to Russia once with a group of individuals. He stated that on this trip they visited a steel mill and that one of the individuals in the group remarked how old the mill was, to which GOLD replied you must never have visited the mills in Pittsburgh, Pennsylvania. GOLD continued his talk relating the assistance he had furnished in forming unions twenty-five years ago and that he would not be happy until the workers got forty years['] pay for twenty years work."

Next he spoke of his recent stay of "approximately four years in Europe," describing the "conditions and contentment of the people" and asserting that Europeans "were having the first opportunity to live under the 'New World.'" Describing "the power the Communists have in all parts of the world except the United States," Gold pointed out that "in

France, prior to the new regime, the French standard of life was very low; however, today, with 1/3 of the French population Communists, they are experiencing much better conditions." He stated that "when one finds one third of a country thinking in the same way, that is power." Referring to the topic that had been gripping much of the nation that spring and that very day on television, he observed that "in France, it would be impossible to hold the type of investigations and hearings conducted by Senator MCCARTHY and his form of investigators and stool pigeons."

Likely alluding to the growing popular backlash against McCarthy, Gold "stated that conditions in this country today are getting to such that the possibility of having a new America is greater now than in the days of Henry Wallace." Wallace, Franklin Roosevelt's vice president until 1944, had run for the White House as the Progressive Party candidate in 1948 but failed to win a single electoral vote. According to Gold, "the people had to stick together and work harder now because the conditions for the new America were coming close."

As the FBI Informant reported, Gold "was encouraged because when he was in Ann Arbor 'yesterday' (May 25, 1954) he had been informed that 120 professors or faculty members at the University of Michigan had signed a petition to do away with MC CARTHYISM. He also advised that approximately 250 people in Ann Arbor had signed an anti-MC CARTHY pledge." Gold's optimistic tone here is consistent with that of a *Masses & Mainstream* article he would later publish about the birthday tour, which concluded that better days for the Left were on the way.

While Gold spoke, a woman named Anne Shore "was actively engaged in selling tickets" for a banquet to be held at Parkside Hall on June 5 featuring the communist lawyer William L. Patterson as guest speaker, and "urged all to attend." Another woman, Rose Gray, was likewise engaged in ticket sales for a concert sponsored by the Jewish Women to be held at the Masonic Temple on June 13. Doug Lee sold copies of the weekly Jewish *Freiheit*. It was announced that "the annual picnic of the *Michigan Worker*, the event sponsor, would be held Sunday, July 4 at Arcadia Park on Wick Road."

Approximately "175 to 200 persons" attended the Gold birthday event, an older audience "consisting largely of people over forty." Both Gold and Hoover would have been interested in the absence of the younger generation that evening. Working on his memoirs just months before he died, the radical writer lamented,

For years the most disheartening thing I knew was when on a lecture tour across the country I would come to one city or another and find myself speaking to an audience of people all of whom were people with lined faces which had seen trouble and white hair as the result of sleepless nights over McCarthy. The audiences were old. We had lost all our youth and no movement lives and continues for a year without the youth. They are the young growing crops that mean life would be sustained in the future. We didn't have it.[21]

In Detroit, the informant noted also that "only a few Negroes were present", and enlarged on this issue, adding that a woman in the audience was overheard commenting on the "poor Negro attendance." She remarked that "Negro Communist Party members had declared to her that they were dissatisfied with the chauvinistic attitudes of the present CP leadership," but she did not elaborate on the forms that chauvinism took and "mentioned no names." These recorded observations point to a defining feature of the FBI under Hoover, which showed an obsessive interest in black activism and evinced a decades-long racist animus that effectively equated blackness with subversion.[22] It is no accident, for example, that the first-ever mention of Mike Gold by an FBI informant came in the file of black Jamaican poet Claude McKay in 1922. It was his association with McKay as coeditor of the *Liberator* that prompted the opening of Gold's FBI file the same year. By May 1954, the bureau had been watching Gold for over thirty-two years; it would continue to do so until his death in 1967.

For Gold, the racial divisions implied by a lack of black attendance would have been deeply disappointing; such discord contrasted painfully with his long-held ideal of cross-racial alliances both artistic and political. As if to compensate for this deficiency, a cash collection taken up at the meeting raised $178.25, "to be used to build the new America that MIKE GOLD had dreamed about." Before the Bureau informant left the meeting at 11 p.m., he added a final note explaining that "all of the speakers referred to each other, when being introduced, as 'Comrade.'"

Appended to the FBI memo were three pieces of surveillance data. The informant, who had apparently taken meticulous notes, listed the names of nineteen "persons [who] were recognized in attendance," including Mike Gold himself. He also listed sixteen names under the heading "the following persons were recognized entering the building." Finally, he included "a list of license plates of cars from which passengers were discharged to enter the meeting." This data included seventeen plate numbers, with owners' names, addresses, and the make and model of their cars, the oldest of which was a 1948 Nash sedan driven by J. Lazare of Burlingame Street, and the newest, a 1954 Ford sedan owned by Morris Auto Sales on Grand River Road. Such were the events of Wednesday, May 26, 1954, at Rainbow Catering Company on Joy Road, Detroit, as summarized and reported to Director Hoover by Special Agent Robert A. Moffatt.

In Washington, it was day sixteen of the Army-McCarthy hearings, during which, in a blow to McCarthy, charges were dropped against two Defense Department officials who had been accused of subverting the senator's investigations. As reported in AP stories that morning, McCarthy had the previous day embarrassed himself by falsely alleging that a chart made by army officials to illustrate evidence in the hearings was "phony" and intended to "deceive the television audience." A young lieutenant had countered the senator's allegation so effectively as to elicit "an explosion of laughter from the crowded hearing room."[23]

Elsewhere in the United States on the day Gold spoke in Detroit, the American Baptist Convention unanimously approved a statement striking out at those "so intent on combating the menace of communism that they adopt the very principles and methods which make communism itself frightening." The article, under the title, "Red Hunters Assailed," spoke of "a tyranny that seems to respect neither rights of individuals nor democratic processes of our nation," and noted that this criticism was "aimed, at least in part, at Senator Joseph R. McCarthy, Republican of Wisconsin."[24]

For McCarthy, the career-killing moment, and the beginning of a rapid physical deterioration that would bring about his death in 1957, took place just sixteen days after Gold's Detroit tribute, when army counsel Joseph Welch challenged the HUAC legal team to turn over to the Justice Department a list of 130 reputed subversives in the Department of Defense. McCarthy responded with insinuations against Fred Fisher, a young lawyer in Welch's own Boston law firm whom Welch had planned to have on his staff for the hearings, and who had once belonged to the left-leaning National Lawyers Guild. Welch informed McCarthy that Fisher had admitted this past association and then fiercely reprimanded the senator for his needless attack: "Until this moment, Senator, I think I never really gauged your cruelty or your recklessness." As McCarthy casually resumed his questioning, Welch angrily interrupted him, saying, "Senator, may we not drop this? . . . Let us not assassinate this lad further,

Senator; you've done enough. *Have you no sense of decency, sir? At long last, have you left no sense of decency?"*

Gallup polls taken just after the Army-McCarthy hearings revealed that the Wisconsin senator's approval rating dropped sharply. In December, the Senate voted sixty-seven to twenty-two to censure Joseph McCarthy, effectively ending his personal reign of terror.

Historical consensus holds that McCarthy was destroyed by the power of television, which put the workings of his character assassinations on mass display in a way that Hoover's never were, at least until the Freedom of Information Act was signed into law in 1966. Though Hoover's modus operandi was secrecy and McCarthy's methods were all about public exposure of ideological crimes, the anti-Communist tactics of FBI and HUAC were products of the same political forces, and up until McCarthy's spectacular demise, their relationship was symbiotic. Hoover's FBI served as the information-gathering arm of McCarthy's subcommittee, putting complete surveillance files into the hands of HUAC members, whose hearings would have been impossible without FBI resources. As bureau insider William Sullivan acknowledged, "During the Eisenhower years the FBI kept Joe McCarthy in business."[25] Experiencing Mike Gold's "Sixtieth Anniversary" celebration through the eyes of FBI informers reveals how the state surveillance apparatus that always functioned jointly with McCarthy derived its power, a power that operated as a major factor in erasing the cultural and historical influence of the literary Left.

Ironically, also included in the Detroit FBI Field Office file was an attractive handbill announcement for the anniversary tribute, which featured two striking quotes that might inspire literary scholars who are curious about Gold's erasure and the present-day meaning of his rehabilitation. On the handbill, Austrian Marxist writer Bruno Frei declared that "None, besides Gorki, has ever described the miseries and hopes of the poor with more emotion than the author of *Jews without Money*. The voice of humanity, speaking through Michael Gold's works, offers testimony for the progressive America in which we place our hopes in this time of decision." Below Frei's words on the handbill, an endorsement from novelist and screenwriter Albert Maltz alluded boldly to Gold's legacy: "What progressive writer in America is there who has not been influenced by him? What critic of the future will not recognize his indelible contribution to American culture?"[26]

Of the simultaneously unfolding events in the nation's capital and in the Rainbow Catering Company, it's hard to judge which is the more compelling. Though the Washington hearings produced high emotion and explosive verbal confrontations, the quieter gathering in Michigan was remarkable in a different way, producing a carefully formal, official synopsis document that is no less disturbing for its meticulous, circumspect version of aggressive authoritarian animus. Considering the identical ideological basis and operant motives in the two locales, the censuring rebuke—*"At long last, have you left no sense of decency?"*—might serve as a response to both.

In February 1967, Mike Gold was hospitalized after a mild stroke at the Kaiser Foundation Hospital in Terra Linda, near San Francisco. Among Gold's visitors in the following weeks, as his health deteriorated, was the folk singer and social activist Pete Seeger.

In his adolescence, even before he learned the five-string banjo, Seeger had subscribed to the *New Masses* and begun reading Gold's regular editorial columns. The two met in the late 1930s, when supporters of the leftist Popular Front were searching for a type of music that could be embraced by Depression-era proletarian culture as a means of bringing about social change. Gold and Seeger's father, Charles, a trained musicologist, held differing views and carried on a theoretical debate in the *Daily Worker* that, by 1935, Gold had won. For the next seven decades, the embodiment of the musical traits and ideals Gold argued for and continued to advocate was Pete Seeger, who in turn often called the proletarian writer his "hero."

Like Gold, Seeger had been blacklisted in the McCarthy era. But by the late 1960s, his revived career was about to reach its peak. In a passionate, nationally televised performance of his song, "Waist Deep in the Big Muddy," Seeger would soon become the symbol, voice, and incarnation of anti–Vietnam War protest.

On the day he came to Gold's bedside, Seeger brought his guitar and serenaded his ailing lifelong friend with "Guantanamera," a work whose beautiful lyrics were composed from the philosophic poetry of Cuban revolutionary writer José Martí. Seeger likely chose this song because both Marti and Gold were prolific writers who dedicated their lives and works to the freedom struggles of the oppressed. Before Seeger performed this beloved song, he always recited from memory an introduction that explained the price Marti paid for his beliefs, including banishment from his own country and death in the midst of a struggle for human rights. Seeger would perform the song in Spanish while pausing to translate key verses:

I am a truthful man

. . .

Before dying, I want to
Share these poems of my soul.

. . .

With the poor people of this earth,
I want to share my lot.[27]

When Mike Gold died two months later, the editors of *The Worker*, who had joined with the San Francisco *People's World* to ensure an outlet and a small salary for Gold's final *Change the World* columns, immediately issued a press release. "We loved this man," the statement read, "who, we knew, spared nothing of himself in his love for country and the ideal of human brotherhood."[28] John Howard Lawson, who'd known Gold since the 1920s, not only helped organize a June 16 memorial service for his friend, he also published a tribute essay, "The Stature of Michael Gold," in that month's *Political Affairs*. He called his subject "a hero of our time . . . a writer of courage, wisdom and—perhaps his greatest quality—stubborn integrity." Lawson used the occasion also to suggest a course of action: "The debt we owe Mike is a just appraisal of his achievement."

Among the great many tributes Mike Gold has received, Lawson's is not unusual for its passion and evident sincerity. It stands out, however, for the implicit challenge it issued for literary historians who would take the measure of the man: "I am concerned about the readers of literary and scholarly publications who have never heard of Mike Gold, and who will be unaware of his death," Lawson wrote. "I wonder about the young people . . . potential rebels, students and angry artists, the troubled desperate crowds in a hundred ghettos, the young who will *change the world*. How many know that Mike wrote a column under that title, and that it was the deepest meaning of the life he lived?"[29]

Chapter Two

Itzhok/Irwin Granich

(1893–1914)

Michael Gold was born Itzhok Isaak Granich on the third floor of a red-brick tenement on Delancey Street on the Lower East Side of New York City, on April 12, 1893. His birth came five weeks after the inauguration of President Grover Cleveland and seven weeks after the bankruptcy of the Philadelphia and Reading Railroad, the first clear warning of the Panic of 1893. That year, in an economic crisis second only to the Great Depression, wheat prices would collapse, five hundred banks would fail, and unemployment would soar from 3 percent to nearly 12 percent nationwide and 35 percent in New York, where soup kitchens were opened to feed the hungry.

He was born in the Jewish ghetto of pushcarts and immigrant crowds bargaining noisily for their daily purchases in the streets. In the 1890s, Manhattan's Lower East Side had the highest rate of tuberculosis of any area in the world, and the highest population density of any city in the world, higher than London's East End, a concentration of human beings roughly equivalent to that of the worst slums of twenty-first-century Mumbai. It was also the largest Jewish city in the world, a place where at one time 70 percent of US clothing was hand-made or manufactured, mainly by Yiddish-speaking toilers in company factories or in-home sweatshops doing poorly paid piecework, supplemented by child labor.

Before Itzhok was old enough to attend school, the family moved to 165 Chrystie Street, a six-story building where twenty-two families lived, with four families on each upper floor and two more on the ground floor behind the storefronts. He spent his days mainly in the streets and back alleys because the stifling interior of a tenement was no place for living. Each apartment had three rooms, one of which was a claustral bedroom barely large enough for a mattress. The kitchen too was cramped and often sweltering. Dominated by a heavy black coal stove, it left room only for a narrow eating table against the wall, a space too small for the family to sit together. On the floor by the stove, under a narrow cot, was a washtub one could pull out and bathe in—if one first removed the fifty pound bags of coal it was usually filled with—by crouching in shallow water with a sponge or cloth. There was no indoor plumbing, only a single water spigot in the refuse-strewn yard behind the building, near a row of four outhouses that were used by residents and the patrons of a nearby street-level saloon.

It was a type of building known as a dumbbell tenement because its rectangular shape was pinched in the middle to create a four-foot wide slot for light and air between the apartments, a space so narrow that one could reach across the shaft and touch a neighbor's hand. Tenements were built this way because a progressive-minded law of 1879 required that there be an outside window in every tenement room.

In practice, the law was a failure. Families on the top floor could look out at the sky, but no healthful sun or fresh air came down the shaft to the lower apartments. Only a dim, vague light reached the cave-like Granich tenement on the second floor. On hot days the residents opened their windows, letting in the harsh or beautiful sounds of domestic life from above and the smells of rotting garbage from below. Besides there being no way to clean the shafts, a place where residents might toss waste or bilge water, they acted as flues that helped spread fires quickly. Urban historians have judged the Tenement Law of 1879 to be a disastrous attempt at reform that helped create the worst type of living conditions ever inflicted on a modern urban community.

But for a sensitive young soul, the airshaft symbolized a longing for freedom and escape. Itzhok would later write plays, stories, and a novel that used the airshaft in just this way. His brother Emmanuel, or Manny, three years younger, once wrote a poem about the airshaft, about the pigeons wheeling over the patch of sky that could be seen only by leaning out the tenement window and how moved he was by the birds' sunlit flight in contrast to his own shadowy confinement.

Itzhok was the first surviving child of Eastern European Jewish immigrants. As a young man he used the Americanized first names Irving and Irwin, then in his late twenties, partly as a response to persecutions of American leftists by the US Department of Justice, he adopted the name Michael Gold, a pseudonym he kept for the rest of his life. The alias was outwardly protective but also expressive of its bearer's ideals; it was taken from a person known to him, a Jewish friend of his father who had been a corporal in the Civil War, fighting for the North in the liberation struggle against the Southern slavocracy.

Itzhok's father, Chaim (Americanized to Charles) Granich, was born in 1861 and came to the United States from Iaşi, Romania, in 1885. He was an erratic breadwinner but a charismatic storyteller, a lover of Yiddish theater and classic drama who inculcated literary values in his three sons. He had left Romania partly to escape the anti-Semitism he experienced as a young man. In his secondary school years he had refused to kiss the hand of a Catholic priest. The Jews were told that a show of submission to the Holy See might save their souls. When it came time to get in line with the other students, Chaim Granich demurred, though he wasn't even particularly religious. His transgression nevertheless militated against everything the dominant culture required of him. After this he realized he had to leave Romania. Teaching his sons about his youth one Shabbat evening when they were very young, he told them he could never eat a tomato because they were used by the Romanians to fling at Jews. He laughed and said he'd come to America to make his way, but really to keep from being pelted with tomatoes.

Irwin's mother, Gittel (Katie) Schwartz, was seven years younger than her husband. She came to the United States from Budapest, Hungary, in 1886. The couple met and married in New York, their union brokered by a Jewish matchmaker. Their first child, a girl, died in infancy several years before Itzhok was born. According to New York City birth records, Katie Granich also lost a second female child, who died at birth in 1894 or 1895. Itzhok's two younger brothers, Emmanuel (Manny) and George, were born in 1896 and 1898.

Katie had been used to hard work in the old country, where her parents had hired her out for farm labor starting at age ten. By the time she reached adulthood, she was slightly stooped from daily toil. A sturdy woman only five feet in height, she carried without complaint the pails of water for washing and sacks of coal for heating and cooking, with strong hands chapped and red from labor. She sometimes helped in the suspender shop but also bought food, cooked, and did her best by her sons when it came to clothing. If there was an emergency of any kind,

Figure 2.1. Gittel (Katie) Granich. *Source:* Granich family.

it was she and not her husband who came to the fore. All the Granich boys knew their mother to be the fighter in the family. A cheerful person who became furious and implacable when aroused by injustice, she was a formidable maternal force, "a brave and beautiful proletarian woman" as remembered by her eldest son.[1]

Among Irwin Granich's earliest published writings was a short sketch that described the circumstances of the author's birth and the conditions that determined his life:

> I was born (my mother once told me) on a certain dim day of
> April, about seven in a morning wrapped in fog. The streets of
> the East Side were dark with grey, wet gloom; the boats of the
> harbor cried constantly, like great, bewildered gulls, like deep,
> booming voices of calamity. The day was somber and heavy
> and unavoidable, like the walls of a prison about the city.[2]

As the mother told her son, her pains had come on "suddenly, dreadfully," after she had washed the dinner dishes. A young doctor, unfamiliar with the vast misery of the Jewish East Side, stayed through the night at her bedside. The father sat under the yellow light of a gas jet in the kitchen of the prison-like tenement, drinking schnapps and weeping.

The long night of pain and waiting passed slowly, "like the solemn pace of a funeral cortege." At dawn, the woman in labor instructed her husband to procure a meal of coffee and rolls for the famished doctor. When the father told his suffering wife he could find no milk, she shouted, "One goes out and gets it at the grocery store, fool! I think you would starve to death if there was no one near to tell you the simplest things."[3]

The father threw on a coat and exited into the gloom. On the tenement stoop, he stumbled on "a huddled thing that rose and accosted him." It was the kind prostitute Rosa, who lived in a single room in the same building and who said she was having trouble sleeping. A friend of the woman in labor, the frail young Rosala asked about the pains and offered comfort to the weeping father:

"It is so terrible a thing to bring a child into the world!" he said. "It *is* terrible," Rosie answered, "And we poor will only be happy in the grave."[4] When the father returned from the grocery he found Rosie writhing and incoherent, lying in a twisted heap on the stoop. He ran and brought the sleepy doctor, but the girl was already "stark and silent." The doctor, picking up an empty phial on the floor near her, could only wonder "why she did it" as he put down her wrist "with an air of finality." The mournful news could not be kept from the mother who, still in labor, wept and lamented "in the heart-rending Jewish manner" for more than half an hour.

Then, Itzhok Isaak Granich was born.

The mother's story ended at noon as the doctor readied to leave. The father, ashamed, could offer only three one-dollar bills for the doctor's fee. "And this is all? . . . Beggars!" cried the physician in disgust, throwing the bills on the table contemptuously and sweeping out the door. "Buy food with it!" he shouted from the stoop. The father picked up the bills and regarded them sadly before shrugging his shoulders and returning to the room where the mother was still weeping with pain.[5]

Though fictionally embellished, this origin story of Itzhok Granich contains basic truths about the world and work of the future Michael Gold. Meant to serve as a prologue to an autobiographical novel, the tale faithfully represents the author's immediate family sorrow and the general struggles of the suffering East Side masses, while symbolically suggesting a fundamental connection between the two. There is a useful insight in the message the Granich boy distills from his mother's mournful tale: "In the same hour and the same tenement that bore me, Rosie Hyman the prostitute died, and the pale ear of the same doctor heard my first wails and the last quiverings of her sore heart."[6] From the beginning, the pained human cry of the future writer-activist is linked in sympathy with the pain of other despairing tenement lives.

Also informative is the depiction of the author's mother, Katie, who would become what scholar Alan Wald termed "a symbol of socialism, albeit a romanticized one."[7] She befriends prostitutes and even in the throes of labor remembers the "poor doctor" who must be fed, while managing the household and instructing her loving but puerile husband.

Itzhok's father, described in the sketch as "a slim, clean-shaven, unusual kind of Jew, who had been the gay blacksheep of his family in Rumania," seems accurately drawn. Charles Granich, loving joy and laughter "as only young thoughtless people can love them," had escaped at age twenty-four to America, only to struggle miserably in the new land. Though he was surrounded by the English language for decades, he rarely spoke it in public and never at home, where both Granich parents spoke Yiddish and their boys answered in English. "The poverty of the golden, promised land had eaten his joy," his eldest son would write. "I knew him as a sad, irritable, weakly sort of father, who drank in troubled times when the family needed him, and who loved us all to maudlinity."[8]

For a time in Itzhok's childhood, Charles Granich ran a small storefront business making suspender fasteners. A cousin, the owner of a clothing business, had established him in a small Chrystie Street workshop, where with the aid of one or two employees, cotton suspender ends were manufactured, usually to fill the orders for the factory of his earlier-arrived and more successful relative. Charles was one of thousands of immigrant entrepreneurs who worked either at home in squalid tenements or in small basements, lofts, or storefront shops—fragile one-family ventures in which children were expected to do their share and help out after school. Frequently ill as a child, Itzhok nevertheless worked often at his father's side.

In those days suspender ends were made with a loop of bundled cotton cord that was cut to size and sewn by hand to fasteners. Beginning when he was a little boy, Itzhok and later Manny and George would help their father by laying out bundles of the cord and cutting them using a table-top machine that had a knife edge and a gage to regulate length. They'd kick the blade down with a foot pedal, then hand on the pieces to their father's employees, who operated sewing machines. These finishers would fold the cord in half, push it through an eyelet, and attach the shank of it in place using heavy thread. The items were fastened into bundles of 144. After coming home from school, it was usually Irwin's job to push the day's cartload of completed suspender fasteners to his father's cousin in the wholesale dry goods district near Broadway and Canal Street.

The job also required the boys to collect the cash payment for the goods and carry it safely home across the Bowery. Time and again they were assailed by a gang and would have to fight their way through. They devised a strategy whereby one brother would clutch the money tightly to his body, backing away from the attackers until he could sprint down a side street, while the other brother would take the battle. They came to expect the attempted muggings as routine and took turns carrying the cash.

One day Itzhok, Manny, and some other boys were shooting craps on the floor of the street-level stoop of an empty building. They were playing for pennies and no one saw a cop approaching until he reached out and snatched their pile of money. The boys froze because they knew the police didn't hesitate to use their clubs on young boys. One of them, Solly Silver, stood his ground to pick up the money and the cop gave him a terrific, thudding whack with his club. Solly did not flinch but turned on the cop, calling him a son-of-a-bitch before running away. Afterward the boy carried out a vendetta against this policeman. He would climb the stairs to the tenement roof with a bucket of water, wait for the policeman to pass the building on his beat, and drop the water on him. This went on for weeks until the cop learned to walk on the other side of the street.

A version of this story was retold in *Jews without Money*, assigning the character the symbolic epithet "Nigger" to hint at connections between the subjugation of Jews and of African Americans. Solly Silver eventually disappeared from the East Side streets for a period of years. As the boys learned later, he'd been in and out of prison, his life criminalized by economic conditions and oppressive state authority. "Is there any gangster who is as cruel as the present legal state?" asks narrator Mikey Gold in *Jews without Money*.[9]

In the suspender shop one workday, Irwin and Manny listened to a conversation between their father and two new employees, young men recently arrived from Russia. It came out that they were on strike and had no place to go. To keep them from starving Charles offered them temporary work, glad to have a fresh audience for his dark humor and storytelling.

This was the great time of unionization in the needle trades and garment industry in New York, and of course suspender making was a related small industry that had been touched by the movement. When the talk turned to unionization and socialism, the machine operators became animated. Charles sent Manny down the street for a big ten-cent pail of beer, which was shared with the workers.

The long discussion continued over several workdays. Itzhok and Manny noticed that their father was not opposed to the socialist theory he was hearing; in fact he was unusually interested but conflicted. In the end he only laughed and said in kidding that when the capitalists get organized no one would be able to pull their tails without paying for it. But the boys could see that he was unsure of himself, questioning which side to take. The conception had not fully blossomed in him, but it was planted in his sons.[10]

Charles Granich was also a minor political official. In a Tammany era and a Tammany district he was approached by a member of the local Republican Party committee to help form a Lincoln Republican Club, after which he was nominated and became vice president. It meant little besides a top-hatted job on election day and a five dollar honorarium once a year for serving as a ballot watcher at the district polling station. Of course he would always come home with elaborate stories about how elections were stolen.

According to his sons Charles was a kind and peaceable man but weak and completely unable to engage in serious confrontation. Once he told his family of an incident that indirectly revealed much about his character. Late on the day of an election he'd heard that stolen ballot boxes were being dumped into the East River, so he hurried in that direction to investigate. On the way he was approached by one of the Democratic watchers, who blocked his path and said pointedly, "It would be better for you not to see this." Charles went away, but when the matter was blasted in the papers the next day, he showed around the article, speaking self-importantly about his attempted intervention.[11]

For all his flaws, Charles Granich lived with passion and was capable of selfless heroism. Once Irwin's younger brother Manny was struck by a horse car, trapping his foot under a metal wheel that cut deeply into his ankle. A crowd of neighbors gathered, debated the situation with great emotion, and came to the consensus that the car would have to be pushed over the boy's foot to release him. Suddenly the immigrant father threw himself beneath the car, placing his head under the wheel beside Manny's foot. "Lift the car!" he shouted. "I won't let you cut off his foot! Cut first my head." After more discussion the crowd found a way to lift the horse car and Manny's foot was saved.[12]

Figure 2.2. Chaim (Charles) Granich and his sons, Itzhok (left), Emmanuel (right), and George, c. 1901. *Source:* Granich family.

Another time Itzhok's father told him about the foul conditions of his steerage passage to New York and a chore he undertook during that ordeal that would symbolize his American struggle. Though he was a manual worker with limited formal schooling, Charles held a reverent passion for the Yiddish drama, going to see his favorite plays multiple times, worshipping his favorite actors, and feeling himself a sensitive dramatic critic. The play he loved most was Schiller's *The Robbers*, which he claimed to have seen thirty-four times in four different languages and could recite from memory. On the way to America, he evolved the idea that the play was unknown in New York and that he would introduce it there. During a storm lasting eleven days, he wrote out the entire play in Yiddish, huddled over loose sheets of letter paper with a lead pencil in the meager light of the reeking lower deck.

Soon after disembarking in New York, he begged an interview with the well-known Yiddish tragedian Sigmund Mogalescu. With great feeling, Charles began a reading of *The Robbers*, only to be interrupted by laughter. "The play is already in my repertoire," Mogalescu said, amused at the greenhorn's notion that such a masterpiece could remain unknown in America. For the rest of his life Charles gloomily repeated the anecdote, adding, "Always I have been too late." Retelling this story in *Jews without Money*, the son of Charles Granich added another character-revealing detail: "I think my father got the feeling at times that he himself was the author of *The Robbers*, and that Mogalescu had cheated him of his rights."[13]

Both Itzhok's parents were among the "huddled masses yearning to breathe free," the class of refugees that poet Emma Lazarus encountered in her charity work among the newly arrived Eastern Europeans, and which she described in her 1883 sonnet, "The New Colossus." They typified the "tempest tost . . . wretched refuse," most of them Jews, who disembarked in the 1880s from steerage at Castle Garden and Ellis Island. But the "golden door" that Lazarus hopefully named as awaiting these refugees with "worldwide welcome" would not be part of Charles Granich's story.

Instead Charles Granich would tell other fantastic tales, learned in his youthful wanderings along the Danube and through the Balkans or heard from bards in Oriental marketplaces and from Romanian peasants. For years, Charles soothed Itzhok and his brothers to sleep with inexhaustible stories that inhabited their waking thoughts and colored their childhoods. Often he told stories of his old-world youth that his children never tired of hearing. Some nights their father's friends gathered in the Granich home, where Charles's voice was heard in the darkness and the tired laborers—peddlers, housepainters, sweatshop workers and other Jews struggling in the Promised Land—listened for hours to thousand-year-old fables. Neighbors dropped in, tired mothers and graybeard grandfathers, who sat hypnotized and then held long debates about each story. His audience did not think it unusual to know hundreds of tales; for Jews from the world of peasant Europe, art was a simple fact of life and storytelling was as natural as breathing.[14] One night Charles's employees, the two striking Russian needle workers, came to enjoy his narration. They had shared the gritty realism of the labor struggle with their boss; in return he offered them an evening of fantasy.

When Itzhok was seven or eight he begged and pleaded with his tired and worried father, forcing him to take him to see Buffalo Bill's Wild West Show at Madison Square Garden. Even Charles thrilled to the magnificence of the spectacle, and Itzhok decided that the Wild West scout was his favorite hero, a greater inspiration for small boys and their elders than President McKinley. He believed that the man on the beautiful white horse shooting glass balls with a rifle wasn't a mere showman but performed real stories and authentic American history.[15]

The early twentieth century was the epoch of another great story-teller, Mark Twain, who was a recurring presence in young Itzhok's real and imaginative life. As a boy he devoured *Huckleberry Finn* under the lantern light and then read it aloud for his father, who loved the book because the raft scenes on the broad Mississippi reminded him of his boyhood near the Danube. Twain paid several visits to the Lower East Side ghetto in the early 1900s and Irwin once saw him in person. The world-famous author, "a magnificent figure all in white," arrived in a carriage to attend a performance of *The Prince and the Pauper* and was recognized by a cheering crowd that included the eleven-year-old Irwin. Twain patted the boys' heads as he passed among them. As Itzhok fondly recalled, "My head he also touched."[16]

Probably Itzhok's oral readings of Twain's novels were dramatic and expressive, for he was already a theater lover like his father. "Since the time I had begun to walk and argue," he remembered, "my father had taken me at least once a week to some theater show." Accounts of his boyhood immersion in Lower East Side Yiddish theater milieu make for entertaining reading but are also a valuable record of a golden age. "The theater was almost a sacred institution on the East Side," he recalled; "Fleeing for their lives in the 1880s from the bloody tsarist pogroms, in haste and trembling, the people yet remembered to pack their theater in the baggage." On the vibrant Lower East Side stage, audiences of poor working people embraced and lived the drama, not as an extravagance but as sustenance, a staple of daily life: "They ate, as the saying went, their *broyt mit teater*—bread with theater."[17]

The Yiddish stage that Irwin knew as a boy was psychologically rich and innovative, tackling subjects like Zionism, socialism, anarchism, and birth control for its mainly proletarian audiences. As Mike Gold wrote later in *Jews without Money*, "The garment workers lived with Shakespeare."[18] What they experienced, scholar Nahma Sandrow maintains, was a drama of the people in an era of the people: "Yiddish writers wrote about poverty because they were hungry."[19] Gold remembered ten or more theaters that were devoted to the serious repertoire of the day, venues that offered productions in many ways the equal or superior to Broadway in artistic depth and sophistication.

Charles Granich possessed genuine theater knowledge and expertise, teaching his sons about the relative merits of legends like Jacob P. Adler, David Kessler, Jacob Gordin, Boris Tomashevsky, and the father of Yiddish theater, Abraham Goldfaden. The claim Charles made to his sons—that he had met and known Goldfaden during his youthful years in Iași—was probably true. Goldfaden had indeed founded a Yiddish theater in Iași in 1876, in time to form a part of that city's theater culture in the years preceding Charles's emigration. These facts in turn lend credence to the claim of the adult Mike Gold that before he was seven, he had seen plays by Gorky, Hauptmann, Tolstoy, Jacob Gordin. and Shakespeare—all of which would have been adapted to Yiddish-speaking audiences and infused with cultural material fresh from the ghetto streets.

Young Itzhok even had what might be called a brief "career" on the Yiddish stage. When the Graniches lived on Chrystie Street, the stage door of Boris Tomashevsky's theater faced their tenement. One summer evening Itzhok was shooting marbles in the alley when a corpulent, bearded man approached, dressed in the long coat, skull cap and the fringed white garment of a Talmud student.[20] This was the great actor-singer himself, who gave the children candy and herded them through a narrow alley-way door, down a dark corridor, and onto a brightly lit stage, where they stood before an audience unseen in the dim theater recesses. In whispers, Tomashevsky instructed them to stand in line, rub their eyes, and try to cry by imagining they were orphans whose mama and papa had just been killed by gentiles. At first the children were unable to produce tears on command, but on listening to the tragedian's echoing soliloquy, which sent the audience into a storm of sobs and wails, they caught the contagion and cried stormily. Immediately afterward they were herded offstage and into the dingy back alley.

The passion formed early in life for the glorious Yiddish stage would be an important aspect of Granich's later life, and the desire to be a play-wright explains many of his early choices. Having once lingered outside the stage door of Tomashevsky's theater in the Bowery, he would later wait outside the Provincetown Playhouse on MacDougal Street, pining for recognition from John Reed, Jig Cook, and Eugene O'Neill, denizens of a world he'd been taught to idealize. If the later plays of Mike Gold were engaging and innovative, this was due in part to a dynamic he'd identified in the milieu of East Side Yiddish drama: "The tight, 'well-made' problem play was not to their liking," Gold recalled much later. "They demanded life in full abundance. They were hefty, solid, real men, real women, who had lived and suffered, therefore could interpret life."[21]

After Charles Granich's suspender business failed, an unknown illness damaged his health, keeping him from other laboring jobs and making him bedridden at the age of forty-five. Itzhok, a talented student, was forced to quit school at the age of twelve to work at menial jobs in vile East Side sweatshop factories. On his last day of school, a teacher who recognized his promise presented him with a collection of Emerson's essays. He had hungered for education, but when he couldn't have it, his impulse was to despise it; out of frustration the boy tossed the book under his bed and refused to read it. The next morning he rose at six-thirty and was out tramping the streets at seven, searching for bread labor to support the family. There were hundreds of jobs but a swarm of thousands battling for them.

His first job was in a Bowery factory that made gas mantles, a "chamber of hell, hot and poisoned by hundreds of gas flames," the air stifling from the reek of chemicals. Decades later he vividly recalled the scene and rendered it faithfully in *Jews without Money*: "Men sat at a long table testing mantles. Their faces were death masks, fixed and white. . . . Little Jewish and Italian girls dipped racks of mantles in chemical tanks. Boys stood before a series of ovens in which sixty gas jets blazed. . . . Everyone dripped with sweat; everyone was haggard, as though in pain."[22] In two months working there, the twelve-year-old boy lost eight pounds.

When he came home at night from the miserable factory to the bottom-of-the-airshaft tenement on Chrystie Street, his kid brother George greeted him at the door with a high-pitched happy scream, throwing his arms around him in grasping hugs. A frail, blond seven year-old with a bright smile, George idolized his older brothers and especially Itzhok, who was a stronger influence on him than their dwindling father. The youngest Granich boy wasn't built for the brutal punishment of capitalist wage slavery, but his turn would come at the age of fourteen, when he took a job in a dilapidated basement cigar factory. Though George "loved nothing more than fresh air and sunlight," Irwin remembered, "he had to work in a miserable hole-like mine under electric light all day."[23] Manny, the middle brother, was Itzhok's nemesis and rival. The obstinate one who felt starved for attention, he regarded his older brother as his chief obstacle on the road of life. Whatever battles the boys fought with each other had to be put away at day's end. The three boys slept alongside each other on a bug-infested mattress in an eight-foot-square room adjoining the tenement kitchen.

Beginning in 1906, Itzhok held various jobs for more than a decade at the Adams Express Company, starting as a driver's wagon helper, sitting high on a heavy truck pulled by a pair of draft horses. He loved all animals but especially horses; as long as he lived he'd recall in his dreams and idle hours the two great Percherons, Brownie and Queenie, which he'd sometimes pretended were his own.[24] The Adams Express branch office and stables were only half a block from his tenement. When he wasn't working in the evenings, he would walk over to get a look at the powerful beasts standing calmly in their stalls.

Figure 2.3. Itzhok (Irwin) Granich, c. 1906. *Source:* Granich family.

Itzhok's driver on the Adams job was "Curley," a sour little Dutchman with a thick mustache who swilled beer throughout the workday and sometimes made Irwin wait with the horses while he took his lunch break in a whorehouse. "If I had any trade other than journalism," Mike Gold said at the end of his life, "it may be that of teamster. Half of my youth was spent working for the Adams Express. I started when I was 13, would quit in a fit of ambition, try for a better job outside, come back when desperate again."[25]

Once in his early teen years he encountered violent anti-Semitism and lost his job because of it. Out on the route one afternoon, his beer-drinking driver broke into a lot of bragging that turned into verbal abuse. The Dutchman had never liked his assistant and Itzhok knew why. It had to do with the boy's having a novel with him and reading whenever he could on the seat next to the driver, who hated books and readers. This "barbarian," Gold said in his memoirs, "chose that particular day to call me a dirty Jew." Stunned, the boy thought of the driver's children and tried to avoid a fight, but it became impossible when the man launched into a vulgar Jew-baiting rant.

The young assistant ended up pulling his boss down from the wagon into the street, putting up the reins, and punching the man, who fell to his knees. The driver repeated his anti-Jewish slurs and howled at the passersby, who heard his insults, stopped, and surrounded him. Some of the Jewish girls slapped and clawed at the Dutchman until an Adams Express inspector came. He fired the driver on the spot but cautiously avoided reprimanding Itzhok before the interested onlookers. The boy was fired when he returned to the Adams Express offices at the end of his shift. Though he would later be rehired by the company as a shipping clerk, it was his last day on the delivery wagon.[26]

Itzhok also loved sports, learning to play baseball and basketball but spending most of his time boxing in the basement gym of a neighborhood Catholic church. He wanted to be a prize fighter and idolized Jim Jeffries, Abe Attell, and Terrible Terry McGovern. His father disapproved of this passion, believing that Christian sports made Jewish boys into gangsters. Even as a young man he knew that his father's fear and misunderstanding of the Lower East Side sports craze was caused by illness and the weakening of the spirit that came with living in the prison-like ghetto tenements, where sport was unthinkable to those defeated by poverty. Told to forget boxing and think only of education, Itzhok had to remind his father that he too had been a skilled athlete, swimming and diving in the Danube in his youth.

His parents' fears about athletics were confirmed when their firstborn son was arrested because of baseball. It happened on a July Sunday in 1908, after a hotly contested game in Van Cortland Park between Itzhok's Chrystie Street bunch and the Forsythe Street team. On the way home in the crowded subway train, the tired, sunstruck boys started giggling and roughhousing. Itzhok, who at fifteen had a gymnast's body and unusual agility, was yelling and doing acrobatics from the subway straps. Suddenly and without warning, a strong adult grabbed his arm: a plainclothes detective was pulling him down and punching him. The policeman's partner helped corral the three other boys and forced them all off the train on a factory street, deserted on Sunday, where the cops gave the Jewish boys a brutal, racially motivated beating before arresting them.

The next morning a Tammany judge took the cops' side and sentenced the boys to five days in the foul conditions of the Raymond Street jail without telling their parents. The incident of police brutality prompted Itzhok's first political writing in the form of an indignant letter to the New York *Globe*. He took responsibility for his disorderly conduct but vehemently protested the assault. Though the letter was never printed, the painful experience instilled what its young writer later termed "hate for the bully . . . then and forever."[27]

As Itzhok interacted more frequently with coworkers and the teachers at the Rivington Street settlement house in his teens, he started going by the name Irving, finally settling on Irwin as his first name for the next several years. In adolescence Irwin also started drinking, heavily at times, to quell a nagging feeling of insignificance and futility as only one of a million other aimless, bewildered, and hungry boys. He'd pick up money from day labor or temporary work as an errand boy in a silk house or shirtwaist factory, then buy cheap gin and escape into poolrooms. He dreamed of running away. For brief periods he took up with the worst hoodlums of his ever-shifting "bunch" and committed indiscretions he'd later refer to only as "unspeakable" things. At other times, thinking of his mother's hopes for him, he prayed on the tenement roof for a Jewish Messiah who would redeem the world.

In these years Irwin's friends were a group of about twenty wild and dirty East Side boys. All day they surrendered to meaningless jobs, but at night they were "free for the poetry of being human." Their turf was at Orchard and Rivington streets, and their haunts the College Settlement, the beer saloon, the public library, the public school, and the "yellow bricked Rumanian synagogue with its Moorish dome" where his parents worshipped. Together, Irwin and his friends were never bored; they boxed in the gym, shot pool, took in the burlesque shows on the Bowery. When there was nothing to do they sang American songs for each other or just rambled around in a group until long after midnight. Forty years later, Mike Gold would remember that though the "bunch" he'd belonged to drove his parents crazy with worry, to him they were "an island of young innocence, upon which beat the vast ocean of social corruption."[28]

Gradually Irwin learned to take what refuge he could in public libraries, immersing himself in Victor Hugo, Robert Burns, Dickens, Tolstoy, and of course Twain, along with reading a good deal of what he later called "romantic junk." Off and on, he supplemented his curtailed formal education by taking secondary courses at Senftner's Astor Place Prep School, where he somehow passed the equivalent of four years of high school English, two years of ancient and medieval history and one year of algebra. He regularly attended lectures at the Rivington Street settlement, which offered evening classes and entertainments with the goal of helping ghetto youth assimilate. Manny noticed that the settlement workers in particular took a shine to Irwin and helped him along, always offering him special encouragement.[29]

For a pair of brothers born almost three years apart, Manny and Irwin shared friends and experiences to an unusual degree, a habit that probably both reflected and contributed to their sibling rivalry. The elder Granich brothers often boxed together, usually at the College Settlement on First Street. Manny was a little taller and heavier than Irwin, and their workouts were intense. Once Manny sparred with local champion Kid Morris and came away with a swollen black eye. That evening he went home to discover that Irwin also had a black eye, from fighting Kid Morris earlier that day. Katie Granich was furious. While fixing dinner that evening, the distraught mother railed and howled at the boys in Yiddish.

Between boxing, basketball, and ping-pong games in the settlement house rec room, Irwin and Manny had roles in a production of Gilbert and Sullivan's *H.M.S. Pinafore*, a project suggested and directed by a charismatic volunteer professor. The Granich bothers loved the experience and always cherished what they'd learned from it. Manny especially was amazed that the poor ghetto friends had had the skill to do something of real cultural value. After they'd imbibed Marxism years later, both brothers viewed the moment in more complex terms, aware that it was, in Manny's words, "a band-aid of the bourgeois to the people of the ghetto in hopes that the rougher spots could be covered over with a nice good-looking plastic veneer."[30]

Whatever elation the boys took from the performance was undercut each night when they returned home to face their father's illness, which worsened significantly in this period. In response to this pain and the impulse to struggle against his environment, Irwin began his creative career by publishing several poems in the settlement house newspaper. If literary art exists for any purpose other than protesting poverty, one would not know it from the apprentice literary efforts of the future Mike Gold. His first brief verse, "The Tenements," opened with the lines, "Like dim muffled bravos they stand / darkly brooding on strange crimes."[31] Thus began a lifelong literary exploration of the cruel effects of economic injustice. The story behind a second poem Irwin wrote for the settlement newsletter would be cited much later as the genesis of Mike Gold's famous theory of proletarian literature:

> I was a shipping clerk in a place on lower Broadway in the cotton goods district. I used to deliver heavy bundles that a truck horse would have rejected. My boss was so stingy he would not even get a hand truck. So we had to carry these heavy bundles which often weighed a hundred pounds on our backs and shoulders. I wrote a poem, on the boss's time, called 'Nails,' and I remember this scrap of paper and the lead pencil that I used then and that I still use for poetry.[32]

In the final year of his life, Gold could no longer recite this verse, but he remembered that "It was a proletarian poem, and it told about the sorrows of the shipping clerk." Pummeled by the hammer-like blows of heavy labor, the worker's body becomes stooped and bent, and the clerk instinctively turns to writing poetry as his only "solution." Gold believed that millions of scraps of this sort of writing were produced every day by workers, but no one observed it. What mattered was that the impulse for such literary efforts was natural, born "not out of theory but out of struggle, out of the actual tortured flesh" of working people: "What else would you call it but proletarian?" he asked, "And what sort of stuff was it made of . . . but life itself?"[33]

The writer's memories of events that took place around 1909, the year he turned sixteen and his father's condition became hopeless, would remain vivid and sometimes troubling to consider even in his later years. At least twice, Irwin came from work at Adams Express to find the home in severe crisis, his father raging loudly with unbearable pain and suicidal urges. "He wants to die!" his mother whispered in tears on one occasion, begging Irwin to "Tell him something good! . . . make him live!" Once in desperation Irwin quickly invented a fable that would bring comfort, a Horatio Alger fairy tale. He told his parents he had met and befriended a wealthy and generous patron who had put him on salary and would make him a lawyer. What made the memory even sadder was the way his mother and father, "like small, trustful children," believed the fantasy. For a few days his father's desire to live was restored. After-ward, Irwin considered studying to become a lawyer just to keep them happy.[34]

On another occasion, returning from a sweltering twelve-hour day on the truck and a late night with his gang, Irwin was stunned awake at three a.m. by the frightened shouts of his mother. He lit the gas and took in the horrific sight of his father, "white as a groaning corpse," his clothes smeared with blood. He'd been seized by one of his recurring "fits of accumulated despair" and had slashed his wrist with a kitchen knife, the second time he'd attempted suicide in this way. Calmly Irwin tried to talk him down and convince him to live, but the forty-eight-year-old invalid was fixated on his rage and out of reach, repeatedly muttering, "Only let me die!" Shaking in trauma, Irwin gave up pleading. He had no idea what to say, when suddenly he remembered Twain. He reached for his worn copy of *Huckleberry Finn* and started reading the "beloved book" aloud until his father gradually forgot his suffering.

After this incident Irwin realized his father was beyond help and found himself agreeing with his death wish. "A chronic invalid is like a running sore in the family that cripples your living. It tears your heart out and fills you with poison. I even found myself hating my father at times, then hating myself more with the guilt of having such evil thoughts."[35]

Two autobiographical short stories, one written for the New York *Call* in 1917 and a second for the *Liberator* in 1922, tell us much about the specific agonies of Irwin Granich's inner world in 1911–1912, a time that would decide his life's future course. The first, "The Trap," opens in the congested tenement at the bottom of the airshaft, with the return from work of Mrs. Kobrin, who "found her husband sitting upright in his humid bed, weeping bitterly, like a forgotten child," a copy of a Yiddish newspaper in his hand.[36] The invalid Mr. Kobrin is sobbing because his son Sammy had come home from his job and passed by his father's bed

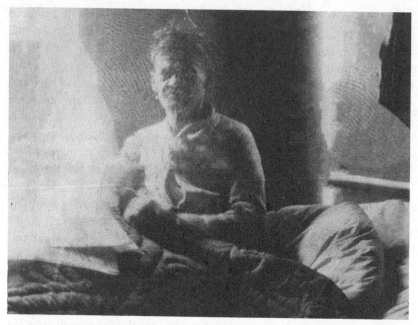

Figure 2.4. Chaim (Charles) Granich in his long illness. Gold described this photo in short stories written in 1917 and 1922. *Source:* Granich family.

without speaking to him. "Every night, . . . Sammy would stop and talk to me, and ask how his poppy was feeling," he tells his wife, "Tonight . . . he passed by me like he hated me! He hated his poppy!" The woman tries to comfort her husband, saying that the young man, who has been slaving for five years to support the family, is simply tired. She passes to the son's bed to entreat him to speak to his father and finds the boy weeping and contemplating suicide, a razor beside him on the bed. "I've got to escape," Sammy says, "I can't stand it any longer! I'll kill myself, I'll do something to get out of this trap." Clearly the son resents the father: "He'll be sick for five years more. He'll go on taking and taking from us, and then he'll die—" At this moment the father's ghostlike, decaying figure staggers from his bed to embrace the wife and son, but the story ends without relief, only the pervasive feeling of "how terrible it was to be poor and friendless in the world." As the family weeps, the sound of their mourning rises into the airshaft, "bringing melancholy to the sad hearts of the neighbors in the tenement."[37] As David Roessel observed in his initial republication and critical treatment of this story in 2010, "the poverty of the tenements and the family situation crushes the life out of the characters," and "there is the suggestion that suicide is the most attractive option."[38]

The same paternal deathbed is the focus of a much longer 1922 story, "The Password to Thought—To Culture." The main character, now called David Brandt, is an overburdened Jewish shipping clerk who, thirsty for knowledge, reads Ruskin "on the boss's time," during his work shift at a busy clothing factory.[39] Sustained by rage and scorn for his boss during the workday, the young clerk returns on a Sabbath evening to his tenement home, where he is not restored but weakened, drained by the suffering that is all around him and concentrated in the ailing body of his father.

While his mother prepares the Sabbath meal, the taciturn young man isolates himself in his room, prompting her gentle reminder, "Darling, you should not do like you did tonight. You should always go and kiss your papa the first thing when you come home. You don't know how bad it makes him feel when you don't do that. He's very sick now; the doctor said today your popper is worse than he's ever seen him."[40]

At the end of the meal, the son has still not gone to his father and remains passively at the supper table. Again the mother suggests, "Be good . . . go speak to him," and the son reluctantly obeys. The vision that confronts David Brandt, as described in this autobiographical story of 1922, would make an accurate caption for the torn photograph found among the personal items of the author at his death in 1967: "The doctor came to see him twice a week, and wondered each time how he managed to live on. He lay in the bed, propped up high against the pillows, a *Vorwaerts* clutched in his weary hand."[41]

As the son realizes, the father is "sucked dry," existing rather than living. What troubles the young man to the point of spiritual paralysis, however, is that the onetime suspender maker, though crushed by capitalism, is still a believer in capitalist fairy tales: "There was only one spark of life and youth remaining in him—incredibly enough—his faith in the miracles of the Promised Land." Like the photo, the conversation between Brandt and his son seems an accurate and poignant index to Irwin Granich's teenage life:

"Davie, dear," he said at last, "why don't you come in to see your popper any more when you get home from work?"

"It's because I'm tired, I guess," David answered.

"No, it ain't that, Davidka, You know it ain't. You used to come
in regular and tell me all the news. Do you hate your popper
now, David?"

"No, why should I?"

"I don't know. God knows I've done all I could for you. . . . I
wanted better things for you than what you've got. . . . I was
always only a working man. Some men have luck; and they
are able to give their children college educations and such
things. But I've always been a schlemozel; but you must try
to get more out of life than I have found."

"Yes."

"David, don't hate me so; you hardly want to speak to me.
Look at me"

David turned his eyes toward his father, but he saw him only
dimly, and heard in the gaslight his father seemed like some
ghostly, unreal shadow in a dream.

"David, you hate me because I'm sick and you have to support
me along with your mother. I know; I know! Don't think I
don't see it all! . . .

"Don't, popper, for God's sake, don't talk about it!" David
spoke sharply.

After this exchange the two sit in uneasy silence. As David moves to leave,
Brandt implores once more: "Davie, dear, tell me why you didn't come
tonight. I must know." The son must now explain that it was because he
argued with his boss. The reaction of his father, who still believes in the
Benjamin Franklin-Horatio Alger success formula, is predictable: "With
the boss? God in heaven are you crazy? Are you going to lose your job
again? What is wrong with you? Can't you do like the other boys and
make a man of yourself?" Unable to tolerate this delusional thinking, the
son escapes, rushing from the room in a rage.

The story ends with a second flight response, this time in reaction to the delusions of David's mother. A version of tenement matriarch Katie Granich, she wears a white kerchief over her hair, with "brown eyes, deep and eager in her wrinkled face." Knowing her son's moods, she asks him why he fought with his father, in the process pinpointing her son's dilemma: "You must be nice to him now; he feels it terribly because he's sick, and that you have to support him. Do you worry because you have to support us?" The son evades this question and instead describes a more generalized despair: "I feel empty and black inside, and I've got nothing to live for." The existential crisis is an end product of the heavy pressures Irwin Granich faced for a time as his family's sole support, but also, for a longer period of time, as the vessel of his father's vapid bourgeois expectations.

It is also a crisis for which the young man's mother offers no relief. She reminds her son of the adolescent vitality he had once possessed in his outings with his wild East Side friends. For his present pessimism and defeatism, she blames "thought and culture," alleging that "those books that settlement lady gave you" are the problem. Ironically, she repeats almost verbatim the angry edict of the young man's capitalist sweatshop boss: "You must stop reading books!"

The son realizes the narrowness of his mother's world of "illiteracy and hope." Not in obedience but in defiance, he gets his hat and coat and leaves the tenement, "wander[ing] aimlessly into the East Side night."[42] David Brandt is not going back to his gang but advancing toward "thought and culture" of an exact nature that is never clarified. We know, however, that his direction is away from his East Side friends and away from faith in capitalist miracles. Father and mother are rejected because the choice they offer him is between two forms of acquiescence, both of which lead to oblivion.

Of course the personal is also political; David Brandt's exodus is the equivalent of Irwin Granich's attempted escape, not only from domestic strictures and pressures but from capitalist hegemony. As anyone who has read the ending of *Jews without Money* might assume, Brandt's wanderings in the East Side streets will lead him eventually to Union Square and to an awakening similar to the one experienced by that narrative's central figure, the Irwin Granich alter ego known in the novel as "Mikey Gold."

The story helps also to explain why at many moments in his adult life Mike Gold continued to struggle with his father's death and why he inserted vestiges of this tragedy even into his final literary efforts of forty

or more years later. The demise of Charles Granich was the great emotional weight Irwin carried in his young life. He rarely spoke of it until his
final years, when he began to sift it directly, first in a series of newspaper
columns in 1959, then dictating into a tape recorder in 1966, when his
eyesight was failing from diabetes. "My father had been the soul of our
home," he realized. "It was hard to accept this stranger as my father, this
struggling invalid with the shrunken face and gloomy eyes. What justice
could there be in a universe that punished so? And there had been no
crime—he was innocent, innocent!"[43]

He may have been innocent, but he died owing money. Manny
remembered his mother staggering home on a dark afternoon a month
after the funeral. She'd been to the butcher and already had a bill run
up against her of about 40 dollars. Manny saw that his mother had been
crying. She told her sons that the butcher had, in her words, "wiped out
the slate." Tearing a page from his account book, he had said, "Look,
we'll start fresh now." To her it was a touching moment but for Manny it
aroused conflicting feelings. "It was such a rich thing to do," he recalled,
"but for me to think this man did that for my mother?" It drove home
realities and left a scar.[44]

After the death, Irwin was the first of the three Granich boys to
embrace radicalism. The East Side streets were filled with soapbox agitators,
and he learned the basics of Marxism and the labor movement at these
street corner colleges. Irwin, Manny, and George got in the habit of arguing
socialism versus capitalism every night at the supper table. George started
out on the side of big business and capitalism but his brothers swung him
over, despite their mother's fears of the dangers that radicalism would lead
them into. As Manny recalled much later, Katie Granich would always
defend the socialist beliefs of her sons before friends in the community.
But at home, the bourgeois side of her would emerge; she wanted their
success and knew the struggles they spoke of would be hard. "But look
you're intelligent kids," she would say. "Why throw it all away?"[45]

The record of Irwin's activities in the two years following his father's
death suggests that his acceptance of a revolutionary worldview was likewise unstable rather than all-consuming, at least initially. His multiple
pursuits at this time were a strange and self-contradictory mixture of
radical politics and conventionally ambitious self-improvement of the type
his naïve father had always preached. Seeking the economic security no
one in his family had known, he enrolled in night-school classes at the
Townshend Harris School of City College and worked as a cub reporter for

the New York *Globe*, then turned these experiences into a year of study at New York University's evening journalism school in 1912–1913. He took reporting assignments for the *Scarsdale Inquirer* and briefly managed the printing plant of the Bronxville Valley Press. Intellectually and spiritually he was embracing radicalism, but in action he was dutifully adhering to the capitalist success path.

On April 11, 1914, the day before he turned twenty-one, something happened to Irwin Granich that would later become central to the personal legend of Mike Gold. He became involved in the radical labor movement when he wandered into an unemployment protest in New York's Union Square, heard passionate anticapitalist speeches, and witnessed an authoritarian crackdown on the right to free assembly. The crowd was attacked by police and Irwin was beaten along with other demonstrators as he attempted to help an injured woman who reminded him of his mother.[46] "I was knocked down[,] . . . booted, and managed to escape the hospital only by sheer luck," he remembered. For years Irwin had been scribbling autobiographical poetry and proletarian sketches without an audience, but soon after this he bought his first copy of the radical journal *Masses* and began submitting politically charged poetry to editors Floyd Dell and Max Eastman.

There is still some uncertainty about whose oratory inspired Gold's conversion to socialism on that pivotal day. In interviews Gold gave in the late 1930s, in speeches he gave for decades, and in newspaper columns in the last years of his life he claimed that the Union Square speaker was Elizabeth Gurley Flynn, the beautiful and fiery socialist-feminist "Rebel Girl" who had risen to national prominence in strikes led by the Industrial Workers of the World. But separate studies of Gold's life give credence to his original claim that the speaker was Emma Goldman, whose anarchist views later made her anathema to the Communist Party.

The event seems to have been consciously mythologized by Gold into a mix of fact and fancy that rendered not literal but emotional truth. Young Irwin had read about Flynn in the 1910s, probably heard her speak several times, and obviously fell in love with her on some level. Manny Granich clearly remembered that in 1912 his older brother took him to hear Flynn at the Manhattan Lyceum on East 4th Street. Manny also suggested that all the Granich brothers admired Flynn. He claimed that around 1914 he encountered Flynn on the Lower East Side, brought her to Chrystie Street, and introduced her to his older brother.[47] Whether or not it was actually Flynn who inspired him in Union Square, Granich/

Figure 2.5. Elizabeth Gurley Flynn, the "rebel girl," in the 1910s.

Gold eventually honored her with this role in the simplified version of his life story. In any case, the words of the Union Square speaker were not the only crucial factor in Irwin's political epiphany. Recalling the incident in 1932, Gold stated, "I have always been grateful to that cop and that club. For one thing, he introduced me to literature and the revolution."[48]

After April 1914, it did not take Irwin long to place his first poem in a large-circulation magazine: "Three Whose Hatred Killed Them" appeared in the *Masses* in August 1914 and marked the beginning of the author's long association with the journal. The poem espouses violence in the cause of labor liberation by extolling three anarchists who were accidentally killed in a New York tenement by a bomb they had made themselves for use against enemies of the working class. The "iron hatred" of the anarchists had "burst too soon," the poet states, but he cautions his comrades to "judge them not harshly." In reminding his audience that "they hated, but it was the enemy of man they hated," Irwin referred to the probable intended target of the bomb, John D. Rockefeller, who had used hired militia to crush a strike in his Colorado coal mines by setting fire to strikers' tents, killing thirteen women and children, in the horrific Ludlow Massacre of April 20, 1914. The poem documents a tragic setback to the revolutionary cause but it eventually finds hope, treating the "undisciplined warriors" in New York as political descendants of John Brown and precursors to renewed radical ardor.

For the remainder of his long career, Granich/Gold's enduring optimism about a worker-led future conformed neatly to Communist Party artistic standards but displeased modernist critics, who saw his revolutionary prophecies as unconvincing and formulaic. His conversion to political radicalism (throughout the 1910s he was a committed anarchist), was also the real beginning of his career as a writer. The movement gave Gold a role, an artistic identity and a message, but it was so much his raison d'être that only when his career was long over did he realize with vague regret that he had never written anything so simple and pure as a poem about love.

The narrative of Irwin Granich's early literary development is best summarized in the 1932 essay, "Why I Am a Communist," the most detailed of the author's multiple accounts of the transformative Union Square incident. The essay seems to assert that Granich was unemployed at the time he "blundered" into the meeting, stating that "in 1914 there was an unemployment crisis in America," and that he "was one of its victims." The national crisis was real, but whether the author was actually laid off at the time is questionable in light of documents he provided to Harvard University some months later and interviews he gave several decades later. The essay states, "I was 18 years old, a factory worker and shipping clerk with five years' experience, and the chief support of a fatherless family." This is generally accurate except for the age given: Granich would turn twenty-one in April 1914. And five years of experience with Adams Express would have put these events in 1912 rather than 1914.[49]

Also, the author's account jumps from the Union Square incident to subsequent phases of his life—his "reading [him]self almost blind each night after work," some "road experiences" and several years of anarchism, along with his presence in several IWW strikes leading up to the period of Russian Revolution—without mentioning a significant detour in his path to radicalism. What it ignores is that, while Irwin Granich may or may not have been laid off from his jobs in April 1914, it is certain that five months later, at age twenty-one, he would voluntarily quit several jobs in New York to pursue a goal that had been "gnawing at" him for years: getting a college education.

Before and after his later-mythologized discovery of "a world movement [that] had been born to abolish poverty,"[50] Irwin spent long hours with a group of friends he'd originally met while attending night classes at Townshend Harris School of City College, including primarily Herbert Feis and Lewis Mumford. Feis was born the same year as Irwin but already held a high-paying job at a New Jersey advertising firm. He would later become an eminent historian and an economic advisor to the State Department in the Hoover and Roosevelt administrations. Mumford was a City College student who was already innovating in the fields of architecture and urban history. Eventually he would write over twenty-five influential books, including a ground-breaking biography of Herman Melville and an urban studies text that won the National Book Award in 1961.

Both men felt substantial admiration for Irwin, qualified somewhat by impatience with his radicalism; Feis remembered him as "a burly, healthy character with a lively mind, and good deal of physical vigor" but somewhat condescendingly pigeonholed his friend as "a rather typical young and ardent Jewish socialist intellectual."[51] Mumford would later say that Irwin could have been "an American Pasternak" but regretted the side of him given over to politics, calling him "a passionate, vehement youth, who was always, before he became a party communist, his own man."[52]

Almost every Sunday when the weather was passable in early 1914, the group made long afternoon excursions on Staten Island, hiking the island's winding network of walking paths at a time when it still retained much of its Old Dutch architecture. They sometimes covered ten miles before stopping at a tavern or café, where they'd buy bottles of cheap wine and have long, animated discussions about art and politics at an outdoor table. "It was that wonderful time of your life when everything is new to you and everything is the subject for an argument," Gold recalled about these afternoons with Feis and Mumford, adding, "And you learn from the arguments. You don't just break down an opponent in brutal fashion, you have a dialogue with him."[53]

One of the discussions was remembered vividly by Gold in the last year of his life:

> Now, in this group, Feis had already made up his mind what he wanted to do next. He wasn't going to spend any more time in

business, but the next term he was going to Harvard. Mumford was also going to Harvard . . . and he urged that I try to go, too. It seemed preposterous to me, for two reasons. I didn't have the college requirements. And I didn't have the money. But these fellows had the Harvard bug bad, and I listened to all this talk, and all my envy was roused, and I knew I would die of frustration if I couldn't go to Harvard College. I had the veneration for a college education that only people who have somehow missed the boat can feel. Harvard was especially an object of superstitious veneration to many Americans, and I was one of them. I was an anarchist then, and talked about it, but I didn't have the knowledge or even the systems of studying. I was all on my own and felt it. If two such academic giants as my friends Feis and Mumford believed that I could make the grade, why then it was almost my duty to do it!

A few weeks after the radical anarchist poem "Three Whose Hatred Killed Them" had made an argument favoring the assassination of capitalists, the author of that poem applied to attend Harvard University as a "special" or provisional student, writing several letters to Admissions Dean John Goddard Hart, including an initial application and two follow-up letters, one of them on Bronxville Press stationery.

His letters of recommendation came from Professor Albert Wilson of the New York University School of Journalism; George Mathew, associate headmaster of the Massee Country School in Bronxville; Elizabeth Williams, head worker of the College Settlement House on Rivington Street; and Marion S. Loken, assistant head worker at the Ruggles Street Neighborhood School on Ruggles Street in Roxbury, Mass. According to the registrar, the recommendations were "uniformly warm and vague," except for the letter from Mr. Mathew which, perceptively, "fault[ed] Granich only with an excess of social idealism, while also recommending that as his strongest virtue."[54]

Irwin's application letter, which he sent very late for a student expecting to study in the fall, revealed that he was news editor for the *Scarsdale Inquirer* from July to September 1914, and that a few days before he sent his application to Cambridge, he had become managing editor. The "managing editor" claim may have been a ruse designed to bolster Irwin's credentials. Manny, who took Irwin's old position as a printer at Bronxville Press beginning a year later, indicated that it was easy to play with the paper's masthead and insert prank or inside joke items because its owner was usually out of town.[55] In any case, Irwin's name appears on the masthead as a "news editor" during most of 1914, confirming his position with the suburban daily. But an editorial column of April 4, 1914, signed "I.G." seems to contradict Granich's implication that he was unemployed at the time of the Union Square demonstration of that month and year.

Perhaps with justification, Granich's application also flaunted a sacrifice he would make in order to pursue his studies: "My present position has financial possibilities," he declared, adding that he was making twenty-five dollars a week, "but I am willing to throw them over—for I know I need Harvard—I want to attain my fullest intellectual stature." To this end, he informed the dean of admissions that he was planning to take a range of general courses. Finally he mentioned what may have been one of his principal reasons for applying: "I want to get into Prof. Baker's playwriting courses especially."[56]

Here Granich referred to the influential George Pierce Baker, whose famous "English 47" workshop course in playwriting was already attracting serious artists who would later author major plays. Baker's courses codified and inculcated the elements of the "well made play" for an early-twentieth-century generation of dramatists, first at Harvard and later at Yale. Granich appears not to have understood that Baker's English 47 was a graduate-level course and that workshop applicants had to submit a completed full-length play to gain admittance. But the fact that Irwin knew of Baker's importance showed that he had retained interest in theater culture since his childhood immersion in the Yiddish stage. In this first concrete indication that he wanted to write plays, he also identified a logical place to learn. As he prepared for Harvard in hopes of studying with Baker, another aspiring playwright was making the same plan. Eugene O'Neill would arrive in Cambridge in fall 1914 for the sole purpose of taking Baker's workshop.

Two weeks later the tenement striver was surprised to be admitted to Harvard as a "special, non-collegiate" student. This meant he was permitted to take instruction in "a particular line of work in which he has already been interested," in this case journalism. As the dean's letter was careful to explain, his acceptance did not include "the privilege of coming to Harvard to do what any regular College student does, and that is general culture." Ignoring the restriction, the young man wrote a second letter, posted as he boarded the night boat for Boston, informing Dean Hart that he planned to take Greek, German, ancient philosophy, lyric poetry, botany, and psychology.

Upon his arrival in Cambridge on September 28, he convinced the receiving clerk to permit his registration for these classes by telling him that the college would find a great loss in mental quality among its newcomers if everyone who wanted to study was turned away because he hadn't gotten a high school certificate.[57] The next day Dean Hart summoned Granich to his office and reiterated that he was a "Non-Collegiate Student," not a member of the class of 1918. At this, the young man pleaded for access to the university's general curriculum. He told and retold the story of Abe Lincoln's education, adding that he'd come to college on his own, with tuition expenses taken from his family's food money.[58]

The inexperienced dean relented. By means of an epic feat of boot-strapping, Irwin Granich became a freshman at Harvard. His registration was accepted for a set of classes including Economics 2A with E. F. Gay, Zoology 1 with G. H. Parker, Psychology 1 with R. M. Yerkes, and Comparative Literature 32 with Bliss Perry. He even got a course with the great George Pierce Baker, though not the acclaimed playwriting workshop. Instead he got a seat in Baker's English 14, "The Drama in England from the Miracle Plays to the Closing of the Theatres." Much later Gold recalled the luck and pluck that had determined the meeting with Hart: "If it had been a more experienced dean he would have seen instantly that I was cut out to be a clothing salesman or a shoe salesman."[59]

There was a final hurdle to clear before Irwin's bold confidence game was complete. Each of his instructors was "asked specifically if they would admit Granich to the named courses." They were "given a summary of his background and situation, and replied agreeably."[60] Perhaps the professors were agreeable because of the evident earnestness of Irwin's application. But the fact that the young man's father had died when he was a mere boy of fifteen, as his application stated, might also have mattered. Not knowing that in fact Charles Granich had died in August 1912, when his eldest son was nineteen, they all accepted this unusual new student to their already running classes.[61] We could say that Irwin fudged his application or we could reason, as Irwin did in his later fiction, that his father's death did occur around 1908, when he wished repeatedly for deliverance while confined to his bed in the stifling Chrystie Street tenement.

All that mattered now was that the ghetto-born child of immigrant Jews was no longer a "special" student; he'd unlocked access to one of the most well-protected privileges of the WASP American elite. At this point it looked truly as if wonder boy Granich, the upwardly mobile Alger hero and Gatsby-like self-creator, had gained entry to what Theodore Dreiser called the "walled city," and that Harvard University might mark the end of the beginning of a great success story.

In retrospect there were warning signs, indications about the stresses of living a double life. At this time, Gold's brothers were more certain of who they were. As Irwin came under the Harvard spell, they were stepping into proletarian manhood. Walking on Second Avenue on a warm night before he left for Boston, Irwin was amazed to see his brother George, just sixteen years old, among the "soapboxers," standing on street corner making a fiery speech for the socialist cause. A few months later, after reading Jack London's *The Road*, George ran away from home, leaving a note to his mother written in red pencil on YMCA letterhead explaining that the electric light in the cigar factory was ruining his eyes. "Please mamma, I want to see the world before I die," he entreated. George stowed away on a steamer for Florida, then lived his bachelor years in the West, where he rode the rails, dodged the World War I draft, and worked the western harvests as a migrant laborer.[62]

At this time Manny was working for Adams Express, a suitable arrangement because the company office was so close to home. His job was delivery boy, not of heavy freight but of company checks and cash-on-delivery invoices throughout the Lower East Side. He would arrive at seven each morning to sweep out the workplace; then get his bundle of checks, route them out by street addresses, and carry them on foot through the business district. At about noon he'd be finished and would stop at home to have lunch, then spend the afternoon at the load and receiving dock, helping get the lighter freight loaded onto trucks because no one could leave until all the day's parcels had gone out. During some periods of the year he'd work fourteen-hour days, as Irwin had, for a salary of twenty dollars a month. Before Irwin left for Cambridge, he agreed to send his brother three dollars of his monthly pay, giving fifteen dollars to his mother and keeping only two for himself.

Manny never approved of what Irwin attempted at Harvard. It may have been easier for him to avoid a class-based identity crisis as a young adult because he hadn't carried the burden of the firstborn son, that of supporting a family of five while existing also as the vessel of their dying father's naive success dreams. Later in life, Manny would express skepticism that the Harvard adventure really happened and doubted whether his brother ever attended a single class. He speculated that Mike saw the war coming and decided that the way to stay out of it was to relocate to the Boston area. Both Mike and Manny sometimes talked as if there was something furtive about it.

It was actually more innocent: a simple acquiescence to the powerful cultural myth of self-creation. Gatsby-like, Irwin Granich was trying to remake his identity and his origins, cleansing away the tenement filth and the shame it carried. In doing so, he was also embracing his father's illusions while forgetting the more indelible lessons his father's tragedy had taught, lessons that were the foundation of his committed radicalism.

Fitzgerald's classic 1925 novel romanticizes James Gatz's response to his destiny in changing his name to Jay Gatsby and calling himself an "Oxford man." Like Irwin Granich, Fitzgerald's "Mr. Nobody from nowhere" had studied briefly at a great university as a special student and had not graduated. But Irwin Granich would never call himself a Harvard man, and when he changed his name, it would be for purposes of distancing himself from the out-of-character belief that he "needed Harvard." The timeline of Gold's life in 1914 suggests that his permanent conversion to radicalism really didn't happen on an April afternoon in New York in Union Square but rather about six months later: in Harvard Square.

Chapter Three

Becoming Michael Gold

(1914–1920)

Irwin's immediate response to Harvard was euphoric; he fell in love with the beauty, order, and tranquility of the setting. He admired the red brick buildings covered with ivy and was charmed by the ringing out of mellow bells for breakfast and lunch. He took daily walks along the Charles River and, passing through the quadrangle on the way home, wished his father could have walked alongside him, wondering whether the son's achievement could have by some miracle saved Charles Granich's health along with his faith in the Promised Land.

At the same time he felt invisible, worried and culturally displaced. For the tenement-born ardent Jewish anarchist, blending in among the sons of the elite in order to successfully "pass" at Harvard would not be possible. Extremely self-conscious, he was humbled amid the "tall handsome bright boys with their college type sweaters and haircuts."[1] From the beginning, the way he spoke, walked, dressed, acted and thought gave him away. He felt an imposter because he was one, and was almost surely given over to soul-splitting effects like those described by Nathaniel Hawthorne, a quintessential New Englander who warned, "No man, for any considerable period, can wear one face to himself, and another to the multitude, without finally getting bewildered as to which may be the true."

Initially Irwin's anguish compelled strenuous approval-seeking. He had taken pride in being a non-scholarly type who preferred action to sedentary study. He now surprised himself with the amount of academic material he could plow through. Though it required heart-pounding bravery for him to ever express a thought during a lecture or ask a question of a professor, he "made it anyway, for a while, and never got low marks."[2]

But from the moment of his arrival in Cambridge, his détente with the great university had been undercut by a pressing problem. He had left New York with about $300 saved from wages, taking nothing from his mother but the hunk of black bread she'd given him for the overnight journey. After buying textbooks and paying $94 for a semester's tuition, along with the rent for his room in a small apartment with Herbert Feis at 81 Highland Street, he was nearly broke. He couldn't afford proper food and ended up subsisting on two meals a day of coffee and a single donut because "sandwiches were too dear." The effects of this diet during a physically strenuous and anxious period included irritability, dizzy spells, and inability to concentrate.[3]

For several reasons, Granich had to face his financial crisis on his own, later explaining that he didn't have the "nerve" to write home for a five dollar bill. Back in New York, Katie Granich was already worried for her sons; she didn't understand the Harvard obsession or why Irwin dropped everything to go there.[4] For some of the same reasons, he couldn't ask more help from 18 year-old Manny, who was nonplussed by Irwin's abrupt departure, a move that ceded the role of family breadwinner to the younger brother. It was a given that Irwin's bold exploit would prompt moments of extreme self-questioning. But the fact that in these moments there was no one rooting for him, along with the thought that he might be wasting three hundred dollars, added considerable burdens of guilt.

Desperate for income, Irwin thought of his newspaper work and brainstormed with Feis, whose family knew the editor of the *Boston Journal*. Feis's father arranged an interview, at which Granich pitched an idea he and his roommate had worked out for an anonymous column called "A Freshman at Harvard" and based on his experience as a class interloper: "You know Boston is full of thousands and thousands of people who never went to college," Irwin explained, "and with Harvard in their lap here, they could want very much to read anything about it."[5] The editor liked the angle and complimented his psychology. Miraculously, he offered Granich $15 weekly for a six-day-per-week column.

The series of articles, which began on October 19 and continued for twenty-nine installments, is remarkable in a number of ways. First it's impressive that Granich was able to function more than credibly as a working professional journalist while barely out of his teens. This is true even when one considers the fact that the time demands of the job almost certainly helped destroy his academic career. The columns may have ensured that Granich could eat, but they cut into the necessary work of passing his courses, if only by robbing him of mental energy and sleep. Second, the content of the articles strikes an interesting balance between an embrace of collegiate life and a firm critical distance, a dynamic that mirrors Granich's uncertain identity and cultural displacement at the time.

Several columns adopt a nostalgia for Brahmin New England culture but contrast the values of an assumed nineteenth-century Golden Age with the shallow commercial decadence of the present day. These pieces depict the titular freshman being taken on imaginary excursions into Cambridge historical locales, sometimes led by a fictional Harvard upperclassman. With the elder student's admonition, "You must not break your little heart searching for this culture you dreamed of in your distant waste of materialism," Granich in effect admonishes his own naive idealism.

Finally the articles are valuable for their still-relevant assessment of higher education from a working-class perspective; they're thus driven by an agenda strikingly similar to that of the *Daily Worker* columns that later made Mike Gold a household name in leftist circles. Undoubtedly one of the reasons the columns could not run very long was that the *Boston Journal* editors got much more than they wanted. They had introduced the series with a front-page lead-in that suggested conventional amusement: "Here's a new story of life at Harvard—a freshman's experiences, a freshman's views of the great institution, told day by day as he comes in contact with the varied activities." What amusement the pieces actually delivered was decidedly subversive.

The first "Freshman at Harvard" column, signed cryptically as all were, "By One of Them," showed Irwin exercising the gifts of discernment any intelligent outsider brings to a new culture. "I have just finished entering Harvard and I confess I do not like all this elaborate college machinery, with its cold, unhuman and mechanical mill of forms and receipts of one kind or another," he wrote in mid-October. It had upset him to discover that the formal admissions process for "special students" pried into "minute details" of personal history and family background. As he would in a number of the columns, Granich created a fictional alter ego, a roommate named Dan Marvin who explained that he'd left grammar school in order to work and was "too poor to have any choice in the matter." Dan said he felt "distressed" at being stigmatized by admissions officials. "They must know that I'm a roughneck printer with no right to

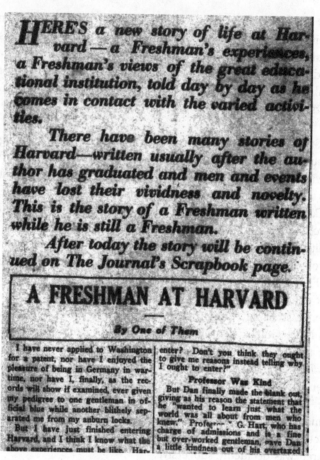

Figure 3.1. *Boston Journal*, page one, October 19, 1914. *Source:* New York Public Library.

be here," he pointed out while implying that he'd been too ashamed to give truthful details about his life.[6]

Another column imagines the roommates discussing the purpose of a new local law prohibiting Harvard students from carrying the university's crimson flag through the Cambridge streets. It falls to the leisure class George to explain that the ordinance was passed after the IWW-led textile strike in Lawrence, Mass., because the red flag "spells anarchy wherever it is raised." According to George anarchy is "where men recognize no law or order, and damage property and do violence to other citizens." Dan is confused because he witnessed the Harvard students doing all of those things after the last football game and wonders why *they* weren't arrested. It is "because they are college men," George responds. "Oh I see," Dan comprehends, "when we damage property and assault individual citizens and police officers, we are college men. When laborers do it they are anarchists. Great life this being a college man."[7]

Irwin's column of November 17 describes the freshman's chance meeting near campus with a lame, elderly mill worker who'd been blacklisted for leading a strike. The man was walking many miles to Waltham to find a friend to stay with, and Dan had sympathized, bought him a meal, and "treated him like a human being." Dan wonders aloud to George "whether either of us could be great enough to throw up a job and lead a strike." Of the encounter he says, "It was ennobling. . . . it made me love the people to see him. . . . brave in his sea of troubles." Irwin's *alter ego* then gets an idea, wishing it were possible to have the frail worker guest-lecture in his economics class on the social problem. "I know that he could give more than any professor," he states, "He would clarify all the maladjustments and brutal disproportions that prevail in our economic scheme of distribution."[8]

Several columns focus also on Granich's experience in a Comparative Literature course taught by Professor Bliss Perry, then an eminent literary authority as former editor of the *Atlantic Monthly*. In Perry's classroom, the one-time East Side factory worker detected a form of timid elitism that trivialized the study of literature: "Heaven knows there are enough profesors who need teaching, too. They are so afraid that life might invade their classrooms, many of them, so afraid of the rude, unbuffered, controversial touch of the dreaded and to be shunned TODAY."[9]

The ghetto-born freshman described a morning lecture during which Perry "held forth . . . on the beauties of the classics" while disparaging the art of British sailor-poet John Masefield. Perry claimed that Masefield's "The Everlasting Mercy," a 1911 poem about "drunken days and weary tramps/From pub to pub by city lamps," achieved a "small touch of beauty" only at the very end when the poet turned away from "brutal, violent, bar-room descriptions" and coarse, contemporary squalor.

Perry's squeamishness prompted the special student's first published defense of the aesthetics of proletarian literature. Noticing that "It was violence the professor mainly objected to," Granich asked Perry whether the *Odyssey* was violent. The *Atlantic Monthly* editor informed him that "it treated of violent subjects but in an extremely artistic manner." Granich's article then quoted a "pleasant and artistic" passage from Homer about bloody mutilation, dismemberment and disembowelment, arguing that the "certain, solid beauty" of the "old classicists" derived from representations of the brutality they imbibed as "thorough livers of their own TODAY."[10]

In a later column Granich continued his criticism of Perry's lectures, this time from a standpoint that alleged a serious flaw in the renowned professor's critical approach:

> I do not like this analytic and microscopic examination of the operations of beauty and poetry. It fulfills no practical end, it seems to me, for no laws have ever nor will ever be thus formalized for the guidance of future artists, who will always have to work, as did their predecessors, by the light of their own inward fires. This process of taking a man's work apart in the tacit assumption that one may thus surprise the secret of his genius reminds me of nothing so much as the small boy who takes apart the works of a watch and then finds he must leave them so.[11]

Here Granich's analysis attacks tenets of the methods known thirty years later as the "New Criticism," a text-centered form of analysis that focuses on the individual psyche and elitist notions of literary merit while studiously ignoring the social concerns of literary works. After the Depression and World War II, these standards were used to formulate a literary canon that broadly excluded working-class experience and radical proletarian art. It's thought-provoking to realize that, as early as 1914, Granich's working-class perspective issued a public challenge to a comparable version of prevailing literary aesthetics. He not only questioned ideas about beauty but asserted the "real-world" element of literary art as the highest justification for its study.

The outlook and values Granich brought to Cambridge from the Lower East Side ensured that pedagogical issues gradually became the main thrust of his columns. His final verdict on Perry's teaching was harsh but theoretically grounded: "Of course, he is an authority on the subject he is handling, 'Lyric Poetry.' But I cannot help thinking that all the warm pulsing life in that great body of emotion called Poetry has died for Bliss Perry. Vivisection usually carries death with it."[12] The working-class columnist implicitly calls for supplementing close analysis of works with attention to the cultural work texts do, and to their social context.

Much later in *Jews without Money*, the "Freshman at Harvard" would write, "Talk has ever been the Joy of the Jewish race . . . Talk is the base-

ball, the gold, the poker, the love and the war of the Jewish race."[13] As a
student in 1914, Granich envisioned the humanities classroom not as a
space for stale lectures but for conversation-based free exchange of ideas
and lively Socratic seminars: "It is shameful . . . that there should be so
little discussion between the professor and students of the subject matter
thus assimilated," he declared, adding,

> Some of the courses have what are called conferences, but they
> are usually recitations for the purpose of ascertaining how
> much of the reading the students have done. There is almost
> no conference in the sense in which Bacon once used it. It is
> just the report of probationers to their probation overseer.[14]

These thoughts led to a sterner indictment of the ivory tower, one
that underscored the basic frustrations of Granich's experience among the
academic elites. "Darn it all," he wrote in a column about core deficiencies in higher education, "the whole process reminds me of one of the
big Hoe newspaper presses. You put your roll of white paper in, get your
forms on, start the motor and then go round to the other end to get your
neatly folded extras. We're the white paper . . . and the profs are the type
forms. That is how they seem to feel about it anyway. It's fundamentally
wrong . . . because it isn't human. We're more than machines, and they
should be more than such to meet us."[15]

A Hoe press is a high speed printing machine of the type Irwin had
been operating just weeks earlier, in the newspaper plant of the Bronxville
Valley Press. That comparison of higher education to a Hoe press shows how
much broader Granich's experience was than that of the genteel students
whose refined lives and behavior he was observing. Taken as a whole, the
"Freshman at Harvard" articles suggest the perceptual advantages of Granich's
frame of reference in the world of hourly wages and manual labor.

By the twentieth column of the series on November 10, the ghetto-born freshman discerned a pervasive obsession with grades that
prompted him to propose an alternate approach to learning altogether.
About "grade gossip," Granich theorized,

> I know students and a university where knowledge and not
> marks are the real end sought. This is the People's Institute and
> Cooper Union in New York City. Every night approximately
> three hundred workingmen gather in its rooms for lectures and
> discussions in economic, sociological, literary, and scientific

courses. They come voluntarily, the act of registration being the only formula of admittance. There is no espionage of any sort for the purpose of forcing these students to fulfill their part in the educational relation.

And yet, any night after 10, one may go in front of Cooper Union and find little knots of these men gathered in fervent prolongations of the discussions that were interrupted in the classroom by the closing bell. Sometimes the instructor is with them—as keenly vibrant with the living touch of his subjects as are they.

I wonder why college students may not be taught on this basis. Is it because they are not as eager to learn as are these hampered workingmen? If that is the case, something is wrong somewhere.[16]

In his final article, Irwin is shocked when his professor says, "There is a continuous sharp competition going on between the departments for the attention of the student." The professor is referring to the divide that's still harming education—the one between the sciences and the humanities. The columnist's next thought is, "I cannot see the prospect of good in such internecine conflict. It must inevitably prove fatal to the development of the full, complete [person] the university is designed to produce." What solution did Irwin Granich propose? He advocated service learning among the underprivileged classes from which he came:

How about the millions who never come inside a university and who do the chores of mankind so as to leave the university free for its work? Isn't there something due them? . . . Why, for instance, shouldn't every man be required to give a prescribed number of hours each week to teaching at some night school or settlement? . . . What good are all these individual dynamos of mental power if they are not being trained to work for the community?[17]

The anonymous freshman makes several concrete suggestions for action but ultimately asserts, "It is enough to point out to the university that it is derelict in its duties."[18]

With this, Granich's column was abruptly terminated. Appended without explanation at the bottom of his 29th installment on Friday, November 21, were the words "The End." Decades later Herbert Feis speculated that the "Freshman at Harvard" experiment was canceled because the columns "strayed so far from Cambridge affairs."[19] But the pieces—touching on campus politics, football, hazing, dormitory life, libraries and union debates—did not actually digress from university subjects. The real reason they were called off, Irwin had to have known, was not because they strayed, but because they had all too much to do with Cambridge affairs. Granich's work—coolly impugning the university's expressed social ideals and undermining the authority of a famous professor while weighing problems of systemic poverty that were absent from its curriculum—was more serious and ambitious than either Harvard or the *Journal* editors could tolerate. It was the first but certainly not the last time Irwin Granich/Mike Gold paid a price for bringing discerning judgments to bear on the literary-academic establishment.

With the consequent loss of income, Granich's high hopes for himself as a student also abruptly ended. He immediately notified the university registrar that he was unable to finish the semester due to "illness and lack of funds." The cited "illness" was both physical and emotional. Overwork and inadequate food were probable contributors to what he later called "a severe nervous breakdown," a crash that certainly had to do as well with his audacious attempt to move in unfamiliar territory where cultural and class background were concerned. Reading these early columns with an awareness of the economic struggle that compelled them, a struggle that would persist in similar form for the next fifty years of the author's life, adds to their meaning, prefiguring the sacrifices that would be made over the decades in order for Mike Gold to churn out hundreds of editorials on deadline in exchange for a living wage.

More than a hundred years later, Granich's multi-level critique of higher education seems prescient. Recent research into the struggles of low income students on elite campuses suggests that entrenched class distinctions manifest themselves not just in the areas of food and clothing but in what these students understand about college, expect of their professors, and imagine for themselves.[20] Lacking both economic and social capital, needier students are still reminded of their assumed inferiority at every turn. Granich's experience suggests how teaching styles and pedagogical choices can intensify this effect, highlighting areas of harmful class-determined bias. In the case of a clearly talented freshman, one who came from the tenement only to soon return there, academic practices and hierarchies operated as micro-aggressions adding spiritual frustration to physical starvation. In other words, the East Side slum-dweller did not fail Harvard; Harvard failed him.

"It was a sort of malaise," Gold said of his breakdown. "Nothing interested me. I did not want to write anything, and so on. If I had been braver and cared less for life I probably would have bumped myself off. There is always a percentage of young people at college who break down in their first year. [. . .] I with my desire for Harvard did not take it easy enough [. . .] and I had only a few friends. I had to do it all on my own."[21] His depression was compounded by setbacks in his romantic life, which triggered a delayed reaction to his father's death. Fifty years later he recalled this period as the low point of his life: "[My father's] memory . . . obsessed me more than did that beautiful girl I was in love with. Every day I thought of him . . . I think the thing that hurt me most was that I had adored him as one of the most brilliant people I had known."[22]

Paralyzed by depression, the "Freshman at Harvard" sold his books and left Cambridge. When the spring semester began in January, Granich was about twenty miles from Cambridge in physical distance but in another world culturally. Ashamed to return to New York, he settled initially in a dingy Boston boarding house until his money ran out and he took to wandering the streets in dirty rags. On March 19 he sent notice of his final separation from the university to the office of John Hart, the Dean who had five months earlier yielded to his passionate appeal for access to Harvard's riches.

There is some irony in the fact that, if Granich had stayed in Cambridge a little longer, he'd probably have met the great John Reed, whose journalism and poetry in the *Masses*, along with his exploits in the 1913 Paterson silk workers strike, were widely known. In March 1915, just after Irwin's self-separation became official, Reed gave a lecture on "Life in the Trenches" for a group of students including John Dos Passos at the Harvard Union. Dos Passos described Reed, who had just returned from Europe, as "a strong lively fellow, with bearing and speech suggesting a football captain's." In describing the speaker's charisma, Dos Passos made observations that may offer a fundamental insight into why Irwin Granich and elite education did not mix:

> Whereas for millions of men the solid rock of everyday life had been shattered by wars and upheavals, we students were living under a bell glass, nourished by the disheartening concoction of ancient cultures. John Reed had escaped from the bell glass. He spoke as if he had never lived under it. Since he had been able to come out from under, others could too.[23]

Judging from his columns of the previous fall, Irwin's stay in Cambridge was doomed from the start. As it happened he reverted to poverty after only about nine weeks under the "bell glass." If the talk by Reed that Granich just missed attending hadn't been sufficient grounds to subvert Irwin's Harvard detour, another factor, also articulated by Dos Passos, eventually would have: "Mike Gold is very lucky to have been born when he was and where he was. The New York East Side before the war was one of the most remarkable phenomena in history, a germ of an ancient eastern-European culture transplanted pure into the body of America. . . . To have been able to live from its beginning the growth of the leaven of Jewish culture in American life may not seem so important now, but from a vantage point of twenty-five years I think it will seem tremendously important."[24]

While Granich was in Cambridge, Dos Passos had been there too, not as a special student but as a legitimate undergraduate. We might think about what it means that they didn't meet at this time, while the young Jew from the slums was class-passing among the sons of the elite. They may have walked by each other on Harvard Square, but they weren't living in the same world. They would meet later in New York. And one day Dos Passos would stroll into the premises of the *New Masses* and offer his services to Mike Gold and that organ of proletarian literary culture he led, thereby reversing their respective positions where authenticity was concerned.

An autobiographical story published in *New Masses* fourteen years after he left Cambridge, "Love on a Garbage Dump," seems to be an intense reaction to the Harvard interval. The narrative begins with a puzzling claim: "Certain enemies have spread the slander that I once attended Harvard college. This is a lie. I worked on the garbage dump in Boston, city of Harvard. But that's all."[25] Though the author did work for a few weeks bailing newspapers at a Boston garbage dump in early 1915, critics unaware of Gold's educational adventures have generally misread this passage, citing it to dismissively charge the proletarian writer with anti-intellectualism. What it actually expressed was its author's status as a rebellious outsider who harbored legitimate hostility toward an American educational system that destroyed rather than nurtured the creative intellect of the laboring classes.

In retrospect, the author's decision to repeatedly locate his crucial and life-determining political awakening in April 1914—five months before he arrived at Harvard—was another way of denying the collegiate experience, suggesting that there had never really been a significant swerving from revolutionary purpose. Considering the brevity of his stay in Cambridge and the critical stance taken in his journalism, the best available record of his inner life at the time, these claims may be justifiable. But one could argue that Irwin's painful break with elite education was the real line of demarcation, a more absolute point of no return even than being beaten by a cop.

Much later, roommate Herbert Feis was still confused about the coming and going of his East Side friend: "Why he decided to leave his job on the Westchester newspaper and come up to Harvard with me, I do not know, for it speedily became evident that he wasn't interested in scholarship or study, but devoted to agitational journalism."[26] Though Feis was essentially correct, what he did not recall was that in between Cambridge and agitational journalism Granich took a year-long hiatus in which he did little besides purge himself of bourgeois ambition and spiritually recuperate among like-minded political radicals.

Despondent, mentally exhausted, and unable to read or write, Irwin spent a period sleeping on the Boston backstreets and begging for handouts. He did odd jobs, delivered packages and took a newspaper route. Once he took a job gardening for an older man, a bookkeeper who gave him a place to stay and then tried to seduce him sexually. After a few months he picked up his writing again and began sending pieces to the *Masses*, earning a single $25 check several months in a row. He re-established ties with the Boston *Journal* and took on a few stringer assignments. At this time Irwin also encountered dozens of husky young members of the IWW and joined that organization, then saved enough money to move into an anarchist commune run by the Boston Leftist Polly Parrot.

Among the anarchists at his boarding house in Bellingham Place, Granich certainly indulged sexual-romantic passions and sometimes gave himself to careless bohemian pursuits among Boston's eccentrics and labor radicals, making up for what youth he'd lost by being forced early into the strenuous role of provider. But he seems not to have lost his social conscience or his need for contact with the hard facts of the working-class movement. In other words, he resumed the life that was real and vital to him.

At Harvard young Granich had turned to journalism to survive. In early 1916 he did the same thing, with the difference that now his focus was not on the "college men" but on the exploited classes. When immigrant operatives struck the Plymouth Cordage Works beginning on

January 17, 1916, Irwin accepted an assignment from Hyppolyte Havel's anarchist newspaper *Revolt* to report on the conflict. As he recalled much later, he "went to visit the Plymouth strike with the people who led the thing."[27] This foray into the front lines of industrial warfare in Massachusetts broadened his political outlook and helped teach him a reporting style that would make him famous.

He later gave this account of his circumstances in the winter of 1916, a time when he was still recovering from the post-Harvard period of self-destructive dissipation but ready to engage with the world again:

> A short powerful Ukrainian house painter, with the blue luminous eyes of a child, said to me in his Slavic accent one day, "We are going to Plymouth. There is a big strike in a cordage factory, and we thought you might like to write it up for the *Revolt*." This was a little anarchist paper published in New York by Hyppolite Havel. Anarchist leaders all over New England were going to go along with us. Police had threatened any anarchist who came in to the city with arrest, and old Luigi Galleani had taken up the challenge. Galleani had made so many eloquent speeches on the subject in little Italian halls around Boston, the meeting places of the anarchists. He had frightened the citizens so badly that it was said that the whole city was buying revolvers.[28]

The revolutionary propagandist Galleani, then fifty-five years old, believed in direct action or "propaganda by the deed," and had been wounded several times in labor actions. Talking with the nervous, disheveled reporter, the notorious anarchist divulged that he was himself carrying a gun. "We have to be prepared," he said. Fifty years later, Gold's memories of the encounter were still vivid. Sitting across from the aging radical in the train, he found it difficult to make eye contact with Galleani and instead looked out a rain-streaked window at the forbidding New England landscape of gray hills laden with wet snow:

> We got out at the station in Plymouth to walk into the biggest police parade I had ever seen. It must have been a hundred cops, some of them with tommy guns. They lined the pavement, and we walked through them with very many mixed feelings. I looked at our little band of young anarchists, innocent and

non-aggressive people of that type of sentimentality that chooses
the stake rather than a gift of a million dollars from some crazy
millionaire. They were idealists and nobody was more idealistic
at any time than a believing anarchist. It was the thing that
had attracted to me to the movement, its innocence.[29]

Granich knew no Italian except for some exclamations and epithets from
the East Side street wars, but he could follow the fiery eloquence of Galleani's speech, delivered to a crowd of several hundred hungry workers
striking for a living wage:

> His eyes flashed and his words sounded, and he threw his
> challenge at the whole capitalist system with the courage of a
> lion who counts no enemy invulnerable because of his passion.
> One of the things that I chiefly remember all these years is
> that he wore a long grey overcoat which had no buttons and
> which was held only by a big brass safety pin fastened at the
> lapels of his coat. He was poor, you could see that. He was a
> poet of the people in their struggle.[30]

The reporter was stirred and awestruck by Galleani, but in later years he
was made "proud" by remembering a second, briefer encounter with a
man whose name would become a by-word in twentieth-century radical
history: "The meeting ended, and people drifted out talking to each other.
It was there at that general introduction that I saw Vanzetti. He was a
young man then, tall with beautiful brown eyes and sort of ascetic face.
I did not talk with him, just hear him talk to one of the friends of my
group."[31] A decade later Mike Gold would be arrested in Boston along
with other literary activists during protest demonstrations for Nicola Sacco
and Bartolomeo Vanzetti when the case culminated in the execution of
the two anarchists.

Irwin Granich's first piece of strike journalism, "Anarchists in Plymouth"—published in *Revolt* on February 5, 1916—gives a sense of the
ardor and outrage that Galleani and the workers ignited: "Plymouth, if
you remember the rubbish taught at school, is where the joy-hating Puri-
tans landed. Now it is a smirchy industrial centre, sprawling and smoke-
belching and hideous with the vile sores of capitalism. . . . Two weeks ago
the helots who make the cordage rose in rebellion, and *Revolt* will rejoice
to know that anarchist tactics and leaders are the spirit of the uprising."[32]

Granich reported that while the cordage company had multiplied its assets more than fifty-fold since the 1890s, the salaries of its wage-slaves had not risen in those same three decades. Workers had been silent because their masters were "of enlightened capitalistic ilk" and had provided the serfs with a club-house, reading room, "fellowship" banquets every year, and ping-pong tables. As a recent convert to political anarchism, Granich took care to praise the "fringe of uncompromising anarchists," for making laborers aware of their exploitation, inserting also a fresh attack on the quintessential elite university: "The men have at last become class conscious. There are two thousand men and women in all, mainly Italians, and they are saying to their charitable masters, 'To hell with your damned ping-pong games. Give them to your feeble-minded sons at Harvard. We must have bread and more liberty.'"[33]

A few months after this reporting, "Irving" Granich was arrested with fellow Boston anarchists in a demonstration for the liberalization of birth control. He also began sending contributions to the Socialist New York *Call*. By summer he had convinced his wealthy friend Van Kleek Allison to found and coedit the *Flame*, a short-lived anarchist "journal of revolution," whose purpose, as stated in its August 1916 masthead, was "to burn against oppression and authority everywhere . . . and to be as pure and merciless as the flower of light after which it is named."[34]

In late 1916 Granich made a second dive into New England labor conflict, traveling to Providence with legendary IWW leader John Avila to help lead a strike of black Portuguese longshoremen. As a teenager, Avila was involved in the great Lawrence Textile Strike of 1911–1912, led by Bill Haywood and Elizabeth Gurley Flynn. Not long after Gold knew him, he was arrested on a blanket charge against all IWW officials, tried in Chicago, and sentenced to ten years. "I can't forget John Avila, . . . we had a great many nights in Boston together," Gold warmly recalled in the *Liberator* in 1921, "He is in Leavenworth now; has been there for four years; and he is my friend."[35] Making friendships with men like Avila was one of the pursuits Granich chose over continuing to attend classes at Harvard.

By the end of 1916 Irwin had finally moved back to New York, where he took regular reporting assignments for the *Call* while completing some short stories and beginning to compose the sketches would appear as *Jews without Money* thirteen years later. One afternoon Theodore Dreiser stopped by the offices of the socialist paper, seeking material for a play about life in the tenements, and asked Gold to show him the life and conditions of the Lower East Side. Gold obliged by escorting the famous author to Chrystie Street and showing him the apartment he still shared with his mother.

Upton Sinclair later wrote sympathetically about Granich in this period. In his 1928 novel *Boston*, a detailed account of the Sacco and Vanzetti case, Sinclair describes the young *Revolt* reporter as "a Jewish lad out of the slums of New York" who came to the Plymouth cordage strike as both a witness and participant, attending radical meetings with a "band of rebels" who were determined to fight on the side of the strikers.[36]

Sinclair's description of Irwin in the same chapter of *Boston* as a "proletarian playwright, a very scarce article,"[37] refers accurately to a contiguous and underappreciated phase of his versatile career. In 1916 to 1917 Granich not only began drafting the sketches that would later become his autobiographical novel, he found further creative outlet as a member of the Provincetown Players, eventually contributing three one-act plays that were produced alongside works by major modernist playwrights including Eugene O'Neill and Susan Glaspell at the Players' theater in Greenwich Village. The Players staged Gold's *Ivan's Homecoming* alongside O'Neill's *The Sniper* in February 1917, and in December of the same year Gold's *Down the Airshaft* was presented on a bill with works by Glaspell and Floyd Dell.

When Jig Cook read *Ivan's Homecoming*, he wrote to Granich immediately, inviting him to a meeting at the at the MacDougal Street premises. Rushing to the theater after a twelve-hour shift on the Adams Express truck, he found Cook sitting alone in the dark with a bottle of whiskey in the office on the first floor. He poured a glass for the newcomer and said, "Welcome! Perhaps you are entering on a career that will give you a lot of grief as it has given me. But this is our destiny, to write and to suffer."[38]

"I am glad to know that you're a worker," Cook said, "and that this is your first play." He told the novice dramatist, "That is what our theater exists for, to give a young writer his forum." As Gold later recalled, Cook's next statements affected him more than the whiskey he was drinking: "You are a member. Your play will be given very shortly. Meanwhile come around, drop in the place, make yourself at home, because it is your home from now on." Irwin Granich, twenty-four years old at the time, would never forget how Cook had "welcomed him, a young man who had never gone to college or written anything . . . as though I were his equal in writing."

Nevertheless the playwright later summarized the one-act that had so impressed Cook in strikingly humble terms, referring to *Ivan's Homecoming* as "a naïve thing I had dreamed up somehow" while recalling its composition, its simple action and its reception by the Players' audience:

It was before the Russian Revolution, but I had read a great many Russian classics, and it was very easy for me to concoct a stage Russian. He was a peasant and his peasant wife was alone there with a child in a hut, and the husband appeared in a sort of dreamy light and spoke to her. They discussed the war. She cursed it and he agreed. They talked about what had happened on their few acres, whether the cow had given enough milk that year to be sold, and whether the corn field prospered. But as he spoke he seemed to grow farther away from her and she was frightened, she thought that he was a ghost and she asked him whether he was alive or a spirit. He said both: "I have died from the battlefield but I am alive in your heart and you will always be alive in my heart." This was all the play was. Some of the people liked it and told me so. I think that was why they liked it. But it was a glorious feeling to be a young author, amidst these talented young writers.[39]

In *Down the Airshaft*, Granich drew from his Lower East Side childhood to tell the story of Sammy Cohen, a boy inwardly torn by a need to earn money for his destitute family and a longing for beauty in the form of flute music heard in a tenement airshaft.[40] The author's summary of the play stressed that it drew on the voices he heard through the airshaft every morning when he rose at six and again at supper at eight or nine. The boy, living with his widowed mother and younger brother, loses his job and is told by his mother that he must find work or they would perish. On the top floor, an old Greek plays his flute and the sound comes down the airshaft as the mother is speaking. "Can the boy express his desire for something greater than the sorrows of the tenement, something like that flute played by the old homesick Greek shepherd?"[41]

No copies have been found of these early one-acts, but O'Neill, who would have seen them performed and had drinks with Irwin afterward, admired them enough to enthusiastically support Gold's career as playwright for the next decade.

A third Provincetown play, *Money*, was performed on a bill with works by Edna Ferber and Djuna Barnes in January 1920 and was published nine years later in *One-Act Plays*, an anthology of short drama intended for use in secondary schools. The simple plot involves a group of immigrant Jewish men living in crowded, gloomy East Side cellar that resembles a basement shop on Chrystie Street where the Granich boys and their father worked for bread during his childhood. Moisha, a cobbler, has lost his savings of $112, a sum he had intended to use to bring his wife and children from Poland. Tormented by this life-and-death calamity, Moisha is unable to sleep for several nights. His obsessive searching awakens the other boarders and turns inevitably to interrogation when he concludes that the savings must have been stolen, and that one of his roommates is guilty. Finally Yonkel, a peddler, cannot endure the pressure; he confesses to the crime and apologizes. The stunned workers are left to consider and debate differences between rich and poor, the Old World and the New, and how the "disease of money" corrupts even fellow Jews with essentially kind hearts.

A key moment comes when a policeman appears, summoned by the loud argument, and Moisha chooses not to report Yonkel's crime. The eldest of the boarders, Abram, offers the double-edged excuse that the men had not been fighting but only talking about money. The policeman departs, greatly amused at the confirmation of the anti-Jewish stereotype. As the play closes, Mendel, the youngest character, tells of a speaker he had once heard, a man standing on an East Side street corner "saying that one day there would be no money, no rich and poor, only everyone working together like brothers and sisters."[42]

Describing the subject matter of the play much later, Gold acknowledged Russian dramatist Maxim Gorki as a strong influence. The immigrant Jews who in Gold's words "starve and suffer in an old basement as many of them did at the time"[43] resemble the wretched lives of the down-and-out characters in Gorki's 1902 drama, *The Lower Depths*, which drew on the Russian proletarian writer's own experience at the bottom of the social echelon. For years, Irwin spoke of a desire to produce an autobiographical "literary masterpiece of the order of Gorki's *Night Lodging*"[44] (an alternate title for *The Lower Depths*). About the composition of *Money*, Gold later explained, "I was obsessed with Russia and with Maxim Gorki and the play was a combination of both, the tragedy of Gorki, and the breadth of humanity that was the great world of Russia." He called *Money* "probably the best one-acter I wrote, of the many," basing his assessment on the idea that the play's "starved, gaunt workers" are crowded into a desperate, "morbidly sad" existence, yet they "achieve a certain greatness as all men must."[45]

It is also interesting that this play, which was performed in 1920 but did not see publication until nine years later, rehearses an ending that has become closely identified with Gold's life, art, and politics. The rhetoric of the East Side street-corner speaker resembles that of the revolutionary speaker who electrified Gold in Union Square in 1914, and it is strikingly similar to the anticapitalist discourse related in the final chapter of *Jews without Money*, the work that made Gold a major cultural figure. With only slight reworking, the plot of *Money* could be inserted seamlessly into the series of ghetto sketches that make up Gold's autobiographical novel.

The correspondence between the early play and the famous novel underscores their long gestation in experiences that were fictionally refined over a long period but found a receptive audience after the stock market crash of 1929. Thomas R. Cook, one of the editors who had found and selected *Money* for its 1929 publication, wrote prophetically of Gold's one-act as a "typically American" play that "succeeded in throwing light on one of our most complex sociological problems."[46]

Until he had a drama accepted by the Provincetown Players and became "a member" of that group in late 1916, Irwin Granich did not even consider himself a writer. But in his lifetime Granich/Gold would complete ten plays that we know of, among them six full-length works, and he left behind drafts of a handful of other dramatic manuscripts, several of which are stage-ready and worth revisiting. Among critics it has been fashionable to claim that Gold was not a very good playwright, but his work was admired and influential in its day.

David Roessel's research into Gold's affiliation with the Provincetown Players focuses on aesthetic similarities and differences between Gold and O'Neill. Roessel shows that while both playwrights participated in a broad movement to dramatize class-based realities, O'Neill disagreed with Gold's overtly political emphasis and consistently advised his activist friend to avoid propaganda in favor of simple realism, which in O'Neill's view was more politically effective. O'Neill believed that if Gold could break away from the financial necessities of magazine editing and journalism, he would be a major dramatist. In 1925 he wrote to the producer Kenneth McGowan, urging him to offer the Communist playwright a contract and adding, "This Gold, as I've told you before, has the stuff!"[47] In hindsight, Gold's association with the Provincetown theater was natural; the group actively sought worker-artists who could authentically express the lives of the downtrodden and bring class war to the stage.

Deeper consideration of the Gold-O'Neill artistic friendship offers evidence that it also had much to do with the life experience they shared as the sons of theater-loving immigrant fathers, and that Gold almost certainly influenced O'Neill, prompting him to explore the possibilities of ethnic theater. Along with his direct experience of poverty and ghetto life, Gold brought to the Provincetown Players a sampling of methods he had learned as a boy from the Lower Manhattan Yiddish theater.

Like the turn-of-the-century Yiddish drama that Gold knew, O'Neill's early plays experimented with a wide range of styles. As in works by Mike Gold and many Yiddish dramatists, O'Neill's characters often came from social classes that had not previously appeared on stage. Gold's sustained interest in writing plays about marginalized groups—not only Jews but African Americans, Irish, and Mexican peons—parallels O'Neill's strong interest in black American life and working-class reality during the same period. O'Neill's sense of belonging to a victimized minority, the Irish, was undoubtedly an important factor that mirrored Gold's sense of otherness as an American Jew. If, as Nahma Sandrow maintains, O'Neill was the modernist playwright whose work had "most in common"[48] with New York Yiddish drama, it was likely because Irwin Granich served as a conduit for influence and cross-ethnic collaboration.

Just as interesting when we consider this period of Granich's career are the associations he formed and maintained in his personal life, which offer evidence that the intimacies of the emerging writer already transcended traditional barriers. During Leon Trotsky's three-month visit to New York in early 1917, the *Call* editors chose Granich to interview the revolutionary leader, believing that Trotsky, a Ukrainian-born Jew, might prefer to speak Yiddish. Irwin's partner on this important assignment was a vivacious and headstrong young Irishwoman, Dorothy Day. Actually Trotsky knew only a few Yiddish phrases and was embarrassed that he had to answer the Jewish reporter in English. But the use of English gave his colleague Day an opening to ask some of her own questions, and the two reporters, who got along well, discovered they made a good team.

They also made a handsome couple: Irwin with a lean muscularity and thick, black, unruly hair, and the lithe, strikingly pretty Day with high cheeks, deep-set brown eyes, and a bearing of youthful energy and confidence. For Irwin Granich, Day's attractiveness had to do with her lack of fear and inhibition. He noticed at once that she never shrank from any human contact with the sick or the poor. Even late at night in Lower Manhattan, she went casually among the tramps, street peddlers, vagrants and immigrants—the rabble. Irwin was surely at home in the ghetto, but he thought of himself as "square" and cautious compared to the spirited Irish girl; she was hard to keep up with and almost too fearless for him. She had a wild, reckless streak in her which made Irwin anxious that she would not lose her life in some brush with the uncivilized section of the Village.[49]

Figure 3.2. Irwin Granich in the 1910s. *Source:* Granich family.

Figure 3.3. Dorothy Day in the 1910s. *Source:* Wikimedia commons.

After work hours on the *Call*, Dorothy and Irwin went to meetings, to picnics, to dances at Webster Hall. They took long walks, then sat and talked into the early-morning hours on the piers over the East River, where every now and then Irwin would sing for her, breaking into Yiddish folk songs or Hebrew hymns. Dorothy could feel Irwin's affection and she became his girl.[50]

Within weeks they were engaged to be married. A new biography of Day by Kate Hennessy, Day's granddaughter, tells a tender story of their cross-cultural love. Irwin brought the Christian girl home to the family tenement to meet his "stern and beautiful Orthodox Jewish mother." When Irwin introduced Dorothy, Katie Granich looked at the girl "sorrowfully, as all three of her sons were dating gentile girls at the time." According to Hennessy, Irwin's mother didn't speak but at once made a formal meal for them, then stood over the couple almost ceremonially with her hands clasped in front of her, and watched the young couple eat. Dorothy stayed the night, sleeping on the narrow parlor sofa. After the gentile girl left, the distraught Jewish mother broke the dish Dorothy had eaten from.[51]

There was a saloon near the Provincetown Players theater, a little one-story wooden house on the corner of Sixth Avenue and Fourth Street, built before the Civil War and known as the Golden Swan but also called the Hell Hole. In a glass case that stood on a table near the entrance, there was a dusty, dirty white swan. The Provincetown Players had the habit of taking the back room of this quaint old Irish gangster hangout, and one night Irwin brought Dorothy there, where she met the talented youngsters of the Players including Cook and O'Neill. It was a dingy little room, where O'Neill would sometimes read from new scripts or, after much whiskey, recite from memory his favorite poem, Thompson's "The Hound of Heaven." Irwin was not a whiskey drinker but Dorothy kept up with O'Neill, and he could see that Dorothy was taken by the brooding Irish playwright. Kate Hennessy gave a charming description of this love triangle and a poignant moment both Day and Granich would long remember:

> The friendship between O'Neill and Day broke Irwin's heart. One night as a fierce blizzard swirled outside the Hell Hole, Irwin poured all his feelings out and told them both how jealous and brokenhearted he was. Gene suggested they go

for a walk and they set out, pushing through the snowdrifts, while Irwin sang songs in Yiddish, and Gene sang sea shanties. Dorothy was Irwin's girl, but she wasn't serious about the engagement and Irwin knew it.[52]

In late April of 1918, John Reed returned from Russia, having witnessed the Bolshevik Revolution, and Irwin Granich was assigned by the city editor of the *Call* to meet him. He hired a carriage and drove with Reed's wife Louise Bryant to the pier, where the two waited for hours while a swarm of Justice Department men detained Reed, going through every piece of his clothes and baggage and putting him through a long interrogation. Reed had been sick with ptomaine and the "inquisition," which almost certainly involved rough physical treatment, was painful. Later, Gold remembered the warmth between Reed and Bryant as they kissed and embraced, and the hungry, homesick look in Reed's eyes as he stared at "the houses, the people on the sidewalk and the New York sky, with his large, honest eyes."[53]

They went to the dining room of the Hotel Breevort, then a meeting place of the Greenwich Village radicals and intellectuals. Scores of friends greeted Reed as they entered, among them a beautiful red-haired actress who hailed him as he passed and drawled, "It seems you've been away, Jack." Reed told her where he'd been and she replied, "Why Russia, Jack?" "There was a revolution," he answered. "A Revolution? Oh! Was it interesting?" she asked. Later Gold observed of Reed, "He had seen famine, war, disease, mental suffering, chaos—everything that the sick and dying past demanded before it would yield to the new," and the actress "wanted to know if it was interesting—as interesting, let's say, as a batik print, or the new edition of Krafft-Ebbing." In response Reed's face flushed. He looked at the beautiful girl who was "too aesthetic" to read the newspaper and sneered, "Interesting. . . . you wouldn't know." For Gold, the heartfelt reaction showed that Reed had not, as anti-Communist critics would later claim, "regretted his revolutionary past."[54]

The story is significant also because it puts Irwin Granich in contact with Reed and Louise Bryant. An artist, feminist, accomplished journalist and original member of the Provincetown Players, Bryant had met Reed in 1915 in Portland Oregon. She then ended her marriage to a Portland dentist and came to live with him in Greenwich Village, where the two were married in 1916. Both she and Reed took lovers outside marriage;

during her New York years Bryant's affairs included Eugene O'Neill and the painter Andrew Dasburg.

After Reed's untimely death from typhus in 1920, both Bryant and Gold would express the desire to write and publish a biography of the romantic revolutionary. Gold had first admired Jack Reed from afar and later up close as a Provincetown Player and as a reporter covering his participation in the *Masses* trial of 1918. Throughout the 1920s Bryant came to resent Gold's efforts to acquire Reed's papers for his biography, a book Louise felt herself better qualified to write. She claimed that her late husband barely knew Gold and "thoroughly disliked" him. One piece of evidence she gave for Reed's animosity was expressed in a November 1934 letter to artist Robert Hallowell:

> I give you briefly the history of Mr. "Gold." He is a draft-evader whose real name is Irwin Granich. His relations with Jack were exactly this: Gold once came to our apartment on West 8th Street one day during the war and asked Jack if he knew ways into Mexico. Jack asked him why he wanted to know. He said he wanted to evade the draft. Jack replied, "Yes, I know ways into Mexico but I also the way out that door. I have respect for conscientious objectors but I have no respect for cowards!" Therefore he pushed him out.[55]

Bryant's story seems questionable, first because Reed was profoundly, irreconcilably opposed to the war in Europe. Having seen its horrors at close range on the eastern front, he was convinced that it represented merely a struggle between rival capitalist interests. At the time the above encounter with Gold would have taken place, Reed was known to be a committed pacifist. It's more likely that if Gold sought Reed's counsel about getting to Mexico, the revolutionary hero would have encouraged rather than scorned him.

"In that struggle the young people had many decisions to make," Gold recalled, referring to the question of draft evasion. "I remember my two brothers' struggles. One of them, Manny, finally escaped to the West and became a cowboy on a ranch. The other, George, became a boxcar hobo for seven or eight years. George always did what came naturally and he just walked away and lived in boxcars. It was pretty tough on youngsters."[56] In 1917 Irwin had been rounded up and questioned by the draft police at least twice.

He left for Mexico in fall 1918 in response to the third draft registration call, which was issued in September. Much later he recalled the
atmosphere of that moment, describing the "senseless idiot joy that flared
through all the capitals as the guns opened the hellish rhapsody" of the
bloody conflict. "The young bank clerks, mechanics, longshoremen and
salesmen were covered with flowers and kissed by the pretty girls as they
paraded along the avenues and sang 'Over There' and the other battle
hymns, and hustled to their tombs and mustard gas."[57]

While living in Mexico for more than a year, Granich learned good
Spanish and immersed himself in a peasant culture involved in its own
form of revolutionary class conflict. He labored in the fields alongside
Mexican peons near Tampico but also did translation work for newspa-
pers and canvased the streets of Mexico City to raise funds to publish a
Spanish-language version of the Soviet constitution.[58]

Gold often said that in Boston he became an anarchist, but Mexico
converted him to communism. Late in her life, Dorothy Day remembered
the still-lovesick Irwin just before his departure from New York, and speculated that in Mexico Gold had met Mikhail Borodin, a Russian Comintern
agent who'd been expelled from the United States. If so it was through
his relationship with M. N. Roy, an Indian revolutionary who befriended
Gold in Mexico City while at the same time sharing an apartment with
the Russian leader. It seems possible that Gold's commitment to "world
socialism" helped ease the pain of his breakup with Day, the Christian
girl from across the tracks whose bond with Irwin was based on what
she called a common interest in "the poorest of the poor, the guilty, the
dispossessed."[59]

Roy remarked in his memoirs that among the hundreds of American
pacifists, anarcho-syndicalists, and socialists of all shades who had escaped
to Mexico, "it was Irwin Granwich [sic] who impressed me the most."
Underneath Irwin's "affected bitterness and cynicism," Roy discerned "a
tolerant temperament" and a kind personality: "From the very first day
of our meeting, I liked him immensely," he recalled.[60] During their shared
exile in the Mexican capital, Granich taught Roy about anarchism and the
IWW while divulging his ambition to write proletarian stories and plays
based on his life in the Lower East Side tenements. In return Roy told
stories of his impoverished early youth in the Midnapore district of West
Bengal. Gold's developing political views at this time were characterized
by Roy as "anarchist Communist"; he had faith in social revolution but
was a skeptic about "the State and political organisation."[61]

In the community of transplanted writers and Bohemians known by the derogatory term *slackers*, Granich struck Roy as an exuberant and adventurous temperament. Teamed with Roy to solicit donations for a printing of the Bolshevik constitution in Mexico City, Irwin recognized and detained a New York acquaintance, the black American prizefighter Jack Johnson: "Say Jack, have you anything against the Bolsheviks?" Granich asked. The great boxer replied, "Nao, not that I know of." Then Johnson pulled out a ten dollar donation with a broad grin, and "wished the Bolsheviks luck."[62]

Though Gold apparently was not an attending delegate at the International Conference of the Socialist Party in Mexico in 1918, he nevertheless made waves. The optics of the event were marred because the Central and South American socialists sent delegations that were devoid of actual members of the proletariat. Instead they were filled with lawyers, teachers, poets and journalists but "not a single industrial labourer or a son of the soil."[63] This was unacceptable to Gold and Charlie Phillips, a New York pacifist who was already known for organizing antiwar demonstrations at Columbia University. As the conference opened, the two went together into the slums to recruit workers and their children, then led hundreds of members of the lower classes into the city plaza, effectively introducing the "respectable" conference delegates to the authentic Mexican proletariat through a mass demonstration of worker strength and solidarity.

Behind "a forest of red flags" and a great banner featuring Lenin, Gold and Phillips led the destitute laborers, who carried signs with slogans that Roy found "striking" for a conference that had leaned toward anarcho-syndicalism rather than communism: "Down with Yankee Imperialism" and "Long Live the Soviet Republic of Mexico." Though Phillips received the largest share of credit for the spectacular demonstration, Gold's Spanish skills and identification with the slums were no doubt instrumental in delivering to the Socialist International "the message that the revolutionary will and might of the working class had triumphed."[64]

Journalist Carlton Beals, also in Mexico City at this time through his affiliation with the city's American High School, saw another side of Gold's character: "Granich's period in Mexico, I am sorry to say, was not very creditable, mostly drinking, whoring around, and 'chewing the fat' with friends." As Beals recalled, Irwin was often broke. When he gave him a job teaching English, Granich showed up for his class in dirty corduroys and a ragged wool shirt, then during the second lesson suddenly said "to hell with this" and walked out. He wasn't much of a teacher but Beals

Figure 3.4. Granich worked for a time in the "wild and rich" oil country near Tampico. "I imagine the Garden of Eden must have been somewhere in this country," he said; c. 1919. *Source:* Granich family.

was impressed with his friend's intellect, noting that he loved poetry and "could quote it by the yard" and that Irwin used to say, 'If I didn't know so much poetry, I'd be a damned fool.'[65]

The following year, Mexico City held its first National Socialist Congress, an event Granich wrote about for a Chicago-based IWW publication, the *One Big Union Monthly*. Despite the reactionary anti-Labor abuses of the Venustiano Carranza government, Gold was optimistic about Mexico's socialist future. Not only was the Mexican worker "unconsciously radical and ready for the message" of the Wobblies, the conference itself was "a workingmen's convention—oil workers, farm workers, miners and city proletariat came in their blue overalls and straw hats."[66] It seemed safe to predict that Mexican regional unions would soon unite with the IWW, adopt its tactics, and therefore "walk steadily" toward the vision Mike Gold held for the next four decades and first expressed here: "One Big Union all over the world." A final hopeful factor remarked on in this interesting article gives some credit for Mexico's progress to exiles like himself, indicating the political activities of draft-evading leftists: "The past two years . . . there has been a renaissance of hope, stimulated directly by the example of Russia and by the influx of hundreds of young Americans of industrialist and Socialist affiliations who escaped here during the war period."[67]

A short story based on Gold's experience among the slackers, "Two Mexicos," dissects the contradictory political views of the country's elite landowning classes and draws analogies between the rural Mexican laborers and those equally exploited in the ghettos of urban America. In the story, a contrast between brothers, Don Felipe and his younger brother, Enrique, represents the contrast between feudalism and an egalitarian future. The elder brother, who abuses the landless peons, seeing them as subhuman and enforcing submission through violence, is the incarnation of "brutal, primitive aristocracy."[68] He rapes and lynches yet claims to value pride and personal valor while bemoaning the Mexican Revolution, which had afforded a modicum of civil rights to the "slaves" on his ranch. Enrique, on the other hand, is a Marxist revolutionary who treats the peasant workers "almost as equals" and has plans to transfer his land to them. While the story's diction emphasizes obvious parallels between systemic worker exploitation in Mexico and in the United States, it does not resolve the conflict between good and evil simplistically. The warring brothers stand "facing each other in the vast, silent moonlight," but the only outcome is implied in the narrator's expectation that there will be "no peace till the younger [brother] shall have forever slain the elder."[69]

Published in the *Liberator* in 1920, this story was later turned into a full-length drama, *Fiesta*, which saw production with the newly commercialized Provincetown Players in 1929 and drew praise from *New York Times* critic Brooks Atkinson, who called Gold "a genuine playwright." The reviewer for the *New Republic*, Stark Young, similarly extolled the author's "genuine poetic feeling for types, fresh feeling, contrasts of personality, [and] raw color."[70] As Wald notes, the sojourn in Mexico was productive, resulting in "a full-length play, a short story, an unfinished novel, and a life-long love of Mexican songs, the spirit of the Mexican Revolution, and the Spanish language."[71]

Before leaving Mexico, Irwin Granich received news of the Palmer Raids, which involved widespread arrests and detentions of radicals and anarchists by the US Department of Justice. This alarming anti-Left atrocity may have been a practical pretext for his permanent name change, but the new identity also resonated in broadly symbolic terms. It's interesting that the pseudonym was taken from a person not only once known to Granich, but still living. The real Michael Gold, a Civil War corporal born in New York, resided in the Bronx until his death in 1938 and, as far as we know, never objected to the borrowing.

To the extent that the name figuratively united the nineteenth-century war against chattel slavery with the twentieth-century struggle against wage slavery, it points to one of Gold's long-standing passions. If there is one aspect of Gold's career as both editor and writer that deserves renewed attention, it is his lifelong effort to espouse and in some ways embody the aims of disparate races and ethnicities by suggesting shared links between the liberation histories of African Americans and working-class Jewish Americans.

As Gold explained in a memoir he wrote just before his death, he had encountered the man behind the alias in his boyhood on the Lower East Side. The first Michael Gold had been the father of a boy Irwin knew in his public school days, before Granich gave up his education to support his family at age twelve. Charles Granich knew him as well. It was at this time also that the Civil War became a subject of fascination for the future activist writer. His school principal was a revered elderly veteran—"white-bearded Colonel Smith"—who shared war stories with the students at morning assemblies. This educational emphasis on the war against slavery elicited an early personal involvement with social principle, inducing the young idealist to seize on a connection between the fight for justice and the Jewish veteran of the Union army, "Corporal Michael Gold."

Apparently the first and "real" Michael Gold was an impressive man. When he died at age ninety-one, a *New York Times* obituary spoke glowingly of his Civil War service as "a Union Corporal stationed outside Appomattox when Lee surrendered." He was a German immigrant who came to the United States in 1864, enlisted, and "became a part of the Second Army of the Potomac." He had met General Grant and perhaps encountered Lincoln as well. He was also a neighbor to the Granich family and a Lower East Side Jew who had escaped outsider status to acquire genuine heroic credentials. A living confirmation of democratic mythology, Corporal Gold suggested that a son of Jewish immigrants could also be a freedom fighter for African Americans. If an appeal to the legend of Lincoln had helped Irwin Granich get a spot at Harvard, becoming Mike Gold would keep this legend—one that neatly and coherently blended the ideologies of immigration and liberation—continuously important in his career as a writer.

A biographical article on Gold published by Marcus Klein in 1981 sees an even deeper potential meaning in the name change. Klein begins by setting aside the notion that Gold took the name only for tactical, "protective" reasons, though he acknowledges that "Irwin Granich" already had some prominence in the leftist press, which certainly could have put the writer in some danger. But Klein speculates, correctly, that if the Palmer men really wanted to arrest Granich under any name, they could have found him. There must have been another motive for naming himself anew. "It must have been the case," Klein insists, "that he changed his name for the additional reason that all genuine revolutionaries did the same."[72]

Chapter Four

From the *Liberator* to the *New Masses*

(1921–1929)

After returning from Mexico in early 1920, Gold began submitting essays and stories to the *Liberator*, the successor journal to the suppressed *Masses* and the namesake of William Lloyd Garrison's famed antislavery newspaper of the antebellum era. Max Eastman, editor of the magazine, described Gold at this time as "a dark-eyed, handsome social mutineer with wide lush lips, uncombed hair, and a habit of chewing tobacco and keeping himself a little dirty to emphasize his identity with the proletariat." Gold was invited to join the *Liberator* editorial staff in January 1921, largely because Eastman recalled what a "close friend" of the old *Masses* Irwin Granich had been, a contributor with a "a rare gift" who had always offered "the very best fruits of his genius."[1]

It also helped matters that, as early as 1918, Granich had celebrated the founding of the *Liberator* and predicted that it would be "more realistic and more concerned with the actual technique of the revolution than was the *Masses.*"[2] Though Eastman believed this prediction accurate, he would eventually decide that "something strange and dangerous began to develop in Mike Gold" after his return from Mexico, an emotional instability that the former head of the *Masses* claimed produced rage and violent mood swings. "We all were anguished about him," Eastman explained in his 1964 memoirs. In the February 1921 number of the *Liberator* he inserted the following announcement:

TO OUR FRIENDS

Michael Gold, formerly a contributor and recently made a contributing Editor of the *Liberator*, has suffered a serious nervous breakdown. Those interested in contributing to his recovery can send money to the *Liberator*.

"It must have resulted in someone's coming forward," Eastman vaguely recalled, for Gold, who was also "dead broke" at the time, recovered in a matter of weeks. Ten years later Gold sent Eastman a copy of *Jews without Money* with an inscription that began, "Thanks for saving my life once" and expressed appreciation for his help with the novel in its earliest stages.

Gold's erratic and troubling behavior—Eastman describes a fit of "shaking convulsions" at the home of Floyd Dell in which Gold threw furniture and broke out a window with his forehead—happened while he was also in the process of changing his name. What this suggests is that the assumption of a new identity was not only gradual but traumatic. The first use of "Michael Gold" in print occurred in the July 1920 *Liberator*. The last work published under the name Irwin Granich came eight months later, in February 1921. The fact that the author wavered before he took the leap and felt emotional distress while doing so confirms the notion that the pseudonym was not really a means of hiding from A. Mitchell Palmer and the Justice Department. It was instead the product of an identity-based inner struggle.

Gold's last article as Irwin Granich was the seminal essay, "Towards Proletarian Art," a complex, impassioned manifesto in which the author formally broke with the liberal-individualist aesthetic theory of mentors at the original *Masses*, Eastman and Floyd Dell. Citing Walt Whitman as "the heroic spiritual grandfather" of proletarian culture, he called for heightened social consciousness in literature and asserted that "a mighty national art cannot arise save out of the soil of the masses." The new art, Granich implied, would express the experience of the poor and without exception be created either by the poor themselves or by artists who had lived sympathetically among them. The American currency of the term "Proletarian literature" dates from the publication of this article, which Michael Folsom described as "a major document in radical literary theory."[3]

Folsom recognized the importance of the piece but somewhat dismissively called it "intellectually callow," perhaps without realizing that the essay was both a professional and spiritual creed, a deeply personal leave-taking with the upward-striving impulse that had once led Granich to Harvard. Whatever embarrassment its author expressed about it to Folsom decades later was probably less a product of its artistic assertions, which Gold never renounced, than of its autobiographical passages, which use a figurative "boy in the tenement" as a rhetorical tool within yet another emotional confrontation with the ghost of his father.

It seems noteworthy and not merely coincidental that this was the last piece published under the old name; Granich locates the essayist's voice firmly in the tenement one final time. Throughout the piece, the author uses the plural pronoun "we," not in reference to radical writers as a collective, but to the two selves battling within him. The essay may be read as an account of his identity struggle and declaration of its outcome. As he defined proletarianism, he defined himself.

"We are prepared for the economic revolution," Granich announces, "but what shakes us with terror and doubt is the cultural upheaval that must come." Having been "bred in the old capitalist planet," the "stuff" of that world is undeniably "in our very bones." Acceptance of capitalist assumptions is instinctive because it is essentially the hegemonic DNA left behind by the author's early cultural formation in poverty. Granich admits to a tendency to cling to the old culture to such a degree that his break with it feels like suicide. "But it must die," he decides, "The old ideals must die." He accounts for his nervous breakdown by treating it, understandably, as a cosmic struggle: "I have felt almost mad as I staggered back under the blows of infinity . . . the endless Nothing. . . . How it has haunted me!" For the artist, the only way out is "to discover what gives them strength and faith," and therefore to choose one's "synthesis for life."[4]

Seemingly predicting the rest of his career, he admits, "I can feel beforehand the rebellion and contempt with which many true and passionate artists laboring in all humanity will greet claims for a defined art." But he asks his audience to remember that what he's experiencing is "a deeper more universal feeling" than most will appreciate. Shifting significantly to the first-person singular, his preamble climaxes with an avowal that he respects "the suffering and creation of all artists" but can write only from the perspective of a child of the ghetto: "I was born in a tenement. . . . It was in a tenement that I first heard the sad music of humanity rise to the stars. The sky above the airshafts was all my sky; and the voices of the tenement neighbors in the airshaft were the voices of all my world. There, in my suffering youth, I feverishly sought God and found Man."[5]

"All that I know of life I learned in the tenement," the soon-to-be former Irwin Granich explains, "I saw love there in an old mother who wept for her sons. I saw courage there in a sick worker who went to the factory every morning. I saw beauty in little children playing in the dim hallways, and despair and hope and hate incarnated in the simple figures who lived there with me."[6]

Choosing his future, he questions the reigning expectation of artists born in poverty, wondering why they are told again and again to go beyond that world for their self-expression. "Life burns in both camps, in the tenements and in the palaces," he admits, "but can we understand that which is not our very own?" And more compellingly, "Need we apologize or be ashamed if we express in art that manifestation of Life which is exclusively ours, the life of the toilers?" For him and his class, art itself is defined as "the tenement pouring out its soul," for the simple reason that this grim world "bore us and molded us through years of meaningful pain."[7]

Concurrent with his binding decision to abandon his name, he makes certain to bear witness to what he can't disown: "The tenement is in my blood. When I think it is the tenement thinking. When I hope it is the tenement hoping. I am not an individual; I am all that the tenement group poured into me during those early years of my spiritual travail."[8]

Another document that offers insight into the terms of Gold's evolution from one persona to another is the previously mentioned short story about his father's illness and despair, "The Password to Thought—To Culture." David Roessel's research shows not only that the earlier version of this story, "The Trap," written by Irwin Granich in 1917, was very different from the one Mike Gold wrote in 1922, but that the differences were related to a shift in the author's identity as an artist.

"The Trap" leaves Irwin Granich's alter ego, and his family, mired in existential stasis, weeping and huddled together in their cave-like tenement in a way that validates the story's title. For Roessel, the concept of "the tenement" in this sketch symbolizes weakness and a brutalizing negation of humanity. The story is a clipped, Hemingway-like treatment of sordidly real conditions that elicits ambiguous, undefined modernist angst. "The Trap" actually compares well with Hemingway's early short fiction and might seemingly have been written by any of the Greenwich Village Bohemians or "lost generation" pessimists. The second version of the story has clearer social priorities. The tenement is now a source of strength in a resistance to clearly defined enemies: his father's childlike faith in the capitalist success myth, and his mother's demand to acquiesce and conform because both the struggle and the knowledge that comes with it are futile.

Roessel's article quotes Carlton Beals, who knew Irwin Granich in Mexico in 1919 and understood that the East Side writer was at this time "fluctuating between literature and Marxianism, Bohemia and the Class Struggle." Roessel's take-away after comparing the two stories is well formulated: "Readers familiar with the assertive voice of Mike Gold" might justifiably take the earlier story "as an indication that Irwin Granich and Mike Gold are actually two different writers, and something more than a change of name happened to the author in the course of the transition from one persona to another." Assuming the name Mike Gold was therefore an announcement to himself and the world that "the fluctuation was over, and Marxism and the class struggle had won."[9]

Part of this book's purpose is to consider how Gold stayed the course in the "class struggle," through abidingly human moments of failure and uncertainty, during a long career. Why did the People's Writer not go the way of so many others and submit? For example Eastman, the famous *Masses* editor and friend of John Reed, ended up switching allegiances in the class war and ridiculing Gold's desire to "produce a really 'proletarian' art and literature."[10] In his 1964 memoirs, Eastman portrayed his former friend's politics during the *Liberator* years as both overly combative and naive, a manifestation of emotional sickness. He implied that Gold's "rabid revolutionism" was little more than an aftereffect of his nervous breakdown, the reflex response to a neurotic "conflict of passions" that afflicted the author of *Jews without Money* throughout his career.

A related claim was that Gold's transformation into a "zealot" about working-class culture, along with his "self-blinding Russia worship," were products of the ghetto-born writer's deep psychic complexes, which desperately required an outlet for his suppressed class-based anger. Though Eastman's phrasing is tendentious, his view is not categorically inaccurate. The main thrust of Eastman's retrospective attack on Gold—that the quintessential proletarian artist was "a man of scars solving his personal conflicts with a rage against capitalism"—is hard to refute. It actually helps to explain why Gold's name change, his return from Mexico, his breakdown, the Palmer raids, and the publication of the "first significant call . . . for the creation of a distinctly and militantly working-class culture"[11] occurred more or less simultaneously. The problems with Eastman's psychology-based analysis are that, first, it is used to assassinate Gold with the grossly misleading label, "an intellectual robot in the cause of communism."[12] Second, it willfully ignores the subject's real humanity: that Mike Gold could be seared and wounded by poverty that did not harm him personally. And third, it does both of these things in an attempt to deny what should not be denied: the man's priceless contributions to American culture and society.

For his part, Gold psychoanalyzed Eastman as well, recalling Eastman's motivations during the brief *Liberator* period of the early 1920s. In his unpublished memoirs, Gold said that Eastman, who had stood bravely in the 1918–1919 *Masses* trials on charges of "treason to American militarism," had begun showing signs of "a sort of intellectual suicide," a moral malaise resulting from the day-to-day pressures of publishing a radical magazine in a repressive political climate. Gold realized that this atmosphere was "one of the most terrible results of an imperialist war" and sympathized with Eastman's dilemma, but he never saw capitulation as an option.[13]

Not surprisingly, a fateful meeting in 1921 at which the management of the *Liberator* changed hands was also viewed differently by the two men. Eastman, who had called the meeting for the sole purpose of deciding the future course of the magazine, fully expected it to be liquidated without conflict or resistance. But as Eastman recalled, the discussion became a personal attack. "On the question of whether I was fit to be editor, Gold rounded up quite a few negative votes. . . . Instead of a debate, therefore, the meeting turned out to be an eloquent discourse by Mike Gold on my lackadaisical spirt and remoteness from the suffering proletariat."[14]

In Gold's recollection of the same meeting, Eastman began by offering arguments about the futility of being "a sitting duck for capitalists under martial law" by continuing to publish antistate ideas, arguments Gold felt were "sufficiently truthful to satisfy anybody." But in Gold's view, Eastman made a mistake in taking it for granted that the editors would "go along with him in the rush for survival, personal survival." When the usually passive editorial board began to resist, Gold "got up to make a fiery little speech" in what he called his "most juvenile style," after which the majority swung to him. "So the editors decided to keep the magazine's flag flying in the winds of freedom," with Gold and Claude McKay as coeditors.[15]

Gold and McKay formally became coeditors of the magazine in January 1922, in a collaboration that would last only six months. Eastman and others have often characterized Gold's relationship with the black Jamaican poet in negative terms. Predictably, Eastman emphasized dysfunctional aspects of the partnership. He described the two men as temperamental opposites who were both "richly endowed with complexes" and used the fact that Gold once challenged McKay to a boxing match to claim that their association "came near to being a fist fight."[16] He further asserted that Gold's zeal for proletarianism alienated McKay and from the "basic temper" of the *Liberator*.

Likewise Harold Cruse's 1967 study *Crisis of the Negro Intellectual* alleged that Gold's proletarian and McKay's New Negro writing operated antagonistically. Cruse accused Gold of being "not sympathetic to McKay's literary work" and depicted the coeditorial relationship as adversarial.[17] He saw Gold as an enemy of the black aesthetic who forced the Jamaican-born McKay to prioritize labor-class cultural standards in opposition to the race-centered artistic criteria of the nascent Harlem Renaissance.

These views have recently been challenged. While it seems true that Gold and McKay were in some ways "temperamentally incompatible,"[18] the actual products of their alliance, according to the research of William Maxwell, bespeak a fruitful concord of goals and priorities. Maxwell's 1996 revisionist consideration of the Gold-McKay relationship, "The Proletarian as New Negro: Mike Gold's Harlem Renaissance," argued that the Jewish Communist and New Negro artist did not represent warring aesthetics but instead reinforced each other in important ways. Both Gold and McKay, for example, saw themselves as proletarian writers and agreed that racism was a threat to the aspirations of all workers. In their unusual cross-racial partnership, Gold and McKay published both poetry and prose that would help initiate the Harlem Renaissance.

As Maxwell pointed out, much of the McKay poetry that later became central to the 1920s black aesthetic was published in the *Liberator*, and the issues McKay and Gold edited together featured articles, poetry, and art by both black and white contributors that dealt with racial oppression and black culture in the United States and the Caribbean. Under their control, the magazine showed that the core values of proletarian literature and the Harlem Renaissance were not mutually exclusive but rather in cooperative alignment. That a Marxist journal with an almost completely white staff was also "one of the small number of magazines in and around which the Harlem Renaissance took shape" is significant.[19] In a general sense, awareness of this dynamic challenges the assumption that proletarian and "New Negro" writing were wholly discrete schools.

It seems possible that Eastman's skepticism about the black-Jewish collaboration was based on unconscious racial stereotypes, or at least on an inability to fathom the totality of a white man's commitment to African American causes at this early stage of Gold's career. It's worth noting as well that the US Department of Justice, which had become obsessed with black subversion during the first Red Scare, was also interested in the unusual arrangement at the *Liberator*. In 1919 the FBI issued a report titled "Radicalism and Sedition among the Negroes, As Reflected in Their Publications." The Justice Department expressed general alarm at "determined and persistent radical opposition" among black journalists and especially at the "identification of the negro with such radical organizations as the IWW and an outspoken advocacy of Bolsheviki or Soviet doctrines."[20] The department seems to have been principally concerned that such synergies could produce, as stated in the report, "no color or caste discrimination whatsoever." If this was what they were looking for, they found it at the *Liberator* in early 1922. The fact that they targeted both editors for surveillance at the same time and mentioned each in the surveillance file of the other would indicate that, unlike Max Eastman, the FBI did not see the Gold-McKay relationship as antagonistic or dysfunctional.

For all that has been written about the conflicts between the coeditors, late in life Gold recounted only favorable impressions: "Claude was a wonderful poet whose songs were as natural as the woodnotes wild that Shakespeare described. . . . He was a charming person covered with all kinds of tragedy. His mind was always unhappy and struggling against internal and external demons. . . . [His] sonnets were like clear crystal songs of a certain kind. And even the indignation against the white racist that boiled in his blood came out with a certain music instead of harshness."[21]

Early in their association, McKay tried to attend a Theatre Guild production for the purpose of writing a review of the play and was refused admission on racial grounds, even by this idealistic organization composed of middle-class progressives. Afterward, his coeditor recalled, McKay wrote a "red-hot" piece for the magazine that Gold considered a masterpiece, "another step in the long road that it took American liberals to realize that liberalism was not enough and that the best of liberals could be an anti-Semite and an anti-Negro of the most filthy kind."[22] Both men saw the incident as a fitting start to their partnership.

Acknowledging Mike Gold's sympathetic responsiveness to black experience also helps to explain a number of his later artistic choices. His 1923 biography of the abolitionist John Brown, for example, has been viewed as a tacit commemoration of his joint editorship with McKay, a book that "situates their collaboration within an old American tradition of interracial revolutionary brotherhood."[23]

The first project Gold tackled after McKay left the *Liberator*, his *Life of John Brown* is a fascinating specimen of radical literature that offers fresh ways of thinking about interracial links and commonalities among historical protest movements. Portraying Brown as "a common man to the end,"[24] a worker-hero and comrade to both white and black proletarians, Gold implicitly offers himself as an inheritor of the abolitionist's militant spirit. Throughout the 1920s Gold referred to Brown as his favorite American hero and returned to his story more than a decade later by transforming *Life of John Brown* into agitprop drama.

Another productive collaboration during the *Liberator* years was between Gold and the great labor reporter Art Shields. The first coke-field strike in more than three decades broke out in 1922, when John D. Rockefeller and other coal barons rejected a new wage agreement with the United Mine Workers, the country's largest labor union at the time. Gold was sent to western Pennsylvania to cover the action for the *Liberator*. On the front lines of an explosive conflict, he teamed up and shared resources with Shields of the Federated Press.

The two would travel together to an area of activity, then separate to observe conditions and conduct interviews. In the evenings they met to compare notes and impressions. On the day they arrived in the town of West Brownsville, they witnessed the moving sight of several hundred black and white workers emerging en masse, singing and shouting with coal soot on their faces, from one of the biggest of the mines owned by U.S. Steel. "This is the first time I've felt like a free man," a youthful Irish miner declared in response to Gold's questioning.[25]

The next day Shields and Gold toured the company towns with two rank-and-file miners. They traveled in a dilapidated Model-T Ford driven by a garrulous, one-legged construction worker who'd been disabled in a work accident. When they reached a mine near the town of Fairchance, they were surprised that the work stoppage had already begun. The strikers had left the mines and were milling around, anxiously waiting for instructions from their leaders. Then, at a hastily organized meeting in an open field, the two reporters were pressed into service as vote counters on the issue of joining the union-led strike. Though the show of hands in favor of the strike appeared unanimous, the organizers insisted on an exact tally. The two reporters darted through the throngs of upraised hands, quickly adding up the more than 400 new union members and announcing the result to excited cheers.

Shields and Gold complemented each other, each bringing distinct perspectives. Gold had a gift for catching the flavor of the workers' dialects and interpreting the significance of domestic details. Remembering the heavy tub of coal in his mother's East Side kitchen, he called attention to an enormous washtub in the kitchen of a Ukrainian miner's crowded home. He stepped forward to explain that the single battered steel basin was where the wife washed the family clothes, and where the husband, wife, and six children took their baths.[26]

For his part, Shields elicited a poignant story from an elderly Hungarian miner who had become a member of the United Mine Workers upon its birth in 1890 and was overjoyed at being able to join again. "It's like coming home," he said, because the moment of his becoming a union worker was also the first time he'd been "treated like a brother" in his American life. The old miner gave a vivid account of how the original union had been "murdered" by the millionaire industrialist Henry Clay Frick, who sent in hired Pinkerton gunman to massacre seventeen Homestead steel strikers near Morewood, Pennsylvania, in 1892. Shields immediately told Gold the shocking story of the strike massacre. Later Shields realized that it prompted his new friend to search for ways to artistically document the grotesque violence of the Pennsylvania coal industry, a search that would later produce Gold's best labor poetry.

As Shields also recalled, he and Gold helped each other with the urgent problem of winning the trust of workers and the officials at the United Mine Worker (UMW) headquarters. What helped them succeed was their willingness to take risks and respond with emotion and humanity to the strikers' experience, a process that was instinctive for Gold, who later told Shields that this was one of the happiest weeks of his life.[27] It is also interesting that this was the first trip on which Gold was followed by Justice Department officials. His FBI file notes that on April 6, the "prolific writer and member of the editorial staff of 'The Liberator' arrived in Pittsburgh" and that the next day he "kept his appointment" with the UMW district officer in Brownsville.[28]

The experiences Gold had while reporting on the 1922 Pennsylvania UMW strikes awakened his interest in the steel industry in general and the city of Pittsburgh in particular. A few months later he returned to the area for further research, intrigued by the ways Pittsburgh surpassed even Chicago in its display of the raw brutality of industrial capitalism.

"Smoke and Steel," an article for the July 15, 1922 *Worker*, is an enraptured consideration of the quintessential steel city, in which Gold envisions the industry—with its blast furnaces and rolling mills situated along the city's fouled waterways—as "the trenches of a great battle," the spectacular evidence of America's world-conquering power. "The material life of the world centers about coal and steel," Gold wrote,

> the lives of the world's millions now hang on the fate of the world's coal and steel; and it was Pittsburgh that battered down Essen and ended the war. It was Pittsburgh and the world it has built that killed Rupert Brooke and John Reed and Karl Liebknecht; it was Pittsburgh that created Carl Sandburg and Eugene O'Neill, Dada Futurism, Bolshevism, Capitalism, Gary and Lenin. Pittsburgh is the material and spiritual capital of the twentieth century world. . . . But oh how monstrous! Oh the horror of these leagues of buildings bursting with flame! . . . Men are fed into these mills as into a giant's maw, and the great jaws eat them, crunch them with cannibal glee, devour their human flesh and bones and dreams![29]

In tone, Gold's fascination resembles the horror expressed by Upton Sinclair on witnessing Chicago's gory meat packing operations: the sight of the killing beds and the sound of the "hog squeal of the universe" as forms of mechanized slaughter. Alternately awed and repelled by the brutalist urban dystopia, Gold nevertheless believed it could be tamed and humanized through the growing power of the labor movement.

When Gold was "severely bounced" from the *Liberator* staff as editor in 1922, Robert Minor and Joseph Freeman were named to take over. But Gold claimed he bore no grudge and did not take it as a repudiation of his work. He was terminated because he deplored on professional grounds the idea of merging the *Liberator*, a magazine "rooted in the intellectual world of artists and writers," with the Party's "completely political" organ, *Workers' Monthly*. "A magazine, like a person, must have some sort of grounded soul," he said. He understood immediately that turning the journal over to "the theorists of communism" was a policy decision made at a moment when the Party itself was weak and confused.

Arriving at home on the night of his firing, he took a big drink of prune juice, realized that there couldn't be two finer editors than Minor and Freeman to keep the tone of the journal alive, and said to himself,

"I'm going to California where the prunes grow because I want to breathe some fresh air and hear some beautiful sounds."[30]

The next day he withdrew from the Workers' Union Bank exactly $105 he'd saved for just this type of situation—his "getaway money" he called it—and bought a bus ticket for San Francisco. He wanted to have moving wheels under him, scenery outside the windows, and perhaps a fellow traveler to talk with about literature and politics. He had always been content with little, and at this moment a bus ride across the continent seemed like "the happiest thing that could happen" to a man who'd just been fired from what he called "a clerical job" he never really wanted.[31]

He spent his first day in San Francisco doing nothing but walking aimlessly with his satchel, enjoying the architectural spectacle of the ornate frame houses in the style the locals called carpenter's gothic. In the evening he found a place on Green Street run by an elderly Italian woman who wouldn't mind his late-night typing.

Only after a few more days of exploring did he feel the inevitable pressure to find work, and he decided, as he had whenever he was penniless, to get back on a paper. He walked all over town and into several press offices, approached workers, and got a handful of leads, noticing at once that the California mood was more hospitable than in New York.

At the *San Francisco Call* he shook hands with Freemont Older and considered this a great honor. With a bushy moustache and a big cigar in his mouth, Older looked like a relic of the Old West, and Gold liked him from the start for his informal manner. Amazingly, the famous newspaperman asked Gold to sit down and the two had a long discussion about Marxism, human nature, and the philosophy of Schopenhauer. Gold didn't believe Older when he said he would call him up "one of these days," but the meeting gave him "a good optimistic start" in his new environment, inspiring him to record that night his hope-filled first impressions of the city and its people in the form of a poem.

Two weeks later, just as Gold was touching bottom and beginning to live on sandwiches and coffee, he got a telephone message from his landlord, called the number and heard Older's deep rumbling voice saying "Is this Mike? . . . Get down here in a hurry. . . . Do you still want to be a reporter on my paper?" He started at twenty dollars a week, good pay.[32]

Fremont Older was one of only a handful of strongly liberal journalists who survived the prioritizing of "commercial" journalism in the staid era of Warren G. Harding's normalcy. Among the many things Gold appreciated about Older was his adventurous and unconventional spirit, which showed in his multiple and varied reform efforts. He exposed graft, defended prostitutes, worked for prison reform, and spent two decades agitating for the release of Tom Mooney, the socialist activist who, along with Warren K. Billings, was wrongly convicted for the San Francisco Preparedness Day bombing of 1916. In Gold's view, "He edited the paper as one would write a poem or run a little hardware, by instinct and by a wide-ranging choice of interest." In other words, he was "the sort of editor a young man always craved to have and he seemed to like me which was a great satisfaction."[33]

Working with Older probably furthered Gold's development as a writer in significant ways. Originally the new reporter took on a general variety of assignments, and for a brief time in winter 1923 these included a column called "The Tenderfoot," which hearkened back to his "Freshman at Harvard" articles by describing the city from the viewpoint of a green newcomer. This experiment did not last long, but its failure forced the author to learn new tricks. At the same time, Gold's reporting assignments and social outings put him in contact with new and stimulating influences. While in California he maintained a correspondence with Upton Sinclair and visited Tom Mooney in San Quentin. He met the poet George Sterling, who shared stories about the late Jack London. He even spent what he later called "a fascinating afternoon" with Harry Houdini.

In early 1924 Gold again ran into Art Shields, who was stopping over in San Francisco on his way to China. Shields's memoir of the period, published in 1986, described a particularly memorable evening, a "poetry night" at which Mike chanted "The Strange Funeral in Braddock," a labor verse that had just been published in the June 1924 *Liberator*. For a roomful of friends, Gold performed the recitative chant to haunting effect:

Listen to the mournful drums of a strange funeral.

Listen to the story of a strange American funeral.

Shields considered "The Strange Funeral in Braddock" Gold's greatest poem and one of the best in the history of the labor movement. The work acquired an especially irresistible pathos when Gold read it aloud that first night for an audience that included not only writers and artists but sailors and longshoremen as well. On that same July evening, Gold and his partner, Helen Black, escorted Shields to a house party where a singing poet named Carl Sandburg performed a long set of folk songs, leaning back in a wooden kitchen chair while cradling a large old guitar and crooning in a gravelly voice. Sandburg was then traveling the country to collect material for his great six-volume biography of Abraham Lincoln.

Gold and Sandburg were "old friends," Shields learned, and he never forgot the conversation he overheard while sipping wine in the parlor of Communist poet Charles Erskine Scott Wood. "You were a revolutionary socialist when I first met you, Carl," Mike said. "I'm sorry you dropped out. You'd be in the Communist Party with me now if you had stayed in." "I quit to concentrate on poetry," Sandburg replied.

"But you did your best poems when you were in the movement," Mike answered. "Your lines still have beauty but they lack the vitality of the *Chicago Poems*. You were in the workers' movement then." As Shields recalled, "Someone interrupted us at this point. The dialogue was never finished."[34]

Shields's memoir also noted that Gold had a female partner at this time and, without naming the woman, repeatedly referred to her as Gold's wife. This was Helen Black, who lived with Gold for several years in the 1920s. A capable writer, she occasionally published reviews and short articles in *New Masses*. Gold and Black appear to have lived together on both coasts and for a time considered themselves husband and wife. Their open marriage was never formalized because Black, three years older than Gold, saw matrimony as a bourgeois institution. Journalist friend Robert Shaw, who knew Gold well at this time, referred to Black as "Mike's wonderful girl who stuck with him through everything."[35] Theodore Dreiser, who kept up a correspondence with Gold in 1923, also acknowledged the union, closing several letters to his friend with, "my regards to Helen Black."[36]

The relationship continued off and on into the 1930s, but Black remained behind when Gold left San Francisco for his first trip to Europe and Russia in June 1924. Heading east, Gold first spent time in St. Paul, Minnesota, where he attended a convention of the Farmer-Labor Party from June 17 to 19, then stopped in Chicago for several days before sailing from Quebec City, and arriving in London in July. While in England he attended a summer seminar run by the Plebs League, a British Marxist organization that advocated syndicalist principles and the need for independent working-class education, causes in which Gold also believed.

After the initial six weeks in England, Gold made shorter visits to Berlin and Paris. Back in London in late fall, he finally sailed for Leningrad. He crossed the North Sea on a battered freighter full to the top deck with unused ammunition from the Great War, now on its way to be sold to other countries so that, as Gold grimly remarked, "there would be no danger of there not being another war soon and more profits."[37]

As the steamer approached Leningrad on a gray afternoon of freezing rain, Gold stood on deck for a first glimpse of Russia. Chunks of ice scraped along the ship's hull as it slowly navigated the Neva River. Alerted by the high needle-like steeple of St. Peter and Paul's cathedral, he scanned the skyline and was transfixed by the sight of the red flag above the square Custom House, an image that reminded him of a great tank with a flag of victory flying overhead. "For years, I had been reading, dreaming, talking, arguing, living in Russia while my body was in New York or San Francisco," Gold recalled, "I was immensely moved to set foot on the gangplank and walk the few steps into the land of the people's revolution."[38]

Exploring the city on foot over several days, Gold passed a number of theater buildings and noticed that the people he met—soldiers and stevedores, engineers and cafeteria workers—spoke passionately about the modern drama. Russian theater culture, whose ardent and knowledgeable followers included common citizens and laborers with no formal education, profoundly impressed Gold and reminded him of the Yiddish theater he'd known as a boy. Yakov, the cook in Gold's boarding house, attended plays nearly every night. He invited Gold to the theater of Vsevolod Meyerhold and even introduced his American friend to the pioneer actor-director.

Figure 4.1. First trip to Russia, 1924–1925. *Source:* Granich family.

Initially Gold was intrigued by Meyerhold's general notion that theater was a conscious art rather than a spontaneous eruption of feeling. Inspired and curious, Gold spent several long evenings in January–February 1925 in intense conversation with the great drama theorist, who spoke excellent English, in the "green room" of the Meyerhold theater. Through these discussions and while attending Meyerhold's plays almost every night for three months, Gold became fascinated by the Russian director's theory of theatrical biomechanics, which united the physiological and psychological processes of stage acting. "Meyerhold's theater was all action," Gold recalled; "They expressed action through the movement of the body, not relying only on words. There was a unity between words and muscular activity."[39] Another element that entranced the American observer was Meyerhold's willingness to fully exploit theatrical space. Staging his productions in a lofty barn-like auditorium with an immense stage, the Russian director constructed sets of several levels in which the actors moved like acrobats, in constant motion from one symbolic setting to another.

Though Gold took many formal lessons from the futurist school of both Meyerhold and the Russian poet Vladimir Mayakovsky, he resisted some implications of their experimentation, namely, the temptation to rely on a basic "feeling for artistic form" that could be rendered without any reference to context other than the mind of the artist. Enemies of Mayakovsky and Meyerhold had tried to reduce their work to pure formalism, but in Gold's thinking the two innovators succeeded as revolutionary artists to the extent that they refused to abandon themes of social and political relevance.

Meyerhold would keep his place in Gold's artistic pantheon. "[He] is the leader of the young Russian theater," Gold reported to American readers later in 1925. "His bare, immense stage is stripped for action, like a steel mill or a factory. . . . All that was static in the old theater is stamped out. This is the theater of dynamics. . . . Drawing room plays have no place here. This theater is the battle-field of life; it is a trench, a factory, the deck of a ship in [a] storm. And the young workers and soldiers adore the futurist director, Meyerhold."[40]

The deep respect Mayakovsky likewise retained was captured in a scene that Gold always remembered and that bespoke the poet's relation to workers and peasants: "It was revealing to see him at a meeting when the workers were crowding around him and came up to shake his hand and say a few friendly words of well wishing. All his gestures were democratic."[41]

One of the last persons Gold saw before leaving Moscow was "Big" Bill Haywood, the great IWW leader who had fled into exile in 1921 after his conviction and sentencing to twenty years in prison on Espionage Act charges. Undeniably it was a bleak and lonely last phase of Haywood's life; overweight, largely immobile, and addicted to alcohol, he had lost his energies but not his will. Gold viewed Haywood, the quintessential IWW agitator, as "a person who never seemed to let any emotion beat him down or affect him in any way that he did not show."[42] Haywood rarely went out, so the two men spent an evening sitting at the table in his tiny kitchen, sharing news, stories, and recollections over beer, which Haywood drank by the gallon because his doctor had warned him off his usual rye whiskey. From this last meeting in Haywood's cramped apartment, Gold internalized life lessons, mainly having to do with the man's resilience and unwavering faith.

The meaning of Haywood's struggle, clearly nearing its end, struck Gold as paradoxical. Threatened with "life imprisonment by the master class," he had been "saved," liberated from prison by American Communists who had raised the money to pay the exorbitant bail imposed by US courts in order to smuggle him out of the country. But Gold couldn't help referring to the man's permanent exile in Moscow as a kind of "life sentence" as well. Haywood still "deeply admired" the Soviet Union, so Gold wondered whether his exile was better described as a homecoming. If he had been ten years younger, Gold thought, he could still have contributed to the building of communism. As it was, he could only give occasional speeches through an interpreter to young Russian workers, explaining to them the sufferings of workers in capitalist countries. Haywood, Gold said, was one of the "Buffalo men," like Charles Erskine Scott Wood or Fremont Older—someone who knew the meaning and background of everything, the long history of the people's movement in its entirety.[43]

Partly due to the Russia sojourn, the 1920s were a productive period for Gold as both fiction writer and playwright. In 1924 the Little Red Library, a pamphlet series underwritten by the Communist Party, published *The Damned Agitator and Other Stories*, a book of short prose that blended autobiographical elements with class-based formulas Gold learned from the *Masses* editors and had refined through direct exposure to Soviet criticism. The title story, originally published in the New York *Call* in March 1917 but updated and revised for reprint, is an impressionistic psychological sketch of an immigrant labor leader. The setting replicates details from a labor action in the New England textile industry and thus from the pre–World War I period of agitation that culminated in a 1912 textile workers' strike led by Haywood in Lawrence, Massachusetts. But while the Lawrence strike ended successfully, the strike led by Gold's Kurelovitch, "a tall, tragic, rough-hewn Pole," seems likely to fail.[44]

The complexity of Gold's psychological portrait of the "damned agitator" matches the untenable set of problems he faces. The story opens when the strike is seven weeks old, scabs are on the way, and the leader's sense is that the action "might soon be a bitter ash in the mouths of the men." As the "woeful conditions" accumulate, it is not surprising that Kurelovitch is under constant threat from police gunmen or that he is accused of "pocketing half the strike funds," as Haywood and other labor leaders often were. But Kurelovitch's deeper predicament is that "his own side" includes an embittered, overburdened wife and fellow workers who have lost hope. The story follows the strike leader through a long day of anguish, ending in a state of exhaustion and alcohol-induced oblivion that will only be repeated: "Never . . . would he be permitted to know sweetness or rest."[45]

An expanded, Russian-language version of the *Damned Agitator* collection was published in 1925. The pessimistic stories were generally disliked by Russian critics, but the Moscow-produced pamphlet managed to reach an audience several times larger than the American version. Haywood himself wrote the introduction for this edition, following a suggestion Gold made at their evening meeting in Moscow. Among Gold's fictional subjects and protagonists—harassed strike leaders, imprisoned Wobblies, and starving coal miners—Haywood surely discerned echoes of his own experience.

A final reworking of "The Damned Agitator," in which Gold changed the nationality of the disgruntled strikers from Russian to French Canadian and softened some elements of the brutal and grotesque, appeared in a collection Gold published in 1929 under the title *120 Million*. Gold's second book of short fiction and poetry showed the author's experimentation and development as reflected in an aesthetic shift from simple, stark realism to a modernist outlook also influenced by his Soviet visit. All told, the stories give evidence that Gold was one of the first to adapt the futurism of Mayakovsky and Meyerhold to American settings, and to do so in works of prose fiction as well as drama and poetry.

In addition to "Two Mexicos," an important work in this collection is "The American Famine," a reworked version of a report Gold wrote for the *Liberator* in 1921 after spending several days wandering among New York City's half-million homeless and unemployed. Impersonating a starving worker, Gold visits the "missions" where charity workers "preach humility to the poor,"[46] talks with men standing in breadlines, and sleeps in Bowery flophouses. The story is valuable for its accounts of persons and conditions in the Bowery YMCA, the reading rooms of public libraries, Union Square, Bryant Park, and the employment bureau in Grand Central Terminal, which offer both a catalog and an interpretation of the misery of the suffering thousands while recording the "unconscious wisdom of the proletariat."[47] The narrative concludes with a comparison between Russian famine, which can be endured because it is temporary rather than systemic or endemic, and American famine, which will continue because for the poor under capitalism there is "no plan . . . no vision."[48] Another story, "Faster, America, Faster," paints American decadence as "a private freight train rushing to Hollywood; violent, profligate, licentious and cruel," blindly advancing toward catastrophe and arrogantly "wasting life."[49] V. F. Calverton's review of *120 Million* in the *Nation* found Gold's fiction crude and violent, but "challenging in its very crudity."[50]

Appended to the twelve short stories in *120 Million* is a section of "Proletarian Chants and Recitations," accompanied by Gold's assertions that such communal theatrical experiments respond to the "needs of American workers" and are "a valuable weapon for propaganda and solidarity."[51] There are chants about the brutal interrogation of a labor leader, the suicide of a pregnant teenage factory girl, the birthday of a long-suffering agitator who would rather die than desert the labor movement, and a recitation excerpted verbatim from the prison letters of Bartolomeo Vanzetti. The book's title is taken from the final chant. It refers to the size of the US population, the millions who are figuratively cataloged by a proletarian poet on a cross-country journey, a people who worship a "Money God" and make war on each other, a people "whose heart is a Ford car, / Whose brain is a cheap Hollywood Movie, . . . / Whose victims die of hunger."[52]

120 Million also reprinted "The Strange Funeral at Braddock," a haunting poem that focuses on three reactions to the horrific death of Jan Clepak, an immigrant worker who was buried alive in molten steel. One observer at the funeral chooses self-destructive despair, another pledges never to let her children work in a mill, and a third, Clepak's widow, responds imaginatively, vowing to transform the death into revolutionary action: "I'll make myself hard as steel, harder! / I'll come some day and make bullets out of Jan's body / and shoot them into a tyrant's heart."

Gold's friend and fellow journalist Art Shields called this elegiac
piece "the most tragically beautiful poem that has come out of the United
States class struggle."[53] Shields thought it important that the story it told
was an actual event Gold had learned about from an aunt who lived in
the Pittsburgh steel district: Jan Clepak, a young Bohemian immigrant,
was enveloped in an avalanche of liquid steel when a cauldron of boiling
metal burst above him while he was at work in a Donora, Pennsylvania
mill. The steelworker's body was completely submerged in a molten coffin.
Later the hardened lump of metal was donated to Clepak's wife and family,
who watched in a state of shock as the 3,000 pound coffin was lowered
into the grave from a company-owned truck. " 'The Strange Funeral in
Braddock' is not just a recital of grim facts," Shields observed; "it is permeated with the grief of Jan Clepak's bride and the fury of Jan Clepak's
fellow workers."[54] Throughout his career, critics tended to characterize
Gold's poetry primarily as overly political and formulaic, little more than
a tool for welding the masses into solidarity. More recent critics including
Alan Wald, however, have expressed strong interest in Gold's verse, noting
that he drew perceptively from Walt Whitman and prefigured the early
Beat poets, making him an important nexus between nineteenth- and
twentieth-century social and aesthetic movements.

By 1927, Nicola Sacco and Bartolomeo Vanzetti—famously described
as "a good shoemaker and a poor fishpeddler"—had become worldwide
symbols of the oppressed proletariat. The Italian anarchists had been
arrested seven years earlier in Brockton, Massachusetts, on charges of
robbery and murder of a shoe factory paymaster and guard. After a 1921
trial that initially attracted little attention, they were convicted, sentenced
to death, and imprisoned while a long series of appeals were initiated on
their behalf. The *Liberator*, under the leadership of Freeman and Minor
but with Gold as a contributing editor, began to publicize the case in 1923.
Over the next several years, a generation of artists and writers had been
swept into the struggle to save the two obscure workers. Through their
long imprisonment and repeated defeat at the hands of a bigoted legal
system, the two immigrant anarchists, clearly being persecuted for their
beliefs, showed sublime heroism. Hundreds of artists and intellectuals in
Europe and Asia wrote protest letters or made public pleas, helping to
further unite American writers in support of the condemned class-war
victims and in protest against the state-sponsored lynching. As Gold
perceived, "This was another and greater Dreyfus case."[55]

With the grim outcome of their long legal battle approaching in
August 1927, Gold stepped forward to transform theory into action in

an important way. A week before the execution, a clerical worker for the *New Masses* suggested that Gold, who had already spoken passionately about the Sacco-Vanzetti case in lectures and public forums, organize a group of writers to go to Boston and picket the State House. Immediately he appealed to the *Masses* editors and writers, asking who was willing to make the trip; he said he was shocked to see the looks of fear that came into the faces of several whom he believed were sincerely committed to justice and to hear the stories they invented as excuses for not going. Gold didn't name the colleagues but admitted that the incident almost made him cynical. Eventually he managed to recruit of a group of eight or nine, including writers and several hands from the garment workers union. Notable among the participants was John Dos Passos, who later used this experience as a focal point for *The Big Money*, the final novel in his great *USA* trilogy.

Testimony to Gold's activity and impact during the Sacco-Vanzetti crisis came also from the black lawyer and Communist William L. Patterson. When the call for volunteers went out in New York, Patterson responded as one who had "followed the Sacco-Vanzetti case with all [his] soul."[56] The only African American on the group's daily picket lines and demonstrations, Patterson was arrested three times in the first week of protests; he sensed the lynching atmosphere in Boston. One day Gold witnessed Patterson being chased by a crazed policeman on horseback "with a loaded club at the ready." Afterward Gold remarked, "A Negro needs twice the courage of a white man in any such struggle."[57]

At the end of an arduous day of shouting and marching that included frantic escapes from police, the demonstrators gathered at their informal headquarters, where Gold approached Patterson, "a stranger and a Negro," to ask if he had a place to sleep for the night and offer him his room. Gold saw this as "an ordinary act of comradeship," but the kindness made a deep impression. To Patterson, the gesture suggested that "true friendship was possible between blacks and whites, if the rottenness of capitalism could be removed." Immediately after returning to New York, Patterson quit his law firm, joined the Communist Party, and dedicated his subsequent career to the International Labor Defense, the legal arm of the CPUSA.[58]

Women were well represented in the ranks of Sacco-Vanzetti demonstrators, with Dorothy Parker, Edna St. Vincent Millay, and Katherine Anne Porter among the most prominent literary names. Also present was Helen Black, who served on the *New Masses* executive board beginning in 1926 and contributed a handful of reviews to the magazine between 1927 and

1931. She added her voice to the historical record in an article published
a week later in the *Daily Worker*, which warned of the possibility that the
two Italian martyrs would be forgotten unless their example inspired the
organization of a strong labor party that would "be a real menace to the
rulers of Massachusetts and the rest of the country."[59] Black later became
affiliated with Sovfoto, an agency established in 1932 to represent Soviet
photojournalism in the West and distribute press photography from the
USSR throughout North America.

Having witnessed and participated in the original Plymouth cordage workers' strike in 1916, Gold felt a personal connection that would
underlie a deep commitment to the Sacco-Vanzetti legal fight from its
beginnings. At the time of the crisis over the impending execution, he'd
been in touch with the case perhaps longer than any other radical writer.
The terse appraisal he gave in the *New Masses* under the title "Lynchers
in Frockcoats" was therefore unique not only in its precisely targeted
outrage but also in its keen discernment of the xenophobia and bigotry of
a "respectable" Boston gentility that Gold had once experienced firsthand
and abandoned in disgust over a decade earlier at Harvard.

"It is August 14th, eight days before the new devil's hour set for the
murder of Sacco and Vanzetti," Gold's report began, "I am writing this in
the war zone, in the psychopathic respectable city that is crucifying two
immigrant workers, in Boston, Massachusetts." At the moment, Gold said,
supporters of the two Italians felt deep despair; "They will burn" Gold
understood, because "respectable Boston is possessed with the lust to kill.
The frockcoat mob is howling for blood—it is in the lynching mood."[60]

The remainder of the article examines ethnic-racial intolerance as
manifested in obsessively monitored markers of cultural and class difference. In Boston, Gold theorized, "if you have a beard, or have dark foreign
hair or eyes, or in any way act like a man who has not had a Harvard
education or Mayflower ancestors, you are picked up on the streets for
suspicion." Speaking of what is now called alterity or othering, Gold
explores the notion of how the hateful process works and manifests: "You
must not need a shave. . . . Six Italians . . . were arrested and held on a
bombing charge because two of them needed a shave." It is interesting
that the othering is based also on geography and perhaps gender: "You
must not look like a New Yorker. Two New York women, Helen Black
and Ann Washington Craton, were arrested and questioned at a police
station for the crime of looking like New Yorkers."[61]

The "well-dressed Boston mob," Gold conclusively asserts, "will kill Sacco and Vanzetti legally," for

> They are determined on revenge. For decades they have been watching wave after wave of lusty immigrants sweep in over their dying culture. . . . They have the subconscious superstition that the death of Sacco and Vanzetti can restore their dying culture and industry. At last they have a scapegoat. . . . They are as passionate against these Italian workers as white Southerners toward the Negro. . . . They are insane with fear and hatred of the new America. . . . [Boston] is in the throes of a lynching bee, led by well-spoken Harvard graduates in frockcoats.[62]

"Lynchers in Frockcoats" was written five days before another moment of reckoning in the struggle. For the rest of his life, Gold vividly remembered the evening he was arrested along with Dorothy Parker. The protest headquarters were at the Bellevue Hotel, where Gold's contingent was welcomed on arrival and joined a large crowd eager for action. A little later that day the group marched in front of the State House, where they were met by an army of police augmented by a crowd of what Gold liked to refer to as "virtuous Bostonian citizens," who shouted down the demonstrators, some of them screaming, "Hang them!" and "Kill them!"—a scene that, in Gold's words, "sort of gave you a feeling that God is not love in the preacher world."[63]

The demonstrators marched past the gold-domed statehouse to a place where the route turned and the march halted, the way suddenly blocked; there in front of them stood an unyielding police captain in breaches and jackboots, a line of patrolmen shoulder to shoulder behind him and his golden badge glittering in the hot sun, to read them the riot act, "a Bostonian convention that often precedes the clubbing of a demonstration," Gold explained. "In a rough barroom voice," Gold recalled, the officer read the order to "disperse or be clubbed." What followed was a few anxious minutes of hesitation. A handful of the pickets stepped out of the line and returned to the safety of Boston Common. Standing next to Gold, Dorothy Parker pulled him toward her, asking if she should step out or keep marching. Gold didn't want to give her advice "because it was every person's problem as all conscience's problems are." Instead he tried to reassure her, saying that probably nothing terrible would happen.

Ultimately Parker, Gold, and the remaining demonstrators in the group were "slung" into a paddy wagon and driven to the Joy Street police station, where they were confined to the bullpens. As Gold recalled, a "literary man" eventually bailed them out.[64]

A few days later, while Gold's group was again marching before Charlestown Prison, Sacco and Vanzetti were executed. As he spoke about this experience on audiotape in May 1966, in his apartment in the Haight-Ashbury neighborhood of San Francisco, Gold paused for several seconds. "Nothing could save them," he said,

> People were asleep in America as they have often been during these last years. I wept when the news flashed that they were executed. All around the world millions of people wept. Those two men had impressed themselves on the consciousness of all humanity more than any case since the Haymarket martyrs, who had been hung on a similar frame up. Frame-ups sometimes make one feel that these are an American institution. But every country in the world has had its frames up of the poor and undefended. When it happens in America it makes you sick, because you have loved America since childhood and you have shared the great majestic dreams of its democratic vision. I know that Sacco and Vanzetti did more to save the democracy of Americans than all the Wall Street and Washington opportunists.[65]

In the mid- and late 1920s, Mike and brother Manny shared a shack on Staten Island three doors down the road from the home of Dorothy Day. They would take the house on alternate weekends, but sometimes Mike would show up on his brother's weekend with groups of friends or George and his family. Manny had built a sturdy rowboat and the three reunited Granich boys would go fishing or dig clams; Dorothy then made the day's catch into fine maritime stews, adding vegetables grown in her garden. Gold's mother Katie even visited once.[66] She who had looked sorrowfully at Dorothy when her son was engaged to her now brought her own kosher dishes, shared her recipes, and took home Dorothy's fresh beets and cucumbers for her soups. At this time Day had a common-law husband and a young daughter, Tamar. When George was there with his wife, Gertrude, their two small children played with Tamar while Dorothy and Mike took long walks on the beach.

Day was glad Gold was near because she was experiencing a painful and tortured, yet sometimes joyful, process of conversion to a public acknowledgment of her Catholic faith, and Mike seemed to understand her misery. As Dorothy said, Mike knew from his own life "that there had to be a price to pay, sometimes a heartbreaking price, in following one's vocation. Neither revolutions nor faith are won without keen suffering."[67] In her anxious time she clung to those who knew her in her Village days. Mike and Dorothy had known each other for ten years and they would stay close for decades to come, but she already considered him her "oldest friend."[68]

In 1927, working with John Howard Lawson and John Dos Passos, Gold secured financial support from the wealthy financier and art patron Otto Kahn to establish the New Playwrights Theatre. For Gold, the origins of the venture were traceable to Russia. "When I got back to New York after three months of seeing these Meyerhold plays and their creator and followers full of enthusiasm at their home in Leningrad, I felt as if something had left my life and must be replaced, by something as close as possible to the original."[69]

Just off the ship from Leningrad with no place to stay in New York, Gold had run into Florence Rauh, Max Eastman's sister-in-law, who was about to leave the city on a trip of her own and offered Gold her small Village apartment while she was gone. Gold accepted and Rauh left with a shy admonishment that Gold "not be idle" in her absence. Assembling paper and typewriter, Gold "almost automatically" began writing a play in the Meyerhold futurist style. "I did not even think about whether it was going to be in the conventional Broadway style," he said, for he knew what he wanted: something that would combine Soviet futurism and Meyerhold's gigantic push toward a new form with an American theme he'd been thinking about for years. He wrote the play in a kind of trance; the work "just happened," Gold said. He then copied it out and sent it to Lewis Mumford and Paul Rosenfeld, editors the *American Caravan*, who thought it was a perfect fit their goal of publishing fresh and innovative new works and accepted it for publication immediately.

Gold's first full-length play, *Hoboken Blues*, is an exuberantly constructivist version of Harlem life subtitled, "The Black Rip Van Winkle: A Modern Negro Fantasia on an Old American Theme." The main character, Sam Pickens, a black child of the Great Migration who came north when his brother was lynched, finds himself unemployed in Harlem and leaves to seek work in Hoboken, N.J., where he achieves success and eventually becomes "president" of the city. He returns twenty-five years later to discover that it had all been a dream, that there "ain't no Hoboken," and sums up the racial and class-based determiners of reality: "Folks, why can't there be a place for de poor men, black and white. . . . Where no one is hungry, where no one is lynched, where dere's no money or bosses, and men are brudders?"[70]

As it is written, Gold's play was groundbreaking in its use of surreal characters, a futuristic visual style, expressivist staging, and the incorporation of modern jazz-dance into what Gold called "simultaneous planes of action."[71] Even more daring was Gold's directive that "no White men appear in this play" and that "where white men are indicated, they are played by Negroes in white caricature masks."[72] This maneuver surpassed many of the risks taken by Gold's theater contemporaries, even in comparison to the innovations of his friend Eugene O'Neill. According to Maxwell, the play attempted nothing less than "to slip the bonds of whiteness and take part in, not merely comment on, the Harlem Renaissance."[73]

As Hoboken Blues was produced, however, it conveyed the opposite of the playwright's radical intentions. When Gold tried and failed to assemble an all-black cast, the production went forward with white actors speaking black dialect, a concession that burdened the play with connotations of a minstrel show despite its enlightened thinking and respectful treatment of black culture. Even in his last years Gold became agitated when discussing the missed opportunity represented by Hoboken Blues, believing with good reason that the play deserved better treatment.

"Like all our plays, it was too ambitious," Gold remarked in 1933 about the works staged by the New Playwright's Theater, with his own play as perhaps the best example. A portent of trouble for Hoboken Blues had come when Gold visited the actor-singer Paul Robeson and personally entreated him to play the main character, Pickens. Gold's agent at the time, Lee Salisbury, suggested soliciting Robeson and sent him the script. A week later Gold had a lengthy discussion with the actor at his small flat in the Village. Robeson had already read the play and admired it, but on the question of taking the lead role, he was conflicted. Part of Mike's pitch was that only Robeson could make it successful, which was probably true. In the end Robeson reverted to his "one self-imposed law" that prevented him from accepting the role: his resolve "never to do a play about Negroes which was totally hopeless, that is, hopeless in spirit." After Robeson added in clarification that "he wanted to do only militant plays," works that displayed "a militant theme of the Negro advancing," Gold said he understood this criticism and resolved to make his future work less concerned with "sadness and trouble" and more "consciously militant."[74]

For present-day theater scholars and historians who have read *Hoboken Blues*, this conversation may be surprising because to many, the work certainly seems militant enough, especially in light of recent scrutiny and intense interest in the historical roots and cultural effects of blackface theatrics. A drama in which blacks play whites in caricature masks had the power to reverse and weaponize the dehumanizing minstrel tradition, or at least to prompt the audience to think about this process because the play's author obviously had. At minimum, the play shows that Gold sought to address problems of racial *representation*: not only the lack or dearth of black representation in drama and other cultural modes but also the distorted form of blackface minstrelsy, which of course did not count as representation at all. By reversing the representational playing field in a confrontational way, *Hoboken Blues* had the potential to interrogate white audiences who refused to see *themselves* in their own monstrous blackface creations.

In today's context, the simple act of following Gold's directive about an all-black cast playing nonblacks in whiteface could prompt fresh thinking about the underside of white modernity that regularly dehumanized black bodies. If, throughout US history, blackface theatrics have served a purpose of confirming a white racist worldview, how might the spectacle of blacks in whiteface be deployed to disconfirm that worldview?

Gold's play, by returning the gaze of whiteness, seems to carry powerful disruptive and subversive possibilities if staged properly. I know of no production of *Hoboken Blues* since 1928, but in summer 2017, I spoke about the play at an international conference of the Eugene O'Neill Society in Galway, Ireland. The audience of about one hundred was attentive and eager to know more about Gold, an underappreciated member of the Provincetown Players. At the moment in my talk when I mentioned the racial composition of the cast and "white caricature masks" in *Hoboken Blues*, there were audible reactions of surprise in the auditorium, followed by a time-limited discussion that I sensed could have continued for quite a while. Some O'Neill scholars said they were puzzled about why we still knew so little about Michael Gold.

In fact, most of the handful of plays produced by the New Playwrights Theatre from 1927 to its demise in 1929 met similarly confused receptions and likewise fell into obscurity. Among the interesting productions that Otto Kahn funded and Gold either wrote or helped produce were John

Howard Lawson's *Loudspeaker*, Upton Sinclair's *Jailbirds*, and Dos Passos's *Airways, Inc.*, all of which closed after disappointingly short runs and generally negative reviews.

Just as their run was ending, in February 1929, the New Playwrights Theater gave a dinner and invited Otto Kahn, the wealthy banker whose money had funded the venture. The playwrights made speeches attacking capitalism and prophesying the triumph of the workers. Gold also stated his belief that the company had succeeded in advancing the cause of a new theater that was radical both artistically and politically. Lawson agreed and unselfishly gave Gold the full credit for conceiving the venture, calling the work of the New Playwrights "an enormously significant experiment, the first workers' theatre in the English language in the United States."[75] Then Kahn, smiling and nonchalant, took the podium for what the press dubbed "the speech of the evening," in which the munificent patron intimated that he gave his money gladly to artistic experiments and was "willing to take a chance on thereby upsetting the social order."[76]

The years 1926–1928 were tumultuous times at the *New Masses*, where Gold was a frequent contributor and one of six editors responsible for the magazine's content. But there was also a ten-member executive board and a fifty-six-member roster of "contributing editors" that included some of the most progressive American writers and artists of the period, including such disparate figures as Sherwood Anderson, Eugene O'Neill, Carl Sandburg, Mary Heaton Vorse, Genevieve Taggard, Lewis Mumford, Jean Toomer, Cornelia Barnes, Edmund Wilson, and Claude McKay. According to Joseph Freeman's memoir, *An American Testament*, only two of the fifty-six were members of the Communist Party and less than a dozen were genuinely sympathetic to socialism.

The range of personalities was bound to lead to disagreements. "Full editorial meetings were marked by sharp debate, reflecting in literary terms the general social conflicts of the period," Freeman noted, "The liberals and radicals were sharply at odds." What Freeman called "class distinctions" between the art for art's sake liberals and the more radical revolutionaries grew wider and became a pitched battle. The liberals wanted intellectualism and a journal of "introspection and doubt."[77] Gold countered by declaring that skepticism was "merely the flower of decay." At one meeting he made a long speech calling for the journal to "set sail for a new discovery of America" by exploring plays, poetry, art, and music from the "world of revolutionary labor," stating, "It is a fact that a proletarian style is emerging in art. It will be transitory as other styles, but it will have its day."[78] Witnessing this and other debates, Freeman noticed that the younger writers were gradually turning toward Gold and concluded that "the war generation of literary radicals was beginning to find its direction," namely, through his notions of proletarian culture.[79]

Then, in early 1927, while several of the left-wing editors were out of the country, a group of the contributing editors held a hasty vote that ousted Gold from the journal altogether. Freeman, who was then in Moscow, heard about the attempted coup and came to Gold's defense, recognizing the conflict as "a struggle between national-liberal ideas and proletarian literature." He cabled Scott Nearing and several others in an attempt to solve the problem. By obtaining proxies from various absent staff members, they rounded up the majority necessary to restore Gold to his editorial post.[80]

For the time being, all that this assured was that the conflict would go on and Gold's voice would continue to be heard. But by early 1928 the magazine was in crisis, riven with dissent, running out of money, and losing readership. At a decisive meeting in April, "finally I was the only one who seemed to want to see the magazine live," Gold recalled, "And all the other editors turned to me and said if you are so heroic and so sure about yourself, why don't you do something to keep it going."[81]

> I had a dream that expressed itself in certain ways and certain elements in my writing. This dream was to have a magazine of young workers describing their daily life and their problems . . . encouraging them to write fiction and sketches of their world. I had actually come into writing because of this great feeling that the young workers of American had no place to express themselves and that it should be the task of the radical magazine to give them elbow room and welcome such expression.
>
> When the last fellow editor advised me to show how all my oratory could be put into practical existence, I jumped to the bait and accepted the magazine. . . . I believed that we must search for the basic material of proletarian life . . . art coming from the working class, and that this could make a special literature that could be called proletarian literature.[82]

The June 1928 issue of *New Masses*, the first under Gold's new management, was reviewed in the *Daily Worker* as one would review a novel, play, symphony, or other unified work of art. "*The New Masses* died in April and has been reborn in June—a lusty infant," wrote A. B. Magill under the subtitle, "Gold Now Editor; June Issue Is Lively." The article noted the disastrous two-year attempt to run the magazine as "a coalition between liberals and revolutionists" and rejoiced that "the liberals have finally been tossed over the wall" and that under Gold, "the *New Masses* will have more than a nominal connection with the American workingclass." Magill pointed to the editor's "strategic reform" of cutting the price of the journal from twenty-five to fifteen cents, saying that it would make "a world of difference." There was elation as well about the editor's pledge that "an effort will be made to enlist the great submerged unpublished voices of America." The issue featured poems from a New Jersey silk weaver, letters from workers, a chapter in progress from *Jews without Money*, and fresh hope. Magill predicted, "Work such as this is in the direction of what may someday be American proletarian literature."[83]

As Gold recalled, "The magazine sold out on the newsstand. We had to increase our printing order by 3,000 copies a month. There had been new advertising too. Over three hundred new subscriptions came in." It gave him great satisfaction, he said, but it wasn't enough. He said he wanted to practice "open diplomacy" with readers from that point forward, recurring frequently to his mantra-like exhortations, "Write as you talk. . . . Heart and mind of the workers."[84]

In late winter 1929 Gold traveled to the Florida Keys for a fishing vacation with Ernest Hemingway, during which he observed the great writer thoughtfully. "Hemingway," Gold decided afterward, "was a giant, boyish figure, a troubled American giant with all the neurotic tendencies of the great powerful nation."[85]

Upon Gold's arrival at the house in Key West, Hemingway's wife Pauline greeted him warmly and told him he could find her husband in his "office," a cramped, sparsely furnished recess under the stairs, where the visitor found his host very much at ease. Immediately Ernest took a bottle of Bacardi from the desk drawer and offered a toast. The two men spent glorious days catching tarpon, bonito, and pompano fish on Hemingway's boat, during which Gold enjoyed swimming and the healthy sun more than the sport fishing. He couldn't resist reminding Hemingway that ordinary working Americans fished out of economic need rather than for entertainment.

One afternoon on the water, Hemingway hooked a big tarpon, then rose from his deck chair and steadied himself in a powerful stance, the

Figure 4.2. On Hemingway's boat, 1929. *Source:* Granich family.

rod bending in half and the sun shining on his shirtless upper body "as if he were the favorite of the gods," Gold recalled vividly. "He was a big husky man, an American with a strong jaw and Viking blue eyes. Muscles of good health and vital enjoyment rippled over his huge frame." Watching him work the rod, Gold wished he'd had a good camera so he could capture this "lord of the sunshine on the rolling waves."

After landing the fish, Ernest sat down with a bottle of Cuban beer, wiped the sweat from his face, and became quiet. The mood changed and the burly fisherman was no longer a glorious sun god. He looked out at the sea for a long time, then turned to his guest. "Mike, I want to show you something," he said, looking suddenly defeated and tragic. He rose and stepped away, returning from the cabin with a heavy revolver that startled Gold, who had no idea what was happening.

Ernest put the pistol in Mike's hand, "Look at this," he said, "what do you think of it?" Gold shrugged uncomfortably, "I don't know Ernest, you know probably." Still standing, Hemingway put a hand on his friend's shoulder and drank off more beer. "My mother sent it to me only this morning. This is the pistol my father used to kill himself six months ago, and now my mother sends it to me. Why would she send it to me? Can you understand that? Does she want me to kill myself too? What does it mean?" Holding the gun, Mike started to invent a soothing answer but

Figure 4.3. While sportfishing, Gold reminded Hemingway that the working people fished out of economic necessity. *Source:* Granich family.

stopped, realizing it was unnecessary. Afterward, Gold wished he'd been composed and courageous enough to tell the great novelist to put away his tragedy and cast the ill-fated pistol into the mighty ocean.

Later that week there was constant activity, including much drinking with other guests, but Hemingway found moments away from the group to ask Gold personal questions about recent developments in the radical movement. It was clear that he had sound knowledge of the class struggle, though even then Gold wondered why that knowledge only rarely and indirectly informed his art.

Gold was surprised when Hemingway told him that as a young reporter in 1919, he covered the Spartacist uprising in Berlin, where he had abjured neutrality and affiliated himself with the radical leftists against the moderate social democrats. If this was true, it meant that Hemingway had put himself in physical danger to side with proletarians, an act the Communist writer instinctively respected.

After dinner one night Gold overheard a conversation between Hemingway and another guest, the charismatic modernist painter Waldo Peirce. The two were discussing Ernest's latest work, an unpublished manuscript that would be serialized beginning that May. Peirce had read the novel and was lukewarm toward it, saying that it was a pretty love story but essentially unrealistic. Taking the manuscript, Hemingway tossed it to Gold, saying, "You try your choppers on that, will you Mike? Tell me how you like it." Gold stayed up all night reading *A Farewell to Arms* and was much moved by it. Perhaps Peirce, a Harvard graduate, was too sophisticated to appreciate it, he thought. To Gold, it seemed a love story that caught the tragic universality of all love.

After this Gold put away his qualms about fishing and managed to catch some big early-season tarpons, describing the process as "all muscle and drag and struggle." He did as Hemingway instructed and hung onto the rod tightly. Later the same day he was disappointed to see a woman weighing about ninety pounds doing the same thing. Eventually he lost interest in the sport, for it seemed to Gold that the real hero of the fight between man and fish was the elderly navigator of the boat, whom he described as "a crusty lean Bahamian with big claws of hands caked open with salt." It was pleasant to observe the relationship between Hemingway and the gentle old seaman, who spoke in a quiet voice as if he would avoid offending any living thing, including the giant fish being dispatched all around him.[86]

The soon-to-be famous author of *Jews without Money* found it very hard not to like Hemingway, who had a charming boyish manner, always putting his strong arms around the shoulders of the people he spoke with, looking at them with big eyes and a wide grin. A part of Gold admired his friend's rugged tastes and dynamic lifestyle. He observed conversations among the guests and noticed that though Hemingway discussed the same topics as anyone else, there was a finality to his sentences that made him seem impressive. And he could switch quickly from his commanding tone to healthy, youthful laughter.

"Hemingway was always horsing around, pretending to box," Gold noticed; "He would take a boxing stance and pack a left jab into your face that could have broken your nose, if not stopped in time by the old maestro." The son of the East Side told Hemingway he'd been crazy about boxing in youth. He'd sparred with professionals in basement gyms but had come away bruised enough to know what a real fighter could do. Gold found it distasteful when Hemingway chided and challenged him, not-so-subtly asserting his superiority. He would put up a fist and push the smaller man from side to side with jabs and hooks and fake knock-out blows. Both men knew it would not have been a fair fight; Gold weighed around 140 pounds to Hemingway's 200.

It was on this trip that Gold discerned the complexity of Hemingway's character, perhaps earlier than most observers of the literary scene did. Even much later, when he attacked *For Whom the Bell Tolls* and wrote columns about the famous author's childish arrogance, Gold did not deny Hemingway's greatness as a storyteller. In his last years Gold remembered with seeming pride that he was one of the first to declare, in print and in person to Hemingway, that *The Sun Also Rises* was a beautiful piece of modern writing.[87] But he saw also that "there were gulfs in Hemingway's nature deeper than even he himself realized." Gold's Jewish leftist background and formation in poverty may have enabled him to perceive things about Hemingway that others missed. He once called Hemingway "a big-hearted boy with many simple suburban prejudices." What he meant was that the red-blooded American youth was vulnerable to the single mistake Whitman had made, believing too readily in the exceptionalism of his country when he "found himself confronted by its crusade for world conquest."[88]

From the beginning of his relationship with Hemingway, Gold saw through the hypercompetitive and gloriously masculine persona. He knew that Hemingway was "deeply melancholy" and thought this should be apparent to anyone who had read his work carefully or knew him as a friend. "Nobody wanted to hurt Hemingway that knew him well," Gold realized, "because he acted like an overgrown Saint Bernard that loved everybody and felt injured when they pushed him away or criticized him. In this Hemingway was after all only reflecting and incarnating the whole character of his people, the Americans."[89]

On the single issue of greatest importance to a committed revolutionary artist, Gold was conciliatory. "I am not saying that Hemingway lacks a deep sympathy for the oppressed in America, the injured and forgotten people," Gold stated late in his life. He added that Hemingway's essential decency about human suffering was shown in the 1930s, when the superstar author contributed several pieces of "passionate" journalism to the *New Masses*. "Hemingway contained all the contradictions," Gold concluded.[90]

When Gold attended a Revolutionary Writers Conference in Kharkov, Ukraine, a year after his Key West visit, Hemingway was still on his mind. Observing the mannerisms shared by a group of Soviet writers who had fought in the revolution and fashioned novels from that experience, he drew an analogy: "The nearest comparison to them in the United States for background, temperament and craftsmanship would be someone like Ernest Hemingway, I suppose. But Hemingway fought in a war in which he was betrayed and raped of his ideals by the capitalists, and he knows it now."[91]

The 1920s had begun with the efforts of Irwin Granich to introduce and advocate proletarian culture, with the *Liberator* as his platform, in opposition to his onetime mentor Eastman. It ended the same way, with a parting from another early teacher, also an editor of the original *Masses*, over a similar set of issues. The unabashed vehemence of Gold's ideas about proletarian culture fueled a long, at times bitter debate with Floyd Dell. While working under Dell at the *Liberator*, Gold spoke, dressed, and acted in ways that heightened contrasts with Dell's middle-class appearance and background. Years later, in *An American Testament*, Joseph Freeman described what he viewed as Gold's working-class posturing: "He affected dirty shirts, a big, black, uncleaned Stetson with the brim of a sombrero; smoked stinking, twisted, Italian three-cent cigars, and spat frequently and vigorously on the floor—whether that floor was covered by an expensive carpet in a rich aesthete's studio or was the bare wooden floor of the small office where Gold's desk was littered with disorderly papers. These 'proletarian' props were as much a costume as the bohemian's sideburns and opera cape."[92]

Throughout the decade, Gold proposed direct contact with workers as the essential ingredient of a new art that would express their lives and struggles. Dell, however, never believed that transforming one's self into a worker was desirable or possible; he developed a profound distaste for proletarian "impersonation" and a defensible argument against it. His antipathy had been publicized as early as June 1922, in a *Liberator* editorial that took issue with Gold dressing like a worker, associating with workers, and living and talking like a worker. Though Gold, as Dell claimed, "really cherishe[d] the romantic delusion that he belong[ed] to the working class," he was actually "a literary man, an intellectual" and a member of the "salaried middle class," whose identification with workers was transparent and shallow. Dell glibly dissected the psychology behind Gold's class-based charade: "Comrade Mike," he explained, "is for some obscure reason ashamed of not being a workingman . . . so he is in awe of the workingman when he meets him and says extravagant things in praise of him."[93]

Dell later acknowledged that he had unfairly mocked the simulation of proletarian identity by radical intellectuals. But his offense against Gold's aesthetic was not without political consequences, especially as the Sacco and Vanzetti case gained currency and began to reinvigorate the proletarian leanings of radicals and even moderate liberals. An important document from this period of internecine conflict is Gold's 1927 *New Masses* article, "John Reed and the Real Thing." In this essay Gold describes Reed—the Harvard graduate who rallied striking silk workers in Paterson, New Jersey, by teaching them college fight songs and staging a workers' pageant in Madison Square Garden before going off to fight for (and ultimately die for) the ideals of the Russian Revolution—in hagiographic terms. The essay also makes clear why the Communist Party founded chapters of the "John Reed Club" to support leftist art. Reed was exceptional, Gold claimed, because he helped mitigate the worker's natural suspicion toward middle-class intervention in labor-class life. Through his sincere amalgamation with laborers at Paterson and elsewhere, Reed had identified himself completely with the working class: "There was no gap between John Reed and the workers any longer." Implicitly disparaging Dell, Gold argued that Reed's greatness could never be understood by the "pale rootless intellectuals . . . who lead wasted, futile lives in their meek offices."[94]

The decade of contention between Gold and Dell did not end as benignly as it might have, with Dell's laconic resignation from the list of contributing editors to the *New Masses* in May 1929. Instead, in characteristic fashion, Gold felt the need to aggressively ostracize his onetime mentor in the July issue of the journal with an essay that Dell's biographer has called "an unrestricted exercise in character assassination."[95] The committed Communist asserted that Dell "had none of the contacts with workingmen and strikes and battles that John Reed made." He was therefore "at no time . . . a real revolutionist" but instead represented a "Greenwich Village playboy" who had tellingly refused to agitate for Sacco and Vanzetti.[96]

Of course Gold knew that the problem was more complex, originating in a polarizing dialectic between bohemian art and revolutionary action, between individualistic and collective consciousness, between Dell's persona as solipsistic artist and the model of a self-abnegating servant to society that all class-conscious radicals tried to embody. But the timing of Dell's casting out was auspicious; the imminent stock market crash and the decade of Depression that followed would dictate a reunification of the literary Left around a newly empowered version of Gold's ideal.

Almost simultaneous with the market crash of October 1929, the first John Reed Club of New York was founded for the purpose of supporting leftist artists and writers. As Alan Wald's research has shown, the formation of the Reed Clubs was not initiated by Communist Party leadership or by Mike Gold individually. Rather, it had been organized after *New Masses* managing editor Walt Carmon had come to the magazine premises one afternoon to find a clique of young radical writers hanging around and getting in his way. He lost his patience and kicked them out of the office, telling them to "go out and form a club," adding, "I've even got a name for you—call it the John Reed club."[97]

The Reed clubs, which expanded into twelve cities by 1931 and reached a peak of thirty chapters two years later, may not have been Gold's idea, but he was undoubtedly the driving force behind the organization's formal manifesto. As part of a determined program to develop leftist literature, that manifesto suggested that each young writer attach himself to an industry for several years so that he or she could write about it as "an insider, not like a bourgeois intellectual observer."[98] First by working in a factory, then by learning to write publicity for strikes, budding writers would acquire "roots in something real," in effect becoming what Gold termed "industrial correspondents" who would give the *New Masses* its "industrial basis" and make the magazine the genuine voice of the working class. As in the years before World War I, it seemed that a revolutionary crisis was looming, and writers with both radical and nonradical inclinations responded by probing the type of class relationships deemed necessary to nurture systemic economic transformation.

Chapter Five

Art for Humanity's Sake

(1929–1935)

The paralyzing economic shock of late 1929 variously affected all class levels but was met by Marxists with complex reactions tempered by their political allegiances. Gold's memoirs recount both widespread misery, from which he was not immune, mixed with an underlying satisfaction that long unheeded warnings had suddenly been validated: "A great panic came to America on November 6, 1929," he recalled, referring to the Wednesday immediately following the more famous October 28–29 market crash. On that day stocks plummeted sharply a second time, confirming the previous week's deep losses and obliterating hopes of foreseeable recovery. "It came like an explosion. . . . It is difficult now for older people to convince some of the younger generation that such a thing actually happened. The American economy—so corpulent, so reckless, so free—had been built in people's minds to a point of Godhood; it was immortal and it would feed luxuries into the most chosen people on earth, for ever and ever." Gold likened the shock to "a crowded theater where flames leaped up from every corner and people began screaming and dying" and implied that the crisis carried a negation of American Exceptionalism, a mental paradigm so deeply felt and comforting to the cultural majority that its nullification produced hysteria.[1]

The Communist reaction was less excruciating: "The only people in America who did not panic were those strange chronic objectors to everything, known in politics as the Left," Gold wrote, "The American Left, like Marxists everywhere, had long been studying and discussing the chronic panics and periods of depression under the conditions then prevailing."[2] Gold's personal response to the crash comprised fears and uncertainties but was inflected also with self-congratulation: "I'm proud to boast that even I, an amateur Marxist, had been able to predict the panic only a short time before it happened." In a *New Masses* column of September 1929, he had warned young writers that bitterly rebellious works would never be acceptable to bourgeois audiences because

> the prosperity of their audiences is based on stock market gambling. One portion of America thinks, saves, and produces in brain-sweat and muscle-sweat the great machines that dazzle and conquer the world. The other portion shoots craps. Our prosperity is based on the next roll of the dice. Was there ever such a stock market? Were there ever such millions of speculators swarming like blue-arsed flies around the world's sugar bowl? It is these crap-shooting bourgeoisie who are the next 'culture' audience.[3]

Weeks later, in the December *New Masses*, Gold returned to the subject with bolder commentary in an article entitled "American Jungle Notes":

> The American capitalist system may last another ten years. It may last another hundred. But when it begins to reel, crack and tumble into chaos, as it must, millions of tiny naïve Americans will buzz around with the same kind of bewildered horror as they did last month when the stock market crashed.
>
> Who would have thought it possible? Who, in California, will admit to himself that another earthquake is sure to come? Beautiful American faith![4]

The Communist editor admitted that on some level he had "enjoyed the recent music of the victims' howls and tears," if only because he'd submitted to "the airs of these cockroach capitalists" for too long. As early as 1921 he'd written about the regular plagues of joblessness in the capitalist world, predicting that "in less than ten years there will be another fierce, dreadful wave of unemployment, another American famine. I am no divinely informed prophet who says this," he added, "Any American workingman will give you the same information."[5] The dawn that proved

Gold right had come, but this mattered less than the systemic problem itself: "The point is," he said, there will come "other crops of suckers and many more crashes before the final crash."[6]

Originally Gold had plans to be out of the country in October 1929; he was scheduled to lead a group of American workers through Soviet Russia on a "Literary Vagabondage" to study cultural trends in the land of the revolution. Instead he ended up spending three quiet weeks in the cottage on Staten Island, recuperating from what he called "my old Tampico malaria."[7] That fall there was still much to do in organizing the Reed Clubs, which were officially founded in November, and in preparing excerpts of "East Side Memories" from his forthcoming novel for publication in Mencken's *American Mercury*.

In retrospect, fall 1929 was a period a period of comparative calm before the excitements of 1930, a time later described by Walter Rideout as "Gold's marvelous year." The publication of *Jews without Money* came in January, followed by a children's book for Harcourt Brace, a writers conference in the Soviet Union, essays defining "proletarian realism" for *New Masses*, and in October, a literary event that many would see as "the 'beginning' of the new school of radical writing," Gold's attack on Thornton Wilder in the *New Republic*.[8]

Early in the year, the Soviet-led International Union of Revolutionary Writers announced a meeting to be held that fall in Kharkov. A scandal of sorts ensued when Gold received a personal invitation to attend the conference, all expenses paid, well before Reed Club officials were even invited to send representatives. This was not Gold's doing, but he worsened matters by arranging for two of his friends, the novelists Josephine Herbst and John Hermann, to have their expenses paid in order to accompany him as observers. Reed Club members were infuriated. The club scrambled to send its own three-person delegation to the momentous gathering, but the enmity some felt for Gold was intense.[9]

Even before the controversy, some younger Reed Club members saw Gold as a personally self-absorbed and undisciplined Communist. He rarely attended meetings and seemed more interested in bringing already-famous writers like Dreiser and Dos Passos into the fold than developing the talent of unknown radicals. As essentially an artistic personality, he might suddenly disappear for a couple of weeks to work on a new idea. Alan Wald's research noted that there was also the feeling, perhaps due in part to professional envy, that Gold was a prima donna. Wald relates the story that *New Masses* managing editor Walt Carmon used a special desk drawer at the magazine's headquarters to store Gold's fan mail, including "scented love letters that poured in" for the unmarried revolutionary writer.[10]

Before things began in Kharkov, Gold made time for a side trip to Moscow to interview Madam Krupskaya, the widow of Lenin, largely because he wanted to hear her impressions and memories of John Reed. He was elated when she confirmed for him in charmingly accented English that her husband had been very fond of Comrade Reed and had great confidence in his revolutionary loyalty and skill. On the same visit he spoke with an "old Bolshevik" who had been on the train with Reed as a delegate to the 1920 Congress of the Peoples of the East at Baku, where the young American revolutionary had made a stirring speech linking the oppression of black Americans and Latin American peoples with the colonialist exploitation of Asian nations. From this witness Gold learned the full story of Reed's boldness when, on the return to Moscow, the delegates' train was halted in a desert valley by the gunfire of White Guards. As the legend goes, Reed had bravely insisted on accompanying the Red Army escorts in pursuit of the White Guard bandits. Only weeks later he died of typhus in Moscow. For Gold, the incident discredited rumors spread initially by Max Eastman that Reed was disillusioned with the revolution at the time of his death.

By several accounts Gold was a favorite at the November 1930 Kharkov meeting. When Manny Granich visited the Soviet Union a year later, he had a list of contacts eager to host the brother of Comrade Mike. One of the reasons he was embraced was that his literary-political views were in close alignment with those endorsed at the conference. For example Gold and the Union of Revolutionary Writers both believed in the importance of winning over big-name literary figures to the Communist cause, or at least in directing their attention to class issues and proletarian culture, rather than driving them away because they were liberals rather than radicals. It was a theory that, in modified form, opened the way to the Popular Front era five years later.

In his dispatch from the conference for *New Masses* readers, "Notes from Kharkov," Gold made it clear to the radicals back home that his views were winning the day. He announced, strategically, that "the general line taken by the conference was not the one taken by our leftists. The congress declared that it was of vital importance to enlist all friendly intellectuals into the ranks of the revolution." Perhaps thinking of the observers Herbst and Hermann, who were assumed to be non-Party members, he wrote that "every door must be opened wide to the fellow-travelers," and that "every artist who comes to us must be stimulated into activity, not inhibited." At the same time he averred that "everything possible must be done to stimulate the proletarian writers. . . . These are the two main tasks, and neither negates the other."[11]

Gold's articles from the conference and recollections from much later capture the atmosphere of a hopeful and confident period for the Communist International, a moment when all things Soviet were tinged with glamour. In one report, Comrade Mike celebrated an excursion into the fields and woods around Kharkov during which the polyglot delegates marched through "a mile of pines and birches" while singing Russian folk songs and frolicking childishly, playing leapfrog and running foot races. Gold also mentioned Whitmanesque scenes of "Red Soldiers in uniform, factory girls munching apples and baloney sandwiches," along with "workers wandering down the street and singing to a guitar and accordion, and no one thinks it strange."[12] His report, published in March 1931, closes with the anticipation of boarding a special train to tour a Soviet engineering project, the world's largest dam at Dneiprostroy.

Before he left the conference, a formal portrait photo of Gold was taken for use as a Soviet postcard, one of a series of world Communist writers. Written in Russian in the upper left corner of the postcard is a quote from Gold that I have not found in his essays: "The war against us is coming. For all who have any hope for the future, there is only one duty: Defend the Soviet Union." Gold's image on the postcard is compelling, his head tilted slightly downward, his gaze intent beneath the signature shock of thick black hair. Alert for battle, he looks much younger than his thirty-seven years.

Much later Gold would say of Kharkov, "It was a notable congress. There were many writers who had to cross to it secretly underground . . . who were living under fascism practically. We had dozens of writers who had come there illegally and who spoke up and described the conditions in their own countries. It was the first gathering of writers from the whole world, to fight the growth of war and fascism."[13]

On his way home Gold stopped in Berlin, a city already roiled with political violence some three years before Hitler's conquest. He was shocked at how emboldened the fascists were becoming, how brazen their antileft persecutions. He witnessed a crowd of Nazis kicking and beating a man while "well-dressed German burghers puffed their cigars and looked on and laughed—the most horrible fat brutal faces I have seen outside of a

Figure 5.1. Gold in 1930. The text on the lower left reads, "Michael Gold—Popular American poet and novelist, editor of the journal *New Masses*, which unites the revolutionary writers of the United States." The logo at the bottom declares, "The writers of the world defend the USSR." *Source:* Nicholas Granich.

nightmare." Gold felt real fear when he saw the Brownshirts cruising the streets in their Volkswagons, arresting or physically attacking anyone they thought was a radical. As he told a German friend, it seemed to Gold at a superficial glance that the Nazis had seized the offensive and the Republic was on the defensive.[14]

At the end of 1931 Gold covered a massive hunger march in Washington, where he met Pete Cacchione, who would become one of his heroes. A short, stocky Italian-American veteran of the Great War, Cacchione was a dedicated Communist and consummate organizer who was later elected by popular landslide to the office of New York City councilman: "He knew the people of Brooklyn so well that though he never hid the fact the he was a Communist, they poured out enthusiastically to elect him," Gold wrote.[15]

Two decades later Cacchione's life was the subject of the last play Gold ever completed, *The Honorable Pete,* a two-act drama scripted in the early 1950s. "I can remember meeting Pete that time when the Hoover police isolated, in January weather, two thousand marchers on a bare hillside. Hundreds of cops with machine guns and tommy guns surrounded us."[16] As Gold recalled, the Washington, D.C., police prepared a trap for the battered trucks and dusty autos of the hunger marchers. They were not allowed into the city but shunted onto an unfinished road on a suburban hill, where the police confined the marchers for two days and nights without food, shelter, or toilets. George Granich was a route captain that year; Gold was worried as he watched his kid brother's frantic attempts to keep the line of trucks on course with waves and shouts out the window of a scout car driving up and down the column of marchers.

The journey to Washington had begun with a send-off meeting at the Bronx colosseum, where ten thousand marchers met and were assigned to trucks. The night before, they'd slept on the floor of armories and union halls. They stopped in Newark first, where the city had granted the marchers a two-hour permit for a meeting in Military Park and allowed the truck caravan to use the municipal piers for parking. Frantic police nevertheless descended on the gathering, ordering its evacuation and threatening to seize the trucks and ship the men back to New York. Gold listened and took notes as the leaders cited the right of free assembly and stood their ground, showing the power of a militant, well-disciplined labor force. In Trenton, as the caravan passed a doll factory where a desperate strike had recently been waged and won, the workers leaned out the windows, waving and cheering them on.

Gold noted that the hunger marchers were followed by Justice Department agents in private cars. The FBI also sent in stool pigeons to dissuade the marchers and spread the rumor that their leaders were pocketing the donated expense money. Gold was appalled at the health and sanitary conditions the marchers endured, which compare to those later recorded by Steinbeck in novels like *In Dubious Battle* and *The Grapes of Wrath*:

> Many suffered from the Hunger March complaint. The hasty bits of food, the bologna which seemed to follow us wherever we stopped, the bread, the coffee, the jogging of the trucks, cramped quarters, etc. all contributed to bound up bowels. Pills that worked their way through cement and steel were the only solution. At various stops numerous people would be attended by the doctor. . . . Such persons would be flushed looking, act a little teched in the head, act-up, get hysterical. . . . They would lie on the cold ground, wrapped in blankets, carefully nursed back to Hunger March militancy. No one wanted to be left

behind and no one wanted to go to hospitals. . . . Our stops
at hamburger stands en route would be marked by streams
of urine which flowed in a common pool seeking the lowest
spots on the frozen ground. A pool large enough to wade in
was created in this fashion.[17]

A second great hunger march in December 1932 was not written up
by Gold but changed the life of his friend Dorothy Day. Gold's brother
George, having followed his older sibling into the labor struggle and
joined the IWW in the late 1910s, was a member of the Unemployment
Councils and an organizer of the march that converged on Washington
that year. At this time Day had been keeping herself financially afloat
as Gold sometimes had, with meager, unsteady earnings from freelance
writing. Mike would stop by to check on her in her East Side quarters,
sometimes with George and his wife, Gertrude. On one visit George mentioned that a group of trucks would soon be leaving from Union Square
for Washington to "present the case of the destitute."[18] Mike's enthusiasm
for the event convinced Dorothy to find a journal that would send her
to cover it. With credentials obtained from *Commonweal*, she hitched a
ride on one of George's trucks for Washington, where she was moved by
the resilience and camaraderie of the starving demonstrators.

    Day's sympathy for the marchers was tainted by indignation that
Catholic leaders were notably absent from this demonstration for social
justice and workers' rights. Her mixed emotions made for a spiritual turning point. In a state of anguish, Day recalled, she "went to the national
shrine at the Catholic University" and there, as the hunger march was still
going on "offered up a special prayer . . . that some way would open for
me to use what talents I possessed for my fellow workers, for the poor."[19]
When she returned to New York she met Peter Maurin and founded the
Catholic Worker newspaper and the identically named movement that
would guide her life.

    During the darkest early years of the Depression, not only George
but Gold himself was active in the Unemployment Councils and regularly
attended their meetings, which were held in unused factory lofts and
warehouse floors that landlords couldn't otherwise lease. The meeting
premises were generally bare of furniture except for rows of wooden chairs
and a small desk from which a secretary took the minutes. Sometimes
the only adornment of the meeting space was a single framed photo of

Franklin Roosevelt or Abraham Lincoln. To Gold, these gatherings were fascinating and moving, "for in this emergency, people opened their hearts and confessed their troubles." One of the teachings of the council organizers had been to reassure workers, to encourage and advise them "not to be ashamed" of unemployment, that "it was not a personal crime but the crime of social structure, of a whole community." More than thirty years later, Gold recalled with emotion a young Puerto Rican man who rose from his chair and struck his breast in the making of a passionate declaration: "We must get up from our knees."[20]

At the council office run by Cacchione, Gold was a regular by choice. "Pete's council was down in the basement," Gold recalled, "and he liked to ask me to speak there, at least twice a month." Cacchione had a good-sized group of husky laborers, many of whom had fought in World War I, who now had nowhere to go; they slept on the floor and made their meals over an old pot-belly stove that could also burn wood for heat. Gold liked this strong but taciturn group because they showed the comradeship and a quiet steadiness of "old veterans who had seen death and wounds on the battlefields of France and Germany."[21]

They also had a feeling for literature, Gold learned. One night he talked and read to them from Stephen Crane's *The Red Badge of Courage*. The out-of-work veterans were moved by Crane's novel: "they took an aesthetic pleasure in its vivid and hard adjectives," Gold said, and they asked him keen and penetrating questions. They compared the fear-driven flight from battle of Henry Fleming to their own feelings about war and were amazed to learn that the book was a work of pure imagination written by a boy of twenty-five. Mike guessed that Cacchione probably encouraged them to attend such readings, helping them to understand that they constituted a step towards the culture that most working men and women crave "because it is a step forward in humanity."[22]

A good way to appreciate Gold's feelings about the work of the Unemployed Councils during the early Depression is to read Act 1 of his circa 1950 play *The Honorable Pete*. Scene 6 occurs in a Brooklyn tenement street, where the shabby furniture of an evicted family is heaped on the sidewalk. Neighbors gather to help the family and an elderly Jewish woman calls the local council. The council leader arrives and recruits the neighbors to help carry the furniture back inside the tenement.

After the group fends off a policeman who had tried to interfere, the council chief addresses the masses: "Fight or die—that's the choice left the American people today—it's how our councils were born—we decided to live—our slogan is Don't Starve—Fight! . . . Our council isn't a fire brigade, or a bunch of specialists in moving furniture. We're just people. Your people. How many of you neighbors will help your neighbor now—and he will help you later?"[23]

Among those who raise their hands in response to this plea is Cacchione. In the same scene Pete, a devout Catholic, meets his future wife, Dorothy, a Brooklyn Jew who joins the antieviction protest. Later in Act 1, Gold depicts the death of Dorothy's Yiddish-speaking mother who, like Katie Granich, emigrated after the pogroms to slave in American poverty. Her husband had been "sick for years," and two daughters had died. She "cooked and swept, cared for us all" and "never had a day of pleasure." Dorothy laments the woman's burdens along with her "worn out hands and poor bowed back." She remembers that her mother feared the neighborhood Italians, Irish, and all non-Jews but "when she came to know a Gentile, she liked him."[24]

At the close of the scene, a growing sense that Gold is writing about his own mother is confirmed. "What was your mother's name?" Pete asks. "Kate," Dorothy replies, at which Cacchione intones a strange Communist blessing: "Peace to the mothers. . . . Peace to the Negro, the Jew, the worker and farmer."[25]

The Honorable Pete also features a rare dramatization of the appalling 1932 attack on the Bonus Marchers in Washington, D.C., narrated from the perspective of the demonstrators and their families in their encampment on Anacostia Flats. With the capitol dome in the background, the World War I veterans and Cacchione witness the ghastly spectacle of General Douglas MacArthur and his troops, fully armed with bayoneted rifles, as they begin setting fire to the tents of the sick and hungry marchers.

"I can't believe it—tactics—war on veterans," says Cacchione. "You can't shoot down your veterans—no country does." To which the African American vet Orlando responds, "I never made the mistake of crediting our lynchers with having a heart." Rocky, an Italian longshoreman from the Brooklyn unemployed council, jeers at MacArthur: "Who me? I'm Mr. America himself—look at all my muscles; my frigidaires, my ottermobiles and flush toilets—I'm so strong I can conquer Anacostia Flats."[26]

In the early 1930s Gold also worked on an unusually modern and somewhat daring play about Soviet life in the period of Stalin's first Five Year Plan. *Moscow Love*, a two-act drama that went through several drafts, suggests that Gold's two trips to Russia had afforded him insights into the country's rapidly shifting domestic life, including an awareness that even in the Soviet Union, women were not yet free from lingering male chauvinism. The main character within the female-centered action is Nadya, the unfulfilled wife of a self-centered husband, Igor, who denies his spouse a role in the nation's Communist transformation by forbidding her to work in a Moscow factory.

A second key character is Elena, Nadya's more liberated friend, who participates in the Five Year Plan through her daily manual toil as a janitor in an apartment building. Elena asserts that she will remain unmarried because she has no time to pamper a husband. She also counsels Nadya, imparting the view that "Men . . . are all alike. They die to win their own freedom, but they would die rather than give us ours." To her it is shameful that the well-educated Nadya, "a grown woman who has been a Soviet worker, allows a husband to crush [her]."[27]

The three men in the play—Igor, his former Red Army comrade Sasha, and Maxime, a prince in prerevolution days who is now a Communist fellow traveler—espouse Stalinism but cling to stagnant conservatism in the domestic sphere. Maxime, for example, sees women solely as objects of romantic fantasy. "Will a man bring roses to a woman locomotive engineer?" he opines; "Can a man whisper his love into the ear of a female longshoreman? Who ever heard of a woman bricklayer having a baby? Why, it's impossible, it's the death of love."[28]

In Act One, Igor is ordered to Stalingrad to build tractors as part of a "shock brigade" of machinists. His absence leaves his young wife time for contemplation. "The truth is," Nadya reveals to Elena, "I am a woman, I have all of a woman's natural desires—I want a lover, I want a home, I want children—all of the normal things. But I also want to lead the life of a Soviet citizen. I want to share in the great work of building a new world. But I haven't found a man . . . who would let me." Elena's diagnosis of her friend's problem is compelling:

> Your mistake is asking them to give you freedom. You cannot
> be given freedom; you must take it. Then, if you are strong
> and free, you will find men changing their attitude toward
> you, accepting you at your own valuation. For instance, it
> is possible to have a baby and go on with one's work if one
> wishes to. How can any man interfere? I'd like to see one try

it with me. No, no, I want nothing to do with men, Nadya. They are all Turks at heart, keepers of harems, selfish egotists and exploiters.[29]

For the bulk of Gold's play, the male characters labor for Stalinism but otherwise lead rootless, ineffectual lives. Meanwhile the focus of *Moscow Love* turns to the life choices of the women, who seek ways to both build the USSR and fulfill spiritual needs. By the end of the play a housing shortage in Moscow brings everyone back to the tiny apartment where the play began. Elena, a tireless worker with the strength of a man, has decided to have a child out of wedlock to retain her independence. She will take Maxime the former prince, not as a husband but in a limited supporting role of helper and unofficial father to her child.

For her part, Nadya finally listens to Elena and resolves to return to the managerial factory work she had once found satisfying. Concerning the problems of life and love, her practical solution is not to remain husbandless but to welcome two husbands into an apartment that is now hers alone. While she resumes her career, the former Red Army comrades Igor and Sasha will share domestic duties, including, it is strongly implied, that of fulfilling her sexual needs.

Michael Folsom, in a letter he wrote to an aspiring PhD candidate in the 1970s, called *Moscow Love* the "most interesting" of Gold's unperformed works and believed that its treatment of women's issues compared well with the second wave feminism of that decade.[30] Many of its assertions about gender still resonate, and while the play is satirical in tone with elements of farce, it serves as an effective, reality-based criticism of complacent masculinity.

The play's depiction of Soviet female workers during the first Five Year Plan seems related as well to an issue Gold touched on frequently in the early 1930s: sexual equality for women in the American labor movement. Gold spoke often about the need to organize unions of female workers on equal footing with men. A *Daily Worker* column of early 1934, for example, argued the point in practical terms and printed a letter from labor activist Grace Hutchins. The *Change the World* column then framed the discussion theoretically, highlighting the need for men to revise patriarchal assumptions: "The bourgeois system trains us to look down on women from the time we are small boys. You can't weed out such feelings overnight, but every real revolutionist must always try to make himself over into a new kind of human being."[31]

Throughout the early Depression years of the 1929 market catastrophe, the massive unemployment crisis, the Bonus March, bank failures, the beginnings of the New Deal, and Hitler's accession to power, Michael Gold was a controversial national figure as best-selling novelist, committed Communist, and vocal advocate of "proletarian realism." A September 1930 *New Masses* editorial column enumerated essential elements of this "new form" of literary expression: "Proletarian realism deals with the real conflicts of men and women who work for a living. It has nothing to do with the sickly mental states of the idle Bohemians, their subtleties, their sentimentalities, their fine-spun affairs." Writers of this genre, Gold insisted, must be workers or must "have the courage of proletarian experience" and "scorn any vague, fumbling poetry, much as they would scorn a sloppy workman."[32] Other elements of the evolving genre included a rejection of sentimentality: "no straining after melodrama or other effects; life itself is the supreme melodrama." Like earlier realists, Gold was suspicious of stylistic maneuvers and preferred simple, direct expression that was now of significance to the class struggle: "We are not interested in the verbal acrobats. . . . The workers live too close to reality to care about these literary show-offs."[33]

Gold's authority for making these declarations was based on his recent publication of a successful work that he believed met his stated realist criteria. *Jews without Money*, Gold's only novel and by consensus his best work of fiction, is a passionate autobiographical account of Jewish life in the Lower East Side tenements. Described by Alfred Kazin as "a great piercing cry of lament and outrage" over the struggles of the poor, the novel is a loosely narrated series of sketches from the author's childhood, told from the perspective of a young "Mikey Gold." As a self-announced "truthful book of poverty," the narrative spares no detail in cataloging slum misery while identifying its cause in the capitalist system: "America is so rich and fat," Gold writes, "because it has eaten the tragedy of millions of immigrants."[34]

The novel went through multiple printings and was instantly recognized as a literary landmark of the Jewish American experience. When Sinclair Lewis mentioned the book in his Nobel Prize acceptance speech in December 1930, he not only credited Gold for his pioneering depiction of the lurid East Side slums but also listed him among the few young writers who offered "hope for the future" by leading the way in American literature—out from "the stuffiness of safe, sane and incredibly dull provincialism."[35]

The tone of Gold's novel, originally titled *Poverty Is a Trap*, is illustrated in its raw yet lyrical descriptions of slum life and its graphic violence, along with economically determined insights that follow from both. In one representative passage, Gold describes tenement-dwelling Jewish mothers who "stopped in the shade of the elevated trains, to suckle their babies with big sweaty breasts," and a bowery bum in "moldy, wrinkled clothes," whose "rusty yellow face was covered with sores . . . like a corpse in the first week of decomposition." The tenement neighborhoods are for Gold a "world of violence and stone" where prostitutes proliferate and "the rose of syphilis bloomed by night and by day," where immigrant girls are gang-raped and a pedophile who assaults a young boy is "kicked, punched and beat with shovels." Later, the victimized boy is decapitated when he falls under a horsecar, his severed head hanging from the bloody axle. On the cruel streets of the Lower East Side, even stray kittens are abused: "We tortured them, they tortured us. It was poverty," Gold explains. The agony culminates when the narrator's six-year-old sister, Esther, is run over by an express truck while gathering stove wood in a snowstorm, prompting the outraged cry of "Shame on America! In Russia we could not live for the pogroms, but here our children are killed!"[36]

The ghetto's pervasive death and misery compel profound sentiments and radical questioning. Gold wonders, "Is there any gangster who is as cruel and heartless as the present legal State?" His heroic, overworked mother declares America "a good land, but not for the poor." A charitable grocery store owner who gives away bread to starving children laments that "kindness is a form of suicide in a world based on the law of competition." Undergoing the shame and humiliation of a fruitless job hunt late in the novel, Gold's narrator concludes, "There can be no freedom in the world while men must beg for jobs." Aside from its central emphasis on class-based injustice, the work is a perceptive critique of urban America, theorizing racism, sexism, and the costs of assimilation for Jewish immigrants struggling with cultural identity in the United States. For its starkly naturalistic presentation of characters caught in a web of economic and social forces, *Jews without Money* has been compared to Upton Sinclair's 1906 muckraking classic, *The Jungle*.[37]

Appropriately, the only light in the book's dark, brutalizing world is the potential for radical change. The novel ends, and the life of teenaged Mikey Gold is given purpose, when he hears and responds to a speech from "a man on an East Side soap-box" about a world movement to abolish poverty: "O workers' Revolution, you brought hope to me, a lonely

suicidal boy. You are the true Messiah. . . . Oh Revolution, that forced
me to think, to struggle and to live. O great Beginning!"[38]

Though the book was a much-discussed, well-timed bestseller, its
initial review in the *Daily Worker* was guarded in its praise and severe
toward Gold in a way that reflected the internecine conflicts of the Reed
Clubs. Under the title "Gold's Book of East Side Senses Revolt," George
Hanon characterized the novel's appeal for a leftist readership galvanized
by anticapitalist sentiment: "What makes this book worth reading by a
worker is . . . that it conveys a deep-going sense of revulsion against this
system of filth and slavery, that it crystallizes an active recognition of the
necessity of destroying it, that it succeeds by means of a simple art form
in stirring up an emotional yet distinctly conscious determination to wage
a revolutionary struggle of annihilation against the capitalist system."[39]

Overall, the reviewer was uncertain about Gold's literary craftsmanship and unwilling to dub the book a powerful novel. Hanon's mention
of the volume's rather steep three-dollar price tag hinted at disapproval.
More troubling, his use of the term "semi-proletarian" to describe its
central characters implicitly questioned Gold's personal authenticity as a
representative of working class, a hesitancy that seemed to recall Floyd
Dell's criticisms of the author's "proletarian imago." What this signified was
that, to some, even Gold's birth and upbringing on the Lower East Side
were not deemed sufficient class credentials because he was no longer a
worker ("if he ever was one" seems to be implicit in the reviewer's tone).
Hanon, perhaps representing the *New Masses* faction who felt Gold was
becoming overly self-promoting, reviews the book almost as if it had come
from a middle-class writer.

Hanon states, for example, that the novel's "subject" or main character
is somewhat highbrow, "a little too much the 'artist' chafing against the
restrictions which capitalism places upon his individuality and looking
forward to the revolution which will remove the fetters from his personal
genius." The *Daily Worker* reviewer wanted to see "more of a line of
demarcation between personal and class revolt" and took issue with the
author's implied personality more than the novel itself. The conclusion that
the novel "definitely helps to awaken class consciousness" is unconvincing
in context. More palpable is a slightly slanderous tone of fault-finding:
"The suspicion of 'pure artist' creeps up on one out of Gold's pages."[40]

The reviewer also seems to have expected more informed treatment
of various Lower East Side cultures. Hanon claims that Gold's knowledge
of "Irish and other non-Jewish residents" as presented in the novel is

"amateurish and second-hand," and that the main character Mikey is "isolated . . . when he finds himself outside his own Jewish land." The problem seems to be that the book's specificity to Jewish life limits its appeal. The accusatory statement that the subject matter "does not guarantee that Gold could have written the story of a native[born] American working-class family" implies a wish to read about something other than Jews and betrays more than a trace of anti-Semitism in the reviewer. The *Daily Worker*, it seems, would have preferred to read "Poverty Is a Trap," not *Jews without Money*.

In contrast, the more bourgeois *Time* magazine had no doubts or reservations about Gold's authenticity. Its brief review of the novel focused on its truthful treatment of poverty and actually stressed Gold's earned credibility: "Forty times he has been chased by cops for taking part in street demonstrations; 20 strikes have had his help." The implicit message of the book's title was correctly interpreted in the review's opening line, in the manner Gold meant it to be: "Not all Jews have money."[41]

It's worthwhile to continue this thought by acknowledging how the title is intentionally disruptive. Gold realized that it was a trigger and that it might strike audiences as distasteful, as if the book's author might himself be an anti-Semite. Obviously he wanted the novel to have the opposite effect, so he appended an explanation to his first published use of it. A prepublication excerpt from *Jews without Money* in the June 1928 issue of *New Masses* anticipated reactions to the book's indelicate moniker and used an added dose of unseemly language that, at minimum, quelled confusion:

> Gentiles believe that every Jew is born with a racial secret that teaches him how to make money. This is an old belief; Jews have been crucified, mothers' breasts have been torn off, Jewish children have been split on Cossack spears for this Gentile belief.
>
> A lie. The Rothschilds are rich, but the Jews are poor. The vast horde has no money, its only secret is poverty. Poverty is in our blood; poverty is in the eyes of the Jewish babies ripening in the womb. . . .
>
> The Jews have been drowning and starving for twenty centuries. Jews are racially desperate. They must fight or die.[42]

Five years after the novel was published, Gold was still calling attention to the title, this time to gauge the novel's substantive effect as a counterweight to fascism. Reported in the "Author's Preface" to the book's 1935 edition is the reaction of a Nazi officer who notices that a German radical he has just arrested had been working on a translation of *Jews without Money*: " 'Ho, ho, ho!' " he roared. 'So there are Jews without money!' And all the Brown Shirts laughed with him at the marvelous joke. How could there be Jews without money, when as every good Nazi knew with Hitler, Jews were all international bankers?"

Gold claimed that he was "first proud" of his novel when he learned that German radicals were translating it "as a form of propaganda against anti-Semitic lies." This exchange shows how its title functions confrontationally to accomplish that.[43]

In the same 1935 preface, Gold takes an autobiographical turn to remember his mother, Katie Granich, the "heroine" of *Jews without Money*, who "died just a year ago this month":

> She lived, to the last, in the same East Side tenement street, and prayed in the same synagogue. This was her world; though her sons born in America were forced into a different world.
>
> We could not worship her gods. But we loved our mother; and she loved us; and the life of this brave and beautiful proletarian woman is the best answer to the fascist liars I know; and it is in the bones of her three sons, and they will never betray their mother, who was a worker and a Jew, nor their race and class, but will honor her dear memory, and fight the fascists in her defense until the bitter end.[44]

The death of his mother in 1934 was likely another factor that gave Gold pride in his novel, perhaps altering its meaning for him by adding new sorrow and pathos to its pages. Alan Wald's thorough research into the genesis and construction of *Jews without Money* indicated that the concept of the book changed significantly during its long gestation, undergoing a "modification in perspective" after the author's 1925 visit to the Soviet Union. An important change, Wald found, was "the creation of a more positive view" of both Gold's parents and particularly his mother.[45] In Gold's early sketches of the Granich household, published in the form of short stories beginning about 1917, his mother is "a symbol of narrowness, a figure to be escaped rather than embraced" (as in "A Password to Thought—To Culture," a 1922 story that shows a mother forbidding her son to read books).

For biographers, the idealized maternal figure of Gold's novel is confusing in light of the information that Gold rarely saw his mother from the 1920s on and did not keep in touch with her during much of his adult life. For example, Gold's unpublished memoirs suggest he did not inform her when he left for Mexico in 1918. But these anomalies are more understandable in light of oral history interviews given in the 1980s by Manny Granich, which likewise venerate Katie Granich while acknowledging that Manny too did not often visit his mother in her last years. In Manny's view, his mother was a beloved "fighter" and "hard worker," but in her widowhood she gradually came to prefer independence and a degree of separation from her adult sons. Manny describes her work as a cafeteria dishwasher for over thirteen years, "almost to the day she died, wanting to be independent of us. Not taking our money, she wanted to live her life."[46] It seems Gold's idealization of his mother into what Wald called a sacred "mother legend," was not inaccurate but simply based on the earlier phase of her life and personality.

It's also interesting that Gold's several published excerpts from his novel included changing versions of the same situations. In one excerpt the adult male character whose failure to sell bananas signifies his failure as an immigrant is not Mikey's father, as in the novel, but his uncle. The author's references to the work as "memories" or "memoirs" reveals that in the final stages of composing a manuscript he'd been tinkering with for over a decade, he still hadn't decided what genre he was working in, though he once estimated that the book was "85% autobiographical" and insisted that it be marketed as an autobiography.[47] This helps explain why the book has confused readers who have taken the family of "Mikey" as Gold's own. After reading about Mikey's housepainter father and the tragic death of Mikey's sister Esther, it comes as a surprise to learn that the author of *Jews without Money* did not have a sister, nor was his father ever a painter.

Though the book made the East Side boy famous, the initial, somewhat sneering, response to *Jews without Money* in the leftist newspaper of record would certainly have troubled him, as did a review in the March 26, 1930, issue of *New Republic* by Melvin Levy, who argued that although Gold was "a sincere, moving writer," his best-selling first novel represented "a failure when judged by the standards of proletarian literature." Levy held that Gold's characters "are not proletarians (though he wants them to be); they are merely poor people." This is because their failures are not inevitable and are instead caused by "individual accidents." There was "no social propulsion in the novel" because of two deficiencies: it didn't sufficiently indict systemic capitalism and didn't include direct treatments of specific events in labor history such as "the great shirtwaist strike and the Triangle fire."[48]

Gold was worked up enough to write a rejoinder to Levy's review that decried the decadence and futility of bourgeois literary culture. After sarcastically congratulating the journal for "permitting" a review of his novel to appear in its "rather academic pages" (which, he added, indicated at least "a stir of life" in the moribund publication), he took issue with "Comrade" Levy's dogmatic application of proletarian canons. He pointed out that proletarian literature took many forms and that there wasn't "a standard model which every writer must imitate." Rehearsing arguments that would make him famous or infamous through many varied iterations over three decades, Gold then made two points: First, he did not include the Triangle Fire or garment strikes because he felt he could describe only what he had seen with his own eyes. Second, he identified a serious issue by pointing out the inherent aesthetic biases of middle-class cultural hegemony. Gold alleged that when bourgeois novelists write "in praise of Catholic theology," or "universal pessimism and mass suicide," their works are deemed artistically worthy by elite critics; but when a "revolutionary writer, even by implication, shows the social ideals that are stirring in the heart of the working class, he is called a propagandist."[49]

Levy had also seen a contradiction in *Jews without Money* because the father character is a worker with "a bourgeois psychology." "Of course he is!" Gold replied; "This is precisely the point of the book." The semifictional Herman Gold is an immigrant who came seeking the Promised Land, only to sink "lower and lower" and discover that "there is no promised land where capitalism functions."[50]

Most contemporary reviews of *Jews without Money* were extremely complimentary, easily good enough to justify the novel's immediate inclusion in book-length scholarly discussions of the Depression-era literary climate. In 1932 the respected critic V. F. Calverton praised Gold and embraced the novel's "more emotional than intellectual" approach, stating that the author "makes his characters live by virtue of their own flesh and blood rather than by virtue of the ideas which they are supposed to convey." As such they are not simple vehicles for propaganda but "better indications of present day society" than those offered in more "intellectual" leftist novels.[51] Picking up the same idea, Edmund Wilson gave credit to Gold's narrative for transcending polemics through realism. In his view the novel's conclusion, where the "lonely, suicidal" East Side boy hears a soap-box orator preaching revolution, is a scene "more moving and convincing than much Communist propaganda."[52]

By 1950 *Jews without Money* had seen twenty-five printings and been translated into sixteen languages. The novel's dual focus on generic poverty and on the Jewish immigrant experience has kept it relevant long past the decade of the Great Depression. That relevance has not had the effect of making the novel widely read in either secondary schools or universities.

Michael Folsom's assertion, quoted in this book's introduction, that Cold War politics operating within the academy had "erased" *Jews without Money*, was exemplified in the change one editor made to the novel's ending, a textual corruption that purged the book of its socialist conversion message. In fact, many formalist scholars and critics have targeted the novel's ending on aesthetic grounds, typically disparaging the scene—in which Mikey realizes, "O workers' Revolution . . . You are the true Messiah"—as either tacked-on or unnecessary and therefore not consistent with standards of literary craftsmanship. Together the two processes might be taken as a hint about how academic and political criteria, which are after all analogous expressions of hegemonic power, often operate jointly to marginalize radical texts.

Undeniably, opinions about Gold's novel often depended on the political views of the critic. In an afterword to the much-maligned 1966 Avon Books reissue of *Jews without Money*, Michael Harrington, an avowed anti-Communist, somewhat coldly assessed the novel as "a moment in the American literary tradition, a social documentation of the miserable, hopeful poverty of the immigrant, and a work of modest, but unquestionable aesthetic value."[53] It's worth repeating that Harrington expressed these views after changing the novel's ending. At the other extreme, Robert Forsythe, a Communist editor, called the novel "an American Classic, not only the best book ever written about the New York slums but a literary achievement of high distinction."[54] While Folsom made cogent claims about the political erasure of *Jews without Money*, he too suggested that politics and aesthetics were part of the same problem. Speculating on the novel's absence from academic reading lists, he observed that as a "truthful book of poverty," *Jews without Money* inhabited "a genus for which there is no accounting in the phylogeny of polite letters."[55]

In response to Folsom, the leftist scholar Barbara Foley offered what seems a useful classification of *Jews without Money*, viewing the book as a paradigm of "proletarian fictional autobiography" that shares key traits with Agnes Smedley's compelling and increasingly popular 1929 novel *Daughter of Earth*. Foley notes that both texts draw to a significant degree on the model of the bildungsroman or novel of education, and that they therefore constitute "a hybrid form, poised between bourgeois and revolutionary discursive traditions."[56] A crucial variation from the norms of the genre is that the learning experiences recorded by Gold and Smedley lead their poverty-stricken alter egos not toward a place in the social order but toward radicalism and revolution, underscoring how the proletarian novel differs in political content from the knowledge gained by the hero of the "classic" bildungsroman.

Gold's book also has much in common with another Jewish American chronicle of the Lower East Side, Abraham Cahan's *The Rise of David Levinsky* (1917), a work often viewed as the quintessential immigrant novel for its representation of a Jewish tailor who becomes a millionaire. Gold reused some characters and elements of Cahan's plot, but he gave them new meaning by associating them with stark economic decline. The character Herman, for example, achieves early business success as a salesman of suspender fasteners, but when that livelihood is stolen, he descends into ever deeper poverty and ends his career as pushcart peddler, the very job with which the greenest of Jewish immigrants usually began life in the New World. The failure prompts Herman's avowal that leaving Romania for New York had been his life's greatest mistake. In essence, *Jews without Money* reverses the trajectory of the archetypal American narrative of upward mobility, recasting the national myth as a family tragedy in which compassion is denied full expression by capitalist material conditions.

In 1988 Richard Tuerk made a major contribution to Gold studies by pointing out that *Jews without Money* is more sophisticated and carefully written than critics have recognized. Studying the novel manuscript and comparing the published and unpublished draft versions of its chapters, Tuerk concluded that it is much more than a series of episodic, factual, rough-hewn sketches with a tacked-on radical ending, and that it was in fact the end product of much revision. Tuerk pointed out places where Gold changed biographical facts to suit his purposes: creating the tragic character of Mikey's sister and reworking the experiences of other East Side Jews in the poignant scene where his father fails to sell bananas from his pushcart. These and other imaginative embellishments, along with Gold's conscious attention to prose style, contribute to the overall effect of the book and especially to its ending, which Tuerk does not find discontinuous with the preceding narrative. The novel's combination of episodic elements and a cumulative plot, along with its use of complex, gradually converging strands of imagery, show that Gold was a capable literary craftsman and that "*Jews without Money* is not a series of rough-hewn memoirs but a carefully worked, unified piece of art."[57]

Michael Denning has written insightfully about Gold's influence, arguing that *Jews without Money* epitomizes the "ghetto pastoral," the most important genre created by the proletarian literary movement. Narratives produced by "plebeian" men and women like Gold, Myra Page, Langston Hughes, Grace Lumpkin, and Henry Roth constituted "a new kind of city novel" not only because they depicted ethnic working-class neighborhoods but also because they were real participants in those settings: Such novels "were not explorations of how the other half lives. Rather, they were tales of how *our half* lives." In Denning's view this type of fiction came to represent at once some of the most powerful works in American literature and "the central literary form of the Popular Front."[58]

My own sense is that Gold's novel should not be seen as an anomaly or outlier but as a significant speaking turn in a crucial long-term conversation in US literary history. In many ways, Gold's subordination of style to subject matter was in agreement with principles espoused four decades earlier by William Dean Howells, whose calls for the "truthful treatment of life" and "art for humanity's sake" were accompanied by a call for writers who were men and women of action who handled words like implements of labor. In the 1880s, Howells had been the first major American writer to side publicly with the Haymarket Anarchists, whose state-sponsored lynching moved him to express a degree of solidarity with labor radicals, slumdwellers, and proletarians in novels like *A Hazard of New Fortunes* and *Annie Kilburn*.

The idea among recent critics that Howells's best fiction about social class was hindered by an inability to fully imagine radicalism due to his identification as a "genteel writer-intellectual" also resonates. It was Gold who famously addressed this very problem by implying that the new realism would better express the experience of the poor because it would, without exception, be created either by the poor themselves or by artists who had lived sympathetically among them. As Gold explained in *Jews without Money*, "There are enough pleasant superficial liars writing in America. I will write a truthful book about poverty."[59]

In previous American literary history, middle-class authors like Howells had been like passengers on the sightseeing bus that rolls down the East Side streets in chapter 4 of Gold's novel. A gang of ghetto kids chases the frightened tourists, calling them liars, yelling "go back uptown!"

and pelting the "frightened sightseers" with rocks and garbage. "What right had these stuckup foreigners to come and look at us? What right had the man with the megaphone to tell them lies about us?"[60] For Gold, who perceived the costs and limitations of the type of middle-class balancing act in which Howells engaged, the cleanest way to address the problem of class outlook and decentralize the genteel perspective was for proletarians to write novels. Until this happened, the challenge for artists was to find ways to demonstrate understanding and empathy genuinely, without condescension and without reinforcing the capitalist order.

∽

The immediate celebrity Gold achieved with *Jews without Money* beginning in early 1930 reached a higher plateau later that year. On his return to New York from the Kharkov conference, he found a major controversy in full swing and himself at the center of it. Just before he'd left for Kharkov, Edmund Wilson, editor of the *New Republic*, had asked Gold to review several novels by Thornton Wilder, including *The Cabala*, *The Woman of Andros*, and *The Bridge of San Luis Rey*. Apparently the clever editor suspected that putting the champion of proletarian realism in contact with Wilder's rather remote, genteel, and cerebral novels during a crisis of capitalism would be an interesting experiment. Gold had never read anything by Wilder but agreed to write the review.

The resulting essay, "Wilder: Prophet of the Genteel Christ," scandalized readers and touched off a nationwide "Gold-Wilder controversy" that played out for several years. "Wilder has concocted a synthesis of all the chambermaid literature, Sunday school tracts and boulevard piety there ever were," Gold declared. His fictional creations depicted "not a world, but a museum." From Gold's perspective, Wilder was "the poet of the genteel bourgeoisie," whose "irritating and pretentious" novels lacked any contemporary relevance because within them "nobody works in a Ford plant, and nobody starves looking for work."[61]

In *The Cabala*, for example, Wilder writes about "a group of people losing sleep over a host of notions the rest of the world has outgrown several centuries ago: the one duchesses right to enter a door before another; the word order in a dogma of the Church; the divine right of Kings, especially of Bourbons." Wilder not only views these characters with "a tender irony," he "makes no claim as to their usefulness to the world that feeds them. . . . He writes with brooding seriousness of them as if all the gods were watching their little lavender tragedies."[62]

In other words, the problem Gold identified in Wilder's art was a class issue. By writing as one removed from his time and from every time, Wilder had exerted a type of privilege that engaged artists from the marginalized classes could not afford. His aesthetic not only did no cultural work; it also consciously excluded the tastes of anyone with more immediate concerns than the "small sophisticated class" of vapid bourgeois that had risen on the corporate profits of the 1920s. "And this is the type and style with which to express America?" Gold wondered, "Is this the speech of a pioneer continent? . . . Where are the modern streets of New York, Chicago and New Orleans in these little novels? Where are the cotton mills, the murder of Ella May and her songs? Where are the child slaves of the beet fields? Where are the stockbroker suicides, the labor racketeers or passion and death of the coal miners?"[63]

In the "historic junkshop" of Wilder's works, Gold asserted, "a genteel spirit of the new parlor Christianity pervades every phase"; the novels, along with Wilder's "petty, tinkling little three-minute playlets," constitute "a newly fashionable religion that centers around Jesus Christ, the First British Gentleman."[64] As per Thorstein Veblen's *The Theory of the Leisure Class*, the purpose of Wilder's entire body of work was to provide status-conferring conspicuous waste for the American bourgeoisie. "Let Mr. Wilder write a novel about modern America," Gold concluded.

Essentially, Gold argued that with unemployment rising and soon to reach fifteen million, it was time for a new cultural order. It was time to relegate novels like Wilder's to the periphery in favor of works about the real material conditions of starvation and strikes. Wilder's anemic, drawing-room aesthetic might be favored by the narcotized middle class, but it had nothing to say about Depression-era American life. Unstated but implied in Gold's jeremiad was a core assumption that the artistic movement he led, with roots in the "vast Whitman" and "rugged Thoreau," was no less legitimate and more democratic than the obsolete "tradition" Wilder personified.

The year 1930 was also a context in which proletarian realities generally vied for notice as a voice in the cultural conversation—for a seat at the mythical table in the Ivory Tower where aesthetic merits and priorities were decided. At this gathering the working class had never had the privilege of representing themselves; they had been represented by others or not at all. With a limited number of seats at the table, someone had to go in order to make room, and it was Wilder. The aftermath of the stock market crash was the right moment to invert the status quo and elevate the novels of factory hands, bus drivers, sharecroppers, and Jews from the East Side slums. If this required a concerted rejection of the caste-based "chambermaid literature, Sunday-school tracts and boulevard piety" of the genteel tradition, so be it. Gold was asking for a new literary culture and canon that looked more like America. He was angry and impolite because he'd been on the bottom of the totem pole and understood the issue as a matter of life and death.

Responses to Gold's review poured in, causing *New Republic* editor Wilson to note that "Perhaps no other literary article published in *The New Republic* has ever aroused so much controversy as Michael Gold's on Thornton Wilder."[65] As Wilson published readers' letters over several weeks, he tried to moderate the conversation, stating that he had nothing against Thornton Wilder and pointing out that Wilder's books had been praised in the magazine "often enough to invalidate this charge." He stated also that the magazine "considers Michael Gold an important writer whose critical opinions have a special interest, since he is one of the only American critics of any literary ability who writes about books from the Marxist point of view."[66]

Wilson's damage control article was titled, "The Economic Interpretation of Wilder." In it he agreed with Gold but extrapolated his message somewhat, suggesting that Wilder's books were indeed "a sedative for sick Americans," and that "the sedative and the demand for it" were products of a precarious economic system that alienated the individual and produced mass neurosis. Though the outraged letters were running strongly against Gold, Wilson defended him as having "raised a fundamental issue," adding that there was "a good deal to be said on his side." Gold's essay, Wilson felt, had exposed "the insipidity and pointlessness of most literary criticism" while making it "very plain that the economic crisis was to be accompanied by a literary one."[67] This was already a meaningful victory for the Left, one that helped define the 1930s as a literary decade. Much later, Joseph North remembered Gold's famous polemic as an "intoxicating credo that clashed with the concept of the Ivory Tower," calling it "a 21-gun salute to the great era of the Thirties."[68]

In 1932 Wilson felt the need to return to the controversy by writing a pair of lengthy articles that retrospectively summarized conclusions: First, Wilson saw no reason why "propaganda" should not be deemed good or great literature. "Much of the stuff we are fed in school and college as classics of the rarest quality . . . are propaganda, pure and simple," he explained. Second, "nine-tenths of our writers would be much better off writing propaganda for communism than doing what they are at present: that is, writing propaganda for capitalism under the impression that they are liberals or disinterested minds." This delayed take on the dispute is fascinating; it reveals much about Gold and Wilder and just as much about the 1930s, a special and discrete period in US literary history in which it was possible to say with confidence, as Wilson did, "Today the culture of Communism is a great intellectual force."[69]

A more recent approach to understanding the Gold-Wilder affair was published in 1981 by historian Marcus Klein. In looking at the reader responses to Gold's incendiary article (before editor Wilson finally called a halt to the debate), Klein noticed that the underlying issue in most of the letters to journal had to do with Gold's identity or status as an outsider to genteel America. What was really being debated, Klein saw, was "the basic appropriateness or inappropriateness of Mike Gold's writing an essay about Thornton Wilder."[70]

The anti-Gold letter writers seemed to be concerned by a question that wasn't specific to Thornton Wilder: "Could a Communist and pro-letarian criticize *literature*?" Gold's defenders thought he was qualified, and the fact that Wilder and Gold were "of different breeds" made for punchy, impolite, non-belletristic invective for which there was certainly a place and time. The majority felt otherwise, seeing Gold variously as "crude," "unkind," "ignorant," "myopic," "enraged," "brutal," "loud," "shallow," "unreasonable," "spiteful," "a third-rate author," "biased," "unqualified," "hurt," "not interested in art," and "dogmatic."

But there was one response that went deeper and in Klein's view, provided "utter revelation" about Mike Gold's position in relation to the American class system. In the November 12 *New Republic* there appeared a letter from a Miss Jeannette B. Peabody of Cambridge, Massachusetts, a town once known to Irwin Granich. Miss Peabody wrote:

> For some years I have been a constant reader of *The New Republic*, generally interested, often disagreeing, but never so infuriated as after reading the article by Michael Gold on Thornton Wilder. Why did you allow such an unfair, vulgar, tainted, poisonous review to be printed? Why did you allow a Jew to write a review of books written by a man who acknowledges himself the apostle of Anglo-Catholicism? A Jew naturally has no sympathy with this point of view. Thornton Wilder would have given a much fairer picture of Zionism! This review seems

to me entirely unworthy of your standards of criticism. It is scurrilous, profane, dirty. The writer shows his vast ignorance of any comprehension of the vision, beauty, ideal for which Thornton Wilder stands. I am not an Anglo-Catholic, nor a parlor-Christian, but I heartily resent, as do many of my liberal friends, this attack on a man who we consider has done some lovely things and who we believe is endowed with a very lovely nature.[71]

Finally the issue was made plain. In Klein's view, "Miss Peabody justified Michael Gold."[72] Her anti-Semitism, her defense of an ideal of beauty in contrast to the vulgarity and poor manners of "a Jew," her claim to liberalism, all of these accounted for and vindicated Gold's "poisonous review." There were a great many Miss Peabodys in the United States and they were precisely why Gold—"scurrilous, profane, dirty"—chose not to mute his voice and wait politely to be admitted to the cultural conversation.

It makes one wonder what Edmund Wilson meant when he claimed in his 1932 reprisal of the controversy that "the people who applauded Gold seemed to be moved by a savage animus; those who defended Wilder pleaded or protested in the tone of persons who had seen a dearly beloved thing desecrated. Strange cries from the depths arose, illiterate and hardly articulate."[73] The closest thing to "savage," we should realize, were the views of Miss Peabody. What Gold wrote was more than just an "economic interpretation" of Wilder or even a simple attack on the Ivory Tower; it was a catalyst in the development of cultural studies, the type of thinking that ultimately, though not in Gold's lifetime, produced a broader literary canon, the end of the New Criticism in favor of more contextualized methods of study, and more democratic trends in the humanities.

Before leaving the Gold-Wilder controversy, we should acknowledge a blind spot in Gold's own rhetoric. He had a habit of resorting to implicit antigay slurs when attacking cultural adversaries. For example the review contains a cringe-worthy reference to Wilder's third novel, *The Woman of Andros*, as "a daydream of homosexual figures in graceful gowns moving archaically among the lilies."[74] In another example of this tendency, a *New Masses* article of 1930 predicts a second world war and blames it on the literary escapism "so beloved among the fairies of Oxford." A decade later in *The Hollow Men*, Gold called out a poet he viewed as a lackey to capitalism as a "poor little homosexual" who despised the proletariat. A handful of similar remarks litter Gold's early *Change the World* columns, supporting the view of critic John Pyros that homophobic tendencies constitute "the one area wherein Gold's compassion failed him."[75] Gold's contemporaries, several of whom criticized the slurs, confirm the notion that Gold thoughtlessly projected bigotry on this issue.

Pioneering leftist scholar Daniel Aaron speculated that the intent of such barbs was to satirize the effete youngsters who shunned confrontation and had no real political or social philosophy. Another source of the apparent prejudice might have been the Communist Party itself, which called for "masculinism" in proletarian writing and rejected what it saw as effeminate in modernist literature. Pyros considers it likely that the blunt remarks reveal more about Gold's lack of self-control once his emotions were triggered than about his actual attitudes toward homosexuality

Gold was a lifelong, committed disciple of Walt Whitman, the "heroic spiritual grandfather" of proletarian culture. On rare occasions Gold noted aspects of Whitman's thinking that he could not accept: the imperialistic implications of Whitman's outlook, for example. He ignored Whitman's erotic ideal of "manly love." There is also evidence that Gold's views later evolved. Speaking with Michael Folsom less than a year before his death, Gold recalled that when he was living as a beggar on the streets of Boston in 1915, a gay man had invited him to his home and attempted to seduce him. He admitted that he was a "prejudiced guy" at the time and that his "impulse" was to physically attack the man, though he didn't do so. Homosexuals "were treated very cruelly then," Gold said.[76]

In 1932, V. F. Calverton conferred on Gold the cultural legitimacy he'd been seeking, treating him as a major writer worthy of participation in the national literary conversation and including him in a rare category of writers who "insist[ed] on seeing America as it really is and not as they were taught to believe it," whose works were therefore "not patriotic" yet "American to the core."[77] The notably liberal critic even acknowledged Gold's political work for New Masses and added that his editorials were "among the best pieces of left-wing writing that America has seen in the last decade." Encouraging laborers to express themselves through literature was a "laudable" enthusiasm. Though it had "not yet succeeded in discovering any great abundance of rich talent," it was nonetheless providing "a training-ground for young proletarian writers."[78]

Calverton did see "an error" that was "thwarting to the development of the proletarian tradition," which tended to forget that the "formal element in art as well as the social" were necessary. With Gold in mind, he warned "the revolutionary proletarian critic" against underestimating "literary craftsmanship." Gold was right to insist that literary craftsmanship alone was insufficient, that the creation of "objects of revolutionary meaning" was equally important. "There must be a synthesis," the critic writes, and when proletarian literature fails, it is not because it is saturated with propaganda, but "because it is lacking in qualities of craftsmanship."[79]

Gold might have agreed with Calverton, but there was a reason for his high tolerance for literature that fell short aesthetically but succeeded politically: definitions of craftsmanship and standards of literary taste were class-determined, consciously and unconsciously skewed toward bourgeois standards by many factors, including the obvious one that only the WASP intellectual elite had a say in their determination. Especially during the heyday of proletarian culture, Gold did his best to expose and counteract this prejudice in a series of *Daily Worker* columns the same year Calverton was treating the issue with such depth and gravity. Under the headline, *What a World* (the name of his regular column before it became *Change the World*), he titled several columns simply, "Examples of Workers' Correspondence." Appearing without any commentary were handfuls of Whitmanesque stanzas, taken verbatim from the letters he regularly received from working-class people. Gold might have argued that his fan mail needed no explanation or critical mediation, and he would have had a point. Here are two examples from 1932:

Hood River, Oregon
The orchardists have made an agreement
Not to gather 25 per cent of the Booc pears
Now thousands of tons rot on the trees
And it makes me mad to see it.
Now, hungry kids could eat up all this good fruit
Mother Nature is big-hearted and free
It is capitalism that makes the famines
I tell you, we must have a Workers' America.

Uniontown, Pa.
Last winter I sent my kids to school barefoot
There was snow on the ground but the school gave them milk
This is our life, though our men were working
We women begged for food at the relief
And our kids picked coal on the slate dumps
Four were killed, do you remember, on the Buffington dump
So now women we cannot afford to lose this strike
Come on out on the picket lines, our men and children need us.

With these pieces, Gold was working to fulfill the prophecy he'd made in the January 1929 *New Masses* editorial, "Go Left, Young Writers!" that a Jack London or a Walt Whitman would soon arise out of the masses of young workers. The excerpts take for granted that lives lived in poverty have intrinsic power and, expressed in plain phrases and unsophisticated diction, attain effortless, arresting beauty. About the motivations of the worker-writer, Gold always believed that "his writing is no conscious straining after proletarian art, but the natural flower of his environment. He writes that way because it is the only way for him."[80] Counseling self-reliance and confidence in the class to which he was born, Gold theorized not solely *what* made literature but *who* made it, striving to convince the people that they were artists: "Write," he told them, "Your life in a mine, mill and farm is of deathless significance in the history of the world. Tell us about it in the same language you use in writing a letter. It may be literature—it often is."[81] The year these pieces appeared, Calverton ranked Gold as "the second most important revolutionary writer" after Dos Passos, adding, "It is very likely that in the book he is now writing, a life of John Reed, his growing literary powers will attain full focus."[82]

The Reed biography had been on Gold's mind for some time. He'd begun talking of the project soon after Reed's death in 1920, though he knew that Louise Bryant intended to write her former husband's biography and had sought a publisher for her book as early as 1921. By the mid-1920s, Gold's interest in the project was widely known, as was Bryant's increasing contempt for the man she'd known as Irwin Granich. When Louise stopped in New York in November 1926, Gold sent a message to her on *New Masses* letterhead, explaining that he'd been trying to get her on the phone and that he was "really curious" to know why she was "angry at the magazine." After offering to meet Bryant, Gold came to his likely point: "I am really anxious to get hold of any of Jack's stuff that you may have."[83]

Gold was also aware at this time that Louise was no longer politically engaged or serious about her writing and that she had already committed the unforgiveable offense of betraying the revolutionary cause for which Jack Reed died. The former revolutionary Bryant had married State Department official William Bullitt and publicly become a rich man's wife, living in idle luxury in Paris. Once a restless bohemian iconoclast, Bryant had suddenly given up her activism to embrace leisure-class values she had earlier repudiated. "Seemingly overnight," observed Bryant biographer

Mary Dearborn, "she had turned her attention from causes to clothes, from politics to parties."[84]

Seeking access to Reed's personal papers, Gold apparently tried to welcome Louise back into the fold, though perhaps half-heartedly, closing his letter to her with, "Also, I would like to make you write for us occasionally" before signing off, "fraternally yours."[85] Apparently the attempt to reach out was fruitless. When Calverton mentioned Gold's book on Reed six years later, its potential author still did not have Reed's letters and manuscripts, which were with Bryant in Paris and were about to become part of a somewhat sad history.

In 1930 Bryant lost custody of her only child in a bitter divorce from Bullitt that also left her without regular income. She suffered as well from Dercum's disease, a rare disorder whose disfiguring effects resemble elephantiasis, causing terrible pain, fatigue, and mental confusion. She increasingly sought refuge from her symptoms in alcohol, leading to bouts of severe paranoia. In 1934 a group of Harvard scholars including Granville Hicks and John Stuart contacted Bryant, who was now living alone in Paris, determined to obtain the trove of Reed documents for the same purpose Bryant was holding them and Gold wanted them.

One of Bryant's responses to these requests, a long letter to artist Robert Hallowell, declared her loathing for the former Irwin Granich while asserting also that Gold knew nothing about Reed. She claimed that she couldn't get a publisher's advance for her Reed biography because Gold had wheedled a large advance of "something like $1500 or $1900" for the project from Coward-McCann publishers. In another letter to Corliss Lamont, she alleged that Gold had been "profiting fatly on the false publicity that he alone is capable of writing of Jack." She said that Gold had spent the large advance sum and had "no idea" how to write about Reed. She even alluded to the invitation Gold had received to the 1930 Kharkov conference, claiming that Gold "also went to the Russians and got free passage all over on the same fake."[86] Bryant also made the apparently inaccurate complaint that on her last visit to New York, Gold gave his "secretaries" at New Masses the order not to accept any submissions from her and added that on the same visit she had "found nowhere any co-operation in work I wanted to do in regard to the book I write about Jack." Since then, she wrote, she had been "usually without money." And so the years had passed. Eventually Harvard obtained Reed's papers, and Hicks's biography, John Reed, The Making of a Revolutionary, appeared in 1936.

At the time Bryant made these charges against Gold, she was unwell and unstable. Her mental state justifies some skepticism about the large advance she claimed Gold had received for the Reed biography. She may have imagined or fibbed about this money in order to use Gold as an excuse for her own inability to write about Reed during the years when she was in possession of Jack's papers and had the cooperation of his family. The fact that she had also turned her back on the revolution might have caused her to feel defensive about the matter.

Nevertheless the story is interesting because it involves questions of income and literary production during a period when Gold was due for a second major book—another novel or the Reed biography—neither of which happened. Of course Gold planned many book projects that never materialized. In addition to his need to survive by selling his best energy to the *Daily Worker*, he was in Wald's view "by temperament . . . simply not suited to sustaining his focus for months or years in isolation on one big project."[87] Wald also mentions Gold's active life and his growing problems with diabetes. Still, there's a good chance that if he'd had access to Reed's papers, Gold would have been passionate about curating that legacy by finishing a biography.

On the subject of Gold's finances at the peak of his career, here is what we know: The early 1930s was one of the few periods of financial stability in his life. Ironically, the worldwide financial crisis that made the author into a famous spokesman for the destitute and dispossessed had also created conditions that helped sell his novel. By the end of 1930, Gold's royalties from *Jews without Money* amounted to $6,000, half of which he used to purchase a piece of land in Bucks County, Pennsylvania, a property he later sold.[88]

The rest of the royalty money seems to have been gradually depleted over the next few years, a time when Gold's income was erratic as he took several breaks from paid journalism to make unsuccessful attempts to produce a second major book. For example he spent more than six months in 1932–1933 drafting several chapters of a never-completed novel about a middle-class Harvard student forced to leave the university when the stock market crash bankrupts his father. At this time Gold probably lived on a combination of royalties from his novel, intermittent work for *New Masses* (where contributors received nothing and staff considered themselves lucky if they received $5 per week)[89] and irregular fees for speaking engagements. He also moved often, taking cheap cold-water flats or living for periods with friends. He had few possessions and had been raised to believe that rent was an inherently wasteful expense.

Nevertheless there were insinuations, some of them tinged with envy as Bryant's may have been, that Mike Gold had money somewhere. In late 1930, Harcourt Brace Publishers, intending to capitalize on the author's sudden celebrity, contracted for a children's book that would reach the market quickly. When the small volume came out, the *Daily Worker* printed a negative and accusatory review that begrudged the author whatever pay he'd earned for it. Under the title, "Digging for Gold," the review alleged that "when a big capitalist publishing house prints a book written by a well-known, allegedly working class writer, all honest workers can be justified for becoming suspicious. 'Charlie Chaplin's Parade' vindicates your suspicions."[90] The implications that Gold was not an "honest worker" and only "allegedly" working class are shocking. The claim that the book is "full of . . . master class propaganda" seems a willful misinterpretation. It fails to notice that the character who espouses the book's "master class" values is clearly treated with ironic disapproval. In 2006 Julia L. Mickenberg more accurately described *Charlie Chaplin's Parade* as "a modernist fable that mocks the corporate order."[91]

According to Wald, Gold was by his own admission a poor self-advocate when it came to negotiating financial matters and understanding his own earning power. Arranging the launch of his *Change the World* column with *Daily Worker* editor Clarence Hathaway in 1933, he was reluctant to accept even fifteen dollars per week, the same modest stipend he'd received almost twenty years earlier from the *Boston Journal* for his *Freshman at Harvard* column. Even when he had leverage, he was the opposite of acquisitive and seemed rather to lack the desire to take financial advantage. This was one of the reasons why he lived his entire life without luxuries, never making a large salary or accruing substantial savings.

If the early 1930s was a period during which Gold had cash reserves, the situation apparently did not last long. Late in his life he recalled his shock on the day bank deposits were frozen by decree, just after Roosevelt's inauguration in 1933. He laughed nervously when he heard the news because at that moment he had ninety-five dollars in an account, "the biggest sum I ever had there," he said, which he immediately tried to withdraw. When the bank cashier refused him the money, he decided to try to use it another way. He went to Roger Peets clothing store off Union Square, remembering how he'd looked in the windows as a boy and wondered if one of those nice suits would ever come his way. He picked out a tan tweed suit and paid with a check that the salesman accepted dubiously, then waited while the elderly gentleman called Gold's bank. "Yes, sir, is there anything else you need?" the salesman asked when he returned. "So I started the Depression with a fine suit of clothes,"[92] he joked. One of the best photos of Mike Gold in action was taken at a May Day celebration in the early 1930s. The first time I saw the photo I remember noticing how well-dressed the speaker was and thinking that he didn't look like a proletarian in that suit.

Figure 5.2. Speaking on May Day, early 1930s. *Source:* Granich family.

The year 1935, in which the Nuremberg Laws divested German Jews of their citizenship and rights and Mussolini invaded Ethiopia, was a time of solidarity for the literary Left and a crucial time in the life of Michael Gold. That year, at the midpoint of the 1930s, the Moscow Comintern officially launched the Popular Front, which urged that all factions of the Left unite to form a solid block against fascism. From this point on, sympathizers, "fellow travelers," and even liberals, who were previously regarded with contempt, were welcomed into the collectivist struggle and encouraged to participate.

In April, Gold addressed the climate of solidarity in his "Author's Note" for a new edition of *Jews without Money*, calling on "every liberal and radical" to defend Jews from "fascist liars and butchers." He attempted to give new meaning to his novel, repurposing the book as anti-Nazi propaganda and dedicating it to the Popular Front purpose of thwarting Hitler's "great lynching party against liberals, radicals and Jews."[93] In late June, the First International Congress of Writers for the Defense of Culture, a mass meeting of intellectuals against fascism, was held at the Salle de la Mutualité in Paris. On a scorching summer afternoon a few days after his arrival in France, Gold participated in the ceremonial opening of the congress, walking several miles in a parade-like procession through the streets of a primarily Communist Paris suburb. He marched in a group of fellow writers behind a fireman's band playing the "Internationale," followed by thousands of workers and their families, several hundred schoolchildren in white shirts and red Soviet-inspired Pioneer kerchiefs, and a troupe of elderly veterans of the 1871 Paris Commune, their crimson and gold sashes shining in the sun. Gold watched and waved as workers cheered and shouted slogans, flourishing their home-made flags and banners from sidewalks, gardens, windows and doors.

The procession's winding way led down a renovated main boulevard that was being renamed after Maxim Gorki. Here the marchers paused for a brief ceremony and Andre Gide unveiled the new name plaque. The procession halted also at the recently built Karl Marx Children's School, which impressed Gold as a beautiful "children's palace, clean happy and bright," especially in comparison to the dismal, prison-like schools of capitalist New York.[94] Eventually the parade reached an outdoor stadium where each writer including Gold was introduced through loudspeakers and made a brief address of salutation, after which a worker stepped forward with a bouquet of roses and gladioli from the local gardens, presenting it with kisses on both cheeks.

Figure 5.3. With Andre Gide in Paris, 1935. *Source:* Granich family.

Gold's formal role in the conference involved participation in a multinational panel discussion on the topic "Nation and Culture" on the evening of June 23, a session cochaired by novelist E. M. Forster and the French essayist and critic Jean Guéhenno. The French representative on the panel was the sixty-two-year-old Communist novelist Henri Barbusse, who was at work on a biography of Stalin and preparing to leave Paris for Moscow, where he was to die of pneumonia eight weeks later. In effect a celebration of the Popular Front, the congress marked a turning point in the decade, the first concerted international effort of a broad leftist coalition of artists and writers for the purpose of opposing authoritarianism.

It was a turning point in Gold's personal life as well. En route to Paris on the British liner *Majestic*, Gold was invited to dine with other single passengers at the captain's table. He struck up a conversation with a smartly dressed French woman in her early thirties, Elizabeth Boussus, a French teacher at Rutgers University who had emigrated to the United States in 1927 and was returning home for a visit. Though twelve years younger than Gold, she found him easy to talk to and noticed his youthful looks and athletic build. Elizabeth Boussus was herself an athlete; at the age of twenty-five she'd won the mixed doubles tennis championship for the state of Vermont. She also had a law degree from the Sorbonne that she didn't use because she preferred teaching, having begun her career by directing the French immersion program at Middlebury College. During the congress the two met often. Though Elizabeth spent part of the time away from the city with her family, she returned to Paris to show him the best of the capital city's culture. By the end of the conference, Gold had impressed Elizabeth by sharing details of his meetings and friendly discussions with Barbusse, Andre Malraux, Andre Gide, and Luis Aragon. Following a civil wedding in 1936, the couple had their first son, Nicholas, that November in Los Angeles, where the newlyweds lived for a several months because it took some time for Elizabeth to adjust to New York. Their second son, Carl, was born in New York in 1940.

Mike traveled home from the Paris congress in early August while Elizabeth remained in France with her family for several more weeks. Before leaving France he had reported on the business side of the proceedings for *New Masses;* at sea on the homeward journey he wrote "A Love Letter for France," a more personal account of an adventure he knew to be significant. As the ship approached New York, the "raw, young city" that Gold "loved painfully," he sent warm parting words to Paris, claiming to understand why Americans were forever fascinated and charmed by that city. He hoped its people would "accept the gratitude . . . of another infatuated American!"[95] No doubt he was also thinking about his nascent relation with Elizabeth, and perhaps already about future encounters with the country and culture of her birth.

Gold also expressed some misgivings about his imminent reimmersion in the American scene. In France he'd observed how one French Communist in particular, Paul Vaillant-Couturier, had managed to balance his multiple artistic passions, including novel writing and painting, with the mundane business of "party work." This was something a number of American Communists, Gold especially, had found difficult.

With good reason, the issue was on Gold's mind in 1935. In the years leading up to the Paris congress he'd more than once been confronted by Party insiders—though probably in a friendly way—about his poor attendance at the meetings of his local Party branch, and perhaps about not setting a good example in other areas related to Party business. For quite a while it had been apparent that, where both bureaucratic and official policy matters were concerned, Gold could be unpredictable and unorthodox.

It was not unusual for the Party to make concessions and compromises that allowed certain artists the option of nonparticipation in day-to-day official business. During and after the Depression decade, a number of openly committed writers who were temperamentally unsuited to formal obligations within the organization were excused from official CP membership dues and obligations because their loyalty was unquestioned. Aware of Gold's substantial value in other roles and that "party work" was among his lowest priorities, members of the Central Committee may have simply decided to allow him his independence.[96]

Though these arrangements were most often settled amicably, Gold's case could have involved some contentious feelings. Manny Granich may have exaggerated only slightly when, much later, he explained the situation this way: "In fact Mike was an ardent member who was kicked out of his branch of the Party because he would never, with his temperament, do what was requested or told to do by his local branch and as a result he worked for about 15 years on the *Daily Worker* without being a Party member."[97]

Manny's assessment would date his brother's break from formal Party duties to about 1933. This may explain why, on the way home from France in 1935, Gold discoursed at length about Comrade Vaillant-Couturier, specifically on the notion that the creative adventures of the prolific novelist-painter had not handicapped his political participation. Somehow Gold's French friend was "up to his neck in party work" but still thriving as an artist.[98]

Apparently something in the humanity and openness to culture of the French Communist movement prompted comparisons. "I wonder what would happen to [*Daily Worker* editor and Central Committee member] Clarence Hathaway," Gold mused, "if he began to write sonnets, or to Earl Browder if he should join the Composers Collective and write proletarian songs." It seems Gold was thinking of his own role in the movement and pushing back at Party functionaries, questioning an American atmosphere in which the choice between political and artistic endeavors was either mutually exclusive or overly regulated. He went on to wonder why comrades who did "political work" in New York were additionally burdened with an obligation to "suppress" their art. "Nobody would have felt that way in France," Gold observed.[99]

A few weeks after Gold's return, Australian novelist Christina Stead added to the lore of the congress by publishing a first-person account that included Gold in a major way. Among the more than four thousand students, workers, and intellectuals gathered in Paris, Stead had found herself "wholeheartedly with the communists." Her invitation to attend the gathering as secretary to the British delegation was likely the result of the ideas expressed in her proletarian-themed first novel, *Seven Poor Men of Sydney*, which had been published a year earlier to positive reviews. Stead's report on the congress in the July issue of *Left Review*, the most emphatic statement she would ever make about the political responsibility of writers,[100] may have had much to do with the strong liking she had taken to Mike Gold.

On the last evening of the conference, June 26, Stead had attended a dinner celebrating the sixty-fifth birthday of Danish writer Martine Anderson Nexo. Among the small group of friends who lingered after dinner in the warm evening breeze on the restaurant terrace was Gold, who seems to have quickly become an infatuation of the Sydney-born novelist. In her *Left Review* article, Stead referred to him as "irresistible Mike . . . with small, swarthy Finnish face and turbulent hair," who regaled the international audience with solo interpretations of American work chants and folk music, what Stead called "the songs of the negroes converted to Lenin in the southern swamps, fields and forests." The thirty-two-year-old Australian novelist sensitively described Gold as "straight-forward, gay, simple" but burdened with regret that "politics" robbed him of "the time he should spend on books."[101]

Of course when Gold said "politics," were holding him back, he was referring in some way to his awkward relation to Party business, but perhaps primarily to his regular *Daily Worker* column, which was really an issue of economics, and which brings this discussion back to money. Throughout Gold's career, newspaper work at low pay was often the only option other than speaking honoraria as a way to make ends meet. The energies required to meet deadlines drained his intellectual resources.

By 1935 he had realized that writing was the single best way he could contribute to the world revolutionary movement, but what he had in mind was creative work: novels, poetry and plays. In a *Change the World* column written just after his return from Paris, he divulged to his *Daily Worker* readers, good naturedly but not jokingly, that he was "completely broke and consistently broke."[102] That year he also applied for a Guggenheim grant for the sole purpose of freeing himself from his column for a year or two. Hemingway agreed to recommend him, and his letter of support indicated a second time, more specifically than in the remarks Stead reported, why Gold had trouble producing another novel. Hemingway wrote,

> I have known [Mike Gold] personally since 1928 and have only the highest regard for his character and ideals. I have been an admirer of his work for many years and would look forward with great anticipation to reading what he would write if given a chance to do creative work for a time, free from the necessity of exhausting himself daily in journalism.[103]

Figure 5.4. With Liz and Nicky at Free Acres, summer 1937. *Source:* Granich family.

The Guggenheim application was not successful, and on January 1, 1936, Gold stated in his *Daily Worker* column a New Year's resolution: "May the author of this column finally write a novel!"[104] As Alan Wald's research found, Gold's letters to Upton Sinclair at this time divulge that he was worried about money and in danger of going back to the days of sleeping on the floors of friends' apartments. Now that he was married and Elizabeth was six months pregnant, he knew this was no longer possible. "I'm afraid that as usual I will have to go back to the *Daily Worker* column," he decided, "which pays a small wage but takes every bit of creative feeling out of me."[105]

Chapter Six

A New Kind of Song

(1935–1941)

In early 2006 Pete Seeger sat for a lengthy interview with journalist Tim Robbins of Pacifica Radio, during which the eighty-seven-year-old folk singer described the origins of American "people's music" and related facts about its early development. Robbins asked Seeger about the Almanac Singers, who had aligned themselves with working-class causes in a brief but historically significant period of activity from 1940 to 1943. In response Seeger referred to the four co-founders of the Almanacs—Lee Hays, Millard Lampell, Woody Guthrie and himself—then immediately called attention to a cultural figure who had worked enthusiastically with the group to promote their art:

> In 1940 we sang at peace meetings and strike meetings and we made two records. [. . .] Lee Hays came and said, "Pete, let's see if we can make up some peace songs" and in one evening we made up three or four of them, and out came three 78 rpm records.
>
> We were famous in the *Daily Worker* crowd. Mike Gold just thought we were the greatest thing. You see Mike Gold was outraged by the Composers Collective. He said "these long-haired musicians don't know how to write music for working people." And along come the Almanacs six or seven years later. And he said, "This is what we need!" And he wrote about [us] in his column in the *Daily Worker*. So in the *Daily Worker* we were famous. [Though we were] unknown elsewhere.[1]

Seeger's name-dropping, which locates the author of *Jews without Money* at the center of a conversation about peace songs and the Composers Collective, probably confused his interviewer and might also surprise some literature scholars. But among historians of twentieth century American folk music it is a well-known story that began almost a decade before the Almanacs came together.

The Pete Seeger-Mike Gold connection originated as early as September 1933 when, as biographer David King Dunaway notes, Seeger "returned to Avon [boarding school] with a subscription to the Communist magazine *New Masses*" and "quickly became a devotee of a firebrand journalist, Michael Gold."[2] The future folk singer, a schoolboy of fourteen at the time, felt thwarted by conformist classmates and teachers who slighted progressives while tacitly approving anti-Semitism. Gold, who was "everything Peter wasn't: ethnic, working-class and politically committed"—became Seeger's ally in rebellion. Music scholar Robbie Lieberman attributes specific meaning to this moment in Seeger's life, stating that the young musician "was conscious of the relationship between art and politics" because of reading Gold's columns.[3]

The fact that Seeger was a Gold fan from his boyhood is significant, but it was only one discreet aspect of a broader 1930s cultural context that actively debated the question of what leftist American music should be. In that debate, Seeger's father Charles was more directly involved than his teenaged son. Pete was correct in stating that Gold "was outraged by the Composers Collective"; what he did not state was that his father, a formally trained musicologist, was a member and leader of the Composers Collective, and therefore Gold's opponent in a philosophical argument the outcome of which has shaped U.S. culture ever since, in ways that are still visible and palpable.

Richard Reuss's 2000 study, *American Folk Music and Left-Wing Politics*, situates American "people's music" in the early 1930s among a welter of cultural organizations devoted to furthering proletarian art, a cause for which Gold was already the most well-known and consistent advocate. From the beginning of the decade, music was seen as a necessary element of the Communist program, but initial production of leftist songs was, according to Reuss, "sporadic and slow," in part because there was no set theory about the form such music should take or how it was to be created.

Not surprisingly, Mike Gold was interested in this problem. Always searching for the proletarian writer-poet who'd become "Shakespeare in overalls," he was outspoken also about the need for American labor music.

He knew and loved the IWW songs he'd picked up from workers in the more than twenty strikes he'd already helped; he would ruminate at length about the need for a "Communist Joe Hill" but didn't know where to look for him.[4] Having no formal musical training, he could initially issue only general directives, but he knew good people's music when he heard it. With help from the Reed Clubs, Gold endorsed art that was both "realistic (as opposed to abstract) in form and agit-prop in character" for the purpose of awakening "class-conscious feelings in the uncommitted masses."[5]

In May 1931, for example, Gold encouraged the New York Reed Club to elect a Music Committee. A month later, Communist Party members established the Workers Music League under the slogan, "Music for the Masses." The purpose of the WML was to bring together artists, composers and trained theoreticians to develop songs that could be weapons in the class struggle. The League began functioning in late 1931 and within a year there were eighteen affiliated organizations in major cities—Boston, Chicago, Philadelphia—with ideological leadership provided especially by the New York Musicians Club and the Pierre Degeyter Club, named after the recently deceased composer of the socialist "Internationale." Within the Degeyter Club there were subgroups of performers, composers, and publishers, the most significant of which in the early 1930s was the Composers Collective.

Formed in 1932, the Composers Collective included, along with Charles Seeger, a group of largely European-trained musicologists such as Wallingford Riegger, George Antheil, Elie Siegmeister and Marc Blitzstein. Seeger was a Harvard graduate who had completed his music education in Germany, conducted the Cologne symphony and held a position as Professor of Music at the University of California, Berkeley, until he was fired in 1916 for his opposition to US entry into the war in Europe. As the chief theorist and driving force of the collective, Charles Seeger looked to the model of Austrian-German Communist Hanns Eisler, a classically trained composer known for elaborate "revolutionary chorales," massive worker choruses of several hundred performers. This type of radical music had been an outgrowth of the demographics of the 1920s Communist Party, whose membership comprised largely immigrant language groups, mainly Eastern European.

Charged with the task of disseminating new and old revolutionary music and establishing methods for the composition of future proletarian-themed works, the Composers Collective published a two-volume collection, the *Workers Songbook*, in 1934 and 1935. The first edition of the *Songbook*

contained thirteen compositions by members of the collective including
Charles Seeger (under the alias Carl Sands). These works may have been
technically masterful, but when it came to their assumptions about musical
form and composition, there was little that was truly revolutionary about
them and little chance they would ever be performed or embraced by masses
of American workers. "Even at a cursory glance," observed music historian
Benjamin Bierman, "much of the material [was] clearly for educated, or
at least experienced, musicians, and frequently has challenging modernist
elements that are problematic for untrained musicians."[6] As another music
historian observed, such musical expression—with ponderous lyrics and
dissonant, complex melody lines and irregular meters—"had few real roots
in American culture."[7] Almost immediately, these qualities were of concern
to Communists hoping to appeal to American-born workers, who noticed
that the particular aesthetic mode the collective chose to work in made its
compositions inaccessible.[8]

To make matters worse the Composers Collective, Charles Seeger
most vocally, was actively hostile to folk music, seeing it, in Eisler's words,
as "a badge of servitude from pre-revolutionary times." What's more, to
the ears of trained musicians of the Composers Collective, folk songs were
technically crude and stylistically inferior. These opinions put them at
odds with pieces in *The Red Song Book*, a publication of the same period
by the Workers Music League, which featured folk-oriented material by
southern activist-artists including songs about the Gastonia textile worker
walkout and Kentucky coal strikes. When the Composers Collective actively
criticized the workers' songs and singer-songwriters of the folk tradition,
"this set up a conflict between the Collective's art music perspective and
the Communist Party's cultural critic, Mike Gold, who felt their attitude
was elitist."[9] With the exception of a few pieces in *The Red Song Book*,
the music presented by both the collective and the WML was in Gold's
view "sterile, cerebral" and "distant from the revolution."[10]

In a *Daily Worker* column of 1934, Gold took an attitude of friendly
impatience with the esoteric approach of the collective. He quoted a union
member complaining that the music of the collective was "unsingable" and
overly complicated. "I think a new content often demands a new form,"
Gold suggested, "reaching the masses is as much a test of Communist art
today as any other test."[11] As the music historian Reuss concludes, "Given
Gold's background and passionate love for 'songs of the people,' it is not
surprising that he was among the most forceful of the 1930s Communists

to hammer at the notion that folk songs were songs of the working people, reflecting their hopes, aspirations, and frustrations—and ought to be
appreciated more in proletarian music quarters."[12]

A telling moment in the early phase of the debate came when Aunt
Molly Jackson, a southern mountaineer folk singer and radical organizer,
was invited to perform at a Composers Collective meeting in 1932. Charles
Seeger recalled that the collective was "more bewildered than inspired"
by the performance and that Jackson was likewise unimpressed with the
collective's works.[13] The Workers Music League sided with Seeger and
disparaged Jackson's songs for their apparent "immaturity" and "arrested
development."[14] Gold disagreed, seeing Jackson as among "the nearest
things we've had to Joe Hill's kind of folk balladry."[15] At another time
his praise for Jackson went even further: "This fine militant mountain
woman with her courageous laughter and deep proletarian love . . . she
ought to be sent around the country to sing her ballads."[16] Of course, it
may have been true that Jackson's songs were technically inferior, and
that their technical inferiority could be demonstrated by a dozen different
scholarly criteria, but none of this mattered to Gold. Having decided to
engage the Composers Collective and the League, Gold declared, "a new
balladry is being created, under our noses, actually the only authentic
folk music of this period."[17]

Jackson's performance for the Composers Collective is often cited
by music historians as "an important turning point in the discussion of
the respective efficacy, as workers' songs, of folk-style music versus art
music."[18] But the philosophical divide it represented did not come to a
head until 1935–36, in a showdown of sorts between Gold and Charles
Seeger in the pages of the *Daily Worker*.

In late 1934, Gold had begun to take a keen interest in the work
of Ray and Lida Auville, Appalachian folk singers with a traditional folk
song repertory who had moved to Cleveland in the early 1930s. Gold had
been thrilled to receive a copy of their radical songs and, evidently gaining
confidence as a music critic, he used his *Daily Worker* column to publish
several detailed arguments for the value of their work. In November of
1934, he thanked the John Reed Club of Cleveland for sending "great
news" about the advent of the Auvilles, exhorting readers to "buy up all
the copies" of their pamphlet of eight songs so that a larger edition of
all the songs would eventually be made. "Certainly this must be done,"
Gold wrote, "Here is the real proletarian art, here is the real America."[19]

In the next day's column Gold printed the verses of several songs and continued his encomium while pointing out the Auvilles' particular nonacademic brilliance:

> Note how timely the themes are, how specific. Note the style, which has the true ring of American balladry. The lines might not be approved by an aesthetic grammarian, but no intellectual poet could hope to imitate them. One has this folk-feeling or one hasn't. Joe Hill had it, and the Auvilles have it.[20]

Two months later, Charles Seeger responded to Gold by offering his own review of the same songs in the *Daily Worker*. Under the name Carl Sands in a long article of January 15, 1935, the music professor and head of the Composers Collective conceded certain merits to the Auvilles but generally lamented their formal shortcomings in a tone of condescension, complaining, "For every step forward in the verse, one takes a step backward in the music." After complimenting the lyrics of one song, he cited two others as simply "pretty bad," sniping, "We are already overburdened with stuff of this sort." Pointing out additional "negative values" of the songs, he somewhat pedantically observed that "the musical idiom is not comparable to the idiom of the language," that the melodies "are not, even in this trite idiom, very good," and that "Broadway . . . has turned out better stuff by the mile." Finally Seeger voiced outright disdain. "Correct evaluation of workers' songs . . . is of paramount importance," he declared, adding, "No one but a musician widely trained in the musical fields of our day and thoroughly conversant with the history of music and its relation to general history can realize how low and how uncritical is the present level of American musical taste." One of Seeger's final insults seemed to specifically assail Gold's enthusiasm by issuing a smug warning: "That one is unaware of it makes it all the more dangerous."[21]

Of course this was catnip to Gold, who took his time responding but eventually did so powerfully. On January 2, 1936, he used his editorial influence at the *Daily Worker* to occupy almost half of that day's page 5, inserting alongside his column the full musical score, complete with guitar chords and five verses of lyrics, to the Auvilles' song, "Rugged, Rugged Individualism." The *Change the World* column began, "Music is of great importance to a people's movement. Songs have a positive value that can almost be calculated in watts and volts of mass-energy and mass-morale. Who will say that the song "John Brown's Body," sung by the first northern troops that marched against the slave-owners, had no little part in winning the Civil War?"

After assessing the recent development of workers music and asserting that even amateurs may produce work that is "serious, loving, disciplined," Gold takes on the Workers Music League and the Composers Collective by name, referring to "a review published on this page some months ago" in which "Comrade Sands had some mighty harsh things to say about the songs of Ray and Lida Auville." Withholding nothing, he accused Sands/Seeger of "sectarianism," by which he meant elitist arrogance that created class-like divisions within the revolutionary movement. "Now I happen to have heard Ray and Lida sing before a workers' gathering in Cleveland," he revealed. Then he mocked the condescending vocabulary

Figure 6.1. *Daily Worker*, January 2, 1936. *Source:* ProQuest Historical Newspapers: *Daily Worker.*

Seeger had used by switching to the vernacular: "Ray Auville fiddles; no, he doesn't play the violin, he fiddles, with gusto and native style . . . And his wife, lovely, soft-eyed Lida, she plays the guitar, and they sing together." Though Comrade Sands "bore down on" the Auvilles "with all the thunder of professional aestheticism," Gold pronounced their work "the real thing . . . workers music coming right out of the soil."[22]

"Really Comrade Sands," continued the comparatively uneducated columnist, "I think you have missed the point. It is sectarian and utopian to use Shoenberg and Stravinsky as a yardstick by which to measure working class music." The point was, Mike Gold had compared the Auvilles' songs with the products of the Composers Collective, and found the music of the Auvilles more valuable and progressive: "Not to see what a step forward it is to find two native musicians of the American people turning to revolutionary themes, converting the tradition to working class uses, is to be blind to progress." Lecturing the purists, he issued a challenge:

> Would you judge the workers' correspondence by the standard of James Joyce or Walter Pater? No, a folk art rarely comes from the studios; it makes its own style, and it has its own inner laws of growth. It may shock you, but I think the Composers Collective has something to learn from Ray and Lida Auville. . . . They write catchy tunes that any American worker can sing and like, and the words of their songs make the revolution as intimate and simple as "Old Black Joe." Is this so little?[23]

One month after Gold's review of the Auvilles, the Workers Music League dissolved, to be replaced by the American Music League. The goals of the new organization included "collecting, studying, and popularizing American folk music."[24] In a related development, the former members of the Composers Collective, which was winding down its operations as Gold wrote, would soon take on new roles to become deeply involved in disseminating folk music.[25] As the music historian Lieberman concludes, "Gold's plea for art rooted in the American vernacular and his call for a 'Communist Joe Hill' began to find a response in the mid-1930s."[26] Admittedly, measuring the influence of a collection of *Change the World* columns, coupled with their author's personal charisma, on the development American music cannot be done with precision or exactitude. But the question of just how meaningful that influence was, and how much it helps to understand the origins of the music culture we now inhabit is worth considering. As I have throughout this chapter, I'll rely on music scholars for insights and answers.

Serge Denisoff, a scholar of folklore and American Studies, stated in 1971 that Gold's article on the Auvilles "was a milestone in that it altered the quest for proletarian music" and that as a direct result, "the attempt to create music for the 'masses' by the tenets of European standards began to disintegrate." In a second study he published the same year, Denisoff gave credit to the *Daily Worker* columnist for challenging the Composers Collective, suggesting that "the work of the Auvilles provided the needed guideposts for future proletarian music," which changed in a generic way soon thereafter, for the sole reason that "Gold's position prevailed." Denisoff states also that the Composers Collective "desired working-class music, yet its model was from across the seas" and that "It required the advent of the popular front, voiced by Gold, to alter this consciousness of proletarian art."[27]

Richard A. Reuss, until his death in 1986 probably the most respected, thorough and objective scholar of Leftist music, argued that Gold's championing of the Auville collection "marks the single most identifiable watershed in the American left's acceptance of traditional songs and lyrics composed in the folk idiom." Looking back on a cultural milieu he had witnessed and participated in, Reuss gave due credit also to singer-songwriter Margaret Larkin but stated that "It was left to others, principally Mike Gold, to develop and sustain a belief in the value of indigenous folk music to a point where it profoundly influenced the course of song activity in left-wing circles." It was Reuss's view that twentieth century American folk music bears to a significant degree Mike Gold's philosophical imprint.[28]

In 1989 Robbie Lieberman, whose father Ernie Lieberman knew and performed with Pete Seeger, Paul Robeson, Earl Robinson and other protest music icons, stated that "The movement's transition from an interest in proletarian music to an interest in folk music was anticipated and encouraged by Communist cultural critic Mike Gold."[29]

In 2010 William G. Roy, a sociologist at UCLA whose work concerns intersections between folk music and race, pushed back somewhat on these views, asserting that Gold's rejoinder to Charles Seeger "was not an epiphany, . . . but looking back we can see an important change from a stance of overt elitism in which the party aspired to bring the working class up to its level to a more compromising attitude in which, artistically at least, they would meet the people halfway." Roy concedes that though "few would have predicted" in 1936 that "the people's music would come to be defined as folk music, . . . some of the pieces were beginning to fall into place."[30]

In 2013, the Benjamin Bierman's chapter in the *Routledge History of Social Protest in Popular Music* named Gold as a figure "who publicized and promoted activist artists in a folk music idiom, [and] propelled the movement away from the use of art music and in the direction of the use of folk style material to promote workers' causes."[31] The important thing about the work of all these scholars but especially Reuss and Lieberman, is that they also acknowledge the effects and legacy of this transitional moment on the present day. Lieberman reminds us that, "Springsteen's work," for example, "is not folk music, but it is certainly unthinkable without that influence."[32]

Springsteen acknowledged the "depth of influence" and "inspiration" of both Seeger and Guthrie by recording the 2006 album *We Shall Overcome: The Seeger Sessions*, a rich folk collection of major significance that will certainly endure. The Boss may or may not have been aware that both Seeger and Guthrie probably could not have been as influential without early-career assistance from Mike Gold. Bierman explains that the line of "succession" that began with the Almanac Singers led eventually to a legacy of "music based on social change by Bob Dylan, Phil Ochs, and Joan Baez." We might rightfully acknowledge also that Gold was the primary reason the Composers Collective gave way to that next link, the Almanacs—and that Gold's proletarianism was undeniably the transforming alembic between Professor Seeger and Pete Seeger.

To whatever degree Gold is due credit, he was clearly a factor at a moment when the general course of American music changed, evincing a shift that also had immediate effects on Charles Seeger. After Gold's public challenge, the musicologist reconsidered his views on folk music and its place in the leftist movement. As biographer Ann Pescatello determined, "He began to look again at folk art with new respect." This transformation, Pescatello asserts, "contributed significantly to his reevaluation of American music and his exploration of the social significance of folk arts."[33]

Just as the Composers Collective was disbanding, Charles Seeger accepted a position with the newly created federal Resettlement Administration and moved to Washington. Part of his new job was to alleviate the difficulties of low-income rural communities by providing the musical component of government sponsored programs in the arts. Eventually

Seeger sent more than 300 trained musicians into Resettlement camps to organize music festivals. In a fundamental policy change for him, he instructed his "music workers" to disseminate repertories of folk music rather than classical or popular tunes.

Charles Seeger's "growing awareness of folk and American music would be the focus of his work for almost two decades in Washington." When his operatives were sent to teach in schools, for example, Seeger gave them a specific caution: "Rather than teaching songs they themselves favored and looking down on the music of the local culture, RA workers were to encourage the singing and playing of songs the children already knew and loved."[34] He also directed and supervised "field workers" in the effort to collect and preserve folk music and workers' songs across the United States.

One of his best field workers, Margaret Valiant, kept a diary that was later published in book form as *Journal of a Field Representative* (1937). In a foreword Seeger wrote for the book in late 1936, he outlined the principles around which he organized his Resettlement Administration music program. The ten principles showed that Seeger had "modified his own musical values and recognized the music values of the people whom he was trying to reach."[35] Among them were the following teachings:

- "Music, like any art, is not an end in itself, but is a means for achieving larger ends."

- "Music as a group activity is more important than music as an individual accomplishment."

- "The musical culture of the nation is, then, to be estimated upon the extent of participation of the whole population rather than upon the extent the virtuosity of a fraction of it."

- "The basis for the musical culture is the vernacular of the broad mass of the people—its traditional (often called "folk") idiom; popular music and processional music are elaborate superstructures built upon the common base."

- "The question, then, should be not 'is it good music?' but 'what is music good for?'; and if it bids fair to aid in the welding of the people into more independent, capable and democratic action, it must be approved."[36]

If the above principles attest also to a conception of music's function in society that closely resembles Mike Gold's theories about proletarian art, it is because they'd been developed in large part through Gold's influence. His interactions with Seeger weren't the first time Gold had attacked elitism in favor of art that does cultural work—as opposed to art that was insufficiently engaged with social struggles—but this time his manifesto had not only succeeded; once announced, it had taken hold largely without further debate.

During this period Gold also championed Woody Guthrie, becoming his unofficial promoter and the first interpreter of his cultural message for East Coast liberals. Due to the anti-Communist Dies Committee, which had already famously subpoenaed Federal Theatre Project director Hallie Flanagan, Guthrie was known simply as "Woody" in a series of articles he wrote for the *People's World* and *Daily Worker* upon his arrival in New York in 1940 (fellow Almanac Pete Seeger became "Pete Bowers" for the time being as well). Introducing Guthrie in his column, Gold wrote that "Woody comes right out of the book by John Steinbeck 'The Grapes of Wrath,' . . . Steinbeck's Okie is not only an Okie. He is a symbol of working class America . . . Welcome to the *Daily Worker*, Comrade Woody."[37]

Gold also became a regular at the Almanac Singers' Sunday afternoon fund-raising parties at their Lower Manhattan loft. He often attended these with his six-year-old son Nickie. The best New York folk musicians came to the gatherings to perform for crowds of up to a hundred. For an admission fee of thirty-five cents for nonmusicians, one could hear not only the Almanacs but Aunt Molly Jackson, Leadbelly, Burl Ives and harmonica player Blind Son Terry, who gave Mike a gift harmonica and taught him to play a little during breaks. Nursing a beer, which was ten cents a cup, Gold would sometimes speak at the Sunday concerts, touting Seeger, Guthrie, Hays, Lampell and their folk-artist guests as spiritual inheritors of Walt Whitman who were finally making communism a singing movement. The Almanacs always dressed the part in jeans and work shirts. Gold loved the fact that the increasingly popular group pooled resources to live communally in a rundown loft, and gave up a gig in the Rainbow Room at Rockefeller Center on principle. As Gold explained, "[Woody] was contracted to sing in the Rainbow Room but refused to shed his honest dungarees and broke the contract."[38]

Guthrie's biographer Joe Klein claims that Gold was "hornswoggled" by the Almanacs' posturing as country boys when all of them except for Guthrie were actually of upper middle-class urban backgrounds.[39] In fact

Gold knew all about the singers' backgrounds but had decided much earlier in his career that sincere voluntary poverty—the "courage of proletarian experience"—could redeem a middle-class outlook.

When internal dissent threatened to break up the Almanacs in late 1941, they decided to have a formal meeting at the New Hampshire estate of Pete Hawes, a collaborator and supporting musician, to hash out disagreements and decide the group's future. The various friends they invited to participate of course included Gold, who turned out to play a pivotal role. Hawes had planned a full-blown seminar of sorts and prepared a lengthy mimeographed agenda. To quote Klein on what took place that day, the meeting agenda "was quickly disposed of by Mike Gold, the columnist, who suggested that the future of the Almanacs should be to keep on writing and singing political songs . . . and that was pretty much that."[40]

For the next year or so, Gold kept up his tireless promotion of the Almanacs, eventually focusing on Guthrie as the group's personification and messenger. "Woody . . . has become one of the true voices of American folk song," Gold wrote, "For years he has traveled the roads with his guitar and made up ballads about American life and sung them everywhere. He is a graduate of the Dust Bowl and made a strong series of ballads on that folk migration." Guthrie was living evidence of Earl Browder's maxim that communism was twentieth-century Americanism; it mattered tremendously that he was both a Marxist and a home-grown democratic voice, the embodiment of "Something that started long ago at Valley Forge, and that needs no communist international to tell it to make its songs of pain and protest." Clearly understanding the appeal of "Woody" as a proletarian symbol, Gold imagined a future for him that transcended artistic boundaries: "A people's theatre in America could be built around someone like Woody."[41]

War-related events would eventually halt the run of the Almanacs just as their audience was growing. They had begun the 1940s as committed pacifists, but after the Axis powers invaded the Soviet Union and the Japanese attacked Pearl Harbor in 1941, their pacifist, noninterventionist stance was obsolete. As Guthrie said, there were "no more isolationists" and they quickly went to work converting all their peace songs to a war footing.[42] In the war mobilization period that followed, the Almanacs would disband. The formal separation came when Pete and Woody both accepted military duties, Seeger in the Army and Guthrie in the Merchant Marine. Gold and his family would long maintain personal and public ties with Seeger and Toshie Ohta, who became Seeger's wife in 1943. In the

decades of World War and Cold War that followed, Seeger often spoke of
Gold with admiration, not only in acknowledgment of their well-aligned
political views, but in gratitude for his friend's work to propagate folk music,
helping immeasurably to curate the cultural space for Seeger's long career.

Guthrie, too, realized he owed something to the *Daily Worker* columnist who had ignited his fame and helped him understand the antifascist
purpose his music could serve. Just before he shipped out for wartime
service, Guthrie's autobiographical narrative *Bound for Glory* was published
by E. P. Dutton and reviewed enthusiastically by Gold in the *Daily Worker*.
That Guthrie responded publicly and effusively was in character for him.
But in light of looming changes in the American political climate, it is
interesting that Hoover's FBI, which had already been watching Gold for
more than two decades, noticed the meaningful bond between the two
and memorialized it in their growing surveillance file:

> The "Daily Worker" issue of 8/10/43, contained an article written
> by Woodroe [sic] Wilson Guthrie which concerned the review
> of Guthrie's book, "Bound for Glory," by Mike Gold. In this
> article, Guthrie stated that Gold's review of his book "Bound
> for Glory" had caused him to write the letter. Guthrie further
> stated that he was shipping out in a few days and that he would
> not be afraid of U-boats as long as there was a whole world
> full of people like Gold to keep things going.[43]

Another unifying thread within Gold's agitational activities of the
Depression decade involved his deepening sympathetic identification
with black proletarian culture. Frequent efforts throughout the thirties to
transcend racial barriers suggest that if John Reed was almost constantly
in Gold's thoughts as an activist model, so was John Brown.

In the fall of 1932, Gold had descended into the urban ghetto to
produce dramatic reportage from the frontlines of the class war in a six-
part *Daily Worker* series, *Negro Reds of Chicago*. "This unemployment is
a famine, a Mississippi flood, a major disaster to the human race," began
Gold's reports, "But the Negro and white capitalists of Chicago, like their
fraternity the world over, have been concerned only with preserving
dividends."[44] In tone Gold's articles were palpably within the Chicago
muckraking tradition of Upton Sinclair. They exposed a coalition of white
and black bourgeois slumlords who caged the poor within the borders
of the Black Belt and suffocated them with exorbitant rents. Gold argued

that this corrupt alliance could only be defeated by a similar multi-racial coalition of revolutionary workers.

Considering Gold's abiding interest in peoples' songs and protest ballads, it makes sense that he also wrote significantly about musical elements of black political expression:

> The negroes were once physical slaves to the white man; they were also made into mental slaves. The chains of a slave religion were fastened on their minds. . . . But on the South Side the old slavish spirituals are being re-written by a new race. The deep yearning that once turned to a mythical heaven for freedom now fights for a real and wonderful future on this earth.[45]

The folk music historian Denisoff noted that Gold's music-related work was innovative because it "placed Negro spirituals in the proletarian tradition."[46] It's also interesting that the type of songs Gold located on Chicago's South Side—linking black spirituals to class consciousness—were being brought to attention at a time when Zora Neale Hurston was making her collecting and recording trips through the Deep South and Communist-affiliated Larry Gellert was in the Carolinas and Georgia gathering the material for his 1936 book, *Negro Songs of Protest*.

Gold's special contribution to this cultural work was to document the transformation of spirituals into activist labor songs in support of communism. "They used to sing 'Gimme That Old Time Religion,'" he noticed, "but now they sing 'Gimme that New Communist Spirit.'" The lyrics he transcribed and published read in part, "It's against the labor fakers, And it's good enough for me./It'll free the world of sorrow, And it's good enough for me."[47]

There were "many such new songs and singers," Gold reported. "At mass meetings their religious past becomes transformed into a Communist present. They follow every word of the speaker with real emotion." The Communist journalist noticed also that the performances retained the 'call and response' rituals of religious service: "they encourage [the song leader], as at a prayer meeting, with cries of 'yes, yes, comrade' and often there is an involuntary and heartfelt 'Amen.'"[48]

Gold's Chicago articles were structured in part around a series of brief "Typical Biographies" of black activists including 21-year-old Claude Lightfoot, a charismatic Garveyite speaker and "patriot" who won a large following at a Washington Park forum, then resisted bribes of both

Democratic and Republican candidates who tried to coerce him to turn traitor and campaign for them. "The work of the Unemployment Councils interested Lightfoot," Gold explained, and he used this fact to highlight the opportunities for cross-racial coalition that the Councils offered: "The fact that white workers fought and shed real blood in defence of Negro workers, gave Lightfoot a new vision of the race question."[49]

Looked at as a whole, the *Negro Reds of Chicago* columns are substantial, riveting journalism based on immersion in black lives and struggles at a time of desperation when the sufferings of white Americans were getting most of the attention. The series, an artifact of twentieth century social history, brought a flood of favorable letters from *Daily Worker* readers, which soon led to a contract for the regular column that would become Gold's signature journalistic achievement.

The series also took Gold deep into the cultural conversation about race, thereby lending credibility to a similar-themed essay, "A Word as to Uncle Tom" completed a few months later and published alongside articles by Arna Bontemps, W.E.B. Du Bois, and several selections by Zora Neale Hurston in Nancy Cunard's massive 1934 tome, *Negro: An Anthology*. "A Word as to Uncle Tom" derives directly from the Chicago journalism and is worth treatment here for what it reveals about how Gold saw himself—his role and his identity—in relation to the Depression era racial struggle.

Negro Reds of Chicago had told of a murder plot hatched by Black Belt slumlord Oscar DePriest (with help from real estate sharks and NAACP lawyers) that had killed three black workers at a moment when thousands were participating in antieviction demonstrations on the South Side. Mass resentment at the murders among black residents swept the district and coalesced into an antieviction fight led by the primarily white Unemployment Councils.

Narrating what he'd witnessed in Chicago, Gold discussed the bitterly ironic spectacle of black real estate owners like DePriest, who had achieved middle-class status only to turn against their own race, arguing, "Thus is the class war revealed in a flash of lightning and murder. It cuts across all the race lines. It is more important than the race conflict. It is the CAUSE of the race conflict."[50]

Gold then considered how and why the "Uncle Tom" phenomenon was not wholly confined to black American life but evinced as well in the historical struggles of the Jewish people. The fate of the few artists or businessmen who achieve success and security "is not the fate of a race," he said: "I, as a Jew, know that." Predictable comparisons of black and Jewish persecution follow, prompting a judgment Gold viewed as personally significant: "it is amazing to see how the history of the two races parallels at so many points." The essay's next maneuver is to articulate two of the author's career-determining core beliefs: First, American blacks "can never be free until there is a social revolution." This was "a hard saying," he admitted, "but let us not avoid reality." Second, any revolution cannot be achieved by whites alone: "The Communists are teaching that there cannot be a strong and successful labor movement in America unless the 11,000,000 Negro workers are included."[51]

These tenets might now seem axiomatic and unsophisticated, but they were applied to political realities and historical phenomena throughout Gold's life in profoundly progressive ways. Concerning the Scottsboro case, for example, Gold notes that both black and white reactionaries were indignant "because the Communists first took up the defence of the Scottsboro accused" and "made of it an international issue like the Sacco-Vanzetti case." What the tories and traditionalists wanted in each case was "a polite, well-mannered lynching." Among the truths nonradicals were incapable of acknowledging were the several revealed by Gold through simple rhetorical questions: "Can you have a fair trial of Negroes in Alabama?" and "Can you have a fair trial for Dreyfus or Sacco-Vanzetti without world-wide publicity?"[52]

Gold's history play *Battle Hymn*, produced during the Federal Theatre Project's initial New York season of 1936, blended socialist realism with elements of expressivist theatricality to assert similarities between the radical abolitionist past and a revolutionary 1930s present in which communism was a mainstream ideology. Though the drama was officially co-authored with Michael Blankfort, anyone who has read Gold's 1923 biography of John Brown will recognize that the play's political philosophy came directly from this text. Already an authority on Brown, Gold enlisted Blankfort for help with the scripting challenges of a mass-scale production that featured multiple large groups of actors. As Folsom saw it, Blankfort "picked up and polished" the completed script.[53]

The play's enormous cast of eighty-four named performers represented a plethora of key historical figures—from Jefferson Davis and Chief Justice Taney to Senator Seward and Abraham Lincoln. Several famed abolitionists, including Boston-based William Lloyd Garrison and Gerrit Smith of New York, were joined on stage by the Concord, Massachusetts antislavery faction represented by Franklin Sanborn, Ralph Waldo Emerson, and the transcendentalist whose public support for Brown surpassed all others, Henry David Thoreau.

In a *New York Times* assessment of the play's May 22 premiere, reviewer Lewis Nichols offered vague praise for the "good solid history" and fine acting of the production. Nichols' remarks about the political implications of the drama sought a tone of neutrality but were somewhat misleading, calling Gold's version of the militant abolitionist "A fair portrayal, avoiding alike the Thoreau deification of Brown, and the reverse theory that he was simply insane."[54] More accurately, Gold's John Brown is a complex character, capable of miscalculation and worried about the death of his sons and his grieving wife. But there is never a question about the sanctity of his cause or the violent acts it necessitates, a factor that allows Thoreau's "deification" to outweigh all other judgments.

The *Times* reviewer also drew attention to a moment of scriptural reverie just before Brown committed to the war in Kansas: "Whoso stoppeth his ear at the cry of the poor, he also shall cry." The idea that Brown's actions were driven not solely by abolitionist frenzy but by outrage at all systemic oppression of the poor and downtrodden accords with the view proposed earlier in Gold's *Life of John Brown*. That text's assertion was that the great abolitionist should be understood as "a common man to the end" and thus a hero of the proletariat, a relevant figure in any period of capitalist-imposed economic crisis. The *Times* reviewer could not fail to notice this message but sought personal distance from it: "Before each act is a prologue, with speakers and chorus, and if the audience wishes to conclude that the events of 1936 are not dissimilar from those of 1856, that is their own affair. The authors don't say it in so many words."[55]

A fascinating ensemble scene in *Battle Hymn* occurs at the home of the New York abolitionist Gerrit Smith just before the Harpers Ferry raid. Brown reveals his daring plan to Ralph Waldo Emerson, William Lloyd Garrison, Frank Sanborn, and Henry Thoreau, who ends the discussion by remarking that the militant abolitionist "acts on a higher law than governments" and lives "in a world with God." In Morgan Himelstein's 1963 critical analysis, *Battle Hymn* clearly indicated that the freeing of black slaves by revolutionary violence was a necessary prelude to the emancipation of the white wage slaves of the North. Gold and Blankfort "thus implied that the agitational activity of John Brown was a predecessor of the current work of the Communist Party and that the Civil War was a forerunner of the coming proletarian revolution."[56]

While the sweeping predictions the play made at the height of the Depression went unrealized, Gold's take on Brown was nevertheless prescient. Assessing the antislavery militant as "almost our greatest American" was a decidedly minority view in the twenties and thirties, but it is becoming the consensus. One reason for this political shift was demonstrated by the republication and reissue of Gold's *Life of John Brown* by Roving Eye Press in 1960, a moment in the Civil Rights movement when cross-racial cooperation was becoming an increasingly viable agitational tactic.

The central argument of *Battle Hymn* probably explains why Cold War-era literary critics left it alone. When Richard Tuerk noticed the play in 1985, it was for the purpose of calling into question the drama's implication that Thoreau and to some extent Emerson were proto-Communist thinkers. But Tuerk made the mistake of defining communism solely as an economic theory rather than as a liberation movement. Relying on Cold War clichés, he argued that Thoreau never would have surrendered to the "loss of individuality" intrinsic to communism.[57] What Tuerk seems to have missed is that Gold's special enthusiasm for Thoreau—nearly equal to his love of Whitman—was not based on economics or politics but on humanity, the compassion for the oppressed that Thoreau felt and expressed by means of his fervent support for Brown. In his *Daily Worker* column of June 11, 1946, Gold called Thoreau, not a Communist, but a "philosophic anarchist." He nevertheless argued that Shelley, Victor Hugo, Whitman, and Thoreau "belong in the natural program of Communism because they help to cultivate the best human beings."[58]

Finally it is worth noting that more than a decade after its initial production, J. Edgar Hoover's Cold War-era FBI became retrospectively interested in *Battle Hymn*, assigning an agent to take a close look at the play's copyrighted script, undoubtedly with the intent of using it against Gold and Blankfort when the time was right. After examining the three-act drama, the reporting agent stated laconically the simple conclusion that it was "historical in character" and that its subject matter was "treated in typical left-wing fashion."[59]

While productions of *Battle Hymn* were still running, International Publishers contacted Gold to express a desire to collect and publish a selection of his *Daily Worker* columns in book form. Sixty-six of the best early *Change the World* articles, including a few pieces Gold had done for

other journals, were published in an eponymous volume of 1937. These
wide-ranging pieces, sometimes bizarrely digressive but often moving and
prophetic, have been called "a storehouse of literary riches" by Gold's first
editor and their historical value remains underappreciated.[60]

One 1935 column in particular, "Just like Lindberg's Baby," antici-
pates the present-day *Black Lives Matter* movement, along with current
debates over access to health care. "In Flemington, N. J., Bruno Hauptmann is being tried for the murder of the child of Colonel Lindbergh,"
the column begins. "Justice is being tested, . . . The air is full of righteous
indignation." As the piece continues, Gold expresses deep outrage at how
race-class distinctions dictate the casual, systemic murder of a destitute
African-American child:

> But there is another crime which no newspaper has reported.
> A child was murdered in Jacksonville, Florida, a three-year-old
> child, and no editor has gone running to the copy desk with a
> flaming editorial calling for the death of the murderer. Eddie
> Lewis was killed the morning of December 13, 1934. He was
> three years old. His parents were poor Negro workers of Orange
> Park, Florida. They were unknown people, who had never done
> spectacular deeds, flown oceans or married colonels. All their
> life long they had toiled obscurely for the benefit and comfort
> of others. They rode in Jim Crow cars in Orange Park. They
> had a difficult time meeting the rent each month. They never
> knew when the jobs they had would end. They never knew
> what tomorrow held for them—what hungers, or miseries.[61]

With their three-year-old suffering from appendicitis, the Lewis family
sought emergency care at several hospitals over a two-day period, only to
be turned away: "The mother's pleas meant nothing. St. Luke's Hospital
cures only the whites. They do not take Negroes, not even dying Negro
children." The family eventually reached a "Jim Crow hospital" but it was
too late: "The new diagnosis was not appendicitis—but death. Little Eddie
Lewis never awoke to know that at last he had been permitted to enter
a hospital. He never learned why he died. He was murdered." Finally the
Communist columnist imagines a form of retributive justice:

> On that day, when the murderers, the class which rules
> America, will stand trial, Eddie Lewis will bear the authority

of a judge. . . . He will sit and preside with Sacco and Vanzetti, . . . [and] with the host of others unknown and nameless
who have been murdered by the ruling class. And among their
voices, the voice of Eddie Lewis will not be least.[62]

The cover image of this book is a cropped detail from a striking
group photo inscribed with the words, "Michael Gold Lecture." The photo
was taken on July 16, 1939, at a Jewish summer retreat in the Catskills.
In the original image, Gold is surrounded by perhaps a hundred admirers, young and old. Among the many interesting faces is a woman at left
who cherishes her copy of *Change the World*, the book in which "Just
like Lindbergh's Baby" was republished. The beauty of the image derives
in part from the thought-provoking evidence it offers that brave essays
like the one about Eddie Lewis were central to the appeal of the people's
writer, for a large and loyal, multigenerational audience.

When the International Workers Order, a leftist fraternal organization
dedicated to promoting multicultural knowledge and understanding among
workers, selected Langston Hughes as the first author to be featured in
its series of literary "pamphlets for the people" in 1938, they also selected
Gold to write the text's introduction. The central message of Hughes's *A
New Song*, a collection of sixteen verses that forged links between the
Popular Front's antifascist labor movement and the aspirations of African
Americans, was contained in the title poem, which prompted white and
black workers to rise together to build a workers' world.

The publisher's choice of Gold as the book's spokesperson and
interpreter was logical; he was an effective conduit for such a message,
as suggested by the anecdote with which he began his introduction. In
1925, Gold recalled, bourgeois poet Vachel Lindsay was "touring America
in the cause of poetry," offering readings to women's clubs, universities,
Chambers of Commerce and other middle-class social gatherings. At
one racially segregated recital for an audience of "governmental elite" at
the Wardman Park Hotel in Washington, Lindsay read several poems by
Hughes, a young unknown at the time. While the recital went on in the
posh hotel dining room, "the young poet so distinguished was carrying
off the dirtied glasses and greasy dishes of the guests. The poet was a
busboy in that white man's hotel."

The story, Gold said, "might well symbolize the strange contradictions" in the life of many a black American thinker and dreamer. After
providing the expected praise for Hughes' poetry—"He has expressed the

hopes, the dreams, and the awakening of the Negro people. . . . naturally, like a bird in the woods"—Gold's introduction picked out and reiterated the more important doctrinal take-away: working-class blacks and whites, both enslaved, were "brothers in suffering and struggle."[63]

When Richard Wright's *Native Son* appeared in bookstores in early 1940, Gold acknowledged the novel's great impact and importance in multiple published commentaries. Gold and Wright had met in 1934 at the John Reed Congress in Chicago, where the columnist remembered the Mississippi-born sharecropper's son as a "shy unformed poet." No doubt the younger black writer had through the years read and taken political cues from Gold in his apprenticeship as a Communist-affiliated writer in both Chicago and New York. When Wright became a bestselling novelist and world figure, Gold was awestruck and elated, considering the transformation "one of the literary miracles."[64]

But the biographical relationship between the two men does not end there. *Native Son* addressed issues that touched Gold deeply, related as they were to his own obvious desire as a white proletarian and Communist activist to know and share the experience of black Americans. It's likely that the psychologically realistic treatment of this dynamic in *Native Son* nudged Gold toward greater self-awareness. Wright's plot, for example, looked microscopically at liberalism and communism through the lens of actual life in the Black Belt, the same topics Gold had explored for the *Daily Worker* in his *Negro Reds of Chicago* series, with some key differences.

"It is a rare and special thing that Wright has done, as no American writer before him," Gold declared in the *Sunday Worker* of March 31, 1940. In the first of four columns he wrote about Wright's blockbuster novel, he predicted that "the story of *Native Son* is one that will burn itself on the imagination of this country, I believe, as no other novel about Negroes since *Uncle Tom's Cabin*."[65]

One of the reasons Gold's congratulatory review wasn't his final word on the novel had to do with gradually growing ambivalence among critics about the brutal acts of protagonist Bigger Thomas. The shift was especially pronounced among a group of leftist blacks that included both Hughes and Gold's close friend Shirley Graham. Hughes, who conceded that *Native Son* was "a tremendous performance . . . a really great book," nevertheless asked pointedly, "Suppose *Native Son's* Bigger Thomas (excellently drawn as he is) was the sole survivor on the bookshelves of tomorrow?"[66]

Responding to similar thoughts in letters from his readers and from Harlem councilmen and *Daily Worker* contributor Ben Davis, Gold reflected on his "recent leap over the deep-end in praise of Richard Wright's great novel." What is interesting is that Davis and Gold were actually discussing different subjects. Davis had questioned Wright's portrayal of Bigger Thomas and noted a danger that the "bourbon enemies" of black America would "seize upon" Bigger's violent character in order to "further their slanders against the whole negro people." Gold acknowledged this concern but went in a different direction by examining the book's portrayal of Party-affiliated Communists and arguing that "self-criticism" was necessary: "Shall we indulge in wishful thinking, or shall we grapple with the more painful truth?" He concluded that proletarian fiction was now "mature" and that Wright's novel exemplified this maturity "because it does not shirk the enormous difficulties presented by the human material." To the extent that Wright produced a "study in psychology" worthy of Dostoyevsky, it seemed "wrong . . . to suggest to the author of such a book that he should have written a simpler agitational novel instead."[67]

Gold was clearly thinking of matters that went beyond Bigger's violent response to the forces of racism in his environment; in wanting to discuss how other "negative aspects" of the book were "offset" by the "heroic character of the Communist lawyer in Wright's book," he hinted at an area of inquiry that led inevitably to himself. For if Bigger's lawyer Boris Max "offsets" anything, it is the extremely negative portrayal of white radicals Jan Erlone and Mary Dalton, a Communist Party member and a fellow traveling daughter of a millionaire capitalist. These two characters unwittingly contribute to Bigger's anger and alienation through naive and condescending violation of his personal dignity.

The novel's opening book describes the attempts of Erlone and Dalton to associate on "equal" terms with the working-class black chauffeur Bigger. Mary not only approaches Bigger closely and speaks to him directly, but asks—in front of her father, Bigger's potential employer—if Bigger belongs to a union. These interactions produce both shame and fear for Bigger, who "knew nothing about unions, except that they were considered bad." Considering the recklessness of her conduct, Bigger's initial reaction to Mary seems justified: "He hated the girl then."[68]

Like Mary, Communist boyfriend Jan immediately assumes a familiar and superficially "equal" relation to Bigger, forcing him to shake his hand and asking Bigger not to call him "sir." Mary's laughing insistence that such gestures of class solidarity are "all right" because "Jan *means* it" (Wright's emphasis) only increases Bigger's anger. He feels "a dumb, cold inarticulate hate" toward Jan and Mary, a reaction that is the direct result of the deluded assumption that for them no class or race barriers exist—they have willed them away in an act of radical defiance.[69]

That evening, Mary says she wants to have dinner in the Black Belt, "to go to a *real* place, one of those places where colored people eat" (Wright's italics). Then, sitting next to Bigger in the front seat on the drive to the restaurant, she touches his arm, points to the slums, and confides, "I've long wanted to go into those houses, . . . and just *see* how you people live . . . I want to *know* those people" (Wright's italics). The impracticable nature of Jan and Mary's request that Bigger treat them as equals, along with the impossibility of their ever actually doing so toward Bigger, is emphasized in a series of dialogues: Mary says she wants to be "friends" with Bigger and then immediately instructs him to take her trunk to the train station; Bigger reveals that his father was lynched, then Jan pryingly asks how he "feels" about it; Mary indicates that she wants to join the ostensibly color-blind Communist Party but observes prejudicially that she'll have be "careful" working among blacks; both Jan and Mary claim an implicit understanding of black culture but admit that they "don't know any [blacks] very well"; Jan and Mary's assertions that blacks "have so much emotion" and "spirit" betray a transparently racial outlook—as do their ridiculous attempts to sing Negro spirituals with Bigger.[70]

Bigger's refusal to sing "Swing Low, Sweet Chariot" with Jan and Mary does more than simply indicate Bigger's nonparticipation in their cross-racial, cross-class joyride; it bespeaks the white characters' complete ignorance of the fact that such cultural material is not theirs for the taking. To the extent that their race- and class-barrier transgressing efforts are both painfully naive and fraught with ulterior motives, Bigger "did not understand them; he distrusted them, really hated them."[71]

Richard Wright's clear intent in *Native Son*—to realistically address the relationship between communism and African Americans—was a task that almost required him to touch concurrently on certain aspects of Mike Gold's life. We've discussed Gold's interest in black spirituals and labor songs. As the spokesperson and driving force of a movement that sought to use and popularize this material, Gold participated in black culture in ways that are indistinguishable from some actions of Wright's white leftists. On at least one occasion, the evening in Paris documented by Christina Stead, Gold sang spirituals—"the songs of the negroes converted to Lenin"[72]—as a representative of black culture for a non-American audience.

Within the actions of CP member Jan Erlone toward Mary and Bigger, Gold would certainly have recognized potent implied criticisms of the Party for which he filled roles of both poet and public spokesman. He also noticed, as stated above, that the rhetoric of Communist lawyer Boris Max redeemed the novel by offsetting the "self-criticism" Wright offered. Gold's identification of Max as a figure of great consequence in the novel was especially fitting. The troubling question Max poses at a coroner's inquest—"Mr. Dalton, do you think that the terrible conditions under which the Thomas family lived in one of your houses may in some way be related to the death of your daughter?"—could have been seamlessly inserted into a great many of Gold's *Change the World* columns, which regularly addressed similar questions. The single interpretation of Bigger's life that is endorsed by Wright is undeniably the one offered by Max, who sounds like Mike Gold when he declares that American capitalist culture is ultimately responsible for the deaths of Mary Dalton and Bessie, along with the legal lynching of Bigger Thomas.

Whether or not Wright had Mike Gold in mind in any specific way when composing *Native Son*, it seems clear from Gold's columns about the novel that he internalized Wright's direct criticism and was grateful for it. Gold is thinking not about Bigger Thomas but about the Party when he observes in one article about *Native Son*, "In Communist politics the workers have always had the habit of self-criticism . . . They know that there is more danger in fooling yourself than in worrying as to what the enemy will say."[73]

One of the reasons Gold loved Wright's book, it seems, was for what it taught him about himself. As the acknowledged literary gatekeeper for the Communist Party, he certainly didn't ignore or obfuscate, as many readers still do, the full weight and import of Wright's message to American society, or his equally direct criticisms of Leftist outreach to blacks. Rather, Gold enlarged upon all of these issues. In his third published reflection on *Native Son*, Gold wrote that in the North, Wright's protagonist is "locked up in segregated ghettos" and in the South, "his life is considered less sacred than a pet dog's." Noting that the U.S. Congress of 1940 had still refused to pass an antilynching law, the columnist offered a truly cosmopolitan interpretation of the meaning of Bigger's life, jarring not only to domestic believers in American exceptionalism but to an international audience perhaps less aware of the country's failed promises:

Fifteen million Americans, born here under a constitution that makes every "native son" a full partner in the democracy are daily robbed, beaten, flouted, cheated, slandered, murdered

and generally treated with the same sort of horrible race-hate
that Hitler and all his Storm Troopers must yet pay for on the
revolutionary guillotine of the German folk. It was Birmingham
that taught Berlin.[74]

It was Birmingham that taught Berlin. And when the play version
of *Native Son* was threatened with cancellation for alleged obscenity in
1942, Gold defended the production with a *Change the World* column in
which he stated that he had both seen the play and "read and carefully
reviewed" the famous novel. "The play is full of the evil and horror of
the American lynching tree and the smell of burning human flesh," he
conceded, but it was not obscene. "Think of Frederick Douglass and
Abraham Lincoln. Were they obscene?"

Additional echoes of shared biographical material and mutual influence between Mike Gold and Richard Wright are available in Wright's
1945 novelistic autobiography, *Black Boy*, a book that bears a great many
resemblances to *Jews without Money*. In fact the two works seem almost
mirror images of each other. Gold's childhood in the Jewish slums served
as a training ground for antiblack prejudice, as illustrated in the character
"Nigger," a Jew so angry and oppressed that he is labeled with the black
epithet, while Wright's childhood teaches him to hate "Christ killers" and
harass the Jewish storekeeper with racial chants. Both works are left-oriented
proletarian autobiographies narrated from a masculine perspective, trac-
ing a path from early poverty toward salvational self-identification with
communism. Certain incidents in *Black Boy*—Wright's discovery of pros-
titution, his youthful forays into Jew-baiting, and the overall structuring
of Wright's book as a mix of memoir with clearly novelistic elements told
from the perspective of an eponymous juvenile central character—recast
famous elements of *Jews without Money*. Gold writes about Jewish life but
uses black experience as a touchstone and reference point for understanding rudimentary elements of a developing critical theory of race under
capitalism; Wright's book on black poverty incorporates Jewish American
social history for the same purpose.

In the winter of 1940 Gold was suddenly hospitalized for more
than a month with severe complications from diabetes, a flare-up that
that was probably related to the multiple stresses of the moment. Elizabeth was in the final weeks of her second pregnancy and Gold had been
fighting a nerve-wracking public battle to justify the Hitler-Stalin Pact.
Initially stunned by news of the pact, he'd stopped writing his column

for a month, then mounted a busy writing and speaking campaign that carried substantial spiritual and physical demands. Giving talks in the evenings meant subway rides and walks home on successive late nights. His bellicose *Daily Worker* columns at this time, brimming with anger at the turncoats and "renegades" who had left the Communist-led cultural movement in the wake of the pact, called up unhealthy emotions, adding to the career-related costs of the essays later collected as *The Hollow Men*. These were among the burdens of the role he'd chosen for himself as the nation's foremost "committed" writer, burdens that apparently wore on him in personal and private ways. On the January 1940 night when Gold's son Carl was born, both he and Elizabeth were hospitalized, and four-year-old son Nick was left alone in their apartment.[75]

While Gold was incapacitated, his old friend Art Shields stepped in and took over his column at the *Daily Worker*. After a February 13 hospital visit, Shields announced to readers that "Mike" had had a "tough fight" with the disease but was "picking up strength" and would be coming back soon "to help in the fight to keep America out of Chamberlain's war."

As Shields noticed, the period of recuperation was also one of contemplation, and news of the ongoing European conflict weighed heavily. Often Gold would turn the conversation to the last "War for Democracy" and its lessons for the current peace struggle. He told his friend about a day in 1917 when he was editing copy for the New York *Call* and saw President Wilson's pro-war slogans coming over the wires. He thought about how the patriotic nonsense from the White House contrasted with the home-front stories in the *Call*: a thousand miners from Bisbee Arizona rounded up and kicked into the desert for being good union men. The lynching of Wobbly leader Frank Little in Butte, Montana, by hired thugs of the Anaconda Mining Company. Police beatings of peaceful socialist demonstrators in New York. All while the country fell into step to the tune of "War for Democracy."

On one hospital visit, Shields noticed that his friend knew all the patients in the crowded ward and had talked with them about their fears. They liked Gold because they were workers and small businessmen, heads of families who also couldn't afford private rooms. Gesturing to the rows of beds, Gold told Shields that "the people" hated war now even more than in 1917. They felt the drift toward the European conflict as a real danger to them and their children.

The two reminisced also about the day they'd first met, on a fact-finding tour of the coke fields south of Pittsburgh in 1922. Shields had

watched Gold make fast-friends with the aged, peg-legged miner who was
maimed in the battle against the gun thugs of industrialist Henry Frick.
What Gold enjoyed most that day, Shields recalled, was the surging vitality
of the old miner as he crouched in re-enactment of the posture he'd taken
in the battle with the strikebreakers. Shields joked that he had almost
missed his deadline because he couldn't pull Gold away from his new pal.

Amused by the evident camaraderie between Gold and his fellow
patients and the ward nurses on the day before his discharge, Shields drew
a parallel: "The author of *Jews without Money*—one of the great books in
American literature—is like Walt Whitman, the old Civil War nurse, in
more ways than one. They are his people, and his column in the *Daily
Worker* is the kind of column they like."[76]

After that hospital stay, Gold was ordered to carefully monitor his
hours of work and sleep, though this proved difficult with deadlines to
meet. For the rest of his life, Gold would have to take sixty units of insu-
lin a day while adhering to dietary limitations including a strict directive
to be careful about drinking, which for Gold meant beer or wine only
in moderation. From this time on he carried in his wallet a "Diabetic
Information" card with his home address and phone number under the
name "Michael Granich." The card read, "I Have Not Been Drinking.
Immediately call a PHYSICIAN or send me to a HOSPITAL."

By the end of the thirties, Gold's theories about art, politics and the
class-race alliances necessary to liberate humanity had not abated but, if
anything, hardened into manifestos. As he was working on *The Hollow Men*
for publication in early 1941, he paid tribute to the memory of John Reed
on the 20-year anniversary of his death. The *New Masses* article, "John
Reed: He Loved the People," showed how Gold's priorities were shifting
in response to a new decade, a context that bore little resemblance to the
years just after the stock market crash. Reed's greatness now had much
to do with his loyalty to the revolutionary cause. Gold wrote the article
to reaffirm Reed's heroic memory against the long-circulating rumor that
before his death, Reed had regretted his path, become disillusioned with
the Soviet Union and lost trust in the revolution.

The evidence that Reed had not been a renegade but kept his faith
is precisely intertwined with the evidence Gold offered in criticism of
the real renegades, the "host of liberals, progressives . . . art for art's
sakers . . . and hyper-aesthetic lilies" who had begun stepping out of the
ranks of the leftist Popular Front by 1940. If emphasizing loyalty was a
solid overall strategy, it was linked also to a new proof of Reed's heroism,

one that reflected the personal priorities Gold had been developing since the beginning of his career, but with special urgency in the thirties. To communicate these priorities, there was one little-known Reed artifact Gold wanted entered into the historical record.

In the midst of the second congress of the Communist International in 1918, Reed hastily scribbled off a brief note to Lenin. The note read, "Comrade Lenin: Do you want me to say something about the American Negroes? I am also on the Trade Union Commission, and so was late. Reed." At the bottom of the note, Lenin scrawled an answer: "*Yes* absolutely I do inscript you into the list of speakers, Lenin." Gold's 1940 article included a large illustration of the handwritten note—a copy of the "rare document" proving that Lenin thought it "absolutely necessary" for Reed to "speak on the American negro."[77]

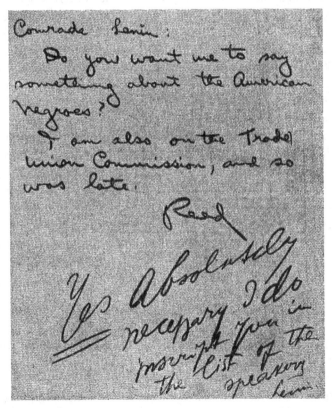

Figure 6.2. *New Masses*, October 22, 1940. *Source:* ProQuest Historical Newspapers: *New Masses*.

At the end of the Depression decade, while he was plugging Hughes and Wright, Woody Guthrie, Pete Seeger and the Almanacs and attacking Roosevelt for leading the nation toward war, Gold was also writing columns that attacked the literary "Hollow Men"—deserters, renegades, intellectuals and bourgeois "apostates, opportunists and lackeys"—in other words, liberals who denounced Stalin and abandoned the Left. The defections had begun in large part as a response to news about the Moscow Trials or Great Purge of 1936–1938, and the Nazi-Soviet Nonaggression Pact of August 1939. In the eyes of many, the Moscow show trials, Stalin's pretext for executing or imprisoning nearly all of his potential political opponents including most of the original actors in Bolshevik Revolution, carried clear evidence of the Soviet leader's brutality, autocratic impulses and willingness to falsify history. Others, including Gold initially, saw the sketchy news about the trials as a possible western-led conspiracy to destroy the Soviet Union, a view that was not incredible at the time.

Obviously, the Hitler-Stalin Pact shocked American liberals and confused Communists, including Gold. Eventually he explained the pact as a justified Soviet self-defense measure, necessitated in part by a clear tendency in the West to view communism as a greater evil than fascism. Stalin saw the danger that Great Britain and the United States, which had stood by while the Spanish Republic fell to fascism, might accommodate Nazi Germany diplomatically while encouraging Hitler to expend his military might against the Soviet Union. For Gold, this view was personified and made viable for Americans in radio priest Charles Coughlin and his Christian Fronters, but also in the figure of Charles Lindbergh, a proto-fascist and anti-Semite with a considerable political following. In essence, if the West wanted to sic Hitler on Stalin, the Soviets would turn the tables and sic Hitler on the West. And as Roosevelt offered American support for Churchill's war effort, U.S. Communists, who heard the anti-Soviet declarations Churchill was making at this time, saw no good options in the coming war. Rejecting both fascism and an alliance of capitalist powers against Sovietism, they took a firm stance of pacifist nonintervention.

For the Left, the moment was thus politically complicated, and it posed special challenges for Mike Gold personally. Mixed in with the geopolitical détente were the notions of proletarian art and culture he had championed since 1921. In separate essays and declarations of 1940–41 the Communist columnist, to whom remaining leftists still looked for guidance, staked out strong opinions from a precarious platform.

As major liberal writers one by one sundered ties with communism circa 1940, they also began a process of denigrating the aesthetic priorities and cultural modus operandi of the very decade that had made Mike Gold's voice significant. He saw what was happening to his legacy and spoke about it in an address to the Fourth Congress of American Writers in 1941. "It isn't sporting to slug a corpse, and I am not going to reassault Mr. Wilder at this time," Gold slyly claimed, both denying and accomplishing the renewed attack, "But ten years after Thornton Wilder occupied our literary sky, a different sort of star appeared there. The success of John Steinbeck's *Grapes of Wrath* is a sensation too recent to need much description."[78] Everyone listening likely knew Gold would also mention Richard Wright, whose *Native Son*, in the speaker's estimation, "made a success as phenomenal" less than a year after Steinbeck. "It is not conceivable," he declared, "that two such novels, based on such proletarian themes . . . could have won the same amazing success ten years earlier."

In the 1930s American literature set forth on "a second discovery of America," Gold said, a period when "the inverted, book-proud intellectuals 'went to the people.'" The result was that new regions and new subjects were opened up: "the Deep South, the daily life in factories, mills, mines, the struggle of the farmer, the souls of black folk, the problems of the recent immigrant and his children."[79] Looking on as collectivism was being written out of U.S. history, Gold resisted the process by declaring that

> The proletarian decade was no misunderstanding or accident, no foreign plot, no feeble aesthetic cult that a few critics had artificially created and now can easily destroy. It was a great movement out of the heart of the American people . . . The present war interrupts the democratic renaissance of the Thirties. But that renaissance and its literature will in turn end the system of war and profit. Let us persist.[80]

Gold already knew that "persisting" no longer meant setting forth, but a static digging in to defend his aesthetics in a changed world. In his personal case, persist also meant becoming by default an unofficial arbiter of the American Communist Party's inflexible artistic standards. This role forced him not only to repeat assaults on artists like Thornton Wilder but to denounce all but a narrow range of modernist literary

works, thereby putting him at odds with scores of writers who had once
been his allies.

In the case of the Gold-Hemingway professional friendship, for
example, an attack on *For Whom the Bell Tolls* crossed a line and proved
destructive. In *The Hollow Men*, Gold used the 1940 novel of the Spanish
Civil War to illustrate a process of "vile and enormous treason" at the
core of the great novelist's "petty-bourgeois renegadism." There was, Gold
acknowledged, "no better story teller in America" than Hemingway, but
because he was "mutilated by his class egotism, the very brilliance of [his]
talents only served to illuminate the poverty of his mind." His characters,
like their creator, too often expressed the attitude of a "spectator without
responsibilities, who holds a box seat the crucifixion of humanity, and is
a connoisseur of the agony and sweat of others." In all of Hemingway's
writing there was nowhere a portrait of a laborer, Gold said, because "he
knows nothing about the factories and fields where men must work and
where the sources of his income arise."[81]

Robert Jordan, a volunteer in the International Brigade who represents Hemingway's own inner life, "cannot work up any real hate of the
fascists." The war to him is "exciting, terrible, dangerous: really a bullfight
on a vast scale." Jordan is blind to the "enormous central fact" of class
conflict and hunger in Spain. The novel, "despite its narrative genius, is
a false picture of the war" and therefore "a minor story." That *For Whom
the Bell Tolls* is "so painfully fair to fascists" but slanders the Republican
heroes profoundly enraged Gold.

Another element of the novel derisively noticed in *The Hollow Men*
turned out to be prophetic in light of personal hardships that awaited Mike
Gold later in the century. Hemingway's text implies that after the war,
Robert Jordan will effortlessly return to his old job of teaching Spanish
at an American university. For the Communist writer, this constituted "a
sign of how ignorant of social reality Hemingway is." A full decade before
McCarthyism, Gold explained that "There were actually a number of university teachers in the Brigade, but when they came home, . . . they found
boycott, persecution, and blacklist." From Gold's perspective, Hemingway
is either unaware or uninterested in the fact that the operations of the
International Brigade overlapped with those of the Dies Committee and
HUAC. In *For Whom the Bell Tolls*, "it is the story of democracy itself
that Hemingway has missed."[82]

While this treatment of the saga of Robert Jordan is a good sample
of the ethos, pathos and logos of *The Hollow Men*, the effect it had on

Gold's relationship with Hemingway was just as representative, causing an alienation that was dramatically enacted and long lasting. On Hemingway's next visit to New York, he remembered that he wanted to see Mike Gold and ordered a downtown taxi to the *Daily Worker* offices on West Twelfth Street. Having once written a glowing recommendation of Gold for a Guggenheim grant, he had now seen *The Hollow Men* and a later *Change the World* column that had repeated the author's harsh criticisms of *For Whom the Bell Tolls* while also attacking Ernest's arrogant posturing as a war hero during the D-Day landing. Biographer Carlos Baker gave an account of the "fiasco" that ensued: "Ernest took the elevator to the eighth floor and told the girl receptionist he wished to see Gold. She answered that he was out and offered to take a message. 'Ok,' said the hulking visitor, 'tell Mike Gold that Ernest Hemingway says he should go fuck himself.'"[83]

Chapter Seven

War and Family Matters

(1941–1950)

Hemingway's reaction to *The Hollow Men* may have been representative but it wasn't universal. Its antithesis came in the *Daily Worker*, which did not always give Gold a free pass in reviewing his books but could have been expected to praise this one. Millen Brand's review, entitled "Mike Gold's Scathing Expose of the Literary Renegades Shows His Love of the People," appeared in May 1941, two months after Gold's big Twenty-Fifth Anniversary Meeting at Manhattan Center. Like the speakers at the meeting and Gold's book itself, Brand linked *The Hollow Men* to the Gold-Wilder controversy, citing the 1930 attack on *The Bridge of San Luis Rey* as "a very important milestone in American criticism" and implying that writers on the Left should "get it out and read it once in a while."[1]

Millen's précis dispensed with objective critical norms in favor of intuitive, spiritual criteria. Of Gold's book he stated, "Others have made broader critical surveys, some have cut with a subtler knife, but Mike we feel resting on the emotion of the people and we trust him. . . . Always the criterion that satisfies in the heart is the judgment that comes out of the love of the people, and Mike has it."[2]

Artists either love the people genuinely or they don't, Millen contended. *The Hollow Men* showed that Hemingway, Dos Passos, Sherwood Anderson, Waldo Frank, Lewis Mumford, Granville Hicks—the renegades whom Gold "pick[ed] off one by one"—claimed such love but had now revealed themselves, becoming what Dostoevsky described as "bourgeois lackeys . . . with a liberal and benevolent exterior." In an interesting passage, the reviewer hypothesized the thought processes of the renegade writers as they coldly embarked on what were essentially slumming adventures. Seeking contact with workers' lives in order to study proletarian pain, bourgeois artists in essence say, "I know how to use this. I'll show how much I love this person so I can lie better about what he's after, so I can say, unions are no good really, war is fine, the Spanish Republicans were a bunch of dumbbells misled by the Communists really—you better believe me because you can see I love humanity."[3] Recent research on the topic of slumming adventures (or "vital contact" with the working classes) shows that a version of this conscious or unconscious thought process manifested in a large number of literary texts in the late-nineteenth and early twentieth centuries.[4]

The purpose of *The Hollow Men* is to expose the duplicity of effete bourgeois intellectuals, "fashioned in the womb of the middle class," who had attempted to impersonate or inhabit the lives of workers, only to misrepresent them in their art because they lacked the compulsory loyalty to the class they were impersonating and representing. As Brand determines, "No evidence of corruption or confusion, no defeats and no wounds in the long battle of the people ever destroy the belief in the people of the honest writer. He isn't 'for the people in his own way.' He is for the people in their way."[5]

Whatever one's opinion of the reviewer's approach, Brand was certainly not the first or last cultural observer to point out the negative effects of slumming adventures or bemoan the rarity of genuine cross-class empathy in bourgeois-dominated society and art.[6] Bringing to bear the shibboleth of "love for the people" as a literary-critical standard was also not new. But Brand's claims and strategy do indicate much about the honored position Gold achieved and retained in the proletarian pantheon. *The Hollow Men* was "crucial to the moment," Brand argued, because its author was a "real and constant" friend of humanity, among the few "who accept the people honestly and not demagogically."[7] Though frustratingly vague and philosophical, Brand's review was an early indication that the leftist literary battles Gold had fought with some success in the 1920s and 1930s would be contested anew in the 1940s, often at a more sophisticated level of debate.

The war years required Communists to adapt rapidly to shifts in the national consensus. The far Left was staunchly antiwar until the major events of 1941 (Hitler's invasion of the USSR, and the attack on Pearl Harbor, and US alliance with the Soviet Union) drove immediate changes in its position and rhetoric. Overnight, militant isolationist radicalism became militant internationalist antifascism, and communism gained some temporary protection from persecution by virtue of the need for wartime unity against the common fascist enemy. For their part, Party leaders recognized common cause with national war goals and largely sublimated their revolutionary agenda for the duration. These political fluctuations—related to and concurrent with the world war in Europe and the Pacific—softened Gold's message in his *Change the World* work at a time when his family life, including his commitments as a father, demanded increasing time and attention.

ᴄᴡ

Gold's initial response to the December 7, 1941, attack on Pearl Harbor appeared in a *Change the World* column of December 9, with a prefatory note explaining that the piece had been written one day before the attacks but that it was "just as timely" now that the country was at war. "The fascists think they can conquer us. Our Lindberghs and Wheelers led them to believe that we were weak and divided. But the bombs that fell on Pearl Harbor were a signal for the mighty mobilization of America. Fascism, whether it be Japanese, German, Italian, Finnish or American, is doomed."

It is interesting that the column as written before the Japanese attack was a diatribe against the Dies Committee, which observers on the Left said was using anti-Semitism and anticommunism to divide and weaken the country at a moment when the "mortal danger" of fascism was apparent and Americans must choose between "national unity or Hitler slavery." In Gold's view, anti-Semitism constituted "not just an attack on American Jews. It [was] a flank attack by fascists on Democracy." Likewise, he urged recognition that red-baiting was "far from what it professes to be," that it functioned as "an attempt to weaken trade unions and schools and destroy unity against Hitler." Gold explained how the coming war would expose such tactics but doubted that the far Right, as symbolized by Lindbergh and "America-first Coughlinites," would join wholeheartedly in American defense.[8]

Five days later, in a column subtitled, "They Hate the Soviets More Than They Love America," Gold elaborated on this warning. "However much the rest of the nation may concentrate on the tragic task of . . . conquering the threat of Hitlerism, these people will spend their energies in war against . . . America's indispensable ally, the Soviet Union." Gold predicted that reactionary forces would soon concentrate on poisoning

U.S.-Soviet relations in hopes of splitting the fighting alliance. Already the red-baiters were parroting the Dies Committee and calling for the suppression of Gold's column: "You would never know from their speeches that we were under attack from Hitler and Japan, and it wasn't the *Daily Worker* that had bombed Pearl Harbor."[9]

Several of Gold's post–Pearl Harbor columns weighed the possibility of Japanese or German air attacks on New York and other East Coast cities, which he saw as likely, though the Coughlinites and Bundists sneered at the probability. "Even if there should be no Nazi bombings, it would be a criminal gamble . . . not to prepare fully for them," he advised. "For more than ten years Communists have been trying to prepare America for this moment. We were called warmongers, loyalists to the USSR and not America. We were persecuted for talking collective security and a united front with Spain and China. I, as one who has written several million words of warning against fascism, should certainly be well-prepared for this moment."[10]

Though not all of Gold's assessments and predictions at the start of the war were accurate, in the case of Charles Lindbergh he offered an immediate, spot-on appraisal. Lindbergh had not only been a spokesman for the America First Committee that advocated neutrality toward Hitler, he had visited fascist Germany and made anti-Semitic statements that echoed Nazi demagoguery. In response to public criticism from Roosevelt, the hero of American aviation had resigned from his post as colonel in the US Army Air Corps. After Pearl Harbor, he offered to reactivate his colonel's commission. Gold, wary of the famous pilot's fascist sympathies, spoke out and issued a strong caution: "Lindbergh has just applied for re-instatement in the army," he wrote in January of 1942. "This notorious Quisling, this frank friend of Axis victory, this anti-Semite and neurotic hater of the common American man, has not even returned the medals given him by Hitler for his treasons to democracy. But they are being very sweet and amiable in Washington about Lindbergh's 'boyish' mistakes. There is an atmosphere of forgiveness."[11] Ultimately Lindbergh was rebuffed by a Roosevelt administration that decided, as Gold and a great many American Jews had, that his duplicitous words and actions carried consequences.

Over the next several years, the gravitas of Gold's wartime columns was occasionally relieved by entertaining detours into personal or domestic matters, most often those involving the raising of his two boys, Nicky and Carl. In a 1941 column that began with a reminder that millions might die before the Nazi beast was exterminated, Gold used his domestic tribulations to lighten the mood: "I cannot always keep my mind on the war because Nicky's mind is on Christmas, and if you have a kid of your own you will know that his mind always wins," he casually opined.[12]

One of the earliest Nicky-Carl columns focused on the piercing cries of three-month-old Carl as Gold typed away at his desk in April 1940. In "Baby's Cries Set Mike Thinking about the World's Problems," the columnist likened his infant son's howling for comfort and food to the cries of Admiral Harold Stark for a budget sufficient to build the world's largest navy, for which five billion dollars would have to be "snatched from the grocery baskets" of the unemployed, with the result that "a lot of unpatriotic babies will keep crying for food." Composing thoughts on national affairs with baby Carl crying in his nearby crib, Gold decided, "It is something indeed to howl over, this capitalist mess of war and hypocrisy."[13]

Later Gold wrote about four-year-old Nicky's fascination with railroad engines and toy trains, saying he was proud to inform his son that he'd spent a summer of his youth on a Pennsylvania section gang with friend Maurice Becker in 1921 or 1922. "It wasn't done for glory, experience or sociology, but for cash . . . we needed to eat," Gold explained to readers. "It was back-breaking and monotonous labor," but it was now "paying dividends as material for some railroad yarns for Nicky."[14]

Figure 7.1. Nicky and Carl, early 1940s. *Source:* Granich family.

In these pieces the columnist almost always succeeded in drawing a quaint moral or insight in keeping with his social convictions. When Nicky became interested in the heroic boys who carried pails of water to thirsty rail workers, Gold, not one to miss such an opportunity, sang for his son a verse from the labor song, "Water Boy," made famous in the 1930s by Paul Robeson. Nicky joked that baby brother Carl was a water boy because his diapers were always wet, then laughed at his own cleverness. "Better than the joke," the father wrote,

> was to know that Nicky contains a sense of humor. . . . He is growing up into a tough world. He will need every laugh he can find in it. May he learn to laugh at all the tyrants, the customs, the exploiters and the stupidities that now rule the earth. . . . Laughter drives out fear, and one great universal blast of laughter by the people at their 'betters' would end the whole sorry show.[15]

Another column revealed that Nicky had commenced talking rather late, at age three, and that "among the first words he learned was the terrible one, Bomb." This detail became the premise for a set of opinions about how progressive-minded parents might talk with their children about war: "There is little a parent can do these days to keep the consciousness of war out of the minds of his children. All one can do is try to explain war as truthfully as possible. . . . You would have to remove your child to a desert island in order to spare him. . . . I just can't afford a desert island for Nicky, so he will have to grow up like the majority of kids and be frightened by war."[16]

A follow-up column counseled, "I do not believe it wise to stuff doctrines into a child. Wait until he asks you a question. Then answer it briefly and truthfully." The illustration of this moral derived from Nicky's habit of asking who made the sky and who made the wind. His father's catchall answer had always been "Nature," but when an older playmate told the boy that "God made everything" and that bad children were burned in God's big fire, the father gently pressed back, asking how the boy's friend knew this kind of God really existed. "She saw him. . . . on a big picture in her church," Nicky answered. Gold was momentarily stumped but responded, "By the way, Grasshopper, who made that picture?" When the child promptly answered, "The workers," the father concluded: "Let's leave it at that for a while."[17]

Eventually the articles dealt with parenting issues in the development of both Granich boys, though it did not take long for the Nicky-focused pieces to become quite popular. Two separately published letters to the *Daily Worker* editors in early 1942 suggest the reasons for their appeal. "Mike Gold's columns on Nick are truly wonderful and I really don't know who should be grateful to whom: Nicky to Mike for his father's great and warm heart, or Mike to Nicky for the son's loyalty and love"[18] A few days later another letter, published under the heading, "Newlyweds Send Request to Mike Gold," came from three young couples "and a host of others" who were regular readers. It stated, "Nicky intrigues us no end— we follow his antics eagerly." As Communists and newlyweds who were soon to be parents, the letter writers claimed "special interest in Nicky's welfare," adding that through Mike's "descriptive" columns, they learned not only political lessons, but "child psychology" as well. "We strongly urge that these articles be continued and as a contribution to the field of literature a collection of all the articles written on Nicky [be published] in pamphlet form."[19]

In 1938 the Granich family had begun paying installments on a cabin in a Single Tax Colony in Plainfield, New Jersey called "Free Acres," which they'd been visiting for years and where brother George and his wife, Gertrude, had been running a children's camp. In the summer months of the war years, the family spent almost as much time there as in New York. They would pack up in early July and travel the thirty miles west to Plainfield on the Lackawanna or Jersey Central line, usually walking with their bags the last two miles down Plainfield Road to their small lot on Emerson Lane. In winter 1941, the house was damaged by an electrical fire. The Sullivan family, who were living there as renters at the time, were friends of the Graniches, and Mike took the loss in stride. Thereafter the space was impossible to rent but still suitable for summer vacations. As Nick Granich recalled, when the news came of Japanese surrender and the end of World War II, the family celebrated with friends on the outside deck of the Free Acres Common House, a meetinghouse and library that had once been a barn.

During the war, the Communist Party under Earl Browder had been a weak force on the domestic front, delaying or softening its revolutionary program in order to support the unified effort against fascism. General secretary Browder, who was released from prison by President Roosevelt in 1942, had adopted a policy of cooperation with capitalist institutions, going so far as to advocate changing the name of the Party to the Communist

Political Association while proposing a corresponding shift in its basic relation to the American political order. As a recent cultural historian claimed, Earl Browder "moved the CPUSA from a splinter political party to an adjunct of the New Deal." Under his proposals, which he advanced in 1944, US communism would essentially cease to be a revolutionary organization, becoming instead one of "peaceful coexistence and collaboration in the same world" with capitalist institutions.[20]

For Gold, ideas such as "pledging aid to capitalism to stabilize itself" and abandoning revolutionary socialism in order to "take a disciplined post in the fighting ranks of the American majority" were, in his own words, "bitter pills to swallow."[21] "Under Browderism," Gold wrote, "Marxism was being liquidated" and left-wing literature "almost destroyed."[22] The push-back against the general secretary from the Communist International was likewise strong. With approval from Moscow, Browder was stripped of executive authority in 1945, expelled from the CPUSA in February 1946, and replaced by the more hard-line class warrior, William Z. Foster.

For some Communist writers, including the highly respected novelist and playwright Albert Maltz, Browder's call to members to defend the US Constitution and Bill of Rights had carried the implication that debate or even dissent on intra-Party cultural policies might henceforth be more permissible. In October 1945, before Browder's final expulsion, Maltz wrote and submitted to the *New Masses* editors a now famous essay, "What Shall We Ask of Writers?" Even as the essay was being prepared for publication, it caused a stir. *New Masses* literary editor Isidor Schneider formulated a critical challenge, titled "Background to Error," as a rebuttal. Appearing on the page just after the offending article and thus almost as a kind of appendix, Schneider's piece cautioned readers to "avoid the mistakes so clearly shown by Maltz."[23] It seems to have been designed not to invite discussion but rather to incite denunciation.

The incendiary nature of Maltz's essay lay in its basic assertion that leftist writers had been for years producing inferior work because they were placing political concerns above artistic ones. "Much of left-wing artistic activity—both creative and critical," Maltz wrote, "has been restricted, narrowed, turned away from life, sometimes made sterile" by a vulgarized version of the 'art is a weapon' theory. It has been understood to mean that unless art is a weapon like a leaflet, serving immediate political ends, necessities and programs, "it is worthless or escapist or vicious," Maltz claimed. He added that for creative writers, Party doctrine was "not a useful guide, but a strait jacket." In current practice, a "thin or inept" novel would be reviewed warmly by Party organs if it expressed "correct political tactics"; other works, no matter how "rich in human insight, character portrayal and imagination," would be "indicted, severely mauled or beheaded" if they implied political conclusions that were deemed "wrong."[24]

When it came to judgments about the merits of authors, a similar canon applied, one that Maltz saw as confusing, self-limiting, and highly "restricting . . . for the creator in practice." Essentially Maltz asked that writers be judged by the works they produce rather than the committees they join; he reminded readers that "where art is a weapon, it is only so when it is art." Overall, Maltz advocated the approach to literature espoused by Friedrich Engels, who had held that it was possible to be a great artist without being "an integrated or a logical or a progressive thinker on all matters."[25]

Some figures of the cultural Left immediately expressed agreement with these points, including Gold's friend Millard Lampell of the Almanac Singers, who thanked Maltz for raising "issues that damn well needed to be raised."[26] But in the days and weeks that followed, more than half a dozen major leftist cultural figures writing in the *New Masses* and the *Daily Worker*—including, Howard Fast, Samuel Sillen, Joseph North, Alvah Bessie, John Howard Lawson, and Gold himself—strenuously rejected Maltz's argument. Lawson's attacks were especially important because he was the head of the influential Party cell in Hollywood, where Maltz was currently enjoying a successful screenwriting career.

As scholar Colin Burnett recently observed, the "storm over Maltz" did not lack a basis in Marxist theory. "The immediate attacks on Maltz by critics like Mike Gold," he notes, "were motivated primarily by the view that a properly Marxist aesthetics must follow, rather than Maltz's Engels-derived ideas, the Leninist-Zhdanovite theory of 'art as a weapon.'" Something all of the attacks on Maltz shared was a rejection of the "para-Marxist" theories espoused by Maltz in favor of the orthodox Zhdanovite-Leninist theory of art that had been officially articulated Communist policy since the mid-1930s.[27]

The assaults that came from Gold were among the most vigorous, strident, and, many would say, disrespectful. In four hostile and repetitive columns of February 12, February 23, March 2, and March 16, he celebrated the achievements of the Communist literary movement, which had "nurtured and created a Richard Wright," as the artistic school that had also "nurtured an Albert Maltz and gave him a philosophic basis."

He expressed sorrow that Maltz had been "poisoned" by the "luxury and phony atmosphere" of his screenwriting career in Hollywood: "Albert's soul was strong when it touched Mother Earth—the American working class." He called Maltz's new aesthetics "abstractions" and "literary evasions of reality," products of the Ivory Tower that did nothing to help trade unionists, African Americans, or "all the rest of toiling humanity who must fight." Maltz's "denial of the social role of the artist" constituted "a veiled attack on the Communist movement" that defended "the liquidators of left-wing literature."[28]

Gold's reference to the "liquidators" is an attempt to establish just how far beyond a "narrowly literary controversy" the issues in Maltz's essay extended. He wanted Maltz to recognize how his positions could only be understood as an endorsement of "Browderism," which Gold saw as a denial of fundamental Marxist class theory because it erased the distinctions between fascist-oriented "Big Capital" and progressivist, democratic "Big Labor." Now that Browder was gone, the Communist movement must "start to rebuild its shattered house. We must again learn to believe in ourselves, and in the independent role of the working class in literature."[29]

Probably the most personally felt of Gold's objections to Maltz stemmed from his sense that the conflict was also about the legacy of the 1930s. Recalling the vast suffering after the crash, Gold called attention to the Party's heroic role in leading the unemployed and organizing hunger marches. At the same time, the literary arm of the Communist movement, led by a dynamic young writer from the Lower East Side Jewish ghetto, "penetrated all the ivory towers," producing proletarian novels, plays and poems, and becoming "a main stream" in national culture. "It was a fighting art," Gold mused nostalgically, "We must rebuild the Marxist cultural front, . . . and plunge literature and art into life and the social realities."[30] In his initial column of February 12, Gold identified a reference to the political committees on which novelist James T. Farrell served as "a bad sign." He was outraged that Maltz's "new personality" had lacked the honesty to call out Farrell's Trotskyism in clear terms and had instead passed it off as a minor or slight offense: "By such reasoning, Nazi rats like Ezra Pound and Knut Hamson, both superior writers to Farrell, must be treated respectfully and even forgiven for their horrible politics because they are 'artists.' "[31]

Suddenly Mike Gold, the worker-poet who had found beauty in the anguish of the slums and who stood up for the art and humanity of lives in the lowliest places, sounds both crass and philistine. At the moment when serious, accomplished writers become "rats" and the term "artists" is used ironically in quotations, a critic must look inward and ponder. Burning and zealous, Gold rejected the notion that "Farrell the author could be tenderly regarded, while Farrell the anti-Soviet warmonger was ignored." The granting of aesthetic immunity to an obvious enemy like Farrell was proof that Maltz had "lost sight of the Communist polar star."[32]

Maltz's implication that the movement was enforcing a "vulgar" course was thus partly justified by Gold himself, who admitted that his attacks were possibly "personal, slanderous and crude."[33] In a rebuttal letter of February 18, addressed to Gold but excerpted in the *Daily Worker*, Maltz castigated his accuser for his insensitivity, correctly pointing out that the assault could only "stultify all discussions and frighten off people who have come to any conclusion . . . that disagrees with acceptable tenets." It was easy, Maltz said, to shrug off Gold's "scarecrow image" of him, but he stressed that the "real victims" of the column were "the younger writers . . . those new to the movement . . . who witness this ferocity, this unbecoming descent to personality slander."[34] In retrospect it was perhaps Gold's weakest moment on the national stage.

To some degree Gold's rash and immoderate invective was surely a product of lockstep conformity to dictates adopted in Moscow by the Stalinist Party. But it was also elicited by more local factors. First, there was the perceived need to rebuild the identity of American Marxism as a revolutionary movement. In the cultural field, this meant retrenchment or recovery from a literary Browderism that Gold saw stepping away from proletarian literature and toward the Ivory Tower, "the floundering in the marsh, the negative and passive literature of the cafes and aesthetic cliques."[35]

Second, most historians recognize the Maltz denunciation as one of CPUSA's adjustments in the face of a more assertive right wing. In other words, the infighting that characterized the affair was related to the onset of a new phase of persecution, one that involved a coordinated effort to justify anti-Left purges under the cloak of national security concerns.[36] Not without reason, the two years between summer 1945 and summer 1947 are a period often described as a "prelude to repression."[37] Isidor Schneider's classification of the immediate postwar era as a moment of "emergency" drew on such concerns, in effect concluding that the right to admire politically suspect artists was a casualty of the threatening context.

As early as 1935, Andrei Zhdanov had offered a blueprint for adaptation to conditions in which Communist cultural institutions were embattled. A central tenet of Zhdanovite orthodoxy held that "a critic has only two functions: he is an interpreter of Party dogma and a discerner of heresy."[38] Though this philistine and narrowly authoritarian modus operandi was completely anathema to Gold's passionately artistic personality, his love of beauty and humanity, and his amplitude of spirit as a poetic disciple of Walt Whitman, in denouncing Maltz he largely followed the Zhdanovite blueprint.

This role was essentially different from the part Gold had played in the critical debates of the 1930s. In a *New Masses* article about Gold's cultural influence, literary editor Isidor Schneider held that what gave Gold's work of the 1930s its impact was its enthusiasm, tenacity, and boldness in applying social criticism to current literary work, with the novels of Thornton Wilder as only the most famous example. With "Wilder, Prophet of a Genteel Christ," Gold had won a major intellectual victory that made placing a work within its social context an obligatory critical move, whatever the critic's political orientation. In Schneider's view, Mike Gold was the most "exemplary" champion of this social critical mode and the first to "challenge . . . the assumptions of the 'esthetic' criticisms of the time, exposing its evasions of reality."[39]

In 1946, Gold, Lawson, and the cultural hard-liners had won a different, intra-Party battle easily enough. Under withering attack, Maltz recanted his views almost immediately, then exonerated himself from Gold's charges of Browderism by writing a rebuttal to his own "mistaken" article and publishing it in the *Daily Worker*. While admitting his errors, he also made an assertion that hearkened back to Millen Brand's review of *The Hollow Men* by reiterating that the only worthwhile artists were those who love the people. After these concessions, Albert Maltz was welcomed back into the fold.

The Party's ideological gatekeepers in the field of literary culture—a group that had included Gold as an influential member since the 1920s—had quelled a substantial challenge and reconstituted order. But they, and especially Gold, had not looked good doing so. For the prolific *Change the World* columnist, the costs included tarnished prestige among readers, both immediately and in the long-term. And the victory won at such a substantial cost would soon become moot. Strong attacks from right-wing institutions—the prelude to repression—were already pigeonholing every tenet of the radical Left as a general threat to the security of the United States. Though the Maltz episode preceded the McCarthy era by about three years, its intensity was a reflection of the strangely uncertain identity of the CPUSA between the periods of Browderism and McCarthyism.

Ironically, in retrospect it seems possible that Maltz's less didactic Marxist poetics might have better equipped Communist cultural workers for the reactionary hysteria to come. The anti-Maltz storm almost certainly alienated some of the Party's liberal supporters while giving ammunition to the Right in the culture wars. As Colin Burnett argued in his 2014 study of the Maltz affair, "In a period of repression, a strategically para-Marxist aesthetics [Maltz's position] would have explored and sanctioned a greater degree of nimbleness among critics as well as artists." This in turn might have helped to at least nominally "sustain . . . a progressive sensibility in American art and life without the overt ties and references to a communist outlook that would, after 1947, become anathema."[40] Perhaps realizing this truth as well as his own unkindness, Gold eventually apologized to Maltz in the late 1950s.[41]

The profanity-laden Hemingway-Gold parting of ways described in chapter 6 has become a well-known anecdote in literary history, repeated in several biographies of the Nobel Prize–winning novelist. A second disaffection of the 1940s, involving another Nobel Prize–winning friend of Gold's who had once recommended the people's writer for a Guggenheim, is worth recounting as well. The relationship between Gold and Eugene O'Neill—formed in Greenwich Village in the glamorous early-twentieth-century atmosphere of the original Provincetown Players—had been a close bond that involved meaningful artistic influence. The two had caroused together at the Hell Hole saloon, shared ideas about radical drama, presented plays on the same bill, and admired each other's scriptwriting. The shift in Gold's attitude toward O'Neill's work carries lessons and insights about the causes of Gold's professional alienation in the last phase of his career.

O'Neill, who was born in 1888 to middle-class privilege, had abandoned that life in his early twenties to make independent forays into the world of the working class, mainly as a sailor but also including, he claimed, a stint doing "manual work for the Swift Packing people."[42] In those years O'Neill signed his letters "Yours for the Revolution" and took extravagant pride in the sailor's jersey he'd received on being promoted to "able-bodied seaman" aboard an American Line cruise ship in 1911. Theoretically O'Neill's pursuit of a type of "vital contact" with working classes, like that of Jig Cook, was understood and approved of by the slightly younger Irwin Granich. Almost as soon as Gold stepped into the role of chief theorist of proletarian culture, he endorsed the process of middle-class writers and artists acquiring such experience—as John Reed had in the 1913 Paterson silk workers' strike, in Mexico, and in Russia.

A crucial issue in these class-crossing exploits, however, was related to the authenticity or loyalty of the down-classer to the class he impersonated. O'Neill's early success as a dramatist had been based on the perception this his identity as a worker was sufficiently authentic, at least in the eyes of middle-class liberals and bohemians. In 1916, five years after his sailing voyages, he donned his sailor's jersey for his arrival in Provincetown and his audition with the Provincetown Players, costuming himself as a seasoned seaman and carrying a sailor's knapsack full of plays. "Dressed slackly like a sailor who had just jumped ship," O'Neill "had come to town trampishly," apparently drawing on a somewhat remote seagoing experience to lend credibility to his current dramatic efforts.[43] His first one-acts, epitomized by "Bound East for Cardiff," attempted to provide audiences with intimate access to working-class reality at almost the precise moment when Irwin Granich, a real member of the working class, was welcomed into the Players by Jig Cook. The Provincetowners accepted and performed O'Neill's plays for the same reason they welcomed Irwin Granich's *Down the Airshaft*: both bespoke an identification with lower-class life that was deep, visceral, and perceived as genuine.

But there were differences between the two. Dorothy Day remembers O'Neill condescendingly teasing Gold about *Down the Airshaft*. Joking about the clotheslines hanging between the tiny tenements, O'Neill sarcastically misquoted English poet Thomas Gray by calling the play's subject matter "the short, simple *flannels* of the poor."[44] A comparable distinction had been on display the winter night in 1918 when Gold, O'Neill, and Day took a long walk in the snowy Greenwich Village streets. As they walked, Gold sang the plaintive Yiddish songs he'd learned as a boy while O'Neill sang the sea chanties he'd learned in his days as a sailor-poet, bound for Buenos Aires aboard the *Charles Racine*. O'Neill had his sea chanties and Gold had his tenement songs, but neither seemed to recognize a disparity in the relation the two men had to the cultural material they were performing.

To pinpoint the distinction, we might look at how it manifested in the context of late 1946, when Cold War tensions were already evident and Gold wrote a *Change the World* column titled "Eugene O'Neill's Early Days." Ostensibly the column was about a recent staging of O'Neill's new play, *The Iceman Cometh*, but actually it was about O'Neill's new status as a literary renegade:

> There are fewer proletarian writers and artists than a decade ago. Repression has taken its toll, and prosperity has killed off a lot of truly creative writing. But I believe the proletarian writers of today are more mature than those of any previous generation. They will be able to give better leadership to middle class writers who will grow in numbers and take their stand for freedom and peace.
>
> Let me give you an example of what I mean. Eugene O'Neill began his career with some sea plays at the little Provincetown Players theatre. I was a member of that group, and they put on some tenement plays I wrote. So I can remember drinking with O'Neill at the old Hell Hole and his showing us a newspaper clipping at which he swore bitterly: "I'll crucify the bastard! I'll crucify him." The clipping reported a speech by a pompous reactionary in the Senate who had called the IWW "apes."
>
> The clipping crystallized into O'Neill's play about a stoker, *The Hairy Ape*. He wrote the play, I am sure, with anticapitalist passion. But if you compare O'Neill's play to young Herb Tank's *Longitude 49*, you will find that O'Neill is a tourist who writes from the outside. He hasn't portrayed a stoker, but himself. Into the mind of a stoker he puts his own middle-class decadence, guilt, and defeatism—a metaphysical haze that belongs in existential cafes, not in an American "foc'sle."[45]

David Roessel's fine research into the Gold-O'Neill relationship cites this passage in order to point out a strange anomaly. In 1922, Gold loved and defended *The Hairy Ape*, calling it "a great play" because it depicted "the poetry of life I have known, the life the great masses of American workmen have known."[46] For Gold, *The Hairy Ape* at that time epitomized his dictate in "Towards Proletarian Art" that the artist of the new millennium "must learn through solidarity with the people what Life is."[47] As Roessel notes, by 1946 Mike Gold was using the same play for the exact opposite purpose: to show that O'Neill "was never really in touch with the working class." The reappraisal was therefore "less dependent on the play, which had not changed, than on the author, whom Gold thought had."[48]

Roessel is correct, but there are more elements to consider, among them the possibility that both men had changed. Gold had actually revised his opinion of *The Hairy Ape* long before 1946, stating in the April 10, 1934 *New Masses* that O'Neill had "committed the aesthetic and moral crime of creating a worker in the author's own image." Writing at the worst period of the Depression, Gold argued that artists must learn something from the stock market crash and the rise of proletarian culture. He had not forgotten that he once approved of O'Neill's play; twelve years later it exemplified outdated art. With fifteen million unemployed it was no longer acceptable to use a giant stoker as a caricature, a marionette "spouting the sort of minor poetry popular among disinherited sons of the bourgeoisie living in post-war Greenwich Village." Gold implied that by not allowing Yank to "fulfill his own destiny," O'Neill had produced a play now visible as a confused, synthetic concoction that reeked of "futilitarianism."[49]

In O'Neill's case, a significant difference between the emerging artist of the 1910s and the world-famous dramatist of 1946 was that the established writer, obviously no longer "yours for the revolution," had come to question his youthful, adventure-driven working-class masquerades, the very formula that had won him Pulitzers and sustained his rise to prominence. In *Long Day's Journey into Night*, which O'Neill began writing in 1939, Edmund Tyrone clearly espouses the social theories of the young O'Neill, while Edmund's father, James Tyrone, just as persuasively expresses conclusions reached by the mature playwright. Like O'Neill at age twenty-three, Edmund has returned from a slumming adventure at sea where he has formed a rudimentary socialist class consciousness. In Act 4 of *Long Day's Journey*, Edmund extols the value of his proletarian experience, claiming that it has enabled him to relate more sympathetically to his father:

> God, Papa, ever since I went to sea and was on my own, and found out what hard work and little pay was, and what it felt like to be broke, and starve, and camp on park benches because I had no place to sleep, I've tried to be fair to you because I knew what you'd been up against as a kid.[50]

Tyrone realizes, however, that his own childhood had been essentially different from Edmund's adventures—"There was no damned romance in our poverty"—and asserts that there is no way Edmund can understand its real consequences:

You said you realized what I'd been up against as a boy. The
hell you do! . . . You've had food, clothing. Oh, I know you
had a fling of hard work with your back and hands, a bit of
being homeless and penniless in a foreign land. . . . But it was
a game . . . It was play.

Tyrone's immigrant childhood in authentic poverty enables him to discern the pretense of his son's voluntary privation. To him it is little more
than a bourgeois "game of romance and adventure."[51] When it came to
the real proletarian life, Edmund/O'Neill was indeed a pretender, tourist,
and outsider.

By the 1940s a good number of American writers, most notably
Richard Wright and John Steinbeck in *Native Son* and *In Dubious Battle*
respectively, had assailed various embodiments of "labor fakers," whose
associations with workers were spurious and ultimately exploitative.[52]
In the case of *Long Day's Journey into Night*, the difference was that the
dramatized labor faker was a version of O'Neill himself.

For Mike Gold, whose childhood was closer to Tyrone's (a character based on the playwright's immigrant father James O'Neill) than to
Edmund's, this class-based acknowledgment mattered. James O'Neill's path
in life had led from extreme poverty to fame and comparative financial
comfort, allowing Eugene to avoid working-class experience except on a
temporary and therefore artificial basis. Undeniably, O'Neill was nurtured,
as Gold put it in *The Hollow Men*, "in the womb of the middle class."
If Gold's opinion of O'Neill changed, it was partly because his opinion
about O'Neill's professed solidarity with the workers had altered. By 1946,
Gold, like O'Neill, took a less idealistic, more complex attitude toward
worker-intellectual associations. Gold's claim that proletarian writers had
learned lessons and were "more mature" by the 1940s was in part a reaction
to the cache of betrayal stories recounted in *The Hollow Men*. *The Hairy
Ape* was a different play in 1946 because Gold was more skeptical about
the slumming expeditions of its author.

So there is a certain logic in the fact that, from Gold's perspective,
the stoker Yank's agony in *The Hairy Ape* looked different in the 1930s
and 1940s, for the simple reason that he could no longer accept the play's
representation of a worker. It also explains why Gold's article, which was
supposedly a review of *The Iceman Cometh*, took the outrageous and
bizarre step of immediately stating that he had not yet seen the play he
was reviewing: "I haven't been to see the Theater Guild's . . . *The Iceman*

Cometh, yet from the reviews I can almost tell what the play is like," Gold wrote.[53]

What could he "tell," and how had he inferred it? For one thing, he could be sure the play wasn't sufficiently about real workers because it came from an artist without genuine proletarian experience, "a tourist who writes from the outside." Gold's assertion that the obscure play *Longitude 49* was better than *The Hairy Ape* was also strategic. It meant that O'Neill's play was now effectively disqualified from a leftist perspective; its author couldn't be trusted—even though he'd spent two years before the mast and had an able seaman's jersey to prove it—because the crucial trait, "love of the people," was absent. In a way Gold was doubling-down on his pronouncements in the earlier Maltz controversy, applying Zhdanovite criteria with full force to register how a change in context translated into a change in meaning.

In the conversations Gold recorded for his memoirs in his final years, he was conciliatory and charitable toward both O'Neill and the Provincetown Players. He reminisced, "If ever a theater however tiny displayed immortal value to the soul of the American, it was the Provincetown Players, surely." He also recognized the true radicalism of its young playwrights and celebrated the ways the collective led by Cook and dominated by O'Neill and Glaspell, but with solid contributions from Irwin Granich, "fit the proletarian mold."[54]

Speaking about the later stages of O'Neill's career, however, the people's writer was less generous. With O'Neill in mind, he formulated a profanity-tinged epithet that packed only slightly less punch than Hemingway's famous farewell to Gold: "I had grown up as a writer knowing that the only forms that can contain the facts of poverty, in America or anywhere in the world, are bitter and real. And anybody who tried to make them only an art form would be a son of a bitch according to my standards, because he neglected the sufferings of human beings for the sake of some Prix Nobel, some jingle bells playing for the amusement of the art dilettantes."[55]

Perhaps Gold ultimately gave wildly conflicting views of O'Neill because, despite class differences, O'Neill's aid and encouragement of the younger writer was once substantial and undeniable. In 1923 O'Neill read Gold's *Life of John Brown* pamphlet and immediately contacted him, explaining that he was leading a new theater collective under the Provincetown name and asking Gold for a play about Brown's exploits, suggesting that he "quicken" that story "into modern art." About a dozen years later this idea bore fruit as *Battle Hymn*, but Gold couldn't get the play ready at the time because he was negotiating with the Brown biography's publisher for a second volume, a never-published life of Lenin.

In 1925, as mentioned earlier, O'Neill wrote on Gold's behalf to producer Kenneth McGowan, plugging Gold's play *Fiesta* and recommending that his friend be given "a decent advance and a contract" that would commission future plays.[56] And more than once, O'Neill counseled Gold on matters of craft, candidly warning him not to taint his plays with overt propaganda and to keep "the artist, Mike Gold, and the equally O.K. human being, the Radical editor, rigidly separated." About the dangers of burdening a play with bluntly political messages, O'Neill advised, "My quarrel with propaganda in the theater is that it's such damned unconvincing propaganda—whereas, if you will restrain the propaganda purpose to a selection of the life to be portrayed and then let that life live itself without comment, it does your trick."[57] Of course O'Neill was right, as his career attested. But Gold might well have seen O'Neill's attitude as a kind of class privilege, a stance much easier for an artist who essentially lived off his father until he was thirty and whose revolutionary ardor was never deeply felt.

In his 1932 essay, "Why I Am a Communist" Gold declared that "nobody who has not gone through this proletarian experience" could ever understand the "fever" that seized him after being beaten by a cop in Union Square and converted to radicalism. "I can never discharge this personal debt to the revolutionary movement," he declared; "It gave me a mind."[58] There are those who will say that it also took away Gold's mind in certain ways, but he knew what he was doing. As Joseph Freeman judged, the "secret" of Mike Gold's "passionate literary style" was simple: "He really cared about socialism more than he cared about his personal career."[59]

Less than six months after the unseemly controversy over Maltz, Gold showed a much gentler demeanor in three *Daily Worker* articles about the death of his brother George, the youngest of the Granich brothers, whose passing from cancer at age forty-six elicited powerful feelings. The emotions of Mike and Manny were probably stronger because the death was unusually sudden. As Manny remembered, George had been having stomach pains for years but refused to seek medical care. "But it reached a stage where he couldn't eat and so doctors came into the deal," Manny remembered.[60] A surgical examination revealed a shocking amount of late-stage cancer, far advanced, through his entire abdomen. The doctors could do nothing but sew up the incision and inform the patient and his wife that he had only weeks to live.

Beginning on September 3, 1946, Gold used three consecutive columns to eulogize his "kid brother" and fellow soldier in the class struggle. "My brothers and I were united in the working class movement from our earliest years, and it strengthened the family bond," he wrote.[61] Though Mike was the first brother to quit school to go to work, George too had done time as a child laborer in a basement factory. Just a few months before Mike left for Harvard in 1914, George had taken up socialism and gone off to see the world. By 1916, he had joined the IWW and become a migrant laborer, following the Western harvests, working the crops as they matured along the Mexican border and into California, Oregon, and the Northwest. One year, his brother recalled, George worked as a cowboy on a cattle ranch, where he was hurt trying to ride an unbroken horse on a dare. Another time a cop found him sleeping in an empty boxcar and he was jailed for riding the rails. Locked up with a violent religious fanatic, he had found a way to escape.

Like all the Granich brothers, George "craved and needed the outdoors." He was "a good farmer, and a skilled carpenter, as well as a good father and active, hard-working Communist," Gold said, taking pride also that his little brother was both a Wobbly and a charter member of the Communist Party.[62]

George's obituary in the *Daily Worker* noted that he spent five years on the road, traveling thousands of miles as a migrant worker and agitator. Later, he and his wife Gertrude had two children, Michael and Bundy, who were active in the Young Communist League and the labor movement. It was to George's son, "Little Mike," that Gold had dedicated *Jews without Money*. The wording of that 1930 dedication had called his four-year-old nephew "a beloved pest" who had helped Gold write the novel by reminding him how proletarian children felt about the world. George's first job after becoming a father was at a Jewish orphanage in Pleasantville, New York, where he sometimes argued with the "drab-minded careerists" who ran the institution, "fighting for the right of kids to be complete human beings."[63] After that he was a taxi driver, then a stage carpenter for the New Playwrights Theater for two years, where he doubtless helped Mike, along with Jack Lawson, Upton Sinclair, and John Dos Passos, realize their elaborate visionary productions.

Gold was particularly proud that George had been instrumental during the early 1930s unemployment crisis, when "the party found its soul and became a national force, the heroic leader of twenty million hungry Americans." He was gratified also that Pete Cacchione, Communist City Councilman and veteran of the Unemployed Councils, came to George's funeral. Gold vividly recalled the 1932 hunger march and the sight of George standing "quiet and steady, as always" at the forefront of the parade as hordes of police approached with tear gas and riot guns.[64]

But the bulk of George's career—more than fifteen years—were spent as an arts and crafts and recreational director for children, work in which he displayed "a sensitive talent that won him the love of hundreds of children and their parents."[65] In the final column Gold wrote about his brother's life, he mused on George's sensitive character and "innocence of heart." Though George was "no weakling," he was neither competitive nor acquisitive:

> He never acquired in 46 years of living any of that dreadful commercial sophistication of today, that talks so glibly about "selling yourself" and how much "money there is" in doing this or that job. . . . He was born ahead of his time in commercial America. . . . George didn't fit too easily into our commercial culture, and millions of plain American proletarians are like him.[66]

As Mike recalled, George was always doing "friendship jobs" because he enjoyed work more when he wasn't doing it for money. Children fell in love with him immediately. "I saw it with my own boys," Gold wrote, "He never talked down to a kid. . . . He taught them how to make things; his hands were always busy, and the kids imitated him." Gold's columns spoke also of Gertrude, George's "comrade-wife," a German-American whose grandfather had participated in the revolution of 1848 and was "one of that breed of German immigrants who brought Marxism to America."[67]

Imparting a farewell, Gold declared that George had never lost faith in the "singing tomorrow" of communism: "Good-bye, beloved brother. You were an artist and a good man and a good Communist! You perished of cancer, and so are millions of other Americans who could be saved, if humanity ruled here ahead of atom bombs and profiteering! Good-bye, you were gentle and good; and your kind will inherit the earth."[68]

The memories Gold came to terms with in these columns were likely among the mix of factors that prompted the Granich family's trip to France less than a year later. Within weeks after George's death, the Free Acres summer house was on the market; its sale for a good price in early 1947 produced a nest egg for travel and living expenses in France. With other small loans from friends, they could make a go of it for at least two years, they determined, while helping Elizabeth's aging grandparents and allowing their boys to learn about their French heritage. Not emphasized around the kids but also undeniably real was the sense of an increasingly threatening political atmosphere in the United States.

In the few weeks between George's diagnosis and his death, another pressing issue was the immediate future of Gertrude and her two children. On this family matter Gold's brother Manny stepped forward. Manny had started out the 1940s as the chauffeur for CPUSA General Secretary Browder while his wife, Grace, also worked for the Party as Browder's personal secretary, and after his expulsion, in another office position. In 1942 Manny took a job in the New York shipyards, where he worked long hours for good pay supervising the repair and refitting of battle-damaged ships.

As soon as the war ended, the couple sought a retreat from city life and politics, deciding on the goal of buying a farm large enough for them to live self-sufficiently in peace and relative isolation. With about three thousand dollars saved from the war years as their down payment, they purchased Higley Hill in Vermont, a 138-acre tract described by Manny as "a little pocket in the hillside with 10 or 12 buildings, two fields immediately apparent and lots of woods, a brook and a chicken house." The buildings were 170 years old, but for Manny, refurbishing them would be pleasant work.

Manny and Grace had planned to make the place into a subsistence farm, but "events changed our direction," Manny later said, referring to George's death. For two years previous to George's sickness, he and Gertrude had been running a children's camp and doing maintenance on a rented farm in the Catskills, but it was clear that Gert couldn't keep this up on her own. Having just closed their purchase of Higley Hill, Manny and Grace suggested that Gert invite the kids from her camp to come to Vermont the next year and they'd see if they could "build a little camp."

This was how the Higley Hill Summer Camp began. Starting with just seven campers in summer 1947, it grew comfortably. By 1950 Grace and Manny would have sixty youngsters at the racially integrated eight-week retreat. Many of the Higley Hill children, including notably Carl Granich, would be sons or daughters of leftists whose parents were being hounded by the FBI or the House Un-American Activities Committee. Once during the oral history interviews Manny gave in 1981–1982, the interviewer said to him, "You weren't so close to George—you were closer to Mike." Manny responded, "No, I was close to George and Mike. . . . There was no division between us."[69]

On May 22, 1947, Mike, Elizabeth, Nick, and Carl gave up their East Twelfth Street apartment and left New York for France, where they would remain for almost three years. The family cat was adopted by Natalie Gomez, Mike's onetime colleague at the *New Masses* who was now a family friend. Before embarking, Gold signed off to his readership in a final *Daily Worker* column that seemed committed to a new project but far from confident, instead hedging bets about his next endeavor: "So long for a time, readers, . . . This author is off again to try to write a novel. It is an irresistible impulse that has to be obeyed. I hope other people than writers will understand the necessity of it. If the novel should never get

Figure 7.2. From left: Manny, George, and Mike, c. 1945. *Source:* Granich family.

written, if nobody ever prints it, if it should never find a single reader, yet the thing has to be attempted."[70]

Though Gold would accomplish substantial writing in France, the novel never materialized, reflecting the basic truth that in professional terms the trip was a retreat and regrouping rather than an advance. The FBI had a theory that the Graniches were going to Europe because Mike Gold was "in the doghouse" with Communist Party officials for having been "a strong supporter of Earl Browder."[71] This seems wildly inaccurate; Gold was on record in opposition to Browder, and he was never seriously reprimanded by the Party because he was not viewed as a serious policy maker. The Party knew he still rarely attended meetings and, well aware of his popularity, they had long ago decided to tolerate the heterodoxy sometimes expressed in his columns.

Contrary to the FBI speculation about internecine harassment, the political threat in 1947 was obviously coming from the Right rather than the Left. In the 1946 midterm elections, Republicans won firm majorities in Congress, adding twelve Republican seats in the Senate and fifty-five in the House. Joseph McCarthy was not yet a factor, but Truman's executive order 9835, issued in response to growing criticism from conservatives and anti-Communists, had initiated loyalty oaths and loyalty reviews for federal employees. Already the names of numerous alleged Communists and sympathizers in the film industry had been published, initiating the Hollywood blacklist that would soon produce subpoenas from the House Un-American Activities Committee.

For their first year in France, the Granich family settled in a dirty Paris suburb, living in primitive conditions on a single floor of a decaying three-story house. It seemed they had miscalculated their expenses and overeconomized. According to Carl, winter 1947 was spent miserably in record-breaking cold at a time when both food and coal were rationed in an economy still recovering from the war. Nick and Carl were frequently sick; the family subsisted mainly on potatoes and at times the boys actually went to bed hungry. In the spring the family moved eagerly into a smaller but more civilized Left Bank pension. For that year Nick and Carl attended a private international school that neither of them liked. Their classmates, though culturally diverse, were the sons and daughters of diplomats; Carl remembered them as somewhat conceited kids from privileged backgrounds. They mocked the boys' New York accents and harassed them by calling them "American gangsters."[72]

The next year the boys were happy when the family moved far from Paris, pooling resources with Elizabeth's parents and renting four large rooms with stone floors in a remote chateau near Nogent-sur-Loir, a town of three or four hundred. Nick and Carl, like their father, loved the countryside. They now attended a small village grammar school half a mile down the road, where they got along well with their classmates, the friendly children of French peasant farmers. It was a simple, orderly, rural community where the pace of life was slow. There were few automobiles and the New Yorkers found the peace and quiet unsettling at first. The chateau they lived in was surrounded by a deep moat that made it possible for the boys to drop a fishing line out their bedroom window.

Gold's health improved in the rural environment. In the mornings he rode a bike to town to buy his Communist newspapers. With the grandparents ensconced in one wing of the chateau, meals were multi-generational, bilingual affairs. Elizabeth's parents were practicing Catholics but forced nothing on the grandchildren. Her white-haired mother, petite and pretty, had a bad hip and could barely walk. Carl recalled that she saw and encouraged his love of music and art, giving him regular careful instruction in how to draw perspective. Both boys, who were now twelve and eight years old, were afraid at the frequent anger and yelling of Elizabeth's father, whom they called *Mon Père*; then they learned he was dying of stomach cancer, for which he was taking only homeopathic remedies, and was in great pain. He had owned a tree nursery that was put out of business by market competition from Italian import farms. He had also owned a photography business, but in 1948–1949 his daily task was to put up a brave struggle against the disease. He would have been a sweet man all the time if it weren't for the cancer, Elizabeth told the boys.

By all accounts Gold got along well with Elizabeth's parents, who came from a semi-aristocratic background but grew up in a family that had adamantly taken the side of Captain Alfred Dreyfus against anti-Semitic French military officials in the fervid political and judicial battle that had divided French society at the turn of the century. As scholar Alan Wald notes, both sides of Elizabeth's family prominently displayed in their homes copies of *J'Accuse*, Émile Zola's open letter of 1898 that exposed a frame-up of Dreyfus and argued successfully for the reopening of his case.

When the French newspapers reported the anti-Red mob attack on Paul Robeson at his concert in the Peekskill, New York, in 1949, Gold's mother-in-law was livid; she "could conceive of no greater crime than to

attack a divine artist like Paul Robeson" and projected the crime onto the
entire United States. Her son-in-law found himself arguing in defense of
his country, explaining that "it was not the people, really, but the scum of
America" who attacked Robeson that day. Gold sadly observed how memories of such atrocities "build up into the great prejudices of the world,"
and that for millions of people living overseas, America had become "only
the land that had persecuted Paul Robeson."[73]

In the French countryside, Gold worked intermittently at several
writing projects. He finished the play *Song for Roosevelt* and began *The
Honorable Pete*. Always an autodidact, he learned French well enough to
read newspapers and speak slowly. As articles that were later published
in *Masses and Mainstream* would show, the trip added much to Gold's
knowledge of world affairs. He was moved by reactions of the people in
the countryside to the French national tragedy of the First Indo-China
War in Vietnam, which was financed largely by the United States. He
wrote with confidence and prescience about the "Dirty War" as the French
called it, and about its effects on postwar sociopolitical matters not only
in France but worldwide.

He traveled as well to Italy, Romania, and Hungary and attended a
writers' conference in Prague, where he met and befriended Welsh poet
Dylan Thomas. In his father's homeland, Romania, Gold dined with Prime
Minister Petru Groza at a congress of writers and scientists and came
away impressed with how well the Socialist leader was genuinely in touch
with his people. At the World Peace Conference in Paris in 1949, he had
a long lunch with his good friend W. E. B. DuBois. For a brief time in
1948 the Graniches lived on the Mediterranean coast in an apartment
near the central square in Hyeres, the town where Elizabeth was born.

Carl and Nick recalled that when it came to physical labor, their dad
"wasn't a worker bee"; he took no pleasure in domestic chores other than
cooking, probably because he'd been forced into brutalizing work when
he was a boy. Gold and Elizabeth could relax in those months because
the household work was done efficiently by a woman in her forties who
lived a mile down the dirt road and stopped by a couple mornings a
week. She was the wife of a dairy farmer and mother of adolescent children, whom Carl remembered as "a nice farm family."[74] During the war
the woman and her husband had taken in a Jewish boy of preschool age
named Claude, risking their lives for the boy's unknown parents because
it was deemed safer out in the provinces. The parents never returned so

the family adopted the chubby, dimple-cheeked boy. When Carl once wondered aloud to Elizabeth why the boy looked so different from his siblings, he was told the story.

The Holocaust, along with its implications for American Jews, seems to have been in Gold's thoughts during the sojourn in France. The play he completed in 1948, *Song for Roosevelt,* explores both European and American fascism as deep-rooted phenomena while offering guidelines for opposing them. The characters in the drama experience religious intolerance and violent intimidation that is both class and race based. Ultimately they find hope in community-based democratic activism that is led in a significant way by women.

The drama is set in the neighborhood Gold knew best, Manhattan's Lower East Side. The action begins on April 12, 1945, the day of Franklin Roosevelt's death. The spokespersons for the playwright's message are two resilient young women who've lived through separate tragedies in the fight against fascism: Theresa is a twenty-six-year-old war widow and single mother whose husband was killed in the 1944 battle against Axis forces at Anzio. Hannah is a twenty-year-old refugee from Nazi Germany whose entire family—her parents and two siblings—died in Hitler's gas chambers.

Adopted by the Shuster family, Hannah had arrived in New York severely traumatized, "afraid of every cop in the street" and panic-stricken when left alone. She heals herself in part by studying American history at the local library. She enters the play as "a vivid, rather shy girl of 20, carrying books and flowers" but also bearing insights derived from pain, along with a question that many are asking today: "I can see America is different from Germany. It could never be another Germany. Just the same, fascism is growing here, also. How can that be?"[75]

The answer to Hannah's question follows from a depiction of New York social history. One of the forces addressed in Gold's setting is the Christian Front, an organization (composed largely of the followers of radio priest Charles Coughlin) that fomented violence against Jews. At one point, Gold's characters discuss the "Christian Fronters who cut up that little Jewish boy on Second Avenue last week." In 1945, such incidents were frequent enough to become the subject of an Oscar-winning short film, *The House I Live In*, starring Frank Sinatra and written (by Albert Maltz) to counteract the brutality.

In the play, Christian Fronters spew Hitlerism while Italian mobsters venerate the memory of Benito Mussolini, the crass and bullying demagogue that Donald Trump most closely resembles. News of Roosevelt's death emboldens anti-Semites, prompting an attack on a barbershop co-owned by Hannah's adoptive father, sixty-year-old Louis Shuster. The assailant is an Italian racketeer who barges in, scuffles with Louis, calls Roosevelt a "Jew lover," then exits, "laughing with brutal triumph" as the elderly man collapses from a stroke.

Months later Louis's son Bernie, age twenty-five, returns from the war against Hitler to learn that his father is paralyzed and comatose. While Bernie vows to avenge the assault, he also forms a close attachment with Hannah, who pleads with him to forgo vengeance and instead recommit to his ambition of becoming a great chemist. "You are a Hamlet and want to avenge your father," she says, "But *Hamlet* is an old story. It does not fit our time! It is too personal. It does not seek the *causes* of the murder, the *causes* of fascism, and fight that!"

Another way to defeat fascists is to live a meaningful life, to "live proudly as a Jew." Hannah's view, informed by the Holocaust, seems newly resonant at a time when anti-Semitic violence is on the rise in the United States: "Don't you see, Bernie, that if Jews are forbidden to be Jews, then nobody else can be free in the world? Nobody can have the right to be a redskin or brownskin, a Mohammedan, a free thinker, an artist, anything different. That's what being a Jew means to me—it means freedom exists for everyone!" While in Europe, Bernie too had witnessed the horrors of the concentration camps. Realizing that even New York is an unsafe place, he weighs questions about how democracies decay: "How can we end the Christian Front and Blackshirts in New York? What protects them in a democracy?"

Also plaguing Gold's characters is the dismissive attitude of public officials toward hate crimes. Hymie, who has worked as a waiter for thirty years, vents his anger by telling of a Christian Front gang that smeared swastikas on the windows of Jewish store. The police captain dismissed it as a meaningless children's prank, prompting Hymie to lament, "Always they protect the Nazis."

"It was like that in Berlin," Hannah responds ominously. "And the South, too," adds Randy, an African American porter who dreams of becoming an inventor. He relates the story of his father's lynching, after which the police arrested his mother rather than the white murderers.

In the play's last scene, a neighborhood meeting is held in the kitchen of the Shuster family's tenement apartment. Before it begins, Max Gottlieb, Louis's partner in the barbershop, wearily reminds everyone that as "a bunch of nobodies," they can't beat the fascists.

Theresa enters the kitchen, "dressed for a summer night, a flower in her hair," and confidently outlines a plan: "Forget the big shots and appeal to the people of the neighborhood. Organize them." Max calls this strategy "childish," but Theresa is unfazed and offers specifics:

> Parades, mass meetings, pressure on the politicians—the whole works—the same things we did to fight the black market and elect Roosevelt. Organize the people, and everything else will begin to happen. It's like unlocking a big dam, freeing the water so it comes rushing down to turn the big dynamos that make power and light for the world!

Hannah's support is immediate and the others are drawn in. Randy testifies, "I've met plenty of people in this neighborhood who was ready to act like brothers with colored people." Mrs. Shuster adds, "When some poor family is in trouble other Jewish ladies and me make up a committee and go from door to door in the tenements. Everybody gives us something."

Bernie too is inspired. "I'll help all I can—I'll do anything!" he says. As he leaves the kitchen to tend to his paralyzed father in the next room, he "suddenly bends down and kisses Hannah in a long passionate embrace."

"It's all stitched together," Theresa continues, "the black market, antisemitism, war, crooked politics, the big trusts, the lynching of Negroes—you can't separate them." Bernie returns, informing his mother in a whispered aside that Louis's lips are moving and he is trembling, signs that the elderly man is dying. Meanwhile Hannah pleads earnestly that the group "please listen" to Theresa's plan.

Randy compares the scene to another famous episode in collective activism: "I was just thinking, . . . this is the way the nine Scottsboro boys got saved—they was framed up in the South, but good people, white and black, got parading for them all over the country, and that's what really saved them."

As the play closes, the voice of the invalid Louis is suddenly heard from the next room. He is not dying but reawakening, revived by the overheard meeting. He speaks for the first time in months, in a voice from offstage: "I'm not afraid of you Blackshirts! You'll never win in this country. Our sons will crush you like they did Hitler. Roosevelt will never die—No, no . . . it's here in our hearts. *Roosevelt, Roosevelt, the people!*"

At this, the neighbors in the kitchen lift their arms and "in harmonious rising chords of triumph" repeat the words, "*Roosevelt! Roosevelt! The People!*"

The play's central message was one acutely felt by Gold in the immediate postwar years, when he and his brothers learned that all but one member of Charles Granich's extended family had been killed in the Holocaust, likely during the Iaşi pogrom of June 1941. The one family member who had been saved, Manny recalled much later, had been away in the Soviet Union studying to be an engineer.

Song for Roosevelt has much to say about some key family matters that impinged on Gold's early and later life and that permeate this chapter. Louis, the bed-ridden invalid, directly recalls Gold's father, and Bernie's devastation at discovering him in a paralyzed condition is yet another indication of how all three Granich boys, and especially Irwin, would have experienced the long illness of Charles Granich. Bernie is devastated and confused by Louis's paralyzed state; as he seethes emotionally, his ambition begins to wane, in danger of being replaced by cynicism. The son of the dying paternal figure may be seen as a composite character, but the Granich brother he most resembles is Manny, who as a young man expressed the desire to be a labor lawyer and would have done so if he hadn't been forced to go West to avoid the World War I draft. Manny's second permanent ambition is the one expressed by Bernie: to become a chemist.

The play's treatment of hate-motivated attacks on young Jews by Catholic Christian Fronters is based on an incident from Gold's family life as well. In 1944, Nicky Granich, whom Gold called his "beloved first born," was beaten up by a gang of Catholic kids in his public school. In a *Change the World* column, Gold explained that the attackers had shrieked at the nine year-old "a horrible lesson learned in New York from their fascist teachers: 'Christ-killer! Christ-killer!'" After this attack, which occurred at nearly the same historical moment in which *Song for Roosevelt* is set, Gold stated, "Antisemitism is breaking forth in every corner of New York, a city where Jews have lived and labored for centuries." He implored his *Daily Worker* readers, "Is it not a symptom and a warning?"[76] The personal account of the attack on Nicky refers directly to yet another true-to-life feature of the drama: the complacent reactions of public officials who downplay hate-driven attacks, calling them "pranks" and "little accidents."

A strength of *Song for Roosevelt* is its message of empowerment, the encouragement to unite and fight against tyranny. The play resembles Philip Roth's 2004 novel, *The Plot Against America*, which envisions a fascist-led government and warns that it can happen here. But while Roth called his novel "an exercise in historical imagination,"[77] there is nothing imaginary about the basic story Gold tells.

Song for Roosevelt also tells us something about the postwar political context of the country to which Gold and his family were about to return. It was almost certainly intended to somehow reach an American audience and aid the campaign of Henry Wallace, Roosevelt's former vice president and the Progressive Party candidate for president in 1948. In that year, a celebration of Roosevelt's social legacy was an argument for Wallace, whose candidacy was supported by the Communist Party. But no liberal wave happened. The Progressives won no electoral votes, a defeat that presaged horrific times and the elevation of a reactionary senator from Wisconsin.

Chapter Eight

McCarthyism

(1950–1955)

It is only a few weeks since two clean-cut young men rang my door-bell. They looked like college graduates just started on a well-rutted bourgeois career. But this time the career was the F.B.I.

They said they had come to find out what I was doing and what theories I now held about proletarian literature and socialist realism, and the names of many literary people I knew, and such matters. I refused to share my thoughts with these bourgeois intellectuals. It is still one's technical right, under the poor old Constitution. So they went away.

Such visits are becoming terribly commonplace in the land of Walt Whitman. If a writer ever emitted in the past a single feeble poem against fascism or lynching he is on the big permanent FBI list of suspects containing, it is said, such names as Eleanor Roosevelt. . . .

Writers are being sent to prison for their opinions, the first time it has happened in America. The American writer begins to understand the feelings of European and Asian writers during their own time of fear, shame and fascism.

—Gold, autobiographical notes, c. 1951[1]

Rest and reconnecting with family were the immediate priorities for Mike and Elizabeth on their return from France in March 1950. Gathering their bags, they took a taxi from Pier 90 to the Mid-town Station and a bus for Wilmington, Vermont, to spend a few weeks with Manny and Grace at Higley Hill.

Figure 8.1. Higley Hill, early 1950s. Gold (upper left) and Manny (lower right). *Source:* Granich family.

By early April, Gold and Elizabeth had found an apartment and the family had finally come home, moving into a modest fifth-floor walk-up at 1783 Topping Avenue in the Bronx, where they would live on the margins of American society for a quiet but stressful six years.

It did not take long for them to realize that the climate had changed. For thirteen-year-old Nick, the day trips he often took with his father and brother were different and confusing. Walking the streets or riding the subway in the 1940s, he'd become used to seeing friends approach his father, a steady stream of well-wishers who shook hands, joked, made conversation, and commented on Mike's *Daily Worker* columns. After the return from France, Nick wondered what had happened. The excursions were strangely silent because people didn't speak to his father anymore. Old acquaintances seemed nervous and no one smiled.

The family's return to the United States coincided with a much weak-ened Communist Party and an atmosphere of pervasive fear, the results of processes that had begun in the Truman years with loyalty oaths, the attorney general's list of subversive organizations, and the criminal indictments of Communist leaders. By 1950 loyalty oaths were not only standard procedure in government agencies but also required in many schools, universities, and private corporations, where the practice of deflecting suspicion by denouncing colleagues was not unusual. FBI files from this period show the vigilance with which the Red Menace was monitored at all levels of society; the files often include handwritten letters to FBI director J. Edgar Hoover from ordinary Americans. Common citizens would frequently forward articles or books they deemed "un-American" while asking for clarification about Communist tactics and urging stricter crackdowns and bans. Hoover did nothing to discourage this practice and instead usually issued polite replies and enclosed helpful brochures that offered strategies for identifying the enemy.

Books and magazines were removed from stores and libraries, foreign and domestic mail was scrutinized for subversive influences, and the nation's artistic-intellectual life was frozen by the effects of both external regulation and self-censorship. In short, a powerful chill on the free expression of ideas hovered over the political landscape. Senator Joseph McCarthy of Wisconsin, a cynical opportunist who emerged as a national figure in 1949 and was therefore a relative latecomer to the witch-hunting zeal of the times, was nevertheless extremely effective at manipulating the media to advance his standing while seizing on mounting general anxieties that went far beyond his specific activities.

Michael Gold had lived through many forms of red-baiting and reactionary harassment; his very name was in part a response to the first Red Scare. But attempting to resume life in the suffocating Cold War climate after almost three years abroad was nevertheless a substantial shock. On his return Gold seems not to have understood, for example, that his newspaper work might now be impossible. Alan Wald speculates that after a brief attempt to fit in again at the *Daily Worker*, he "fell victim to staff cutbacks possibly connected with internal political struggles."[2] An unnamed FBI informant reported in April 1950 that Gold had "recently returned to work for the *Daily Worker* but that the *Daily Worker* did not pay Gold a salary, therefore a reception is being held to raise funds to pay Gold for his work on the paper."[3] Something went awry with this plan and Gold never worked for the paper again.

For a while, Gold kept up his usual busy calendar of speaking engagements, the first round of which were justified as part of his homecoming celebrations. But the cycle of his career and its related public activities—a routine he'd grown accustomed to and that once seemed permanent—was broken, and the matter of simply paying his rent became a struggle. To make ends meet, Gold accepted small fees for speaking engagements and gave guest lectures for literature courses at the New School for Social Research, the Jefferson School, and a few other Left-oriented New York colleges and night schools. For a short while he worked for Telepress, a Polish news agency, assembling news summaries from various daily papers. He took a job in a print shop and offered an evening writers' workshop with a tuition fee of a dollar per session. He even tried work in a venetian blinds factory but lasted less than a day.[4] After that he talked often about the idea of opening a coin laundry that would allow him to write a novel while patrons washed their clothes.

He spent parts of a season or two at Higley Hill, one of a handful of leftist camps that offered a refuge for children from the city whose parents were targets of McCarthy and red-baiting. These camps, whose story constitutes a little-known but fascinating piece of radical social history, provided a culturally rich, racially integrated environment that inculcated socialist ideals and culture among a generation that would eventually make major contributions to progressive causes in American society.

In 1953, Gold applied for summer work at Camp Unity in upstate New York, a multiracial, Communist-affiliated camp similar to Higley Hill. In the 1930s and 1940s, Gold had regularly been invited to speak and lecture at the Wingdale, New York, camp, sometimes as the headliner of its annual opening celebrations and visiting days. Now he worked as a clerical assistant, handing out towels and room keys to arriving guests, arranging accommodations, and performing duties that included cashiering in the camp restaurant, where Liz was also employed as a waitress.[5]

In July 1954 at Camp Unity, Gold would certainly have met Lorraine Hansberry, a young poet he'd read about in Paul Robeson's newspaper, *Freedom*, and would later admire for her spirited activism. Hansberry was the twenty-four-year-old director of Camp Unity's outdoor music and theatrical programs. That summer, which was the last one Mike and Elizabeth spent at the Wingdale camp, Hansberry wrote a letter to her husband, Robert Nemiroff, in which she shared her frustrations about the finances of the camp, explaining that some of the staff would have to be fired and how it angered her to have to do the dirty work of dismissing them.[6] The possibility that Hansberry and Gold, who at another time in history would have eagerly shared so much of value to them both, had to waste one of their potentially rich interactions at opposite ends of

Figure 8.2. Mike and Elizabeth worship the sun at Camp Unity, 1953. *Source:* Granich family.

an awkward staff cutback decision symbolizes the poisonous effects of McCarthyism.

Gold was not unproductive as a writer during the early 1950s; his work for *Masses & Mainstream*, with occasional articles in the *Guardian*, would have been enough for a writer without mouths to feed. But in reality, Elizabeth Granich accounted for most of the family's income as dictated by the blacklist. In addition to waiting tables in the summer months, she held a custodial job at a New York art gallery and later worked in a garment factory. With her law degree from the Sorbonne, she was overeducated for the jobs she accepted. But it should be remembered that, as Carl Granich pointed out in a 2018 phone interview, "She was blacklisted too."[7] According to her sons, Elizabeth was endlessly faithful and dedicated to her husband's literary work, never questioning the time and energy he gave to increasingly taxing and laborious projects that were invariably either unpaid or underpaid.

While there is ample evidence that financial realities deeply frustrated Mike, Liz's steadiness no doubt helped shield the boys from worry. As their father struggled to provide, the children "never heard him complain about it. He was happy most days," Nick recalled.[8] Carl agreed that the

mood in the Granich household was better than one might expect and
explained why:

> We lived close to the ground, but we lived a very rich life.
> Because of my dad's friendships, because of his cultural richness,
> we did everything with no money. We lived on the East Side
> in an ordinary cold-water flat and then in a modest walk-up
> in a five-story. But we'd go to Florida in the winter, and then
> I'm going over to take art lessons from Hugo Gellert and Fred
> Ellis, and banjo lessons from David Sear and Jerry Silverman.
> So we had this rich cultural life. We'd get Dodger ball tickets
> from Lester Rodney, the *Daily Worker* sportswriter. And then,
> one of the best doctors in New York would take care of my
> dad because he was a comrade. And the dentist would take
> care of our teeth for nothing. So we had this communistic,
> socialistic safety net that you couldn't put down on paper
> because it wasn't money. It was friendships.[9]

At home Mike and Elizabeth largely avoided discussing McCarthyism,
but the boys were instructed to be careful on the phone. They were told
about wire taps, and a clear rule was to never give names to unknown
callers. Ten-year-old Carl once thought he was talking to a family friend
and answered the questions of an FBI caller. The agent quizzed him about
his father's whereabouts, place of employment, and companions. "After I
hung up I realized what I'd done wrong," Carl recalled, "I told my dad,
and I was crying over that because I felt like I had disgraced the family."[10]
Unmarked cars with men inside were regularly parked outside the Topping
Avenue apartment building. Around this time Carl remembers walking
with his father in Manhattan when a friend approached from behind,
nodded, and said in passing, "Hey Mike they have a guy following you.
Yeah, there's a guy tailing you."

That Carl felt fear and shame after speaking with the FBI highlights
a problem distinct to Communist families, in which the children carried
the weight of what they often called "the secret" of their parents' political
beliefs. In some families this secret had to be kept from all but a very few
close friends, but for families of known leftists like Gold, a consciousness
that surveillance was a fact of life carried an added, at times overwhelm-
ing burden for children. Cultural histories indicate that in the McCarthy
period and especially around the time of the Rosenberg executions, young

children of Communists worried they would reveal information, either accidentally or under torture, that could make them responsible for the death of their own parents.[11] As they grew older, however, the fear and confusion felt by "red diaper babies" like Nick and Carl was compensated for by pride in their nonconformity and an awareness that Communists were more progressive and enlightened on many social justice issues than the compliant cultural mainstream.

Though FBI observation was constant, Bureau files of this period suggest that the agency actually ascertained little of value about Gold's personal life. A status update sent to Hoover in 1951 observed only that "Granich is always in his apartment and does not seem to be employed." The next year's annual memo to the FBI director was slightly more bleak: "Unemployed, does occasional writing, suffers from diabetes."[12] Where the ascertainment of private or personal knowledge is concerned, FBI documents of this period are notoriously inaccurate, containing puzzling errors that have prompted some who experienced surveillance to retroactively dismiss the constant attention as only a minor nuisance. But David Wellman, who lived under FBI scrutiny at the same time the Granich family did, believes that the voyeuristic forays into the lives of Communists should be classified as "state terrorism," an abhorrent act with significant human consequences: "They were trying to put fear of police power in the minds of the people they spied on," Wellman observed, and "to a large degree, it worked."[13]

In October 1951 a pair of FBI agents, perhaps the "clean-cut young men" described at the start of this chapter, arrived unannounced in order to catch Gold at home at the Topping Avenue apartment. They reported that Gold "readily admitted his identity, and also admitted that he and his wife had attended the founding meeting of the Peace Information Center held on April 3, 1950, at the home of Mr. and Mrs. DAN RUBENBERG, 100 Riverside Drive, New York City." Gold no doubt yielded these responses because he surmised that the agents knew this much already. But for the rest of the interview he obfuscated and evaded. "The subject claimed that he and his wife attended the meeting in the belief that it was to be a social affair," read the FBI memo of the encounter. "He stated that he was unable to furnish any information as to the proceedings of the meeting as he could not recall anything about it." And of course Gold divulged no names: "He also said that he had no recollection of the identity of any other person who had attended the meeting."[14]

What Gold "could not recall" was that the April 1950 meeting, which took place just three weeks after his return from France and while the

"Welcome Home Mike Gold" events were still going on, was organized in order to prepare for a May Day for Peace rally sponsored by the D.C.-area Party and held at a Jewish Cultural Center in the capital.

Prominent among Gold's associations at this time was the Peace Information Center of the American Peace Crusade. This organization, which the House Un-American Activities Committee described as "an organic part of the Communist Peace offensive," had been identified by HUAC as responsible for the circulation of the Stockholm Peace Petition, which demanded a worldwide ban on atomic weapons while declaring also that "any government which first uses atomic weapons against any other country whatsoever will be committing a crime against humanity and should be dealt with as a war criminal." To aid and advance the U.S. peace movement, Gold had attended the April 3 meeting and the subsequent May 5 Washington rally with W. E. B. Du Bois, Shirley Graham, Howard Fast, and Elizabeth Moos.

This event was of special interest to the FBI, not only because of the prominence of those attending, but because HUAC documents saw the World Peace Congress as a "front group organized under Communist initiative in various countries throughout the world as part of the campaign against the North Atlantic Defense Pact." By August 1950 the Justice Department was sending threatening letters requesting that the organization be registered as an agent of a foreign power. In early 1951, Du Bois replied that they were acting as Americans for America and their work was supported by funds raised solely in the United States.[15] Du Bois and four others would nevertheless be indicted and charged under the Foreign Agents Registration Act in February 1951.

Several FBI informers attended the May 5 rally in DC, where Gold was the main speaker. He was introduced by *Daily Worker* Washington editor Robert Hall, who stated, "To those acquainted with and active in the revolutionary movement, it is known that Mike Gold is ours, and that he is one of the great proletarian novelists." Gold then spoke about his experiences in France, Romania, Hungary, and Czechoslovakia, referring to the "new democracies" of these countries, in which the citizens were receiving from the state newspapers the "socialist truth" that in the United States was only printed in the *Daily Worker*. One point Gold made, which probably elicited a strong audience response as it was particularly apt at the outset of the 1950s, was recorded verbatim by FBI observers: "I did not see any Iron Curtain in Eastern Europe," Gold declared; "The only Iron Curtain I know of is the one I saw in New York, on my return."[16]

The FBI harassment and his daily economic struggles help explain why Gold experienced some periods of frustration and writer's block in the early 1950s. But he managed to complete both his own articles and regular editorial work for *Masses & Mainstream*, where he served alongside notables such as Paul Robeson, Du Bois, Shirley Graham, Meridel Le Sueur, Joseph North, John Howard Lawson, and the emerging poet-playwright Lorraine Hansberry. Gold also wrote poetry, published a series of articles in the *National Guardian*, and completed *The Honorable Pete*, a substantial and interesting play about the life of Communist New York councilman Pete Cacchione.

Under the mistrustful atmosphere of McCarthyism, there was a general tendency among the blacklisted or marginalized members of the Old Left to seek each other out for reassurance and safe haven. In Gold's case, the job of remaining upbeat at home seems to have left a need for outside commiseration with a friend of his youth, someone who had known him in his Irwin Granich days. In 1950 he reached out to his one-time fiancée Dorothy Day, whom he hadn't seen since the 1930s, with visits and a series of letters.

The lifelong friendship of Mike Gold and Dorothy Day is a poignant story. They had met and became lovers in Greenwich Village, working tirelessly for the *Call* and the *Masses* in the time of the Great War and the Russian Revolution when, as Day remembered, "We were young, we had found ourselves, in that we had a cause, and we served it on our writing."[17] Though their engagement was brief, they shared a bond that kept them in each other's thoughts through difficult times. For Day, it mattered that Gold encouraged her to write for the *New Masses* and, more important, came to see her on Staten Island in the late 1920s while she was unhappily contemplating the sacrifices necessary for her religious conversion. Staying with brothers Manny and George in a bungalow just down the road, "Irwin" as Day liked to call him, was an unselfish listener as they walked and talked on the beach through the time of Dorothy's anguish. Though their breakup in 1918 had been hard for Gold, he never for a moment tried to dissuade Day from the step she would take, something for which she would always be grateful. According to Day biographer Kate Hennessey, "Coming from an Orthodox Jewish family, Mike never appeared to be concerned or afraid of Dorothy's religiosity. He had seen and identified it years before."[18]

While still in the hospital after the birth of her daughter Tamar in 1926, Day wrote an account of her childbirth experience that she sent

Gold, who at the time was editor of *New Masses*.[19] Gold made the article famous by sending it out for reprinting in Soviet newspapers and Marxist outlets all over the world. In fall 1927, despite Day's family commitments, she and Gold also saw each other in Boston while both were protesting the execution of Sacco and Vanzetti.

Kate Hennessey's book, *The World Will Be Saved by Beauty*, adds much to what we know about the relationship between the two great radicals. Hennessey, who is Day's granddaughter, sees significance in the fact that her grandmother never denied the "special bond" she had with Mike, though she was sometimes accused of being a Communist because of it. When they were engaged to be married in 1917, their connection had only begun, and it somehow reached deeper levels than a fairly serious romantic love implied; ten years later, Gold was the best man at the wedding of Day's sister Della. The enduring friendship "helped change Dorothy's life" because Gold exemplified for his friend the costs and difficulties of following one's conscience. As Hennessey concludes, "Of all Dorothy's friends, it was Mike Gold, she felt, who understood the misery she was going through during her conversion to Catholicism."[20]

In the late 1930s their beliefs and ideals took them in opposite directions, and Gold stopped visiting because he believed that now that Day was a Catholic, she was aligning with the fascists in the Spanish Civil War. Gold's columns didn't publicly criticize Dorothy's political stance, but Hennessey senses that his "faint praise" for the *Catholic Worker* as "an earnest little paper" and for Dorothy as an "honest person" may have been hard for her to bear. As Hennessey explains, "It didn't help that in 1936 the *Catholic Worker* published an article critical of Russian totalitarianism, and Mike Gold would not hear any criticism of the Soviet Union."[21]

The hiatus in the Gold-Day relationship lasted from the Spanish Civil War until March 1950, when Mike renewed the friendship with a visit to the *Catholic Worker* office on Chrystie Street. He had just returned from France and hadn't seen Dorothy in fifteen years. Liz was with him; they both embraced Dorothy, took turns telling stories about their travels, then showed pictures of their two sons, the first named "Nicolai," Day recounted, "after Lenin."

After the reunion they corresponded, and in 1952 the Granich family spent a busy afternoon and evening at Day's Catholic Worker farm on Staten Island, where the boys played baseball, and then hungrily devoured the French bread Day had baked for them herself. Gold presented Dorothy with a print they'd brought from France, a painted representation of a pilgrimage to the shrine of St. Anne of Brittany that Dorothy later had framed and hung in the farm dining room. On the same visit, Dorothy gave Mike a copy of her beautifully written autobiography, *The Long Loneliness*. He read it quickly and wrote her an extended letter about it, saying that "much of it was very good" while honestly and sharply disagreeing with aspects of Day's outlook that he saw as historically regressive.

In that letter, Gold then pulled back from his critical tone, perhaps remembering that with tyranny all around them, it was best for radicals to cultivate solidarity: "I wish there were five million Catholics like you and your friends in this country," he wrote. "The Senator McCarthys could not exist then. The world would be spared another atomic war and extermination." Then he waxed nostalgic, inviting his old girlfriend to vicariously relive the better times of their youth: "Well Dorothy, to hell with it. I am sentimental and like to think of you on my old street. Do you remember or don't you that I once took you to call at our home on Chrystie Street? I believe you stayed overnight with us and my mother fed you and marveled over the unknown from across the tracks."[22]

In closing, Gold broached the economic pressures of blacklisting that he'd likely suppressed during their visit: "Liz has been looking for a job again. So have I. When I saw some of the poor victims on your farm I was again reminded of the heartless way capitalism treats human beings. Western civilization—bah! The member of an African tribe had better security and brotherhood. Give our best to the farm friends."[23]

Later that year, another missive from Gold to Day took a casual tone that suddenly turned plaintive: "The economics of the moment has me stymied," he wrote. "Our oldest boy works after school; Liz has done odd jobs, and I have worked for weeks in a little factory, a printshop, and other odd jobs. It is lousy. Am trying to get a camp job for the summer. Have done a few writing bits. Sometimes I think jail will be a relief from this futility."[24]

The financial hopelessness was severe enough to produce a solipsistic, almost existential, anguish: "Dorothy, if I was a bachelor again I would not marry but would come down and occupy a bunk on your farm and write poetry for the rest of my life." This passage might sound like an insult to Elizabeth, but Gold was probably reacting to a combination of financial stress and unrealized literary ambition rather than marital or family conflict. Later in the letter, perhaps to atone for the self-indulgent venting of frustrations, he made a small monetary offering: "Dorothy I enclose a buck for the paper or whatever—have been getting the paper for the past year without payment." Since the 1930s Day had been sending Gold gratis copies of the *Catholic Worker* for reasons personal and political. "Though I know it is a propaganda effort," Gold said, "I think I should pay something for paper and printing at least."

A final letter to Day from this period began, "Delighted you can come Wednesday night" and gave detailed directions to the Topping Avenue apartment. Gold then poured out his complex and self-revealing emotions:

> Dorothy I had some poems in the *Mainstream* for July—did you see them by chance? I was glad that in my advanced age I could still feel strongly enough to write poetry—it is really the basis of literature—I have been reading a history of Irish writing—did you ever hear of the O'Rahilly, one of the Hedge Poets, a bitter, wandering man who chanted in inns and cursed poverty and the British in Gaelic rhymes—he was blind and homeless at the end—I wish I had one of his last poems here to type out for you.[25]

Here Gold is conflating the Hedge schoolmasters, who kept Irish culture alive by writing and teaching in Gaelic in the nineteenth century, and Michael Joseph O'Rahilly, an Irish republican nationalist hero killed in the 1916 Easter uprising. "Irish history has a fascination for me," he continued, "because the people seemed to combine rebellion with poetry and suffered through the centuries almost as much as the Jews—it is a pity how this great tradition of poetry and rebellion seems to have died among the U.S. Irish—they were better people in our youth, I seem to remember."[26]

The passage is deeper than it sounds, carrying hints and implied meanings. Addressing an Irish companion of his youth, Gold isn't really generalizing about Irish Americans; instead he is making statements about specific people. In their younger days, Irwin and Dorothy had both known Eugene O'Neill. Dorothy had been taken by O'Neill and would speak often, even in her later years, about the time when she, O'Neill, and Gold were a close group of friends. Writing to Dorothy and thinking about the Irish of his youth would have made Gold recall the heartbreak and jealousy that preceded his exile in Mexico, when the talented, brooding playwright came between them. Without having to name these poetic and revolutionary "better" Irish, Gold was sharing with Dorothy his memories and reflections about her and O'Neill. And when it came to the current generation's decline, it wasn't even necessary for Gold to name the bullying, decidedly antipoetic Irish American who was on everyone's mind in 1952, the counterrevolutionary senator from Wisconsin.

The fact that the Gold-Day friendship was renewed under McCarthyism seems significant, and it tells us something about the kind of radical commitment the two shared. Kate Hennessey's stance, that it was something about the "hardening times" that led those from the radical past to seek one another out, is likely accurate. "And perhaps," Hennessey muses insightfully, "it was because Dorothy kept moving in the face of the hostility . . . unperturbed, unshaken, and unafraid. Along with Mike Gold, she was a radical who endured, who never got tired."[27]

In his letters to Dorothy Day, Gold also called attention to his recent poems in *Masses & Mainstream*. He had reason to be pleased with these works, which comprised a series of six verses that appeared under the title "Spring in the Bronx" in the July 1952 issue. They offer a fascinating window into Gold's inner life while he was still readjusting culturally after his time in France. From a notably global perspective that sensed and judged the cultural egocentrism of the United States, he weighed varied phenomena, including a booming consumer economy, a new wave of immigration, and the war in Korea.

The first poem in the series, "The Killers," considered the effects of American militarism as a hegemonic concept that saturated popular material culture and penetrated even into child development, with eventually violent consequences worldwide:

A mother wheels her baby down the street
he wears the stylish two guns and western holster
made so fashionable by toy merchants this year
the baby shoots and shoots at his proud mother
nobody is surprised to see a baby shoot his mother

. . .

it is free enterprise
the murder of truth and innocence
it is big business
my heart is troubled when I see
this baby shoot a mother in Korea

The final line, which presents a sudden and striking extension of Gold's meaning, ties together in a cause-effect relation the opening domestic image with the global consequences of Truman's attempt at Communist "containment" on the Korean Peninsula.

The next work, "The Buds Are Open," continues the antiwar theme by directly addressing "Mister Faraway President" with the words, "not all the garbage in the Bronx / is as dirty as your war / your napalm massacre war / your son-destroying war!" Both this and the first poem's allusion to the Korean conflict show that warnings about the disastrous combination of militarism with the seeking of corporate profits—the "military-industrial complex"—were current long before Dwight Eisenhower's farewell address of January 1961 gave the name to that nexus, which, despite the warnings, later helped escalate and determine American intervention in Vietnam.

While in France, Gold had witnessed firsthand the disastrous effects on the French culture and people of the First Indo-China War. In July 1950 he had published an article on the atrocity known in France as "the dirty war," declaring that "the French people are paying for this forerunner of the Wall Street attack on Korea with their blood and living standards" and that "There's many a lesson in their experience for the American people today."[28] Long before Dien Bien Phu, Gold predicted the failure of the American-financed French war in Vietnam. His attacks and protests against the Korean War constitute early and fierce criticisms of the direct US intervention he also foresaw in Vietnam.

Gold's third poem in the series, "Boom Industry," records and comments on a form of hypocrisy specific to domestic US society in the McCarthy period:

The churches call with a sweet clang of bells
. . .
America's number one informer has been given another award
just made Professor of Christian Ethics in a Bronx university
can Christ hope to build brotherhood on such rotten foundations
the project is dubious I do not think it can succeed

This informing has become a new American boom industry

While Gold's title forged a valid figurative link between economics and obedience to antidemocratic Cold War orthodoxies, the poem also offers interesting images of the world just outside his Bronx apartment, a location from which it was easy for a semi-imprisoned poet to sense his society's "rotten foundations" of hypocrisy.

The fourth poem, "The Happy Corpse," offers a new take on the old issue of Jewish cultural assimilation by depicting

> a gray little Chaplin refugee
> escaped from the Hitler furnaces
> to become a Fuller Brush salesman here
> now he is 100 per cent American
> with stern faith in our toilets frigidaires and autos
> he worships in the chromium temple of success
> Hitler's victim now believes in the Chase National Bank.

It's hard not to read these lines as in some ways a micro-version of the journey that took the ghetto-born Itzhok Granich from Old World immigrant culture to disorienting modern consumerism. The Marxist theories that Gold adopted consistently expressed faith in machines and industrial technology to meet the material needs of the masses, but at the same time, he resisted certain innovations. Gold never learned to drive a car and was fond of half-jokingly saying, "I was born in the horse and buggy era and I'll stay there."[29]

"Bronx Express" offers a gritty snapshot of the proletarian and bourgeois masses packed into a subway car "like stockyard cattle." It also comments on the cultural influence of Hemingway, whom Gold had described in *The Hollow Men* as the nation's best storyteller nevertheless "ignorant of social reality."[30]

> be they sick or well strong humble or foolish
> all are kneaded into a dough of exploited flesh
>
> . . .
>
> truckmen in eisenhower jackets
> Jewish Italian Puerto Rican needle trade workers
> reading newspapers that preach atombomb war
> low wage clerks in neat blue suits doing crosswords
> and crisp young stenos with silken legs
> dodging reality in a brave Hemingway novel
> a longshoreman dozes darkly in his dungarees
> electricians teachers domestics and bookkeepers
> nobody is a tall elegant Hemingway hero

Gold uses the final poem in the series, "Ode to a Landlord," to
consider his current economic hardships alongside his place in New York
history and his role as an inheritor of the city's artistic, social and political
movements:

> New York is mine
> New York is my village
> every street has known my grief and joy
> . . .
> landlord of the white eyelashes and fat nervous mouth
> you really can't evict me from my home
> I was born over a Bowery saloon
> and peddled papers along that street of the damned
> I worked in office factories and on trucks
> I raised corn peas and roses by Raritan bay
> and dug clams for the nightly chowder there
> lived too by the Coney Island beach
> where Walt Whitman once chanted Homer
> to the startled seagulls of Brooklyn

It's worth noting that these images, which could be seamlessly inserted
into the text of *Jews without Money*, also represent the McCarthy-driven
realities of a mid-century world in which Gold must have felt once again
impoverished, once again a Jew without money. But despite what he'd
called "advanced age," he retained the ability to "feel strongly" and observe
dynamically in celebrating new expressions of multiculturalism:

> But you can't own Walt Whitman or his people
> . . . . we are always getting fresh reinforcements
> now the Puerto Ricans are arriving to our help
> starved and perscuted and exploited
> like earlier immigrant Jews or Italians
> they bring us new valor and song
> hurrah for the brave Puerto Ricans
> with their bright colors and lovely girls
> they renew our song and solidarity
> my family is a big brave family
> . . . . maybe you will evict me into one of your jails
> where you are throwing my family nowadays

as a magic cure for your fatal disease
but I will be happier than you
more secure and with healthier roots in life
owning more of New York than you
though I cannot pay my rent

As the case of Julius and Ethel Rosenberg became an international cause in 1953, Gold was among the writers, artists, actors, poets, and scientists who went on record with pleas for clemency. He was present also at the mass meeting in Manhattan on Friday, June 19, the evening of the execution. Along with thousands of protesters who had tried to gather at Union Square, he was forced by a barrier of police into a narrow area on Fifteenth Street between the Square and Fifth Avenue. As Hugo Gellert recalled, the crowd, hemmed in and restless, began watching the clock on the tower of the Metropolitan Life building. As eight o'clock, the hour of execution, approached, the cries of the multitude grew in a steady crescendo, changing from shouted slogans to intermittent piercing screams, followed by a final low wail that visibly terrified the police, who could contain the bodies of the demonstrators but not their echoing lamentations.

Understandably, the author of *Jews without Money* was shaken by the gruesome case of the Rosenbergs, in which the Jewish American parents of two young sons were brutally scapegoated for the loss of hydrogen bomb technology to the Soviet Union. Gold wrote a lamentation about the judicial lynching titled, "The Rosenberg Cantata," which appeared soon after the execution. Like the chants and recitations Gold published beginning in the 1920s, the poem foregrounds a need to hear the cries and "voices" of human victims above the clamor of bestial capitalist culture:

The Beast

I have muddied the People's brain with movies and television
I have deafened their hearts with money and dead art
I have deafened them to the great voices
The People can never hear you
And every bank and steel mill has sworn
That this is the American Century
And the Rosenbergs must die.

. . . .
Confess only that you stole the Bomb.
I need your confession
It is a battle won
In the war for the American Century
          (a silence)
Here is the key to your prison
Confess and live.
You can gain the bright crown of success
Confess daily at treason trials and on television
Become famous informers rich and admired like Hollywood
    stars
And your children will have joy.
          (a silence)
Be practical, make a deal and live,
Justice and truth are commodities
The world is a jungle,
Its only law victory or death.[31]

Thirteen-year-old Carl Granich was also traumatized by the Rosenbergs' ghastly fate. An hour before sundown on the night of the execution
that has been called "the most savage moment of the American cold
war,"[32] Gold's younger son walked alone to a Bronx synagogue, where he'd
been asked to participate in a memorial gathering for the doomed Jewish
parents. Playing his guitar to accompany the hymns of lamentation, he
was frightened and unnerved, as the police and protesters on Fifteenth
Street had been, by sounds of grieving and observable misery of especially
the older Jewish women. "It was one of the first times I'd played for an
audience, and I wondered why they had asked me," Carl recalled.

Included in the family news Gold had sent to Dorothy Day a year
earlier was the report that "we have lots of music around these days" and
that Nicky and Carl were experimenting with various instruments. Gold
played harmonica and concertina, Liz played the piano, and the Granich
family often sang folk songs at home. But the primary musical influence
on the children was a role model they'd seen so often that he became
an honorary uncle. When Carl showed an interest in music, his father
encouraged him and told him to pick an instrument. Carl said, "I want
to learn guitar and banjo because I love Pete Seeger."[33]

While Gold was on a national speaking tour in May 1954, he visited Seeger in San Francisco. After the meeting, Pete sent a letter to the Granich boys; it was a short note that reveals quite a lot about his relationship to the family:

Dear Nicky and Carl (and all the musicians at home):

It was terrific to see Mike and talk to him. Heard all the dope about you two. Congrats to Carl on M & A. and I hope Nick, old boy, that you get into City. Maybe it will be a better joint with a few more HH'ers there.

California is wonderful. I could write for pages on it but won't. If you ever decide to travel à la Danny North come see us in Cal. The weather is just dreamy if you like fog. When Mike gets back don't let him mislead you about Marl de Mumza. That's my dog. He and Mike just didn't quite make it but he (the dog) is a good hound at heart. This is just a note so I'll end it, much love to your mom. And my best to everyone even Ester F. if you see her.

Wish I could hear you fellows at a hoe-down.

With an eye on what the future may bring.

Fraternally,

Pete

P.S. Love to Mace and Granny if you see them.

To the younger Granich boy, Seeger sends congratulations "on M & A," New York's famous High School of Music and Art on West 135th Street in Harlem, where Carl had just been accepted and where he began studies in music and drawing that fall semester. A magnet for talented students and teachers, the school had already produced a large number of notable alumni. Actor Billy Dee Williams was in a class two years ahead of Carl, writer Erica Jong was a year behind him, singer Diahann Carroll had just graduated, and artist Stephen Stiles arrived in Carl's second year there.

Seeger also wished luck to Nick Granich on getting into "City," or City College of New York, where the seventeen-year-old would attend classes that fall. He also hoped Nick might meet "more HH'ers" there: alumni of the Higley Hill summer camp where Seeger always sang and where Nick and Carl spent enriching summers. It was natural that many children of Higley Hill would find their way to CCNY, a school sometimes known as "the Harvard of the proletariat."

Seeger also said he wanted to hear Gold's sons play at a "hoe-down," a term that can mean either a type of square dance or a folk music social gathering, the latter of which was obviously Seeger's meaning. At any other time, Seeger probably would have used the word "hootenanny," which would have been a more potent near-synonym. He and Woody Guthrie had first heard this term during their 1940s travels in the Pacific Northwest, and they had since developed the leftist "hootenanny" into "a new form of participatory music."[34] As Seeger famously defined them, hootenannies brought together amateur and professional musicians young and old, while fusing the roles of performer and audience to achieve an elevating, communal, often euphoric experience. Instructing audiences about the rituals of the "hootenanny"—both in person and in a pamphlet published in the bulletin of the group he helped found, People's Songs—was a key part of the "naming work"[35] Seeger did during his several decades as the most important advocate of American folk music.

The well-attended "hoots" of the People's Songs artists had received national attention in the late 1940s. Since then, however, the FBI surveillance and targeting of leftist musicians by HUAC had become more threatening. The intentionally depoliticized songs of the Weavers were a response to these pressures. By gearing their work to popular taste, the Weavers had sold more than four million records between 1950 and 1953. But investigations into past associations and song lyrics quickly caught up even with chart-topping artists. By 1954 Seeger's career had been brought to a standstill by the powerfully effective blacklist of the House Un-American Activities Committee. When he caught up with Mike Gold and wrote this letter to the Granich boys, Seeger was on a forced hiatus during which he did intermittent concerts at obscure venues in the San Francisco–Palo Alto areas while awaiting the HUAC subpoena that would come in early 1955.

In this context, "hootenanny" had become a highly charged term, a specific, named irritant of anti-Communist agencies and organizations at a time in which, as Seeger knew, the eyes and ears of the state were everywhere. Whether out of reflexive fear or conscious choice, Seeger substituted the politically safer term "hoe-down," even in this personal letter.

Nevertheless Seeger was communicating the desire to share with Gold's sons what a hootenanny offered. A central purpose of the ritual form Seeger had cultivated to perfection was for well-known leftist performers to initiate new "people's artists." In New York, for example, the first fall hootenanny was billed as a summer camp reunion that picked up where camps like Higley Hill or Camp Unity had left off. Hootenannies also gave vital emotional support—what Mario Casetta termed "sustenance, strength and morale"[36]—to Communists at a time when the movement was in crisis.

As folk historian Robbie Lieberman argued, group singing "was clearly an effective internal 'weapon,' helping to build and maintain the collective self-confidence necessary to challenge the dominant culture."[37] Carl Granich's banjo teacher David Sear characterized the euphoria of these events as "the most exciting musical experience of my life in many ways."[38] People's Songs artist Ernie Lieberman explained that participative music "reinforce[d] the feelings of the people on the Left, that what they were doing was right . . . and that they would win."[39] In effect, Pete Seeger's letter imagines sharing this ritual with Carl and Nick.

Seeger signs off "fraternally," a fitting sentiment because his letter had affirmed close bonds with "all the musicians" in the Granich home. It's striking also that the affirmative, ecstatic experience the letter alludes to is the opposite of the frighteningly mournful musical ritual Carl had experienced exactly a year earlier on the night of the Rosenberg execution. Substantively, Pete Seeger's reaching out to the Granich boys replaces fear with elation to offset the boys' fears and satisfy a deeply human need.

In the letter's postscript, Seeger assumed the role of a family insider, in part by remembering Gold's brother and sister-in-law in a joking, familiar way: "love to Mace and Granny." They had all spent time together at Mannie and Grace's summer camp. Seeger's standard charge for a night of singing at leftist camps was fifty dollars, but he always sang for free at Higley Hill. At the cabin the Seegers were building in Beacon, New York, Nick and Carl met Pete's wife, Toshi, and passed a working weekend, mixing batches of mortar and sleeping in cots on the back porch.

In this period, the Granich family had a Thanksgiving dinner at the Brooklyn Heights home of W. E. B. Du Bois and Shirley Graham Du Bois, who had just experienced a particularly caustic Cold War trauma. Despite Du Bois's advanced age—he was eighty-three and Graham was only fifty-five—the couple had married in 1951. The civil ceremony was rushed because of Du Bois's indictment for alleged violation of the Foreign Agents Registration Act, but really for his expressed belief that "In modern war all contestants lose" and that the hydrogen bomb should be banned.[40] The wedding was moved up because Graham wanted to ensure she would have the visiting rights of a legal spouse by the time Du Bois was arraigned and incarcerated. Two days after the ceremony, Graham broke into uncontrolled sobs at the sight of her venerable octogenarian husband being frisked, fingerprinted, and handcuffed.[41]

After Du Bois was freed on bail, he and Graham spent most of 1951 organizing and touring with a national committee to raise defense funds for the upcoming trial. The final result was that Du Bois barely avoided a prison term: charges were dismissed in November, after nine months of proceedings in the case, when it was clear that the state lacked evidence and that public opinion was turning against the prosecution. Du Bois recalled that the Department of Justice "had made a frantic last minute search of all possible sources of information" and that "practically every person" connected with the Peace Information Center "was visited by FBI agents, often two or three times." The aforementioned knock on Gold's door in October 1951 had been part of that last minute search, and its details support Du Bois's attendant claim that "little was discovered."[42]

With the nightmare over, Du Bois and Graham pooled their dwindling financial resources to make a down payment on a house in Brooklyn Heights, just across the East River from lower Manhattan. In their search for a home in spring 1952, they had used an "anonymous purchaser" out of fear that no one would sell to them directly, and they were lucky to find a well-maintained property owned previously by playwright Arthur Miller.

To recuperate from a tumultuous phase, the couple made a conscious effort to create a comfortable, secure domestic refuge and invited Michael Gold's family as guests for their first Thanksgiving in the new home. On the morning of the holiday, Mike, who had been doing most of the family cooking, got up early and made a Romanian eggplant dish. At midday, he, Elizabeth, Nick, and Carl took the downtown train from the 175th Street station. Around the table that evening was a diverse multigenerational group, brought together by difficulty but bearing up under the weight of persecution.

Like Gold, Du Bois was still on the Cold War blacklist and unemployed. His ties to Communists of Gold's ilk continued to arouse suspicion; he had been abandoned even by the NAACP, an organization he had helped create. For his new wife as well, who had an FBI file even more extensive than her husband's, the Red Scare had taken a toll. On Graham's national fund-raising tour for her husband's defense fund, she had more than once felt the threat of physical violence; her books were banned and her speaking engagements greatly curtailed. The careers of certain writers who were in accord with the prevailing conservative atmosphere were being elevated, while all others suffered correspondingly. Many in the latter category, as Graham's biographer notes, "were Jewish or African American."[43] Many of their old friends had ostracized them. The State Department had revoked the passports of both Graham and her husband.

The potentially bleak Thanksgiving gathering was remembered fondly by Nick and Carl Granich, who felt the genuine warmth of their hosts and their evident happiness. Despite his reputation for aloofness, Du Bois showed a kind interest in the Granich boys, inquiring about their schoolwork and experiences in Paris, quizzing them jokingly on the French language. He spoke French with Elizabeth while Gold helped Graham in the kitchen. Graham's twenty-seven-year-old son David was there also; as his mother knew and regretted, he too had been suffering the effects of the antileft hysteria because of his filial ties.[44] After dinner Elizabeth played the piano. As the evening wore on, Graham's doting on her husband became a friendly joke. Carl, a budding artist as well as a musician, presented their hosts with a drawing he'd made, and Nick recited a Luis Aragon poem in French.

The occasion, in which countercultural, defiant families took strength from each other, is all the more thought-provoking in light of the fact that Graham was then undergoing a crisis in her racial thinking. On finding herself subject to multiple and intersecting forms of intolerance as a black female Communist, Graham had decided that there were very few whites she could trust. She had been denying the requests of white researchers for access to her husband's papers, alleging that the "frantic interest in Negroes" of certain whites was nothing more than "a tool to perfect the machinery of control and to continue . . . enslavement," adding, "White America has forced me to this position."[45] Having learned through long experience the need for self-protection, she had also, through her marriage, willingly accepted the role of protecting Du Bois. But on this Thanksgiving, as she and her husband recovered from a series of painful reminders of their vulnerability, the great race-feminist welcomed the Graniches across the color line and into her carefully arranged domestic life.

It seems these family-centered, cross-generational, and often cross-racial bonds were an important feature of a decade in which spiritually sustaining relationships among radicals were a necessity. Dorothy Day, for example, believed it significant that she had gathered shells on the Long

Island beach, not only with Irwin Granich in the 1920s, but also with Elizabeth Granich in the 1950s. Day, Du Bois, Seeger, and Gold surely knew as well that the ties they formed and nurtured could confirm negative suspicions and further alienate them from conformist sensibilities. Being consigned to the margins was the price paid by a long list of twentieth-century artists whose creativity was inseparable from their activism.

In 1951, Manny and Grace Granich were identified as "communist functionaries" by two former Party members testifying in the ongoing House investigations. They received word of a subpoena that August, while Gold's son Carl was with them as a camper at Higley Hill. Manny and Grace were called before the House Committee on Un-American Activities to "answer charges of having engaged in Communist activities both here and abroad." They had almost expected the HUAC subpoena because months earlier, the Justice Department had sent agents to conduct audits of all the Higley Hill financial records, apparently looking for Moscow Gold. They thought the committee was interested in their activities in China, where they had published an openly pro-Communist English-language magazine in the late 1930s, and perhaps in activities at Higley Hill, where the couple unapologetically inculcated progressivism. But Manny and Grace were surprised that the HUAC committee members were apparently not interested in the couple's time in China or in Manny's visit to the Soviet Union. "They were just using us to confirm that members of the State Department were in touch with Communists," Manny said afterward. "They were acting only on McCarthy's prodding to get at the State Department."[46]

In his testimony Manny refused to discuss his activities or to say whether he was or ever had been a member of the Communist Party. He was called a "very uncooperative" witness and threatened with a citation for contempt of Congress. Grace took the stand next, but the committee recessed for the day before she was asked the key question about party affiliation. The next day she told the told the congressional committee that she was "a very loyal citizen of the United States" but joined her husband in taking the Fifth Amendment. As the congressmen questioned her, they repeatedly referred to Higley Hill as a "communist school" and Grace repeatedly corrected them, pointing out that it was a summer camp. After being called "a constant and continuing menace to the security of the United States," she too was threatened with a contempt citation that did not materialize.[47]

Though Manny and Grace would resist HUAC attempts to label their camp a school, it is certain that Mike Gold's son Carl learned things at Higley Hill that could not be matched in any formal educational setting. Carl Granich would come to love Higley Hill, where he spent the summers from age ten until he was fifteen. In 1955 he and his best friend, the future Oscar-winning screenwriter Marshall Brickman, worked as counselors for that year's ten to eleven year-old group. There Carl also met and shared activities with Eric Foner, the son of the prolific Marxist labor historian Philip Foner. Eric, who was born in 1943, knew Carl Granich at Higley Hill from 1952 to 1955 and later became a two-time winner of the prestigious Bancroft Prize for his works on race and social conflict in post–Civil War US history. Foner, who is now a professor at Columbia, remembers Higley Hill fondly, not only for the usual camp activities such as swimming and ping-pong, but also for the security it offered young people of leftist backgrounds as "a kind refuge from McCarthyism."[48]

Bettina Aptheker, a Higley Hill camper in the early 1950s who grew up to become a nationally known professor and social activist for feminism and free speech, wrote in her 2006 memoir that the camp's educational programs had a "huge emotional impact." Not only was the camp integrated, she recalled, but "racial equality and civil rights were emphasized in our everyday activities, in the songs we sang and in the stories we were told." The white and black campers, she recalls, "sang freedom songs and spirituals, and were taught their meaning embedded in the history of slavery." Of course Mike Gold had been a forceful advocate of these songs before Bettina Aptheker was born. She fondly remembered Seeger's singing visits to Higley Hill and the clear emphasis of his songs on peace and social change, along with camp movie nights that included antifascist films like *How Green Was My Valley* and *The Grapes of Wrath*. In the McCarthy years, she remembered, excited discussions of social issues often continued long into the night through whispered debates from the campers' bunk beds.[49]

Manny likewise commented on the educational philosophy of Higley Hill, explaining that it was an atmosphere in which the children felt free to take any personal problem to him and Grace at any time night or day, and where the campers helped plan each day's activities, often based on what kind of animal care was needed, what new play could be performed, what speaker or musical performer was visiting, what the campers had learned or discovered on the day before, or what new problems they were having. When the armistice halting the Korean War was accepted on July 27, 1953, one of the campers, a boy of twelve, approached Manny as he was making the announcement and asked, "Does this mean there'll be no more Jim Crow?" Manny's reaction was to schedule on open, all-camp discussion of that issue the next day. When camp was over in late August every year, saying goodbye was difficult. Manny remembered that when the buses came to pick up the campers for the ride back to New York, just making eye contact with the children would often cause the tears to flow.

The year after their HUAC testimony, Manny and Grace were asked to add to their camp roster the recently orphaned sons of Julius and Ethel Rosenberg. This was logical because the camp specialized in offering unconditional love to the children of parents victimized by Cold War hysteria. But the request, made by friends of the Meeropole family, who had adopted the boys, was changed at the last minute when it was decided that ten-year-old Michael and six-year-old Robert would be safer in the long run at a more "bourgeois" Massachusetts camp that did not carry the stigma of leftism. Manny implied that he and Grace would have gladly accepted the Meeropole boys though it might have caused some tensions for the parents of other campers during that summer's session, which began just two weeks after the horrific execution.

The fact that one of the party members who had identified Grace and Manny as "functionaries" was Louis Budenz, Gold's former editor at the *Daily Worker*, prompts the question of why Gold himself was never called to testify before HUAC, as Pete Seeger, John Lawson, Albert Maltz, and many of Gold's colleagues were. A possible reason is that Gold's influence had waned during a period of comparative inactivity while in France and McCarthy had more immediate targets to pursue. His never-disavowed Communist views were on record in hundreds of articles, and it may have been clear that he would be an uncooperative witness, though perhaps capable of sparring with the committee. According to Carl and Nick Granich in separate interviews, the likely reason was that their father had no job that McCarthy could take away. He was publishing only in the already closely watched *Guardian* and the small circulation quarterly, *Masses & Mainstream*. Having lost even his position with the *Daily Worker*, he was already effectively blacklisted.

Probably for related reasons, the writing Gold did produce in the 1950s has either been ignored or disrespectfully described as the "tired" scribblings of a declining writer. This does not seem accurate, and in fact an argument can be made that the 1950s accounted for some of the most finely crafted and affecting prose he ever produced. A case in point is "The Troubled Land," Gold's personal account in *Masses & Mainstream* of his 1954 "American Tour."

The nine sections of this beautiful essay comprise a cultural counternarrative that effectively offsets stereotypes about leftist American life in the 1950s. They relate the author's physical and spiritual journey in concise, muscular language. Billed as the "result of my sixtieth birthday" (though Gold was actually sixty-one at the time), the month-long tour was described as "a good approach to the solemn sixties, a firm hand clasp with my America!"[50]

The alternative, radical, "troubled" America that Gold describes is a vision more honest and compelling than the fantasy of conformist prosperity that has been popularly adopted as a shallow substitute for real knowledge of the 1950s. Chicago, Gold's first stop on the tour, "looked even shabbier and filthier than twenty years ago, when I had visited it during the depression." In 1932 Gold spent several weeks in the city's South Side black belt, attending demonstrations, witnessing evictions, touring factories, and earning trust in the African American homes he visited. While immersing himself in the realities of black life, he had produced a powerful six-part *Daily Worker* series under the title, "Negro Reds of Chicago." In the 1930s he described the South Side masses as "so fed up with misery, so desperately hungry and oppressed, that it has to be restrained by the leaders, rather than pushed forward." In 1954, he saw that the tenements of the "Negro ghetto" were "still the same rotten, unpainted wrecks, paying superprofits to criminal landlords and their bought politicians."[51]

But there are telling differences in the two decades. First, as Gold explained, "Now the Korean War boom has given the people jobs but not houses or equality." Second, the "progressive movement" had declined in Chicago because "people are frightened by McCarthyite fascism. It is obviously dangerous to think." And third, Gold could see plainly that the FBI was everywhere, "like roaches in the neglected house—tapping phones, gathering auto license numbers, watching the mails, frightening employers into firing the victims of informers." Echoing one of his letters to Dorothy Day, he asserted that "prison is not the worst thing that happens to people in America today. The walking death of being made jobless because of a fascist frame-up is often worse than jail."[52]

Characteristically, Gold was hopeful to the extent that he saw strength
and resolution in the anonymous proletarian masses: In 1932, progress for
humanity was visible in "the first mass revolutionary movement among
Negroes" that, as such, was "of world importance" because black and white
American workers had found a new enemy, and it was not each other,
but capitalism. Twenty-two years later, despite McCarthy, an audience of
800 gathered at the anniversary meeting of the New York *Jewish Morning
Freiheit* to hear Mike Gold speak. "At such meetings every night all over
Chicago," Gold realized, "people brave the blacklist to fight the fascist
danger."

"I like that proletarian look of Chicago," Gold continued, "the big
men and women doing big things, a match for the roaring fires and metal
monsters of industry." He noted optimistically that all Chicago newspapers,
"from the pale, liberal Sun to the vile old reactionary Tribune," opposed
the American intervention in Asia, and that this represented "the new
disgust of the people with futile, costly and risky adventures like Korea."[53]

With the narrative about Chicago as a rhetorical paradigm, Gold
proceeds to acknowledge courage and beauty everywhere. In Minneapolis,
he celebrated his host, a Finnish machinist with "a wonderful wife, and a
college daughter engaged to a young soldier half sick with the separation."
He praised fellow socialist writer Meridel LeSueur, a regular contributor
to *New Masses* in the Depression decade, as a "true voice" of Minnesota.
Unlike native sons Sinclair Lewis and F. Scott Fitzgerald, who "simply
never saw or described the region," the socialist LeSueur is "involved in
the freedom struggles of her people."[54]

In Detroit, as in Chicago, Gold recalled the city in the 1930s, when
it resembled "a French city occupied by the Nazi devil" and Henry Ford's
"storm troopers"—an army of trained thugs, spies and informers—"occupied every minute of a worker's life." Twenty years later he noted that
segregation had "been dealt some heavy blows" in Detroit and increased
black political participation had redeemed the city: "The bosses concentrate on superprofits, the workers think about schools, segregation, decent
homes and peace." And twenty miles away in Ann Arbor, the University
of Michigan "leads the nation's schools in resistance to fascism."[55]

"I can't express all my admiration for the outlawed Hollywood people
I met on this visit," Gold wrote in his segment on Los Angeles. "Some
are driving taxis or working as carpenters and machine hands." They are
inspiring people who have "proved to themselves and others what they are."
Despite the blacklist, "their creativeness burns bright. It will shine through

America and the world. Wait and see!" To the city itself, Gold bestows an eloquent paean in the tone of a beat poet: "Beautiful mixed-up city of smog and orange blossoms, of stool pigeons and moral heroes, of the people's genius struggling and degeneracy of the masters! . . . I believe you to be a confused young giant, on the way to glory . . . *Avanti*, Los Angeles!"[56]

In Seattle, when a troupe of young actors presented an hour of dramatized selections from his writings, Gold was moved by "the chords of sympathy and comradeship here by Puget Sound, in the rugged city of fisherman, lumber jacks and Alaskan cannery workers." Later he was encouraged by a trend that might have brought to mind the rebel girl ideal of Flynn, who had inspired his political conversion exactly forty years earlier: "I have noted on this trip that more and more women seem to be taking over places of responsibility in the anti-fascist fight. It was that way in resistance Europe, too. The emergency brings out the hidden reserve of the people."[57]

The essay closes with an encomium to San Francisco, which Gold later adopted and claimed as his favorite city. Standing on Telegraph Hill, he looks down on "the Bay and its shining expanse of blue water, amid the sensuous hills covered in spring with poppies and lupine, in summer tawny as lions." The vista's beauty has "one cancer on its face," Alcatraz. The Rock "can be seen wherever you stand" and offers a grim reminder: "Morton Sobell [sentenced as a coconspirator of the Rosenbergs] is chained to that Rock, like a modern Prometheus. The tragedy haunts the city."[58]

Gold's true encomium in the essay is to the "Troubled Land" in its entirety: "I felt better about the country after seeing it again at close hand. . . . The roots are still sound in America. . . . Nowhere did I hear or see mass demonstrations for war or fascism. The people want peace." Having stayed in the homes of "ordinary Americans, bearing the common burdens," he observes sympathetically, "Yes, their bodies break down with worry and sickness—they have doubts, fears, hesitations." Thinking of Whitman, Gold notices also that they yet "persist in their pioneering" and concludes with an affirmation of faith: "Slowly, the People's Front against Fascism is being born in America. It is the green signal in the desert. It is the American spring, it is the resurrection of our McCarthyized democracy."[59]

Gold found equally hopeful signals in the early civil rights movement, but he could not ignore the often violent Southern responses to the 1954 *Brown v. Board of Education* decision. In 1956 he published an analysis of William Faulkner's shifting stance on civil rights issues that exposed Faulkner's vacillation on race questions while showing that Gold's own commitment to African American advancement had, if anything, grown deeper through the decades. "A Reply to William Faulkner's 'thinking with the blood,'" which appeared in the April 7 issue of the *National Guardian*, took sophisticated positions far in advance of conventional thinking at the time.

The article gave Faulkner credit for denouncing "the rat-like killers of Emmett Till" and for producing several novels that had "broken through" the conditioned patterns of American racist thinking. "Faulkner was never a Nazi," Gold declared. But the advancing civil rights movement—with the *Brown* decision, the Montgomery bus boycott, and the spring 1956 attempt of Autherine Lucy to attend the University of Alabama—apparently overwhelmed the Mississippi liberal. "I was formerly against segregation," Faulkner had said, "now I am just as strongly against compulsory integration." Revealing his ignorance of actual social conditions, he also stated his belief that Northern judicial intervention in the Southern way of life would make whites the "underdog" and blacks the new "topdog"—a prospect that, as Faulkner claimed, forced him to join with "a segment of that white embattled minority who are our blood and kin."[60]

Shocked at Faulkner's bigotry, Gold intervened to demolish the Nobel laureate's reactionary logic: "This surely is thinking with the blood . . . the sort of 'thinking' that loomed large in Nazi ideology, and has long kept the South in pauperism." It was, Gold explained,

> painful that a writer of Faulkner's great stature should easily desert reason and be ready to accept the leadership of Kluxers and Dixiecrats, the vile Eastlands and Milams! For that is what he is telling us, this strong, honorable artist, the Southern man who had groped for justice and understanding! Are these really his kinfolk, these haters of culture, and torturers and killers of little boys?

Faulkner also made a naive attempt to portray the South as the victim by repeating the plaintive call to delay justice and "Stop now for a time." Gold counterargued that social movements couldn't be shut off like a tap and were not, as Faulkner defensively implied, stirred up by a cabal of extremists. What Faulkner was really asking of blacks, Gold said, was "to halt their history." And by mentioning J. W. Milam and referring to "tortures and killers of little boys," Gold compared Faulkner with the brutal murderers of fourteen-year-old eighth grader Emmett Till.[61]

In appraising the Nobel Prize winner, the Communist theorist brought to bear the type of sociological insight Herman Melville had relied on to explore the unconscious racism of Captain Delano in the 1855 novel *Benito Cereno*. With sadness, Gold perceived that Faulkner was

> biologically conditioned by a group fixation that the Negro is inferior, that the Negro is a born servant. He can feel tenderly toward the Negro servant, but the Negro who rejects that historic status and demands his full humanity wounds the fixated white to the core. It is a great shock; the foundations of his psychology seem to be crashing.

Gold also summarily dismissed Faulkner's attempted reliance on the "state's rights" mantra, calling such a stance "the familiar old evasion of the slaveowners of 1861, who couldn't face the ugly fact that they were fighting to preserve a slave system. They, too, built up a state's rights mythology to conceal the reality even from themselves." He concluded by asserting, "This is just demagogy," and added that if Faulkner couldn't "face" the race crisis, it was because "feudal dogmas weigh him down."[62]

The evasive rhetoric was jarring because "it [had] looked as though in Faulkner the Southern people were finding a strong new voice in a time of agony and change." Gold was stunned by the notion that all it took to reverse the great writer's thinking—and prompt him to declare that he would "fight for Mississippi against the United States even if it meant going out in the streets and killing Negroes"—was the attempt of a black woman to attend university classes in Tuscaloosa. Justifiably, Gold wondered whether Faulkner might be headed "back to the Klan."[63]

Undoubtedly a literary artist of the first rank, Faulkner was also a traditionalist, a type Mike Gold had made a specialty of unmasking in the name of social progress. In the mid-1930s, for example, another established giant of American literature had lost his bearings on a momentous social issue, prompting Gold's intervention. When Theodore Dreiser stated anti-Semitic views in a 1933 public symposium, then reiterated those opinions in letters printed in the *Nation* in 1935, most progressives reacted with silent acceptance of the famous writer's inane musings. Gold stepped in to express outrage at Dreiser's dangerous notions.

As Gold explained, Dreiser had long been a leftist sympathizer and was probably not a true anti-Semite (as Faulkner was not a Nazi). But he was without doubt insufficiently aware of racial justice issues. In an almost child-like way, the famous novelist had "stumbled in some manner upon the Jewish problem," which Mike Gold knew profoundly as a "blood-stained question." Dreiser had glibly echoed the vulgar prejudice that Jews were rich and "money-minded"; "Shame to you, Mr. Dreiser," Gold retorted, "Can't you understand that the Jews are a race of paupers?" Dreiser had groused that Jews should either assimilate or leave the country; Gold observed that this preoccupation with "pure" Americanism was "shocking" coming from the son of German immigrants, and that "Any theory of nationalism which forces cultural assimilation of its citizens is a big step toward fascism." After relating these lessons in history and sociology, Gold observed that Theodore Dreiser had "damaged his own great name and the cause of the oppressed by his carelessly spoken words." Particularly vexing for the former Irwin Granich was his recollection of Dreiser's visit to the Lower East Side more than a decade earlier, during which the Gentile outsider had been escorted through the back alleys and dark hallways to experience the primitive conditions of his family's tenement, then given the great compliment of a Sabbath meal prepared by Katie Granich. It seems certain that Gold now sensed the great novelist's failure to compassionate the private life he had exposed to Dreiser's view, and he felt betrayed. In expiation, the *Daily Worker* columnist recommended that the celebrated artist "now undo the damage" and rehabilitate his reputation through "years of devoted battle against anti-Semitism and fascism."[64]

Gold has long been denounced for his unseemly attacks on other writers—mainly for their betrayal of the workers' struggle or apostasy toward the Soviet Union—but the confrontations with Faulkner and Dreiser show that such attacks came in more than one form. At various moments he functioned as a kind of aggressive social conscience for the headliners of American literature who clearly needed correction. As a radical gadfly whose purpose was to reform society, Gold had the genuinely progressive credentials that figures in the literary pantheon sometimes lacked. Like few others, he also had the temerity to bring the geniuses down to earth, schooling them on social issues and reminding them essentially to either be part of the future or get out of the way.

Comparing the civil rights stances of William Faulkner and Mike Gold therefore seems almost unfair; the aristocratic Southerner was bewildered, trapped in the nineteenth century, paralyzed by racial fear, ultimately unable either to work for social justice or accept its mandates; the ghetto-born Communist had been advocating civil rights for more than three decades, never expressing any ideal other than complete social equality for all races and religions.

The treatment of Faulkner demonstrates that Gold had discerned early on the meaning of the civil rights movement, quickly understanding that "what we are beholding is a new stage of American history, the rolling tide of a new consciousness." American blacks, he believed, were "praying to live together in peace. But they will no longer wait." About the nascent culture of nonviolent protest, he wrote presciently: "I am willing to prophesy that one of these days the South will be fired by a great revival spirit as it enters modern times." Indeed, certain passages in Gold's response to Faulkner would not seem out of place in the oratory of Martin Luther King Jr. The movement, Gold wrote, "will pray and fight, sing ballads and dance reels—fathers, mothers and children. . . . It is coming."[65]

The essay also bravely subverted the single most distasteful of Faulkner's notions: his recourse to the ties of blood. In its visualization of multiracial brotherhood, Gold's dream for America was comparable to King's, with the difference that the Communist preferred not to soften certain truths: "The Negro will be one of the kinfolk, as by white rape through the years he actually is." Gold probably knew that the American majority wasn't ready for such rhetoric. But he was right to point out that one did not have to be an apologist for the South to deny visible evidence that calls for segregation in the name of racial "purity" were based on an abject hypocrisy that has defined American civilization.

Gold's critique is valuable for its prophetic interpretations of specific events, but also for its offering of a general Marxist reading that exposes capitalist complicity in Southern race-class hierarchies through the proxy of Wall Street corporations. Northern monopoly capital, the actual owner of the South's natural resources, "controls the price of the fertilizer every little sharecropper must buy," a business relation that ensures and perpetuates poverty in the region. Equally meaningful for Gold is the fact that the "super octopus of the North" owns the racist Southern media and therefore controls the Southern mind: "It is they who preserve Jim Crow."

Characteristically for Gold, these references to economic conditions are not digressive; they supply the necessary linkage between his reading of race issues in American history and his reading of class issues in American literature. In *The Hollow Men* he excoriated the cowardice of literary turncoats who had claimed solidarity with oppressed workers only to return to their class-based roots in the bourgeoisie. Gold no doubt recognized this familiar pattern in Faulkner's withdrawal of support for black aspirations in deference to race-based allegiances. To the genteel ex-comrades of 1941 and the genteel civil rights defector of 1956 he sent essentially the same message: "The manifesto of retreat belongs to the past."[66]

Mike Gold was sixty-three when he wrote his reply to Faulkner, a piece that could only have come from a formidable thinker and in itself offers good reason for reading Gold today. Treating this essay in some detail seems worthwhile also because it belies the impression that Gold embodied a rapid and pathetic professional decline in the 1950s. He felt the pressures of a reactionary time but remained hopeful and committed.

Moreover, while for some time diabetes had been weakening Gold physically and dictating a more sedentary life, he seems to have been more intellectually engaged than ever, and still learning. In June 2018 I spent an evening in Nick Granich's home in San Francisco, going through the personal library his father had accumulated in the last stage of his life, after the family's return from France. I was impressed by the great number of African American writers and topics in black studies that were represented. Two boxes, which I carried from Nick's closet to the kitchen, held only works on black culture; there was writing by Sterling Brown, Ann Petry, Chester Himes, Lorraine Hansberry, and Richard Wright; Paul Robeson's *Here I Stand*; Ralph Ellison's *Invisible Man*; and essays by James Baldwin that Nick said were especially important to his father. There were academic titles by Du Bois, and African American biographies by Shirley Graham Du Bois, alongside works about black social history by the white academics Philip Foner and Herb Aptheker.

Stacking up these books on the kitchen table with Nick, a retired longshoreman with a PhD-level vocabulary whose knowledge of leftist history went far deeper than mine, was exciting for us both. We talked about his father's lifelong passions and what they meant, forgetting to eat dinner until late in the evening, when I found some bread and made sandwiches. Hanging out with Nick and looking at the priceless stack of his father's books in front of us, I was revisited by a feeling I'd had when I first saw a grainy black-and-white film of Richard Wright speaking in Paris in 1958. I thought it meaningful that the person born to the dehumanizing world described in *Black Boy* was now responding in fluent French to questions from international journalists about his latest novel. Wright, I thought, had come a very long way from a Natchez sharecropper's shack. That evening with Nick was a reminder that Mike Gold, too, had traveled quite well and quite far from the Lower East Side tenement, at the bottom of an airshaft, where his life began.

Chapter Nine

"One Brave Hello"

(1956–1967)

Sometime before taking final leave of the fifth-floor Topping Avenue apartment that had been visited by both Dorothy Day and FBI agents, where he'd lived out the McCarthy years, endured sickness, and spent far too many hours home alone in an attempt to remain a writer while Elizabeth worked and the boys were in school, Gold composed the following fragment from a never-published poem. Some might judge these lines as self-pitying, but I believe they help round out the picture of what it meant to live "close to the ground" as Carl Granich phrased it; it meant used clothing, unhealthy food, a worried, insecure family, and a father whose thoughts about death prompted a tighter grip on life:

from "Americans Want to Be Loved"

We wear second hand shirts and shoes and we eat poorly
And a knock on the door often sets our blood beating
I am a man of heart and therefore suspect in America
Women and men of heart and socialism are prey now of the FBI
I have diabetes to suffer as well as the FBI
So the problem remains will I and my petty troubles outlast
Wall Street America and its grandiose conflicted contradictions
You see I still have a sense of humor
And make a joke or two on my gallows
Behind these ribs I have still a heart

I am proud of its warm glowing newness
I have been cheated in life I have been betrayed
I have seen hundreds of stronger men than I go down
Dead of poverty and lack of faith
But I have been loyal to the people
And it has kept my heart in good repair
I am proud I can still feel it glow
It grows old strongly for justice
And burns with rage anew.[1]

The faith and loyalty described in these verses had already been tested many times and would be tested again in June 1956, when the *New York Times* published the text of the "secret speech" that First Secretary Nikita Kruschev had delivered that February at a closed session of the 20th Congress of the Communist Party of the Soviet Union. Under the title, "On the Cult of Personality and Its Consequences," the speech revealed to the world the immeasurable horrors of Stalin's rule, including mass murders of intellectuals and political opponents, deportations of minorities, repression of original Bolsheviks, rejection of collective leadership, grave corruptions of Leninist principles, and, in Krushchev's terms, "brutal violence toward everything that opposed him."[2]

The news sent shock waves throughout the Soviet Union and Soviet bloc but was just as devastating to the organized Left worldwide. Within weeks of its publication, 30,000 U.S. Communists quit the Party. Most of those who remained expressed confusion, sadness, and bewilderment. Undoubtedly it was a trying time for Mike Gold, who had not previously written or spoken about Stalin's crimes. The matter was all the more vexing because Krushchev not only verified Stalin's cruelty, megalomania, and insanity; he also confirmed evidence that had been gradually reaching the West since the late 1940s.

Nine days after Krushchev's speech, on June 14, 1956, the Washington, D.C., office of FBI director Hoover sent an AIRTEL registered message to the New York and Detroit Field Offices: A source "who has furnished reliable information in the past" had "orally advised that MIKE GOLD, an author from New York City," was to speak the next evening in Detroit at the Amalgamated Plant Guard Union Local 114 Hall on 13722 Linwood. The informant advised that "the sponsor of this affair was unknown" but that the topic of Gold's speech was to be "Jewish Culture in the Soviet Union."[3]

It would have been understandable if Gold had canceled speaking engagements for some weeks—or longer. He might have decided to speak about anything but the Soviet first secretary's de-Stalinization campaign. But by the time the event took place, the title of the lecture had become "What Happened to Jewish Culture in the Soviet Union," a slight change that increased the expectation that it would treat Comrade Krushchev's revelations. As one of the lecture's organizers noted, the topic had been chosen because at this time Gold "preferred to speak on world-wide events."[4]

Two FBI informants attended Gold's talk and submitted separate accounts, which were received by the Detroit field office on June 25. Gold was introduced to an audience of "approximately 65 persons" as "a widely known author, lecturer, world traveler, former assistant editor of the 'Daily Worker,' and a contributor to leftist magazines internationally." He then immediately "told the audience that he was sure that they had been confused and uncertain in regard to the events that had taken place among Jewish intellectuals in the Soviet Union, as disclosed by KRUSHCHEV's speech against JOSEPH STALIN."[5]

Gold related that "it was unfortunate that the news of the Jewish purge had to reach the American Jews indirectly" and repeated, "We should have known, our leaders should have known." With the term "Jewish purge," Gold was referring to the executions of thirteen prominent Yiddish writers on the "Night of the Murdered Poets" in August 1952, which was now confirmed to have been carried out on the orders of Stalin. "We should have been making inquiries about the silence from the Jewish writers and the Jewish theatre groups," Gold lamented. (Yiddish theaters, publishing houses, and schools, along with the Jewish Museum in Vilnius and the Moscow State Jewish Theater, had been closed between late 1948 and early 1949.) "We should have known something was wrong," Gold stated. "I do not know why our leaders did not ask, did not keep in close touch," he said.[6]

"But because of this, we must not lose faith in Socialism," he continued, "for now that STALIN is condemned for his crimes against Jewish writers, Jewish artists, now that the menace is removed and Jewish culture is again beginning to flourish in the Soviet Union our purpose can again be singlefold, our aims strengthened and our hearts as one as typified in a Socialist democracy." According to the FBI informant, "Gold asked [his audience] not to be disillusioned by what happened to the Jews in Russia under STALIN, and not to believe all the irresponsible theories being published as to the reason for KRUSHCHEV'S disclosure at this late date."[7]

The Party of Lenin itself remained pure and bore no responsibility for the aberrations, about which Lenin had presciently warned in his suppressed "testament" concerning Stalin's flaws as a human being and leader. In fact, Gold's speech was as much pro-Lenin as it was anti-Stalin.

One of the informants in attendance described the gist of Gold's self-positioning this way: "In answer to the question as to why KRUSH-CHEV and BULGANIN did nothing to stop STALIN's crimes, GOLD stated that they were ignorant of them. . . . GOLD also stated that the condemnation of STALIN's acts by the present Russian leaders have removed the barriers which had previously existed between the several leftist organizations—and these groups, with minor exceptions, could now work together in furthering worldwide Socialism. He said that unification is now in progress and gaining momentum rapidly. GOLD closed by urging renewed faith in Marxist Socialism and the support of its leaders."[8]

The second informant gave a comparable synopsis, stating that Gold "commented on the crimes committed against the Jews in Russia and stated that this was the work of STALIN and a few of his men. He stated that the Russian people knew nothing of these crimes . . . because they are the kindest people in the world . . . [and] that Socialism is here to stay and that it is stronger than ever before."[9] Having earlier been reluctant to believe certain truths about Stalin, Gold now transferred his remaining faith to Krushchev and to the Party.

To be sure, Gold's acceptance of a role of public authority on a new and developing situation was a difficult assignment, as was shown in the "discussion period" that followed the talk. Gold was asked, "What is relationship of the status of Jews in America with the Jews in the Soviet Union?" The first-mentioned informant reported that Gold "pretended to misunderstand the question and gave the man a rambling answer on the number of Jews in American and in Russia." The second reported that Gold had in fact addressed this relation, stating that "the crimes against the Jews in Russia are no different from those committed in the United States against the Negroes." Krushchev's "recent speech," Gold said, shows that "this position has changed" and that "the Russians are trying to right this wrong."[10]

When asked how American Communists could "be sure such a thing would not happen again," the speaker gave an answer that sounded effective but may have shown a too willing acceptance of Krushchev's stated motive: "KRUSHCHEV would not have made his speech if he did not intend to change the conditions." At this point an audience member,

Ray Franklin, seems to have come to Gold's aid. He "got up and stated that the best way to judge is by what is presently taking place in such places as Poland where they now have a non-Communist paper and in the Soviet Union where there is a revival of Jewish cultural activities."[11]

Both informants stated that Gold pointed optimistically to the health of socialism outside the Soviet Union and especially in France, as he had during his talk in Detroit in 1954. One account also made note of a strange moment in the lecture when Gold told a story from "a time when he was on the staff of the *Daily Worker*," which would have been while Stalin was still in power:

> [Gold] had disagreed with a certain [Stalinist] policy and asked for clarification. . . . After not getting any satisfaction, he had dropped the subject. However, he was told later by a friend that if he had said another word, he would have been "torn limb from limb" by other followers. GOLD said that showed what a leader could "get away with" with a following of his own and explained why STALIN could do to the Jews what he did in Russia without the Russian people being aware of what went on.[12]

This quote is thought-provoking because it is difficult to imagine Mike Gold, who was always more volatile than doctrinal in his Marxism, being able to negotiate Stalinism in Russia without severe risk. The Stalin-era Soviet postcard mentioned in chapter 5 and featuring a youthful Gold at the Kharkov conference had sanctified the single duty of all who had hope for the future: "defend the Soviet Union." Living up to this dictum might have been a challenge in 1930, but it was certainly a harder task twenty-five years later. Alan Wald's 2003 study of leftist literary history, *Exiles from a Future Time,* offered this insight into the general trajectory of Gold's world socialist "vision": "In the excitement of the early 1930s, the vision seemed to be working for others as well. Unfortunately what Gold believed to be the opening of a new epoch, leading forward to socialism, was but an anomalous moment in a sequence of unexpected events, a series of limited victories to be followed by many serious defeats."[13]

Krushchev's demolition of the Stalin cult in early 1956 had been one such defeat; a possibly worse crisis erupted only months later. In October–November, an anti-Soviet protest in Hungary escalated into a bloody revolt against the Marxist-Leninist satellite government. After student demonstrators demanding the withdrawal of Soviet troops and a new government under Imre Nagy were fired on by Soviet secret police, the government collapsed and the revolt in Budapest spread quickly across the country. The Politburu initially expressed a willingness to negotiate the withdrawal of Soviet forces, then reversed course and moved to violently suppress the pro-democracy movement. As historian Lara Vapnek noted, the Hungary crackdown had the effect of "stripping off any democratic gloss that might have remained on the Soviet Union from its fight against fascism during World War II."[14]

At this time Gold did not engage in public soul searching, for he was not actively writing or speaking, preoccupied instead with sudden plans to take Carl out of high school and move the family to San Francisco. Along with the stresses of this major transition for the sixty-three-year-old, there is evidence of some newly felt domestic tension. Recalling the situation, Carl described a moment when, at the age of sixteen, his politics first diverged from his father's: "After Krushchev's speech and the Hungarian uprising, I had my reservations about the Soviet Union. My dad and I didn't talk politics after that."[15]

As Gold's son was quick to explain, "Mike was a sweet person in all ways, except when it came to politics." Carl felt lucky that he and his father talked so often in his childhood and adolescence, but he had seen his father lose patience even with friends when the discussion turned political, which Carl said was "the only time he could be angry or harsh." Unsure of his father's exact thinking about the dual crises of 1956, he was certain that Mike remained a believer in the Soviet Union and speculated that he was staying loyal out of deep disappointment with those who had "turned their backs on the movement" during the McCarthy period. "I'm sure he had reservations and didn't think everything was perfect but he wasn't going to be a turncoat," Carl said.[16]

By late 1956, Mike, Elizabeth, and Carl had moved to San Francisco, where they took up residence on 448 Waller Street near Buena Vista Park in the Lower Haight-Ashbury neighborhood. For a few months they divided their time between their new home and Los Angeles. Gold loved the City of the Golden Gate, but he and Elizabeth were sun worshippers and Venice Beach was worth a bus ticket down the coast. It seemed the Graniches might be seeking a place to retire, though Liz was still willing to take jobs and Mike apparently had part-time work in mind. He opened registration for a "Mike Gold Writer's Workshop" beginning on January 16 in San Francisco. As Gold advertised it, the workshop would be "a place where students can grow in the crafts of writing by means of constant experiment, mutual criticism, and advice and inspiration of an experienced leader. The atmosphere will be not that of a classroom, but of a group of craftsman helping each other."[17] Tuition for the ten-week class was ten dollars per student.

At this moment the editor of the San Francisco *People's World*, the thoughtful and dedicated revolutionary Al Richmond, was doing his best, as Gold was, to manage the crisis caused by the "Kruschev thunderbolt." The *People's World* was losing circulation—at one point dipping to a nadir of 6,000—and the paper became a target of "the natural focus of the angry eruption" after the Hungarian crackdown.[18] Richmond's memoirs metaphorically summarized a dilemma felt almost universally at this time by the remnants of the embattled Left: "It is very difficult to keep a steady helm when a ship is buffeted by stormy waves," and this was especially true if one is "not sure of what compass to steer by."[19] Having no alternative, Richmond committed stubbornly to the idea that he had to keep the ship afloat.

In his memoir, *A Long View From the Left*, Richmond recalled that, among the "many goodbyes" said in a mood of "dispiriting turmoil" as the *People's World* staff disbanded, there was "one brave hello."[20] This was from Michael Gold, who appeared in the newspaper's office one day to offer his services. Richmond had known Gold as an almost heroic figure, the "prophet" of proletarian literature and "incandescent light" of the 1930s whose *Change the World* column was now what Richmond considered a warm but fading memory. Richmond and associate editor Adam Lapin now encouraged Gold to revive the column. Somehow they also pieced together a modest syndicate—the *Worker* and the New York *Jewish Morning Freiheit* also agreed to pick up the column—an arrangement that would assure Gold fifty dollars a week.

For Gold, now in his mid-sixties with declining health, the passion was still there. The latest incarnation of *Change the World* was as fresh and fiercely partisan as ever. Only occasionally did Gold reminisce about the heyday of the Left; mainly he showed how young he still was, observing the life around him from the streets of Haight-Ashbury to the Soviet Union, Mexico, and Vietnam. In 1958 he wrote about a long visit to Mexico City; years later he catalogued the atrocities in Southeast Asia; he wrote about the civil rights "Freedom Fight" that was then reaching a climax in the South; about the beatniks outside his window, who never bathed but were "morally cleaner than the makers of the dirty wars in the Congo, Vietnam, and Santo Domingo"; he titled one column "Bob Dylan—Voice of America's Youth." Gold was likely gratified by a published letter about his columns from "two teenagers" who wrote to the editors in 1958 saying, "In particular we would like to commend Michael Gold for his beautiful and thought-inspiring columns which add a warm touch of personality to the paper. . . . Both of us feel the immense sincerity of this man."[21]

At this time occasional letters also arrived from the Soviet Union, usually from curious or admiring literary historians who no doubt reminded Gold that it had been decades since his last visit. In April 1961 he and Elizabeth left San Francisco for a six-month sojourn in the USSR as guests of the Soviet Writers' Union. In Moscow they toured schools and factories, met writers and artists, and attended a reception for cosmonaut Yuri Gagarin. Gold was amazed at how much the people knew about American life, and in one of his columns he lamented the dangerously blind leaders of the West who still assumed that well-formed culture did not exist in the Soviet Union. "There can be no peace in the world while such stupidity and non-realism reign in the high places of the western world," he declared.[22]

The trip was longer than expected because Gold had a flare-up of his old ailment, high blood sugar, and had to spend over twelve weeks in a sanatorium, where he got a close-up view of the Soviet medical system and found it impressive. He said he had never received such a careful and complete examination. Elizabeth was also hospitalized, spending several weeks in the same Moscow facility to receive treatments for a leg ailment, taking exercises with Mike as part her daily routine. The fact that every citizen received such thorough care in a modern medical system was in Gold's view "one of the great achievements of a great revolution."[23]

Eventually the Writers Union invited Mike and his wife to stay in Moscow for at least another year. They offered him a job as the main consultant for a series of volumes they were planning on the topic, "American literature, past, present and future." Gold was tempted and said he would stay if he could find enough research material and if his health could take a Moscow winter at the age of sixty-eight. In Moscow's largest libraries he found all the research material he needed, but when cold weather came in late October, both he and Elizabeth got very sick. "I had to give up the best job I ever was offered in my life," Gold said, but the proposition gave him the idea for a book about the literary culture of the 1930s, which later became his memoir project.[24]

With the death of Elizabeth Gurley Flynn in September 1964, Gold dedicated a *Change the World* column to the "courage" and "noble leadership" of the original IWW "rebel girl," who had inspired several generations of revolutionaries and gone to prison for her beliefs, musing, "Dear Elizabeth, I wish I could write something worthy of your great soul."[25]

At about this time Gold was contacted by Michael Folsom, the PhD candidate at the University of California at Berkeley who had wanted to write his dissertation on Gold but was told by the Berkeley English

Figure 9.1. Mike and Elizabeth Gurley Flynn celebrate Flynn's birthday. San Francisco, early 1960s. *Source:* Granich family.

Department, then chaired by Henry Nash Smith, that the subject wasn't worthy of scholarly attention. Despite this setback, Folsom dedicated immense energies to writing a biography of Gold, with the intention also of editing the memoirs of the "father of proletarian literature."

The story of the young academic motorcycling across the Bay Bridge to Gold's apartment on weekend afternoons in 1965 and 1966, picking up a bottle of wine or some quarts of beer along the way, in order to put a microphone in the aging Communist's hand and prompt him to tell about his life, is part of this book's narrative as well. On one of his visits to Gold, Folsom brought with him his fiancée, Marcia, also a Berkeley PhD candidate in literature who later became an expert on Jane Austen. In a 2017 interview at her home in Boston, Marcia Folsom remembered Gold's tenderness, which was in keeping with a man who loved youth, embraced change, and always welcomed the future.

Though Folsom was not able to complete the well-begun Gold biography, he published an indispensable collection of Gold's best essays, short stories, and poems in the 1972 text, *Mike Gold: A Literary Anthology,* which included material chosen, introduced, and sometimes retitled with Gold's help and approval. During this process Folsom discovered *People's World* columns about Gold's early years in the ghetto and published them under the title, *A Jewish Childhood in the New York Slums.* These late-career gems were not only a sequel to *Jews without Money* but a reminder of Gold's real genius, the artless, sincere humanity Gold drew on "before he got tangled in the life of literature and politics."[26] They also remind us of what his devotion to the Party had cost him. The fact that Gold could not complete another novel after 1930 was inarguably due in part to the sacrifice of his creativity at a subsistence wage to the working-class liberation movement. "He could have done a newspaper or magazine column that would have made him rich and famous," journalist Robert Shaw wrote to Folsom in 1967, adding, "But my prediction is that when all the hired apologists for the status quo are dead and forgotten, the name of Mike Gold will be known to millions of people around 2067."[27]

A consideration of Gold's struggles after the 1930s to remain an artist and to support his family while being vilified as a political outcast—or, in Folsom's term, "the pariah of American letters"[28]—makes one wonder whether, by aspiring to be simultaneously a loyal Communist and a respected writer in a reactionary and philistine country, Gold had attempted the impossible. Gold's comment in 1932, "I want socialism so much that I accept this fierce, crude struggle as my fate in time,"[29] indicates that he may have wondered about this himself.

Unlike most of the literary leftists of his generation, Michael Gold did not eventually disavow his radicalism, though his refusal to soft-pedal his artistic or political opinions earned him enemies in the cultural establishment. Perhaps more brazenly, Gold never gave up the cause of what he termed "world socialism," instead retaining throughout his life the hope, expressed in the epiphanic ending of *Jews without Money*, that a worker's messiah would come. What Mike Gold explained about his spirit and temperament at the advent of his fame—"The tenement is in my blood"—was as true in the author's final days as in 1921.

By the mid-1960s Gold's eyesight had deteriorated from the effects of diabetes. Nearly blind, he continued to write for the *People's World* and the Jewish Communist *Freiheit*, dictating articles to Elizabeth and using a tape recorder to work on a never-completed autobiography. A sampling of thoughts recorded for those memoirs, typed up by Elizabeth less than a year before his death and left among the author's papers, do not reveal anything close to a political change of heart. But they do reveal a bit of the unmasked Mike Gold he intended to make public in his autobiography: a man capable of introspection, self-criticism, and some regret. At one point he contemplated his "Greenwich Village period," which was really another term for his youth:

> I have often thought about that period of my life and have not liked that period too well. I felt like I wasted many years of strong feeling, of useless emotion, of misunderstanding of the general world and confinement to a narrow little beatnik society. . . . It seems such a waste of life as I look back on it later. I should have kept on writing hard and furiously and writing about the things that moved me the most. The Village did not move me as the strikes did at the time, the great social injustices. I really felt that with all my heart and soul, as I did not feel the prettiest woman in the Village.[30]

He thought also about a part of himself he had repressed or left undeveloped, one that happened to be tender and human:

> In thinking over these things I came on a curious fact that I had never really written one love poem in all my writing. . . . I wrote quite a few poems, . . . and they were all poetry of the class struggle. This will make me out to be sort of a freak, I suppose, but it is a form of freakishness which has seized

hundreds of writers since that early time when I was one of the four or five writers of proletarian poetry in America.[31]

Recalling his brief time at Harvard and the lingering consequences of that failure, he realized that he'd sometimes judged human beings unfairly because of his pain and anxiety:

> As I look back I see that one of the troubles of my character was formed then. I began to have too much of the outlaw temperament. I didn't think I had any friends so I became too extreme in my self-defense, . . . too extreme in my attack on people who believed in capitalism. I did not learn to judge them by their own special character. I have found so many kindly, good and talented people who were not radicals since that time, that I feel I must explain it sometime or other and I will in this book, I hope.[32]

On another occasion, he looked back on literary history to take a long view on the fates and factors that, he felt, had made him a scapegoat. Now he likened his literary life to forced estrangement from a "family"—a painful process that was, thankfully, only temporary:

> During the time of McCarthyism in America a great vacuum was formed in the thinking of the Left. Actually the only political party who was haunted by McCarthy was the Communist Party. That party was practically driven underground by the endless persecutions and its publications were not seen any more on college campuses or otherwise, and this created an intellectual vacuum in the type of great debate on history that continuously goes on in a healthy nation.
>   Into the vacuum flocked the numerous little splinter parties and groups whose chief aim in life seemed to be to help the McCarthyites destroy the Communist Party. The strange thing was, after McCarthyism had been wiped off the scene, the intellectual vacuum still went on for years, and for instance one of the things that was taught in many of the English departments of the colleges, was the confidently and elaborately conceived fiction that there had been no literature

of the Thirties. Yes, these teachers of truth had actually created a fiction that so many in the collegiate world took for gospel.

Another less important fiction that was widely spread was that proletarian literature was a mechanical literature written on formulas which had no art or science. I was somehow mixed up in this fiction by reason of the fact that every anti-communist intellectual needed a whipping boy for the theory that no literature was produced and that it was a mechanical literature, and that I was the chief commissar of the conspiracy to destroy real literature and to substitute proletarian literature for it. This was also widely believed by hundreds of innocent young freshman who had taken their first classes in literature and world literature. It is not a pleasant thing to be a scapegoat. I can testify I got sick of reading these descriptions of myself as a beetle-brow gangster commissar snapping the whip over the innocent victims of a party of commissars who were taking over American literature by every manner of brutal means.

In the last four or five years, however, I had the delightful luxury of seeing this myth peter out like dying in the desert of thirst. It just withered away and I had quite a few young college students writing a thesis on some form of literature of the thirties come to see me as if I was a grandfather, which I am, telling them stories of the old battle. The thirties has been rediscovered by the American youth, . . . I felt often a new pride burning in my veins when I came across evidence that they didn't look down on me and my writing, but accepted it as a worthy specimen of a new time. Yes, it is a wonderful feeling to have your family reunited.[33]

Gold's last *Change the World* column was published on July 31, 1966. He signed off to his readers, saying, "I am giving up, with your permission, the writing of future columns." Keeping up the pieces while working on his memoir was becoming too difficult: "I think it would be better for everyone if I don't attempt the impossible at this moment," he said, adding, "I am and I will always remain loyal to the tradition of working class journalism in which I have labored for almost 50 years." In the supposedly temporary leave taking, there was a palpable feeling of permanence and finality: "With a warm comradely handshake to the

young and old readers, to the wise, witty, militant, optimistic and fearless
ones who read this paper and guarantee that it will never fail to survive
the storms of social change, Your friend, Mike Gold."[34]

The following February Gold suffered a major stroke that left him
bedridden and partly paralyzed. In March the *People's World* updated
his condition for readers, announcing that he was having transfusions
and in need of blood donations. The paper gave an address for sending
"messages of cheer and concern."[35] On April 29 Richmond ran a second
announcement about the need for blood donations, reporting also that
Gold was making progress toward recovery and was "slated for another
operation this week."[36]

On May 14, 1967, Gold died of complications following the stroke
at the Kaiser Foundation Hospital in the San Francisco suburb of Terra
Linda. He was seventy-three. A memorial service was held June 2 at
Golden Gate Park, with Harry Bridges, hero of the 1934 San Francisco
General Strike, delivering the main tribute.

Two weeks later a memorial service was held in New York. The list
of those who came to pay respects represented surprisingly varied strands
of American life. The presence of "voice of America" Carl Sandburg, who
sang for Gold in San Francisco in 1923 but never answered his question
about why he left the movement, confirmed that Gold had once touched
many in the cultural mainstream. The famously blacklisted John Howard
Lawson, one of the Hollywood Ten, had once been Gold's associate at
the Playwright's Theater; he not only spoke but published a tribute, "The
Stature of Michael Gold," in that month's *Political Affairs*, calling his subject
"a writer of courage, wisdom and—perhaps his greatest quality—stubborn
integrity."[37] Gold's lifelong friend Dorothy Day, the most notorious of all
Catholic radicals, also attended. In the June 1967 *Catholic Worker*, she
eulogized Gold as "a gentle and loving spirit."[38] The folksinger and social
activist Pete Seeger, who had been reading Gold's work since the 1930s
and would soon become the embodiment of Vietnam War protest, came
to both the San Francisco and New York tributes with his wife, Toshie,
to celebrate the man he had often called his hero. Of course Art Shields
was there, forty-six years after befriending Gold in the coke fields of
Pennsylvania. His tribute article was titled, "Mike Gold: Our Joy and
Pride." "Mike's drumbeats of struggle went on for more than 40 years,"
Shields wrote, "They beat in the hearts of many thousands of workers."

The Uruguayan American woodcut master Antonio Frasconi was
present too; he would have credited Gold as an inspiration for his visual

art, which relentlessly addressed racism, poverty, violence, and social injustice. Frasconi shared with Gold a love of Henry David Thoreau and Walt Whitman, and, like Gold, he wrathfully called attention to the "ugly things in life" in a quest for truthful art. At the time of the memorial Frasconi was exhibiting a set of woodcuts condemning the impact of the deadly US war machine on the impoverished people of Vietnam. One of Frasconi's definitions of art—"the direct expression of a man who is angry about something"[39]—describes as well Gold's creative motivations and deepest convictions.

While the memorials were still going on, earnest contestations had already begun about the complicated question of what this American life meant. The day after Gold's death, the *San Francisco Chronicle* published a sloppy and insulting obituary that classified the deceased as "a free-lance writer" and "outspoken literary apologist" for communism who eventually "became disillusioned with Party." This egregious mistake was the product of lazy thinking by an editor who no doubt felt safe in assuming that every relic of the Old Left later abandoned Marxism and radical idealism.

Mike Folsom, Gold's great defender, wrote to the *Chronicle* editors, allowing that Gold was "too rambunctious an individual to ever get along with persons or parties without friction" but correcting the fundamental error: "To do his memory justice, it should be noted that he proudly died—as he had lived almost fifty years of his life—a communist." Five days later in *The Worker*, Gold's long-time colleague Joseph North chimed in: "The lad from the East Side was a proud American and Communist to his core, to the end of his days."[40]

Now that this was settled, a new set of issues arose as Folsom carried out the crucial task of compiling and publishing an anthology of Gold's writings. As soon as Folsom drafted his introduction to the anthology, an essay titled "The Pariah of American Letters," he sent a copy to Elizabeth Granich for her approval. Gold's widow liked and trusted Folsom; she did not disagree with the title but was saddened by it, and felt a need to voice her feelings in a typed response:

> Mike may have been a pariah of American letters, but he was adored and respected by his readers of his prime who remained faithful to him. The young generation is another affair; they had not read him from the beginning. Yet it is to them that Mike wanted to appeal, he was looking toward the future, had faith in the future of the Young, and in that sense

he never despaired and he did not care how much praise or readers he still had. It was the principal of social change and [the] everlasting spring of progress nursed by the Young that mattered to him.[41]

When Folsom's extraordinarily valuable anthology was published in 1972, Art Shields, who had covered labor conflicts and witnessed strikes at Gold's side throughout the 1920s and 1930s, was both pleased and disappointed. Shields wanted to address what he felt the professors and the academic world were misunderstanding. In a review for the journal *Political Affairs*, he wrote that he agreed with Folsom in many ways: "I think no American writer ever struck such a powerful blow against anti-Semitism as Mike Gold, author of *Jews without Money*." But he saw that Folsom's standards of judgment were more academic than Gold's and wondered why more *Daily Worker* columns weren't included: "Many of Mike's admirers, especially his working-class admirers—think some of his best writing is found in his *Change the World* columns," he noted, "Unfortunately the editor thinks these remarkable columns are not literary enough."[42]

Shields was shocked by Folsom's claim that Mike was "a little cynical" after disappointments like the truth about Stalin. "This is outrageous. The cynic and Mike were two opposite poles. . . . There is nothing cynical in the letters Mike wrote to me and other friends before his death."[43] He also took issue with the term "pariah." This was how academics might have viewed him, but not the people. No Communist writer won the hearts of young people like "our beloved Mike," Shields said. He felt that all scholarly viewpoints missed the essentials about Gold; namely, his appeal to common people and the pride they still feel in him. He and Folsom couldn't satisfactorily work out their disagreement. They both loved Gold but were looking at him from different vantage points.

Another reviewer of the anthology, W. T. Lhamon of the *New Republic*, wanted to talk about the audacity of Gold's attacks on Wilder in the 1930s, on the "renegades" in 1941, and on Maltz in 1946. He offered a final take on the debate between "art for art's sake" and "art for humanity's sake" that had permeated almost every phase of Gold's career.

Lhamon did not condemn Gold's rudeness toward other artists. "The fight was very real," he asserted, by which he meant that politeness wasn't necessary. The attack on Wilder "wasn't a petty argument" because the renegades, by allying themselves with the workers' struggle in ways that ultimately did harm to their liberation movement, effectively revealed the cultural and class allegiances they had held all along. The flirters with the proletariat were returning home to their bourgeois backgrounds, and this was not a harmless or cost-free maneuver. The act of switching allegiances sent a signal.[44]

Lhamon admitted that in a general way, perhaps the Party did coerce people into "speaking its own line—which it claimed was the voice of the people." But "bourgeois literature worked no less culpably or diligently to promote its own class-serving values." Literary works function as "an organizing force," he wrote, and "implicitly urge readers to behave in certain ways, notice certain things, forget certain impulses." In other words they have substantial shaping power, determining how we view and respond to the social world.[45]

The celebrated masterpieces of the "genteel tradition" have a certain subversive potential because of their complexity, sophistication and their "expressed possibilities," but this only makes the "drawing room sensibility" they offer as a substitute version of reality more enticing. The process of perpetuating capitalist hegemony is actually more weaponized because the American bourgeois worldview has an advantage; as Lahmon put it, its enticements, coercions and seductions are "a shillelagh whose handle is carved for the middle-class." Two metaphors defined the effects of that bourgeois culture: it was "a hard rain dampening everything" and it was a "strong odor" that "pushed out and covered everything else."[46]

What Mike Gold did successfully and consistently for his entire career was to express for those willing to discern it "how dominated America was by the values of its predominant class." His steadfastness and consistency, articulated in blunt and discomfiting ways, "proved that there was a genuinely different culture in America, other than the official, consensus one"—an undeniably significant achievement. To Lhamon, Folsom's anthology was a "corrective book," one of its great uses being that of helping readers to see for ourselves how Gold managed the challenge of proving the existence of another America, and how difficult it made his life.[47]

All these sentiments involve class theory, but Gold was capable of framing the issue in largely aesthetic terms as well. In letters to Louis Untermeyer early in his career, he discussed his choice to become a revolutionary artist in the first place. He was repulsed by the many writers who had failed "to stay with the masses," instead selling their souls to the elite, and admitted to labelling poets who only poeticize "criminals."

He realized this was "raw" but explained, "I cannot help getting peeved at their eternal arrogances" and ended the letter with a question that is still relevant: "What sort of instincts can anyone have who is not seared and wounded by the sight of poverty, even when it does not hamper him personally? It is such an offense to the sense of beauty and love which the poet is supposed to have a monopoly on."[48]

Since the debate over Gold's legacy that was incited by Folsom's anthology, the twin claims made by John Howard Lawson at the time of his friend's death—that there were many readers of literary and scholarly publications who had "never heard of" the once-famous Communist and that Mike Gold had "suffered brutal misjudgments and cold neglect from the cultural establishment"[49]—have been validated. But reclamation work goes on, and one early twenty-first-century testimony to Gold's impact from a perhaps unanticipated source offers perspectives at once deeply interesting and historically revealing.

In her best-selling 2003 memoir, *Reading Lolita in Tehran*, the Iranian-American author Azar Nafisi wrote about Gold with insight and a curious mixture of sympathy and disdain. Nafisi, who holds a PhD in literature from the University of Oklahoma, completed her doctoral dissertation on "The Literary Wars of Mike Gold" in 1979, just before she returned to Iran and witnessed the start of the Iranian revolution.

Reading Lolita in Tehran describes a meeting Nafisi had with the head of the English Department at the University of Tehran before her first semester teaching a course in Western literature. When asked about her dissertation, Nafisi explained that she had initially envisioned "a comparative study of the literature of the twenties and thirties, the proletarians and non-proletarians." It was obvious that the best person to represent the 1920s was F. Scott Fitzgerald, but identifying a writer who would serve as Fitzgerald's "counterpoint" was difficult until she came across "the real proletarians, whose spirit was best captured by Mike Gold." In the end Nafisi left Fitzgerald out of her dissertation and wrote solely about Gold, analyzing why the proletarian writer's cultural view "took over" in the 1930s and forced out writers like Fitzgerald. Nafisi, who in her student days protested the Vietnam War and embraced leftism, accounted for Gold's appeal on a personal level: "I was a revolutionary myself. I wanted to understand the passion that drove the likes of Mike Gold."[50]

A month before this meeting took place, in July 1979, Nafisi had sent a copy of her dissertation to Michael Folsom, thanking him for his advice on the project and asking for his comments. With the manuscript she enclosed a personal note that affirmed her deep commitment to the Communist writer: "I feel close to Gold because of his passion for his people," she wrote, "because I think he never once forgot them or their vision. . . . I love Gold."[51] Not surprisingly, when the fall academic term began weeks later in Tehran, Nafisi did something Folsom had been calling for since 1959: she took the bold step of incorporating Gold into her survey of twentieth-century fiction, teaching his stories alongside those of Fitzgerald and Hemingway and affording him the stature of a major writer.

But at some point between 1979 and the publication of *Reading Lolita in Tehran*, Nafisi's thinking underwent a fundamental change, transforming her love for Gold into contempt. The author doesn't say how Gold was received in the Iranian university classroom (though she remarks that her copy of *Jews without Money* caused consternation during a search of her belongings at the Tehran airport). Instead, in the memoir published more than two decades later, one purpose of which is to expose the corruption and tyranny of the Islamic Republic of Iran, she equates Gold's communism with the fundamentalism of Ayatollah Khomeini. After witnessing the brutal imposition of state authority in her homeland, "now, in retrospect," Nafisi decides, "the revolution Gold desired was a Marxist one and ours was Islamic, but they had a great deal in common, in that they were both ideological and totalitarian." To prove her point, Nafisi quotes out of context a few sentences from Gold's essay "Towards Proletarian Art," referring to the passage disparagingly. She then delivers a decisive stroke: "Such sentences could have come out of any newspaper in Iran."[52]

The stunning transformation of Nafisi's literary standards from one decade and context to another replicates the arc of Michael Gold's career, exposing the contradictions behind his marginalization as a literary figure. Nafisi's unstable appraisal of proletarian art has several implications for Gold's present and future standing. First, it serves as a general reminder of the politics of canon formation as they operate now and always. Second, the text's thinly disguised warning that neglect of our "great writers" in favor of Gold could produce a form of totalitarianism in the United States analogous to what Nafisi found in Iran reflects the reactionary processes by which Michael Gold was erased from cultural memory.

A final, contemporary object lesson to be derived from *Reading Lolita in Tehran* involves the recognition that the extremism Nafisi criticizes in Iran resembles twenty-first-century examples of US political intolerance more than many are willing to recognize. The text, after all, articulates Nafisi's passionate argument to Iranian students in 1979—but actually to well over a million American readers in 2003—that Mike Gold is still unworthy of acceptance by the literary establishment, and still dangerous.

In a period of corporate control, wealth disparity, and the mainstreaming of proto-fascism, Michael Gold should be more than ever of interest to a cultural establishment whose attention to his work has been insufficient. But whether the voice we privilege in *Reading Lolita in Tehran* is that of the twenty-nine-year-old PhD in literature who loved Gold or the middle-aged famous author who likened his ideals to tyranny and brutality, Nafisi's text suggests reasons to read and reconsider the literary pariah, both globally and at home. Meanwhile, the paradox Nafisi explained to her colleagues in Tehran, a statement that came from the Nafisi who loved Gold, is still true and bears repeating: "You may not believe it, but he was a big shot in his day."[53]

Nafisi's insight about the best American writer that is still largely unknown to Americans would seem a viable way to bring this study to a close. But if we've learned anything about Mike, the people's writer, we know he wouldn't have been pleased at giving the last word to a defector from world socialism. In fact he'd have been outraged, though not surprised, that yet another revolutionary had turn red baiter. Better, maybe, to quote from a proletarian letter, a form of writing first granted the status of literature by Michael Gold, whose life was a long battle for just such militant visibility for marginalized people. In the book review section of the *Liberated Guardian* of July 1972, there is a letter in response to the just-published Gold anthology, from a person identified only as "a member of the collective":

> In reading this book I got an excited sense that I was reading what my history was about—not the explorers and wars shit they teach you in school, but the history of poor and working and minority people, the history of the revolutionary movement. This is the history they don't tell us in school or on television, the history that is dangerous for the Man to let us know about. We need to get to know our history and we need to get in touch with the strength that comes from knowing our past. Mike Gold's stories are part of a strong, proud heritage of ours.[54]

NOTES

Introduction

1. Sinclair Lewis, "The American Fear of Literature," Nobel Lecture, 12 Dec. 1930.

2. Alan Wald, *Exiles from a Future Time*, University of North Carolina Press, 2002, p. 55.

3. Michael Folsom, "The Book of Poverty," *Nation*, 28 Feb. 1966, p. 242.

4. Folsom, "The Book of Poverty," pp. 242, 244.

5. Michael Folsom, unpublished manuscript, Gold-Folsom Papers, University of Michigan, Ann Arbor.

6. John Pyros, *Mike Gold: Dean of American Proletarian Writers*, Dramatika Press, 1979, p. I.

7. Alfred Kazin, "Introduction," *Jews without Money*, by Michael Gold, Carrol & Graf, 1996, p. 4.

8. Paul Berman, "East Side Story: Mike Gold, the Communists, and the Jews," *Village Voice*, Mar. 1983, p. 39.

9. Stanely Burnshaw to Alan Wald, 10 Dec. 1990, quoted in Alan Wald, *Exiles from a Future Time*, University of North Carolina Press, 2002, p. 63.

10. Gold, "A Bourgeois Hamlet of Our Time," *New Masses*, 10 Apr. 1934, pp. 28–29.

11. Gold, "Go Left, Young Writers," *Mike Gold: A Literary Anthology*, edited by Michael Folsom, International Publishers, 1972, p. 186.

12. Gold, "Go Left, Young Writers," p. 189.

13. Richard Reuss, *American Folk Music and Left-Wing Politics, 1927–1957*, Scarecrow Press, 2000, p. 72.

14. Reuss, *American Folk Music and Left-Wing Politics, 1927–1957*, p. 72.

15. Art Shields, "Mike Gold, Our Joy and Pride," *Political Affairs*, vol. 57, no. 1, Jul. 1972, p. 49.

16. Reuss, *American Folk Music and Left-Wing Politics, 1927–1957*, p. 72.

17. Shields, "Mike Gold, Our Joy and Pride," p. 58.

18. Reuss, *American Folk Music and Left-Wing Politics, 1927–1957,* p. 72.

19. Gold, "The Troubled Land," *Masses & Mainstream,* July 1954, p. 4.

20. Art Shields, "Mike Gold, Our Joy and Pride," p. 49.

21. Richard Ruess, *American Folk Music and Left-Wing Politics, 1927–1957,* p. 72.

Chapter One

1. Handbill event announcement, "Mike Gold Anniversary Meeting," 2 Mar. 1941, Gold-Folsom Papers, University of Michigan, Ann Arbor.

2. Telegram from "A Group of Mens Clothing Workers," 2 Mar. 1941, Gold-Folsom Papers.

3. "Browder Calls Gold 'Poet of the People,'" *Daily Worker,* 3 Mar. 1941, pp. 1, 5.

4. Art Young, tribute message, 2 Mar. 1941, Gold-Folsom Papers.

5. Gold, "Change the World," 8 Apr. 1940, p. 7.

6. West Virginia coal miners, telegram, 2 Mar. 1941, Gold-Folsom Papers.

7. Gold, unpublished memoirs, 3 Nov. 1966, Gold-Folsom Papers.

8. Michael Gold, *The Hollow Men,* International Publishers, 1941.

9. Joseph North, "Mike Gold Back Home," *Daily Worker,* 10 Mar. 1950, pp. 3, 9.

10. "Reception for Mike Gold Thursday at Manhattan Towers Hotel," *Daily Worker,* 19 Apr. 1950, p. 11.

11. "Reception for Mike Gold."

12. Edmund Wilson, "The Literary Class War: II," *New Republic,* 11 May 1932, p. 348.

13. "Browder Calls Gold 'Poet of the People,'" *Daily Worker,* 5 Mar. 1941, p. 5.

14. "Browder Calls Gold 'Poet of the People,'" *Daily Worker,* 5 Mar. 1941, p. 5.

15. "Rubles Flow as Mike Gold Gets 2d Wind," unsigned article, 1941, Gold-Folsom Papers.

16. *Daily Worker,* 23 Mar. 1950, p. 7.

17. *Daily Worker,* 28 Apr. 1950, p. 7.

18. David Platt, "Mike Gold Is 60—Tributes Pour In," *Daily Worker,* 14 Apr. 1954. Quoted in Alan Wald, *Exiles from a Future Time,* University of North Carolina Press, 2002, p. 40.

19. Mike Gold, FBI file specific to the Detroit Field Office, obtained under provisions of the Freedom of Information Act, assorted documents ranging from 1950 to 1956. Internal case file no. 100-DE-18926.

20. Gold FBI file. Unless otherwise noted, all quotes from accounts of the 26 May 1954 Gold birthday meeting in Detroit are from reports contained in the Detroit Field Office FBI file.

21. Gold, unpublished memoirs, 19 May 1966. Gold added, "And now we are reaching the youth again and as I said it is a wonderful feeling."

22. See William Maxwell, *F. B. Eyes: How J. Edgar Hoover's Ghostreaders Framed African American Literature*, Princeton UP, 2015.

23. W. H. Lawrence, "Three Officers Dispute McCarthy Charge of Phony Charts," *New York Times*, 26 May 1954, p. 1.

24. "Red Hunters Assailed," *New York Times*, 26 May 1954.

25. William Sullivan, *The Bureau*, W. W. Norton and Company, 1979, p. 45.

26. Handbill event announcement, "Mike Gold's 60th Anniversary," Mike Gold FBI file.

27. Jose Fernandez Diaz, "Guantanamera" (original music and lyrics), arranged and adapted by Julian Orbon, Hector Angelo, and Pete Seeger, 1949, 1963, 1964.

28. Press release, *San Francisco People's World*, 16 May 1967.

29. John Howard Lawson, "The Stature of Michael Gold," *Political Affairs*, June 1967, p. 14.

Chapter Two

1. Gold, unpublished memoirs, 19 May 1966.

2. Michael Gold, "Birth," *Masses*, Nov.–Dec. 1917, reprinted in *Mike Gold: A Literary Anthology*, edited by Michael Folsom, International Publishers, 1972, pp. 44–48. The story is subtitled, "A Prologue to an East Side Novel."

3. Gold, "Birth," p. 47.

4. Gold, "Birth," p. 47.

5. Gold, "Birth," p. 48.

6. Gold, "Birth," p. 44.

7. Alan Wald, *Exiles From a Future Time: The Forging of the Mid-Twentieth-Century Literary Left*, U of North Carolina P, 2002, p. 47.

8. Gold, "Birth," pp. 44–45.

9. Gold, *Jews without Money*, 1930, reprint, Carroll & Graf, 2004, p. 128.

10. Manny Granich, Oral History Interview Transcripts, Grace and Max Granich Papers, Tamiment Library and Robert F. Wagner Labor Archives, New York University.

11. Manny Granich, Oral History Interview Transcripts.

12. Michael Gold, "A Jewish Childhood in the New York Slums," 1959, reprinted in *Mike Gold: A Literary Anthology*, edited by Folsom, p. 309.

13. Gold, *Jews without Money*, pp. 87–88, 103.

14. Adapted from *Jews without Money*, chapter 7.

15. Gold, "Change the World," *San Francisco Peoples World*, 3 Aug. 1958.

16. Gold, "A Jewish Childhood in the New York Slums," p. 307.

17. Nahma Sandrow, *Vagabond Stars: A World of Yiddish Theater*, Syracuse UP, 1996, pp. 77, 91.

18. Gold, *Jews without Money*, p. 88.

19. Sandrow, *Vagabond Stars: A World of Yiddish Theater*, pp. 165–66.

20. Gold, "A Jewish Childhood in the New York Slums," p. 310.

21. Gold, "A Jewish Childhood in the New York Slums," p. 311.

22. Gold, *Jews without Money*, p. 307.

23. Gold, "Change the World," *Daily Worker*, 3 Sept. 1946.

24. Gold, "A Jewish Childhood in the New York Slums," p. 293.

25. Gold, unpublished memoirs, 15 Sept. 1966, alternate version in "A Jewish Childhood in the New York Slums," by Gold, p. 293.

26. Gold, unpublished memoirs, 15 Sept. 1966.

27. Gold, "A Jewish Childhood in the New York Slums," p. 295.

28. Gold, "A Jewish Childhood in the New York Slums," p. 297.

29. Manny Granich, Oral History Interview Transcripts.

30. Manny Granich, Oral History Interview Transcripts.

31. Gold, unpublished memoirs, 19 May 1966.

32. Gold, unpublished memoirs, 19 May 1966.

33. Gold, unpublished memoirs, 19 May 1966.

34. Gold, "A Jewish Childhood in the New York Slums," p. 303.

35. Gold, "A Jewish Childhood in the New York Slums," p. 308.

36. Gold, "The Trap," New York *Call*, 17 Jun. 1917, p. 6, reprinted in "Three Early Stories by Mike Gold in the New York *Call*" by David Roessel, *Resources for American Literary Study*, vol. 33, 2010, pp. 133–53.

37. Gold, "The Trap," New York *Call*, 17 Jun. 1917, p. 6.

38. David Roessel, "Three Early Stories by Mike Gold in the New York *Call*," *Resources for American Literary Study*, vol. 33, 2010, p. 139.

39. Gold, "The Password to Thought—To Culture," *Liberator*, Feb. 1922, reprinted in *Mike Gold: A Literary Anthology*, edited by Michael Folsom, International Publishers, 1972, p. 103.

40. Gold, "The Password to Thought—To Culture," p. 105.

41. Gold, "The Password to Thought—To Culture," pp. 105–06.

42. Gold, "The Password to Thought—To Culture," p. 110.

43. Gold, "A Jewish Childhood in the New York Slums," 308.

44. Manny Granich, Oral History Interview Transcripts.

45. Manny Granich, Oral History Interview Transcripts.

46. Gold, "The *Masses* Tradition," *Masses & Mainstream*, vol. 4, no. 8, Aug. 1951, p. 46.

47. Manny Granich, Oral History Interview Transcripts.

48. Gold, "Why I Am a Communist," *A Literary Anthology*, edited by Folsom, p. 203.

49. Gold often gave 1894 as his birth year.

50. Gold, *Jews without Money*, p. 309.

51. Herbert Feis to Michael Folsom, 1 Oct. 1971, Gold-Folsom Papers.

52. Quoted in Michael Folsom's unpublished manuscript, *Mike Gold: A Literary Life*, n.d., Gold-Folsom Papers.

53. Gold, unpublished memoirs, 1 Sept. 1966.

54. Application summary provided by Harvard University Admissions Office to Michael Folsom, n.d., Gold-Folsom Papers

55. Manny Granich, Oral History Interview Transcripts.

56. Application summary provided by Harvard University Admissions Office to Michael Folsom, n.d., Gold-Folsom Papers.

57. Gold, unpublished memoirs, 15 Sept. 1966.

58. Gold, unpublished memoirs, 15 Sept. 1966.

59. Gold, unpublished memoirs, 15 Sept. 1966.

60. Application summary provided by Harvard University Admissions Office.

61. In his passport application before his 1930 trip to the Soviet Union, Gold stated that his father had died in August 1912, which makes Gold nineteen years and four months old at the time of Charles Granich's death.

62. Gold, "Change the World," *Daily Worker*, 3 Sept. 1946.

Chapter Three

1. Gold, unpublished memoirs, 1 Sept. 1966, Gold-Folsom Papers, University of Michigan, Ann Arbor.

2. Gold, unpublished memoirs, 1 Sept. 1966.

3. Gold, unpublished memoirs, 1 Sept. 1966.

4. Gold, unpublished memoirs, 1 Sept. 1966. When it came to Harvard, Gold said, his "poor mother . . . never knew what all the shouting was about."

5. Gold, unpublished memoirs, 1 Sept. 1966.

6. Gold, "A Freshman at Harvard," 19 Oct. 1914.

7. Gold, "A Freshman at Harvard," 13 Nov. 1914.

8. Gold, "A Freshman at Harvard," 17 Nov. 1914.

9. Gold, "A Freshman at Harvard," 20 Oct. 1914.

10. Gold, "A Freshman at Harvard," 20 Oct. 1914.

11. Gold, "A Freshman at Harvard," 5 Nov. 1914.

12. Gold, "A Freshman at Harvard," 5 Nov. 1914.

13. Michael Gold, *Jews without Money*, H. Liveright, 1930, 2nd. ed., Carroll & Graf, 1996, pp. 112–13.

14. Gold, "A Freshman at Harvard," 3 Nov. 1914.

15. Gold, "A Freshman at Harvard," 3 Nov. 1914.

16. Gold, "A Freshman at Harvard," 10 Nov. 1914.

17. Gold, "A Freshman at Harvard," 29 Nov. 1914.

18. Gold, "A Freshman at Harvard," 29 Nov. 1914.

19. Herbert Feis to Elizabeth Humeston (née Elizabeth Granich), 7 May 1971. Gold-Folsom Papers, University of Michigan, Ann Arbor.

20. See Megan M. Holland, *Divergent Paths to College: Race, Class, and Inequality in High Schools*, Rutgers UP, 2019. See also Anthony Abraham Jack, *The Privileged Poor*, Harvard UP, 2019.

21. Gold, unpublished memoirs, 1 Sept. 1966.

22. Quoted in Alan Wald, *Exiles from a Future Time: The Forging of the Mid-Twentieth-Century Literary Left*, U of North Carolina P, 2002, p. 50.

23. John Dos Passos, *Monde* (Paris), 18 Jan. 1930, p. 3.

24. John Dos Passos, "The Making of a Writer," *New Masses*, Mar. 1929, p. 23.

25. Gold, "Love on a Garbage Dump," in *Mike Gold: A Literary Anthology*, edited by Michael Folsom, International Publishers, 1972, p. 177.

26. Feis to Humeston, 7 May 1971.

27. Gold, unpublished memoirs, 1 Sept. 1966.

28. Gold, unpublished memoirs, 1 Sept. 1966.

29. Gold, unpublished memoirs, 1 Sept. 1966.

30. Gold, unpublished memoirs, 1 Sept. 1966.

31. Gold, unpublished memoirs, 1 Sept. 1966.

32. Irwin Granich, "Anarchists in Plymouth," *Revolt*, 5 February 1916.

33. Granich, "Anarchists in Plymouth."

34. Irwin Granich and Van K. Allison, eds., *The Flame*, Aug. 1916.

35. Gold, "Thoughts of a Great Thinker" *Liberator*, Apr. 1922, reprinted in *Mike Gold: A Literary Anthology*, edited by Folsom, p. 114.

36. Sinclair, *Boston*, A. & C. Boni, 1928, p. 77.

37. Upton, *Boston*, p. 79.

38. Gold, unpublished memoirs, 19 May 1966.

39. Gold, unpublished memoirs, 19 May 1966.

40. David Roessel, "'What Made You Leave the Movement?' O'Neill, Mike Gold, and the Radicalism of the Provincetown Players," *Eugene O'Neill and His Early Contemporaries*, edited by Robert Dowling and Eileen Hermann, McFarland, 2011, p. 237.

41. Gold, unpublished memoirs, 19 May 1966, quoted also in Roessel, "'What Made You Leave the Movement?'" pp. 236–37.

42. Gold, *Money*, One-Act Plays, edited by Barrett H. Clark and Thomas R. Cook, D. C. Heath, 1929, p. 229.

43. Gold, unpublished memoirs, 19 Oct. 1966.

44. M. N. Roy, *M. N. Roy's Memoirs*, Bombay, Allied Publishers, 1964, p. 110.

45. Gold, unpublished memoirs, 19 Oct. 1966.

46. Thomas R. Cook, Introduction, *One-Act Plays*, edited by Barrett H. Clark and Thomas R. Cook, D. C. Heath, 1929, p. xvi.

47. Eugene O'Neill to Kenneth McGowan, *The Theatre We Worked For: The Letters of Eugene O'Neill to Kenneth McGowan*, edited by Jackson Breyer, Yale UP,

1982, p. 90. Quoted also in Roessel, "What Made You Leave the Movement?," p. 243.

48. Nahma Sandrow, *Vagabond Stars: A World of Yiddish Theater*, Syracuse UP, 1996, p. 201.

49. Gold, unpublished memoirs, 26 May 1966.

50. Kate Hennessy, *Dorothy Day: The World Will Be Saved by Beauty*, Scribner's, 2017, p. 10.

51. Hennessy, *Dorothy Day*, p. 10.

52. Hennessy, *Dorothy Day*, pp. 15–16.

53. Gold, "Reed: He Loved the People," *New Masses*, 22 Oct. 1940, pp. 8–11.

54. Gold, "Reed: He Loved the People," pp. 8–11.

55. Louise Bryant to Robert Hallowell, 19 Nov. 1934. Virginia Gardner Papers, Tamiment Library and Robert F. Wagner Labor Archives, New York University.

56. Gold, unpublished memoirs, 19 Aug. 1966.

57. Gold, unpublished memoirs, 19 Aug. 1966.

58. Wald, *Exiles from a Future Time*, p. 51.

59. Dorothy Day, "Michael Gold," *The Catholic Worker*, June 1967, pp. 2, 8.

60. M. N. Roy, *M. N. Roy's Memoirs*, p. 110.

61. M. N. Roy, *M. N. Roy's Memoirs*, p. 120.

62. M. N. Roy, *M. N. Roy's Memoirs*, p. 117.

63. M. N. Roy, *M. N. Roy's Memoirs*, p. 143.

64. M. N. Roy, *M. N. Roy's Memoirs*, p. 144.

65. Carleton Beals to Kenneth W. Payne, 23 Feb. 1971, Gold-Folsom Papers.

66. Michael Gold, "Sowing the Seeds of One Big Union in Mexico," *One Big Union Monthly*, vol. 2, no. 1, Jan. 1920, p. 36.

67. Gold, "Sowing the Seeds of One Big Union in Mexico," p. 36.

68. Gold, "Two Mexicos," *Mike Gold: A Literary Anthology*, edited by Folsom, p. 54.

69. Gold, "Two Mexicos," p. 61.

70. Quoted in John Pyros, *Mike Gold: Dean of American Proletarian Writers*, Dramatika Press, 1979, p. 73.

71. Wald, *Exiles from a Future Time*, p. 51.

72. Marcus Klein, *Foreigners: The Making of American Literature, 1900–1940*, U of Chicago P, 1981, p. 234.

Chapter Four

1. Max Eastman, *Love and Revolution*, Random House, 1964, p. 265.

2. New York *Call*, Jan. 1918, quoted in Eastman, *Love and Revolution*, p. 266.

3. Gold, "Towards Proletarian Art," *Mike Gold: A Literary Anthology*, edited by Michael Folsom, International Publishers, 1972, pp. 67, 70, 62.

4. Gold, "Towards Proletarian Art," pp. 62, 63.

5. Gold, "Towards Proletarian Art," p. 64.

6. Gold, "Towards Proletarian Art," pp. 64–65.

7. Gold, "Towards Proletarian Art," p. 65.

8. Gold, "Towards Proletarian Art," p. 65.

9. David Roessel, "Three Early Stories by Mike Gold in the *New York Call*," *Resources for American Literary Study*, vol. 33, 2010, pp. 141–42.

10. Max Eastman, *Love and Revolution*, p. 267.

11. Michael Folsom, editor, *Mike Gold: A Literary Anthology*, International Publishers, 1972, p. 62.

12. Max Eastman, *Love and Revolution*, p. 268.

13. Michael Gold, unpublished memoirs, 5 Aug. 1966, Gold-Folsom Papers, University of Michigan, Ann Arbor.

14. Max Eastman, *Love and Revolution*, pp. 268–69.

15. Gold, unpublished memoirs, 5 Aug. 1966.

16. Max Eastman, *Love and Revolution*, pp. 269–70.

17. Harold Cruse, *The Crisis of the Negro Intellectual*, William & Morrow, 1967, p. 49.

18. Alan Wald, *Exiles from a Future Time: The Forging of the Mid-Twentieth-Century Literary Left*, U of North Carolina P, 2002, p. 51.

19. William J. Maxwell, "The Proletarian as New Negro: Mike Gold's Harlem Renaissance," *Radical Revisions: Rereading 1930s Culture*, edited by Bill V. Mullen and Sherry Linkon, U of Illinois P, 1996, p. 100.

20. U.S. Department of Justice, "Radicalism and Sedition among the Negroes, As Reflected in Their Publications," *New York Times*, 23 Nov. 1919.

21. Gold, unpublished memoirs, 5 Aug. 1966.

22. Gold, unpublished memoirs, 5 Aug. 1966.

23. Maxwell, "The Proletarian as New Negro: Mike Gold's Harlem Renaissance," p. 100.

24. Michael Gold, *Life of John Brown*, Haldeman-Julius Publications, 1924, p. 3, reprint, Roving Eye Press, 1960.

25. Art Shields, *On the Battle Lines, 1919–1939*, International Publishers, 1986.

26. Art Shields, *On the Battle Lines, 1919–1939*, p. 77.

27. Art Shields, "Mike Gold: Our Joy and Pride" *Political Affairs*, vol. 51, no. 7, July 1972, pp. 41–58.

28. Mike Gold, FBI file obtained under provisions of the Freedom of Information Act, assorted documents ranging from 1922 to 1967, internal case file no. 1385228-0.

29. Gold, "Smoke and Steel," *The Worker*, 15 Jul. 1992.

30. Gold, unpublished memoirs, 5 Aug. 1966.

31. Gold, unpublished memoirs, 5 Aug. 1966.

32. Gold, unpublished memoirs, 5 Aug. 1966.

33. Gold, unpublished memoirs, 5 Aug. 1966.

34. Shields, *On the Battle Lines, 1919–1939*, p. 94.

35. Robert Shaw to Michael Folsom, n.d., Gold-Folsom Papers, University of Michigan, Ann Arbor.

36. Theodore Dreiser to Michael Gold, n.d. (1923), Gold-Folsom Papers, University of Michigan, Ann Arbor.

37. Gold, unpublished memoirs, 20 Sept. 1966.

38. Gold, unpublished memoirs, 6 Oct. 1966.

39. Gold, unpublished memoirs, 13 Oct. 1966.

40. Michael Gold, "Theater and Revolution," *The Nation*, vol. 121, no. 3149, Nov. 11, 1925, pp. 536–37.

41. Gold, unpublished memoirs, 13 Oct. 1966.

42. Gold, unpublished memoirs, 19 Oct. 1966.

43. Gold, Unpublished memoirs, 19 Oct. 1966.

44. Michael Gold, *The Damned Agitator and Other Stories*, Daily Worker Publishing, 1924, p. 4.

45. Gold, *The Damned Agitator and Other Stories,* pp. 3, 16.

46. Michael Gold, *120 Million*, Modern Books, 1929, p. 62.

47. Gold, *120 Million*, p. 69.

48. Gold, *120 Million*, p. 70.

49. Gold, *120 Million*, p. 140.

50. John Pyros, *Mike Gold: Dean of American Proletarian Writers*, Dramatika Press, 1979, p. 20.

51. Gold, *120 Million*, p. 170.

52. Gold, *120 Million*, pp. 191–92.

53. Shields, *On the Battle Lines, 1919–1939*, p. 126.

54. Shields, *On the Battle Lines, 1919–1939*, pp. 93–94.

55. Michael Gold, "The Education of John Dos Passos" *The English Journal*, vol. 22, no. 2, Feb. 1933, pp. 87–97.

56. Michael Gold, "William L. Patterson, Militant Leader," *Masses & Mainstream*, vol. 4 no. 2, Feb. 1951, p. 38.

57. Gold, "William L. Patterson, Militant Leader," p. 38.

58. Gold, "William L. Patterson, Militant Leader," pp. 38–39.

59. Helen Black, "Will They Be Remembered?" *Daily Worker*, 30 Aug. 1927, p. 6.

60. Gold, "Lynchers in Frockcoats." *New Masses*, Sept. 1927, reprinted in *Mike Gold: A Literary Anthology*, edited by Folsom, p. 148.

61. Gold, "Lynchers in Frockcoats," p. 150.

62. Gold, "Lynchers in Frockcoats," p. 151.

63. Gold, unpublished memoirs, 5 May 1966.

64. Gold, unpublished memoirs, 5 May 1966.

65. Gold, unpublished memoirs, 5 May 1966.

66. Kate Hennessy, *Dorothy Day: The World Will be Saved By Beauty*, Scribner's, 2017, p. 37.

67. Dorothy Day, "Michael Gold," *The Catholic Worker*, June 1967, pp. 2, 8.

68. Day, "Michael Gold," pp. 2, 8.

69. Gold, unpublished memoirs, 19 Oct. 1966.

70. Gold, *Hoboken Blues: The Black Rip Van Winkle: A Modern Negro Fantasia on an Old American Theme*, *The American Caravan: A Yearbook of American Literature*, edited by Van Wyck Brooks, Alfred Kreymborg, Lewis Mumford, and Paul Rosenfeld, Literary Guild of America, 1927, p. 626.

71. Gold, *Hoboken Blues*, p. 548.

72. Gold, *Hoboken Blues*, p. 549.

73. Maxwell, "The Proletarian as New Negro: Mike Gold's Harlem Renaissance." p. 106.

74. Gold, unpublished memoirs, 19 Oct. 1966.

75. John Howard Lawson, "The Stature of Michael Gold," *Political Affairs*, vol. 46, no. 6, June 1967, p. 12.

76. "Ghetto," unsigned book review, *Time*, 24 Feb. 1930, p. 82.

77. Joseph Freeman, *An American Testament:. A Narrative of Rebels and Romantics*, Farrar & Rinehart, 1936, pp. 379, 381.

78. Quoted in Freeman, *An American Testament*, p. 85.

79. Joseph Freeman, *An American Testament*, p. 381.

80. Joseph Freeman, *An American Testament*, p. 635.

81. Gold, unpublished memoirs, 19 May 1966.

82. Gold, unpublished memoirs, 19 May 1966.

83. A. B. Magill, "Rebirth of New Masses," *Daily Worker*, 2 Jun. 1928, p. 5.

84. Gold, unpublished memoirs, 12 May 1966.

85. Gold, unpublished memoirs, 13 Jan. 1966.

86. Gold, unpublished memoirs, 13 Jan. 1966.

87. Gold, unpublished memoirs, 13 Jan. 1966.

88. Gold, unpublished memoirs, 13 Jan. 1966.

89. Gold, unpublished memoirs, 13 Jan. 1966.

90. Gold, unpublished memoirs, 13 Jan. 1966.

91. Gold, "Notes from Kharkov," *New Masses*, Mar. 1931, pp. 4–6.

92. Freeman, *An American Testament*, p. 257.

93. Floyd Dell, "Explanations and Apologies," *Liberator*, Jun. 1922, p. 25.

94. Michael Gold, "John Reed and the Real Thing," *New Masses*, Nov. 1927, reprinted in *Mike Gold: A Literary Anthology*, edited by Michael Folsom, pp. 203–08.

95. Douglas Clayton, *Floyd Dell: The Life and Times of an American Rebel*, Ivan R. Dee, 1994, p. 253.

96. Michael Gold, "Floyd Dell Resigns," *New Masses*, Jul. 1929, p. 10.

97. Norman MacLeod and Rose Marmon, quoted in Wald, *Exiles from a Future Time*, p. 105.

98. Michael Gold, "A New Program for Writers," *New Masses*, Jan. 1930, p. 21.

Chapter Five

1. Michael Gold, unpublished memoirs, 5 Feb. 1966, Gold-Folsom Papers, University of Michigan, Ann Arbor.

2. Gold, unpublished memoirs, 5 Feb. 1966.

3. Michael Gold, "Notes on Crap Shooting, etc." *New Masses*, Sept. 1929, p. 10.

4. Michael Gold, "American Jungle Notes," *New Masses*, Dec. 1929, p. 8.

5. Quoted in Joseph Freeman, *An American Testament: A Narrative of Rebels and Romantics*, 1936, Octagon Books, 1973, p. 238.

6. Gold, unpublished memoirs, 5 Feb. 1966 and 7 Mar. 1966.

7. Michael Gold, "Letter from a Clam-Digger," *New Masses*, Nov. 1929, 1p. 0.

8. Walter Rideout, *The Radical Novel in the United States, 1900–1954*, Harvard UP, 1956, pp. 151, 153.

9. See Alan Wald, *Exiles from a Future Time: The Forging of the Mid-Twentieth-Century Literary Left*, U of North Carolina P, 2002, pp. 103–05.

10. Wald, *Exiles from a Future Time*, p. 104.

11. Michael Gold, "Notes from Kharkov," *New Masses*, Mar. 1931, p. 5.

12. Gold, "Notes from Kharkov," p. 6.

13. Gold, unpublished memoirs, 11 Aug. 1966.

14. Gold, unpublished memoirs, 11 Aug. 1966.

15. Gold, unpublished memoirs, 18 Mar. 1966.

16. Gold, unpublished memoirs, 18 Mar. 1966.

17. Michael Gold, "Notes on Hunger March," manuscript fragment, Gold-Folsom papers.

18. Dorothy Day, *The Long Loneliness*, Harper & Rowe, 1952, p. 162.

19. Day, *The Long Loneliness*, p. 166.

20. Gold, unpublished memoirs, 18 Mar. 1966.

21. Gold, unpublished memoirs, 18 Mar. 1966.

22. Gold, unpublished memoirs, 18 Mar. 1966.

23. Michael Gold, *The Honorable Pete*, unpublished manuscript, c. 1952, Gold-Folsom Papers, p. 45.

24. Gold, *The Honorable Pete*, pp. 58–59.

25. Gold, *The Honorable Pete*, pp. 62–63.

26. Gold, *The Honorable Pete*, pp. 54, 52.

27. Michael Gold, *Moscow Love*, unpublished manuscript, c. 1931, Gold-Folsom Papers.

28. Gold, *Moscow Love*, unpublished manuscript, c. 1931, Gold-Folsom Papers.

29. Gold, *Moscow Love*, unpublished manuscript, c. 1931, Gold-Folsom Papers.

30. Michael Folsom to John Brogna, 7 Apr. 1976, Gold-Folsom Papers.

31. Michael Gold, "Change the World," *Daily Worker*, 12 Feb. 1934, p. 5.

32. Michael Gold, "Proletarian Realism," *Mike Gold: A Literary Anthology*, edited by Michael Folsom, International Publishers, 1972, p. 206.

33. Gold, "Proletarian Realism," p. 208.

34. Gold, *Jews without Money*, 1930, reprint, Carroll & Graf, 1996, pp. 2, 71, 112.

35. Sinclair Lewis, "The American Fear of Literature." Nobel Lecture, 12 Dec. 1930.

36. Gold, *Jews without Money*, pp. 57, 58, 53, 15, 60, 64, 284.

37. Gold, *Jews without Money*, pp. 128, 159, 243, 305.

38. Gold, *Jews without Money*, 309.

39. George Hanon, "Gold's Book of East Side Senses Revolt," *Daily Worker*, 31 May 1930, p. 3.

40. Hanon, "Gold's Book of East Side Senses Revolt," p. 3.

41. *Time* magazine, vol. 15, no. 8, 24 Feb. 1930, p. 82.

42. Michael Gold, "*Jews without Money*: From a Book of East Side Memoirs," *New Masses*, June 1928, p. 11.

43. Students who have read *Jews without Money* in my literature courses over the years have commented about feeling uncomfortable reading the book in public and have told about looks or comments they've received. A situation similar to the one Gold recounted in Germany happened to Iranian American writer-scholar Azar Nafisi, the author of *Reading Lolita in Tehran*, who claimed that Gold's book, found among her belongings during a customs inspection in the Tehran airport in 1979, worried Iranian officials to a degree that complicated Nafisi's return to the country of her birth.

44. Gold, *Jews without Money*, pp. 11–12.

45. Wald, *Exiles from a Future Time*, p. 56.

46. Manny Granich Oral History Interview Transcript, Wagner Labor Archives, New York University.

47. Wald, *Exiles from a Future Time*, 45.

48. Melvin P. Levy, "Michael Gold," *The New Republic*, 26 Mar. 1930, pp. 160–61.

49. Michael Gold, "A Proletarian Novel?" *New Republic*, 4 Jun. 1930, p. 74.

50. Gold, "A Proletarian Novel?," p. 74.

51. V. F. Calverton, *The Liberation of American Literature*, Charles Scribner's Sons, 1932, p. 465.

52. Edmund Wilson, "The Literary Class War: I," *New Republic*, 4 May 1932, p. 322.

53. Michael Harrington, Afterword, *Jews without Money*, by Michael Gold, Avon Books, 1965. Quoted in Michael Folsom, "The Book of Poverty," *The Nation*, 28 Feb. 1966, p. 244.

54. Robert Forsythe, Foreword. *Change the World!* by Michael Gold, International Publishers, 1937, p. 9.

55. Folsom, "The Book of Poverty," p. 244.

56. Barbara Foley, *Radical Representations: Politics and Form in U.S. Proletarian Fiction, 1929–1941*, Duke UP, 1993, p. 284.

57. Richard Tuerk, "*Jews without Money* as a Work of Art," *Studies in American Literature*, vol. 7, no. 1, spring 1988, p. 77.

58. Michael Denning, *The Cultural Front: The Laboring of American Culture in the Twentieth Century*, Verso, 1997, pp. 230, 231.

59. Gold, *Jews without Money*, p. 71.

60. Gold, *Jews without Money*, p. 55.

61. Michael Gold, "Wilder: Prophet of the Genteel Christ," reprinted in *Mike Gold: A Literary Anthology*, edited by Michael Folsom, International Publishers, 1972, pp. 201–02.

62. Gold, "Wilder: Prophet of the Genteel Christ," p. 197.

63. Gold, "Wilder: Prophet of the Genteel Christ," pp. 200–01.

64. Gold, "Wilder: Prophet of the Genteel Christ," pp. 198, 199, 200.

65. Edmund Wilson, "The Economic Interpretation of Wilder," *New Republic*, 26 Nov. 1930, p. 31.

66. Wilson, "The Economic Interpretation of Wilder," pp. 31, 32.

67. Wilson, "The Economic Interpretation of Wilder," p. 32.

68. Joseph North, "Mike Gold Won World Fame as Proletarian Writer," *The Worker*, 21 May 1967.

69. Wilson, "The Economic Interpretation of Wilder," p. 32.

70. Marcus Klein, *Foreigners: The Making of American Literature, 1900–1940*, University of Chicago Press, 1981, p. 247.

71. "Homage to Michael Gold," *New Republic*, 12 Nov. 1930, p. 353.

72. Klein, *Foreigners: The Making of American Literature, 1900–1940*, University of Chicago Press, 1981, p. 248.

73. Edmund Wilson, "The Literary Class War: I" *New Republic*, 4 May 1932, p. 319.

74. Folsom, editor, *Mike Gold: A Literary Anthology*, p. 200.

75. John Pyros, *Mike Gold: Dean of American Proletarian Writers* Dramatika Press, 1979, p. 116.

76. Gold, unpublished memoirs, 15 Sept. 1966.

77. V. F. Calverton, *The Liberation of American Literature*, Charles Scribner's Sons, 1932, p. 40.

78. Calverton, *The Liberation of American Literature*, pp. 457, 458.

79. Calverton, *The Liberation of American Literature*, pp. 458–59, 460.

80. Michael Gold, "Go Left, Young Writers," *Mike Gold: A Literary Anthology*, edited by Folsom, p. 188.

81. Gold, "Go Left, Young Writers," p. 189.

82. Calverton, *The Liberation of American Literature*, pp. 463–64.

83. Gold to Louise Bryant [Mrs. William Bullitt], 15 Nov. 1926, Virginia Gardner Papers, Wagner Labor Archives, New York University.

84. Mary V. Dearborn, *Queen of Bohemia: The Life of Louise Bryant*, Houghton Mifflin, 1996, p. 228.

85. Gold to Louise Bryant [Mrs. William Bullitt], 15 Nov. 1926.

86. Louise Bryant to Corliss Lamont, 30 Oct. 1935, Virginia Gardner Papers.

87. Wald, *Exiles from a Future Time*, p. 59.

88. Wald, *Exiles from a Future Time*, p. 58.

89. Wald, *Exiles from a Future Time*, p. 103.

90. Si Gerson, "Digging for Gold," *Daily Worker*, 17 Jan. 1931, p. 4.

91. Julia L. Mickenberg, *Learning from the Left: Children's Literature, the Cold War, and Radical Politics in the United States*, Oxford UP, 2006, p. 297.

92. Michael Gold, unpublished memoirs, 5 Feb. 1966, Gold-Folsom Papers, University of Michigan, Ann Arbor.

93. Gold, *Jews without Money*, p. 9.

94. Michael Gold, "A Love Letter to France," *Mike Gold: A Literary Anthology*, ed. Folsom, p. 240.

95. Gold, "A Love Letter to France," p. 242.

96. I am grateful to Alan Wald for his insights on this issue. In his extensive interviews with CPUSA members and officials, Wald learned that key Party members did not know Gold to pay CP dues or attend regular party branch meetings. Wald suggests that Gold was among a number of writers attached or committed to the CP who didn't need to join because of their unquestioned loyalty. Wald named Ella Winter, Muriel Rukeyser, and Josephine Herbst as other possible examples of writers who were "trusted" in this way.

97. Manny Granich, Oral History Interview Transcript, Tamiment Library and Robert F. Wagner Labor Archives, New York University.

98. Gold, "A Love Letter to France," pp. 237–38.

99. Gold, "A Love Letter to France," p. 238.

100. Hazel Rowley, *Christina Stead: A Biography*, Henry Holt, 1995, p. 173.

101. Rowley, *Christina Stead: A Biography*, p. 177.

102. Michael Gold, "Change the World," *Daily Worker*, 30 Aug. 1935.

103. Gold-Folsom Papers, University of Michigan, Ann Arbor.

104. Michael Gold, "Change the World," *Daily Worker*, 1 Jan. 1936, p. 7.

105. Quoted in Wald, *Exiles from a Future Time*, p. 59. Wald's citation is "Gold to Sinclair, marked 'Early Fall 1936,' Sinclair Papers."

Chapter Six

1. "Pete Seeger Talks about the Almanac Singers," 2006, https://www.youtube.com/watch?v=RX3aP1DAH-c.

2. David King Dunaway, *How Can I Keep From Singing: Pete Seeger*, McGraw Hill, 1981, p. 46.

3. Robbie Lieberman, *"My Song Is My Weapon": People's Songs, American Communism, and the Politics of Culture 1930–1950*, U of Illinois P, 1989, p. 23.

4. Joe Klein, *Woody Guthrie: A Life*, Knopf, 1980, pp. 145–46.

5. Richard A. Reuss, with JoAnne C. Reuss, *American Folk Music and Left-Wing Politics, 1927–1957*, Scarecrow Press, 2000, p. 43.

6. Benjamin Bierman, "Solidarity Forever: Music and the Labor Movement in the United States," *The Routledge History of Social Protest in Popular Music*, edited by Jonathan C. Fredman, Routledge, 2016, p. 35.

7. Reuss, *American Folk Music and Left-Wing Politics, 1927–1957*, p. 46.

8. Robbie Lieberman, *"My Song Is My Weapon": People's Songs, American Communism, and the Politics of Culture 1930–1950*, U of Illinois P, 1989, p. 29.

9. Benjamin Bierman, "Solidarity Forever: Music and the Labor Movement in the United States." *The Routledge History of Social Protest in Popular Music*, edited by Jonathan C. Fredman, Routledge, 2016, p. 36.

10. Gold, "Change the World," *Daily Worker*, 14 Jun. 1934, p. 5.

11. Reuss, *American Folk Music and Left-Wing Politics, 1927–1957*, p. 73.

12. Reuss, *American Folk Music and Left-Wing Politics, 1927–1957*, p. 72.

13. Bierman, "Solidarity Forever: Music and the Labor Movement in the United States," p. 36.

14. Quoted in Reuss, *American Folk Music and Left-Wing Politics, 1927–1957*, p. 71.

15. Michael Gold, "Change the World," *Daily Worker*, 21 Apr. 1935, p. 5.

16. Gold, "Change the World," *Daily Worker*, 22 Nov. 1934, p. 5, quoted also in Serge Denisoff, *Great Day Coming: Folk Music and the American Left*, U of Illinois P, 1971, p. 47.

17. Gold, "Change the World," *Daily Worker*, 21 Apr. 1934, p. 5, quoted also in Reuss, *American Folk Music and Left-Wing Politics, 1927–1957*, p. 73.

18. Bierman, "Solidarity Forever: Music and the Labor Movement in the United States," p. 36.

19. Gold, "Change the World," *Daily Worker*, 22 Nov. 1934, p. 5.

20. Gold, "Change the World," *Daily Worker*, 23 Nov. 1934, p. 5.

21. Charles Seeger, "Songs By Auvilles Mark Step Ahead in Workers' Music," *Daily Worker*, 15 Jan. 1935, p. 5.

22. Gold. "Change the World," *Daily Worker*, 2 Jan. 1936, p. 5.

23. Gold. "Change the World," *Daily Worker*, 2 Jan. 1936, p. 5.

24. Lieberman, *"My Song Is My Weapon": People's Songs, American Communism, and the Politics of Culture 1930–1950*, p. 35.

25. Lieberman, *"My Song Is My Weapon": People's Songs, American Communism, and the Politics of Culture 1930–1950*, p. 36.

26. Lieberman, *"My Song Is My Weapon": People's Songs, American Communism, and the Politics of Culture 1930–1950*, p. 35.

27. Serge Denisoff, "Folk Music and the American Left," *The Sounds of Social Change*, Rand McNally, 1972, p. 112; Denisoff, *Great Day Coming: Folk Music and the American Left*, U of Illinois P, 1971, pp. 49, 50.

28. Reuss, *American Folk Music and Left-Wing Politics, 1927–1957*, pp. 74, 72.

29. Lieberman, *"My Song Is My Weapon": People's Songs, American Communism, and the Politics of Culture 1930–1950*, p. 35.

30. William G. Roy, *Reds, Whites, and Blues: Social Movements, Folk Music, and Race in the United States*, Princeton UP, 2010, p. 97.

31. Bierman, "Solidarity Forever: Music and the Labor Movement in the United States," p. 41.

32. Lieberman, *"My Song Is My Weapon": People's Songs, American Communism, and the Politics of Culture 1930–1950*, p. 162.

33. Ann M. Pescatello, *Charles Seeger: A Life in American Music*, University of Pittsburgh Press, 1992, p. 132.

34. Pescatello, *Charles Seeger: A Life in American Music*, pp. 135, 140.

35. Pescatello, *Charles Seeger: A Life in American Music*, p. 146.

36. Pescatello, *Charles Seeger: A Life in American Music*, pp. 145–46.

37. Gold, "Change the World." *Sunday Worker*, 21 Apr. 1940, p. 5.

38. Gold, "Change the World." *Sunday Worker*, 21 Apr. 1940, p. 5.

39. Joe Klein, *Woody Guthrie: A Life*, Knopf, 1980, p. 194.

40. Klein, *Woody Guthrie: A Life*, p. 211.

41. Gold, "Change the World," *Daily Worker*, 10 Aug. 1943.

42. Klein, *Woody Guthrie: A Life*, p. 216.

43. Mike Gold FBI file obtained under provisions of the Freedom of Information Act, assorted documents ranging from 1922 to 1967, Internal case file no. 1385228-0.

44. Michael Gold, "Negro Reds of Chicago." *Daily Worker*, 28 Sept., 1932, p. 4.

45. Gold, "Negro Reds of Chicago." *Daily Worker*, 30 Sept. 1932, p. 4.

46. Denisoff, *Great Day Coming: Folk Music and the American Left*, p. 46.

47. Gold, "Negro Reds of Chicago," *Daily Worker*, 30 Sept. 1932, p. 4.

48. Gold, "Negro Reds of Chicago." *Daily Worker*, 30 Sept. 1932, p. 4. Denisoff notes that songs in this category "were quickly forgotten" in the period of the Composers Collective, only to be revived after the demise of the Workers Music League and its replacement by the folk-oriented American Music League, the prime example being Gellert's book, *Negro Songs of Protest*, published by the AML in 1936.

49. Gold, "Negro Reds of Chicago," *Daily Worker*, 28 Sept. 1932, p. 4.

50. Gold, "A Word as to Uncle Toms," *Negro: An Anthology*, edited by Nancy Cunard, Continuum Publishing, 1934, 1970, p. 136.

51. Gold, "A Word as to Uncle Toms," p. 137.

52. Gold, "A Word as to Uncle Toms," p. 138.

53. Michael Folsom, "The Education of Mike Gold," *Proletarian Writers of the Thirties*, edited by David Madden, Southern Illinois UP, 1968, p. 223.

54. Lewis Nichols, "The Play: John Brown," *New York Times*, 23 May 1936, p. 12.

55. Nichols, "The Play: John Brown."

56. Morgan Himelstein, *Drama Was a Weapon: The Left-Wing Theatre in New York, 1929–1941*, Rutgers UP, 1963, p. 94.

57. Richard Tuerk. "Recreating American Literary Tradition: Michael Gold on Emerson and Thoreau," *Markham Review*, vol. 15, fall–winter 1985–86, pp. 6–9.

58. Gold, "Change the World," *Daily Worker*, 11 Jun, 1946, p. 5.

59. Mike Gold FBI file.

60. Samuel Sillen, Introduction, *The Mike Gold Reader*, by Michael Gold, International Publishers, 1954, pp. 15–16.

61. Gold, "Just Like Lindbergh's Baby," *Change the World*, by Michael Gold, International Publishers, 1937, pp. 173–74.

62. Gold, "Just Like Lindbergh's Baby," pp. 174–75.

63. Michael Gold, Introduction, *A New Song*, by Langston Hughes, International Workers Order, 1938, pp. 7–8.

64. Hazel Rowley, *Richard Wright: The Life and Times*, Henry Holt, 2001, p. 192.

65. Gold, "Change the World," *Sunday Worker*, 31 Mar. 1940.

66. Langston Hughes, "The Need of for Heroes," *The Crisis*, Jun. 1941, pp. 184–85.

67. Gold, "Change the World," *Daily Worker*, 17 Apr. 1940.

68. Richard Wright, *Native Son*, Harper & Brothers, 1940, p. 58.

69. Richard Wright, *Native Son*, p. 76.

70. Richard Wright, *Native Son,* pp. 78–79, 88.

71. Richard Wright, *Native Son*, p. 81.

72. Hazel Rowley, *Christina Stead*, 177.

73. Gold, "Change the World," *Daily Worker*, 17 Apr. 1940.

74. Gold, "Change the World," 29 Apr. 1940, p. 7.

75. Wald, *Exiles from a Future Time*, p. 60.

76. Art Shields, "They Won't Be Fooled As They Were in '17." *Daily Worker*, 14 Feb. 1940, p. 7.

77. John Gold, "John Reed: He Loved the People," *New Masses*, 22 Oct. 1940, p. 10.

78. Michael Gold, "The Second American Renaissance," *Mike Gold: A Literary Anthology*, edited by Folsom, p. 244.

79. Gold, "The Second American Renaissance," p. 244.

80. Gold, "The Second American Renaissance," p. 253, 254.

81. Michael Gold, *The Hollow Men*, International Publishers, 1941, pp. 87–88.

82. Gold, *The Hollow Men*, pp. 95–96.

83. Carlos Baker, *Ernest Hemingway: A Life Story*, Scribner's, 1969, p. 459. There is also this, in a letter from Baker to Michael Folsom of July 1971, located in the Gold-Folsom Papers: "[Hemingway] had his innings with Eastman and Gold. The enmity towards Gold is all mixed up with the Spanish Civil War, as you know. Gold was never one to spare the adjective, especially the vituperative, and EH (a non-adjective man) resented them all." (Gold-Folsom Papers)

Chapter Seven

1. Millen Brand, "Mike Gold's Scathing Expose of the Literary Renegades Shows His Love of the People," *Daily Worker*, 4 May 1941, p. 4.

2. Brand, "Mike Gold's Scathing Expose of the Literary Renegades Shows His Love of the People," p. 4.

3. Brand, "Mike Gold's Scathing Expose of the Literary Renegades Shows His Love of the People," p. 4.

4. Patrick Chura, *Vital Contact: Downclassing Adventures in American Literature from Herman Melville to Richard Wright*, Routledge, 2005.

5. Millen Brand, "Mike Gold's Scathing Expose of the Literary Renegades Shows His Love of the People," *Daily Worker*, 4 May 1941, p. 4.

6. Other recent academic treatments of slumming and vital contact include Laura Hapke, *Labor's Text: The Worker in American Fiction*, Rutgers UP, 2001; Keith Gandal, *The Virtues of the Vicious; Jacob Riis, Stephen Crane, and the Spectacle of the Slum*, Oxford UP, 1997; Mark Pittenger, "A World of Difference: Constructing the Underclass in Progressive America," *American Quarterly* vol. 49, no. 1, 1997, pp. 26–65; and Eric Schocket, "Undercover Explorations of the 'Other Half,' Or, the Writer as Class Transvestite," *Representations*, vol. 64, fall 1998, pp. 109–33.

7. Millen Brand, "Mike Gold's Scathing Expose of the Literary Renegades Shows His Love of the People," *Daily Worker*, 4 May 1941, p. 4.

8. Gold, "Change the World," *Daily Worker*, 9 Dec. 1941, p. 7.

9. Gold, "Change the World," *Daily Worker*, 16 Dec. 1941, p. 7.

10. Gold, "Change the World," *Daily Worker*, 11 Dec. 1941, p. 7.

11. Gold, "Change the World," *Daily Worker*, 6 Jan. 1942, p. 7.

12. Gold, "Change the World," *Daily Worker*, 18 Dec. 1941, p. 7.

13. Gold, "Change the World," *Daily Worker*, 24 Apr. 1940, p. 7.

14. Gold, "Change the World," *Daily Worker*, 14 Jan. 1941, p. 7.

15. Gold, "Change the World," *Daily Worker*, 14 Jan. 1941, p. 7.

16. Gold, "Change the World," *Daily Worker*, 30 Jan. 1941, p. 7.

17. Gold, "Change the World," *Daily Worker*, 12 Apr. 1941, p. 7.

18. "A Letter of Appreciation," *Daily Worker*, 19 Jan. 1942, p. 6.

19. "Newlyweds Send Request to Mike Gold," *Daily Worker*, 27 Jan. 1942, p. 6.

20. Ron Capshaw, "The Recantation of Albert Maltz: A Pre-History of PC Stalinism," *Tablet*, 27 Oct. 7, 2016.

21. Gold, "Change the World," *Daily Worker*, 29 Dec. 1944, p. 7.

22. Gold, "Change the World," *Daily Worker*, 23 Feb. 1946, p. 7.

23. Isidor Schneider, "Background to Error," *New Masses*, Feb. 12, 1946, p. 25.

24. Albert Maltz, "What Shall We Ask of Writers?," *New Masses,* Feb. 12, 1946, p. 19.

25. Maltz, "What Shall We Ask of Writers?," pp. 22, 20.

26. Quoted in Ron Capshaw, "The Recantation of Albert Maltz: A Pre-History of PC Stalinism," *Tablet*, 27 October 2016, and in David King Dunaway, *How Can I Keep from Singing: Pete Seeger*, McGraw Hill, 1981.

27. Colin Burnett, "The 'Albert Maltz Affair' and the Debate over Para-Marxist Formalism in *New Masses, 1945–1946*," *Journal of American Studies*, vol. 48, no. 1, 2014, pp. 229–50, 223, 240.

28. Gold, "Change the World," *Daily Worker*, 12 Feb. 1946, p. 7.

29. Gold, "Change the World," *Daily Worker*, 12 Feb. 1946, p. 7.

30. Gold, "Change the World," *Daily Worker*, 16 Mar. 1946, p. 7.

31. Gold, "Change the World," *Daily Worker*, 16 Mar. 1946, p. 7.

32. Gold, "Change the World," *Daily Worker*, 16 Mar. 1946, p. 7.

33. Gold, "Change the World," *Daily Worker*, 23 Feb. 1946, p. 7.

34. Albert Maltz, quoted in Gold, "Change the World," *Daily Worker*, 23 Feb. 1946, p. 7.

35. Gold, "Change the World," *Daily Worker*, 23 Feb. 1946, p. 7.

36. See Burnett, "The 'Albert Maltz Affair' and the Debate over Para-Marxist Formalism in *New Masses, 1945–1946*," pp. 227–28.

37. See the title of chapter 7 of Larry Ceplair and Steven Englund, *The Inquisition in Hollywood: Politics in the Film Community, 1930–1960*, U of Illinois P, 2003.

38. Quoted in Burnett, "The 'Albert Maltz Affair' and the Debate over Para-Marxist Formalism in *New Masses, 1945–1946*," p. 230.

39. Isidor Schneider, "Probing Writers' Problems," *New Masses*, 23 Oct. 1945, p. 22.

40. Burnett, "The 'Albert Maltz Affair' and the Debate over Para-Marxist Formalism in *New Masses, 1945–1946*," p. 228.

41. Wald, *Exiles from a Future Time*, p. 68.

42. Philip Mindil "Behind the Scenes," *Conversations with Eugene O'Neill*, edited by Mark Estrin, U of Mississippi P, 1990, p. 4.

43. Harry Kemp, "Out of Provincetown: A Memoir of Eugene O'Neill," in *Conversations with Eugene O'Neill*, ed. Estrin, p. 95.

44. Quoted in David Roessel, " 'What Made You Leave the Movement?' O'Neill, Mike Gold, and the Radicalism of the Provincetown Players," *Eugene O'Neill and His Early Contemporaries*, edited by Robert Dowling and Eileen Hermann, McFarland, 2011, pp. 230–50, 237–38.

45. Gold, "Change the World," *Daily Worker*, 27 Oct. 1946, p. 8.

46. Heywood Broun, "It Seems to Me," *New York World*, 25 Apr. 1922, p. 13, quoted in Roessel, "'What Made You Leave the Movement?' O'Neill, Mike Gold, and the Radicalism of the Provincetown Players," p. 241.

47. Gold, "Towards Proletarian Art," *Mike Gold: A Literary Anthology*, edited by Michael Folsom, International Publishers, 1972, p. 64.

48. Roessel, "'What Made You Leave the Movement?' O'Neill, Mike Gold, and the Radicalism of the Provincetown Players," p. 246.

49. Gold, "A Bourgeois Hamlet of Our Time," *New Masses*, 10 Apr. 1934, pp. 28–29.

50. Eugene O'Neill, *Long Day's Journey into Night*, Yale UP, 1956, p. 109.

51. O'Neill, *Long Day's Journey into Night*, pp. 146–47.

52. See the chapter, "Alternative Initiatives of Dos Passos, Steinbeck and Wright," in Patrick Chura, *Vital Contact: Downclassing Journeys in American Literature from Herman Melville to Richard Wright*, Routledge, 2005.

53. Gold, "Change the World," *Daily Worker*, 27 Oct. 1946, p. 8.

54. Gold, unpublished memoirs, 3 Nov. 1966, Gold-Folsom Papers, University of Michigan, Ann Arbor.

55. Gold, unpublished memoirs, 3 Nov. 1966.

56. Jackson Breyer, ed., *The Theatre We Worked For: The Letters of Eugene O'Neill to Kenneth McGowan*, Yale UP, 1982, p. 90.

57. O'Neill, *Selected Letters*, p. 206.

58. Michael Gold, "Why I Am a Communist," *Mike Gold: A Literary Anthology*, edited by Folsom, p. 210.

59. Joseph Freeman, *An American Testament: A Narrative of Rebels and Romantics* (Henry Holt, 1936, r. Farrar Strauss and Giroux, 1973), p. 633.

60. Manny Granich, Oral History Interviews, Grace and Max Granich Papers, Tamiment Library and Robert F. Wagner Labor Archives, New York University.

61. Gold, "Change the World," *Daily Worker*, 3 Sept. 1946.

62. Gold, "Change the World," *Daily Worker*, 3 Sept. 1946.

63. Gold, "Change the World," *Daily Worker*, 7 Sept. 1946.

64. Gold, "Change the World," *Daily Worker*, 7 Sept. 1946.

65. Gold, "Change the World," *Daily Worker*, 10 Sept. 1946.

66. Gold, "Change the World," *Daily Worker*, 10 Sept. 1946.

67. Gold, "Change the World," *Daily Worker*, 10 Sept. 1946.

68. Gold, "Change the World," *Daily Worker*, 10 Sept. 1946.

69. Manny Granich, Oral History Interviews.

70. Gold, "Change the World," *Daily Worker*, 26 May 1947, p. 6.

71. Michael Gold, FBI file obtained under provisions of the Freedom of Information Act, assorted documents ranging from 1922 to 1967, Internal case file no. 1385228-0.

72. Carl Granich, personal interview, 9 Jan. 2018.

73. Gold, "Change the World," *The Worker*, 6 Oct. 1957, p. 7.

74. Carl Granich, personal interview, 9 Jan. 2018.

75. Michael Gold, "Song for Roosevelt," unpublished manuscript, c. 1948, Gold-Folsom Papers, University of Michigan, Ann Arbor. All quotations from the play are from this manuscript.

76. Gold, "Change the World," *Daily Worker*, 14 Jan. 1944.

77. Philip Roth, "The Story Behind 'The Plot Against America,'" *New York Times*, 19 Sept. 2004, p. 10.

Chapter Eight

1. Gold, autobiographical notes, c. 1951, unpublished manuscript, Gold-Folsom Papers, University of Michigan, Ann Arbor.

2. Wald, *Exiles from a Future Time: The Forging of the Mid-Twentieth-Century Literary Left*. U of North Carolina P, 2002, p. 61.

3. FBI memo dated 21 Apr. 1950. Mike Gold FBI file, obtained under provisions of the Freedom of Information Act. Assorted documents dated 1922 to 1967, internal case file no. 100-14207.

4. Al Richmond, *A Long View From the Left: Memoirs of an American Revolutionary*, Houghton Mifflin, 1973, p. 383.

5. See Gold's FBI file and Wald, *Exiles from a Future Time*, p. 61.

6. Imani Perry, *Looking for Lorraine: The Radiant and Radical Life of Lorraine Hansberry*, Beacon Press, 2019, p. 68.

7. Carl Granich, personal interview, 9 Jan. 2018.

8. Nick Granich, personal interview, 4 Jun. 2018.

9. Carl Granich, personal interview, 15 Nov. 2017.

10. Carl Granich, personal interview, 9 Jan, 2018.

11. Judy Kaplan and Linn Shapiro, *Red Diapers: Growing up in the Communist Left*, U of Illinois P, 1998; Paul C. Mishler, *Raising Reds: The Young Pioneers, Radical Summer Camps, and Communist Political Culture in the United States*, Columbia UP, 1999. See also Robbie Lieberman's review of these works, "*Raising Reds: The Young Pioneers, Radical Summer Camps, and Communist Political Culture in the United States. By Paul C. Mishler. (New York: Columbia University Press) and Red Diapers: Growing Up in the Communist Left. Ed. by Judy Kaplan and Linn Shapiro. (Urbana: University of Illinois Press) (book reviews), Journal of American History*, vol. 87, no. 2, Sept. 2000, pp. 717–18.

12. Mike Gold FBI file obtained under provisions of the Freedom of Information Act. Assorted documents dated 1922 to 1967, internal case file no. 100-14207.

13. David Wellman, "Mistaken Identities," *Red Diapers*, edited by Kaplan and Shapiro, p. 174.

14. Mike Gold FBI file.

15. W. E. B. Du Bois, *In Battle for Peace*, Masses & Mainstream, 1952, p. 152.

16. Mike Gold FBI file.

17. Dorothy Day, "Michael Gold," *The Catholic Worker*, June 1967, pp. 2, 8.

18. Kate Hennessey, *Dorothy Day: The World Will be Saved by Beauty*, Scribner's, 2017, pp. 62–63.

19. Dorothy Day, "Having a Baby," *New Masses*, Jun. 1928, pp. 5–6.

20. Hennessey, *Dorothy Day: The World Will be Saved by Beauty*, pp. 252–53.

21. Hennessey, *Dorothy Day: The World Will be Saved by Beauty*, p. 85.

22. Mike Gold to Dorothy Day, n.d., 1952. Marquette University Raynor Memorial Library Special Collections.

23. Mike Gold to Dorothy Day, n.d., 1952.

24. Mike Gold to Dorothy Day, n.d., 1953.

25. Mike Gold to Dorothy Day, n.d., 1953.

26. Mike Gold to Dorothy Day, n.d., 1953.

27. Kate Hennessey, *Dorothy Day: The World Will be Saved by Beauty*, p. 186.

28. Gold, "The French Call it the 'Dirty War,'" *National Guardian*, 23 Jul. 1950, p. 8.

29. Nick Granich, personal interview, 4 Jun. 2018.

30. Michael Gold, *The Hollow Men*, International Publishers, pp. 96, 88.

31. Martha Millet, *The Rosenbergs*, by Martha Millet, Sierra Press, 1957, n.p.

32. Martha Millet, Introduction, *The Rosenbergs*, by Martha Millet, Sierra Press, 1957, n.p.

33. Carl Granich, personal interview, 9 Jan. 2018.

34. William G. Roy, Reds, Whites and Blues, *Social Movements, Folk Music, and Race in the United States*. Princeton UP, 2010, p. 5.

35. Roy, *Reds, Whites, and Blues, Social Movements, Folk Music, and Race in the United States*, p. 136.

36. Robbie Lieberman, *"My Song Is My Weapon": People's Songs, American Communism, and the Politics of Culture 1930–1950*, U of Illinois P, 1989, p. 124.

37. Lieberman, *"My Song Is My Weapon": People's Songs, American Communism, and the Politics of Culture 1930–1950*, p. 125.

38. Lieberman, *"My Song Is My Weapon": People's Songs, American Communism, and the Politics of Culture 1930–1950*, p. 118.

39. Quoted in Lieberman, *"My Song Is My Weapon": People's Songs, American Communism, and the Politics of Culture 1930–1950*, p. 125, from a 1983 interview with Ernie Lieberman.

40. W. E. B. Du Bois, *In Battle for Peace*, Masses & Mainstream, o. 49.

41. Gerald Horne, *Race Woman: The Lives of Shirley Graham Du Bois*, New York UP, 2000, p. 135.

42. Du Bois, *In Battle for Peace*, p. 152.

43. Horne, *Race Woman: The Lives of Shirley Graham Du Bois*, p. 148.

44. Graham said that David's "passport was taken away and he had other difficulties" because of "the oppression and senseless hysteria sweeping our country." Shirley Graham Du Bois to Roselyn Richardson, 3 Jan. 1954, Roselyn Richardson Papers, quoted in Horne, *Race Woman: The Lives of Shirley Graham Du Bois*, p. 148.

45. Horne, *Race Woman: The Lives of Shirley Graham Du Bois*, p. 148. It is not clear to whom Graham referred in the cryptic comment, "In the final analysis I trust only one white American."

46. Manny Granich, Oral History Interview, Transcripts, Grace and Max Granich Papers, Tamiment Library and Robert F. Wagner Labor Archives, New York University.

47. See "Granichs Bar Reply to Red Tie Queries," *New York Times*, 17 Jan. 1952, and "Mrs. Granich Refuses to Tell if She Is a Red," *New York Times*, 18 Jan. 1952.

48. Eric Foner to Patrick Chura, email, 16 Sept. 2019.

49. Bettina Aptheker, *Intimate Politics: How I Grew Up Red, Fought for Free Speech, and Became a Feminist Rebel*, Seal Press, 2006, p. 49.

50. Michael Gold, "The Troubled Land," *Masses & Mainstream*, Jul. 1954, p. 1.

51. Gold, "The Troubled Land," p. 2.

52. Gold, "The Troubled Land," p. 2.

53. Gold, "The Troubled Land," p. 2.

54. Gold, "The Troubled Land," p. 4.

55. Gold, "The Troubled Land," p. 5.

56. Gold, "The Troubled Land," p. 8.

57. Gold, "The Troubled Land," p. 8.

58. Gold, "The Troubled Land," p. 9.

59. Gold, "The Troubled Land," p. 10.

60. Gold, "A Reply to William Faulkner's 'Thinking with the Blood," *National Guardian*, 7 Apr. 1956, p. 7.

61. Gold, "A Reply to William Faulkner's 'Thinking with the Blood," p. 7.

62. Gold, "A Reply to William Faulkner's 'Thinking with the Blood," p. 7.

63. Gold, "A Reply to William Faulkner's 'Thinking with the Blood," p. 7.

64. Gold, "The Gun Is Loaded, Dreiser!," *New Masses*, 17 May 1935, *Mike Gold: A Literary Anthology*, edited by Michael Folsom, International Publishers, pp. 226, 228, 229.

65. Gold, "A Reply to William Faulkner's 'Thinking with the Blood," p. 7.

66. Gold, "A Reply to William Faulkner's 'Thinking with the Blood," p. 7.

Chapter Nine

1. Michael Gold, unpublished manuscript, Gold-Folsom Papers, University of Michigan, Ann Arbor.

2. "Text of Speech on Stalin Released by State Department," *New York Times*, 5 Jun. 1956.

3. Mike Gold file specific to the Detroit Field Office, obtained under provisions of the Freedom of Information Act, assorted documents ranging from 1950 to 1956. Internal case file no. 100-DE-18926.

4. Mike Gold file specific to the Detroit Field Office.

5. Mike Gold file specific to the Detroit Field Office.

6. Mike Gold file specific to the Detroit Field Office.

7. Mike Gold file specific to the Detroit Field Office.

8. Mike Gold file specific to the Detroit Field Office.

9. Mike Gold file specific to the Detroit Field Office.

10. Mike Gold file specific to the Detroit Field Office.

11. Mike Gold file specific to the Detroit Field Office.

12. Mike Gold file specific to the Detroit Field Office.

13. Alan Wald, *Exiles from a Future Time: The Forging of the Mid-Twentieth-Century Literary Left*. U of North Carolina P, 2002, p. 57.

14. Lara Vapnek, *Elizabeth Gurley Flynn: Modern American Revolutionary*, Westview Press, 2015, p. 164.

15. Carl Granich, personal interview, 9 Jan. 2018.

16. Carl Granich interview.

17. Mike Gold Writer's Workshop, registration form, n.d., Gold-Folsom Papers.

18. Al Richmond, *A Long View from the Left: Memoirs of an American Revolutionary*. Houghton Mifflin, 1973, pp. 367, 369.

19. Richmond, *A Long View from the Left: Memoirs of an American Revolutionary*, p. 369.

20. Richmond, *A Long View from the Left: Memoirs of an American Revolutionary*, p. 382.

21. "Teenagers Like Mike Gold," *The Worker*, 27 Apr. 1958, 7.

22. Michael Gold, "Soviet Readers' Interests Include Lenin, Salinger" *The Worker*, Feb. 18, 1962, p. 7.

23. James Jackson, "Mike Gold Back, Tells of Progress in Soviet Union" (interview), *The Worker*, Jan. 7, 1962, p. 6.

24. Jackson, "Mike Gold Back, Tells of Progress in Soviet Union," p. 7.

25. Michael Gold, "A Vivid Recollection of Elizabeth Flynn," *People's World*, 26 Sept. 1964, p. 9.

26. Michael Folsom, editor, *Mike Gold: A Literary Anthology*, International Publishers, 1972, p. 292.

27. Robert Shaw to Michael Folsom, 12 Jun. 1967, Gold-Folsom Papers.

28. Mike Folsom, "Introduction: The Pariah of American Letters," *Mike Gold: A Literary Anthology*, edited by Folsom, International Publishers, 1972, p. 7.

29. Michael Gold, "Why I Am a Communist," in *Mike Gold: A Literary Anthology*, edited by Folsom, p. 214.

30. Gold, unpublished memoirs, 11 Aug. 1966, Gold-Folsom Papers.

31. Gold, unpublished memoirs, 11 Aug. 1966.

32. Gold, unpublished memoirs, 11 Aug. 1966.

33. Gold, unpublished memoirs, 3 Sept. 1966.

34. Gold, "Change the World." *San Francisco People's World*, 31 Jul. 1966.

35. "Mike Gold in the Hospital," *People's World*, Mar. 25, 1967, p. 12.

36. "Blood Still Sought for Mike Gold," *People's World*, 29 Apr. 1967, p. 3.

37. John Howard Lawson, "The Stature of Michael Gold," *Political Affairs*, vol. 46, no. 6, Jun. 1967, p. 11.

38. Dorothy Day, "Mike Gold." *The Catholic Worker*, Jun. 1967, p. 8.

39. Nat Hentoff, Introduction, *Frasconi against the Grain*, by Antonio Gransconi, Macmillan, 1972, p. 13.

40. Joseph North, "Mike Gold Won World Fame as Proletarian Writer, *The Worker*, 21 May 1967, p. 3.

41. Elizabeth Granich to Mike Folsom, 3 Dec. 1970, Gold-Folsom Papers.

42. Art Shields, "Mike Gold, Our Joy and Pride," *Political Affairs*, Jul. 1972, pp. 41–58.

43. Shields, "Mike Gold, Our Joy and Pride," p. 51.

44. W. T. Lhamon Jr., "In History's Ashcan." *The New Republic*, 27 May 1972, pp. 27–29.

45. Lhamon, "In History's Ashcan." P. 29.

46. Lhamon, "In History's Ashcan," p. 29.

47. Lhamon, "In History's Ashcan," p. 29.

48. Undated letter Mike Gold to Louis Untermeyer, 1920s. Quoted in Wald, *Exiles from a Future Time*, p. 317.

49. Lawson, "The Stature of Michael Gold," p. 11.

50. Azar Nafisi, *Reading Lolita in Tehran: A Memoir in Books*, Random House, 2003, pp. 87–88.

51. Azar Nafisi to Michael Folsom, 28 Jul. 1979, Gold-Folsom Papers.

52. Nafisi, *Reading Lolita in Tehran: A Memoir in Books*, p. 109.

53. Nafisi, *Reading Lolita in Tehran: A Memoir in Books*, p. 107.

54. Anonymous, "Mike Gold," *The Liberated Guardian*, Jul. 1972.

SELECTED BIBLIOGRAPHY

Works of Michael Gold

Fiction and Poetry

"Three Whose Hatred Killed Them," *Masses*, Aug. 1914. Reprinted in *Mike Gold: A Literary Anthology*, edited by Michael Folsom, International Publishers, 1972, p. 22.

"The Trap," New York *Call*, 17 Jun. 1917, p. 6. Reprinted in David Roessel, "Three Early Stories by Mike Gold in the New York *Call*." *Resources for American Literary Study*, vol. 33, 2010, pp. 133–53.

"Birth," *Masses,* Nov.–Dec. 1917. Reprinted in *Mike Gold: A Literary Anthology*, edited by Michael Folsom, International Publishers, 1972, pp. 44–48.

"Two Mexicos." *Liberator*, May 1920. Reprinted in *Mike Gold: A Literary Anthology*, edited by Michael Folsom, International Publishers, 1972, pp. 49–61.

"The Password to Thought—To Culture," *The Liberator,* Feb. 1922. Reprinted in *Mike Gold: A Literary Anthology*, edited by Michael Folsom, International Publishers, 1972, pp. 100–10.

The Damned Agitator and Other Stories, Daily Worker Publishing, 1924.

"The Strange Funeral in Braddock." *Liberator*, Jun. 1924. Reprinted in *Mike Gold: A Literary Anthology*, edited by Michael Folsom, International Publishers, 1972, pp. 126–28.

"Love on a Garbage Dump." *New Masses*, Dec. 1928. Reprinted in *Mike Gold: A Literary Anthology*, edited by Michael Folsom, International Publishers, 1972, pp. 177–85.

120 Million. Modern Books, 1929.

Jews without Money. H. Liveright, 1930, 2nd ed., Carroll & Graf, 1996.

Charlie Chaplin's Parade. New York: Harcourt Brace, 1930.

"Spring in the Bronx"; "The Killers"; "The Buds are Open"; "Boom Industry"; "The Happy Corpse"; "Bronx Express"; "Ode to a Landlord"; *Masses & Mainstream*, Jul. 1952, pp. 15–20.

"The Rosenberg Cantata." *The Rosenbergs*, edited by Marsha Millet, Sierra Press, 1957.

Nonfiction

"A Freshman at Harvard." *Boston Journal*, 19 Oct.–21 Nov. 1914.

"Anarchists in Plymouth." *Revolt*, 5 Feb. 1916.

"Sowing the Seeds of One Big Union in Mexico." *One Big Union Monthly*, vol. 2, no. 1, Jan. 1920, pp. 35–37.

"Towards Proletarian Art." *Liberator*, Feb. 1921, reprinted in *Mike Gold: A Literary Anthology*, edited by Michael Folsom, International, 1972, pp. 62–70.

"Thoughts of a Great Thinker." *Liberator*, Apr. 1922, reprinted in *Mike Gold: A Literary Anthology*, edited by Michael Folsom, International, 1972. pp. 111–16.

Life of John Brown, Haldeman-Julius Publications, 1924, reprint, Roving Eye Press, 1960.

"Theater and Revolution." *The Nation*, vol. 121, no. 3149, Nov. 11, 1925, pp. 536–37.

"Lynchers in Frockcoats." *New Masses*, Sept. 1927, reprinted in *Mike Gold: A Literary Anthology*, edited by Michael Folsom, International Publishers, 1972, pp. 148–51.

"John Reed and the Real Thing." *New Masses*, Nov. 1927, reprinted in *Mike Gold: A Literary Anthology*, edited by Michael Folsom, International Publishers, 1972, pp. 152–56.

"Floyd Dell Resigns." *New Masses*, Jul. 1929, pp. 10–11.

"Notes on Crap Shooting, etc." *New Masses*, Sept. 1929, pp. 10–12.

"Letter from a Clam-Digger." *New Masses*, Nov. 1929, reprinted in *Mike Gold: A Literary Anthology*, edited by Michael Folsom, International Publishers, 1972, pp. 190–93.

"American Jungle Notes." *New Masses*, Dec. 1929, pp. 8–10.

"A New Program for Writers." *New Masses*, Jan. 1930, p. 21.

"A Proletarian Novel?" *New Republic*, 4 Jun. 1930, p. 74.

"Proletarian Realism." *New Masses*, Sept. 1930, reprinted in *Mike Gold: A Literary Anthology*, edited by Michael Folsom, International Publishers, 1972, pp. 203–08.

"Wilder, Prophet of the Genteel Christ." *New Republic*, Oct. 22, 1930, reprinted in *Mike Gold: A Literary Anthology*, edited by Michael Folsom, International Publishers, 1972, pp. 197–202.

"Notes from Kharkov." *New Masses*, Mar. 1931, pp. 4–6. "Why I Am a Communist." *New Masses*, Sept. 1932, reprinted in *Mike Gold: A Literary Anthology*, edited by Michael Folsom, International Publishers, 1972, pp. 209–14.

"Negro Reds of Chicago." *Daily Worker*, 28 and 30 Sept. 1932.

"The Education of John Dos Passos." *The English Journal*, vol. 22, no. 2, Feb. 1933, pp. 87–97.

"A Word as to Uncle Toms." *Negro: An Anthology*, edited by Nancy Cunard, Continuum Publishing, 1934, reprint, 1970.

Change the World! International Publishers, 1938.

"Just Like Lindbergh's Baby." *Change the World!*, International Publishers, 1938.

Introduction." *Langston Hughes, A New Song*, International Workers Order, 1938.

The Hollow Men. International Publishers, 1941.

"William L. Patterson Militant Leader." *Mases & Mainstream*, Feb. 1951, pp. 34–43.

"The Masses Tradition." *Masses & Mainstream*, Aug. 1951, pp. 45–55.

"The Troubled Land." *Masses & Mainstream*, Jul. 1954, pp. 1–10.

"A Reply to William Faulkner's 'Thinking with the Blood.'" *National Guardian*, 7 Apr. 1956.

A Jewish Childhood in the New York Slums. Individual essays first published in *People's World*, Apr.–Oct. 1959, reprinted in *Mike Gold: A Literary Anthology*, edited by Michael Folsom, International Publishers, 1972, pp. 292–319.

Flame masthead. N.d., Gold-Folsom Papers, University of Michigan, Ann Arbor.

Published Plays

Hoboken Blues: The Black Rip Van Winkle; A Modern Negro Fantasia on an Old American Theme. The American Caravan: A Yearbook of American Literature, edited by Van Wyck Brooks, Alfred Kreymborg, Lewis Mumford, and Paul Rosenfeld, Literary Guild of America, 1927, pp. 548–626.

Money. 1929. *One-Act Plays*, edited by Barrett H. Clark and Thomas R. Cook, D. C. Heath, 1929.

Battle Hymn: A Play in Three Acts, Prologues, and an Epilogue, with Michael Blankfort, Samuel French, 1936.

Unpublished Manuscripts

Unpublished memoirs. Gold-Folsom Papers, University of Michigan, Ann Arbor.

"Fiesta" (play). 1929, Gold-Folsom Papers, University of Michigan, Ann Arbor.

"Song for Roosevelt" (play). C. 1948, Gold-Folsom Papers, University of Michigan, Ann Arbor.

"The Honorable Pete" (play). C. 1952, Gold-Folsom Papers, University of Michigan, Ann Arbor.

Anthologies

The Mike Gold Reader. International Publishers, 1954.

Mike Gold: A Literary Anthology. Edited by Michael Folsom, International Publishers, 1972.

Papers

Mike Gold and Mike Folsom Papers, 1901–1990 (bulk 1930–1967). Joseph A. Labadie
    Collection, Special Collections Library, University of Michigan, Ann Arbor.
Grace and "Max" Granich Papers. Tamiment Library and Robert F. Wagner Labor
    Archives, New York University.
Virginia Gardner Papers. Tamiment Library and Robert F. Wagner Labor Archives,
    New York University.

Interviews

Folsom, Marcia McClintock. Personal interview. 14 Sept. 2017.
Granich, Carl. Personal interview. 15 Nov. 2017.
———. Personal interview. 2 Jan. 2018.
———. Personal interview. 9 Jan. 2018.
Granich, Nicholas. Personal interview. 4 Jun. 2018.
———. Personal interview. 5 Jun. 2018.
Granich, Reuben. Personal interview. Mar. 2017.

Critical and Biographical Studies

Aaron, Daniel. *Writers on the Left: Episodes in American Literary Communism.*
    Avon Books, 1961.
Berman, Paul. "East Side Story: Mike Gold, the Communists, and the Jews." *Village
    Voice*, Mar. 1983, pp. 39–53.
Bierman, Benjamin. "Solidarity Forever: Music and the Labor Movement in the
    United States." *The Routledge History of Social Protest in Popular Music,*
    edited by Jonathan C. Fredman, Routledge, 2016, pp. 31–43.
Brand, Millen. "Mike Gold's Scathing Expose of the Literary Renegades Shows
    His Love of the People." *Daily Worker*, 4 May 1941, p. 4.
Brogna, John J. *Michael Gold: Critic and Playwright.* 1982. University of Georgia,
    PhD dissertation.
Burnett, Colin. "The 'Albert Maltz Affair' and the Debate over Para-Marxist
    Formalism in New Masses, 1945–1946." *Journal of American Studies*, vol.
    48, 2014, pp. 229–50.
Calverton, V. F. *The Liberation of American Literature.* Charles Scribner's Sons, 1932.
Chura, Patrick. *Vital Contact: Downclassing Journeys in American Literature from
    Herman Melville to Richard Wright.* Routledge, 2005.
Clayton, Douglas. *Floyd Dell: The Life and Times of an American Rebel.* I. R.
    Dee, 1994.

Cruse, Harold. *The Crisis of the Negro Intellectual*. William Morrow, 1967.

Day, Dorothy. "Mike Gold." *Catholic Worker*, Jun. 1967, p. 8.

Dell, Floyd. "Explanations and Apologies." *Liberator*, Jun. 1922, pp. 25–26.

Denisoff, Serge. "Folk Music and the American Left." *The Sounds of Social Change*, edited by Denisoff, Rand McNally, 1972.

———. *Great Day Coming: Folk Music and the American Left*. U of Illinois P, 1971.

Denning, Michael. *The Cultural Front: The Laboring of American Culture in the Twentieth Century*. Verso, 1997.

Eastman, Max. *Love and Revolution*. Random House, 1964.

Freeman, Joseph. *An American Testament. A Narrative of Rebels and Romantics*. Farrar & Rinehart, 1936.

Foley, Barbara. *Radical Representations: Politics and Form in U.S. Proletarian Fiction, 1929–1941*. Duke UP, 1993.

Folsom, Michael. "The Book of Poverty." *Nation*, 28 Feb. 1966, pp. 242–45.

———. "The Education of Mike Gold." *Proletarian Writers of the Thirties*, edited by David Madden, Southern Illinois University Press, 1968, pp. 221–51.

———. "Introduction: The Pariah of American Letters." *Mike Gold: A Literary Anthology*, by Michael Gold, International Publishers, 1972, pp. 7–20.

———. *Mike Gold: A Literary Life*. Unpublished manuscript, n.d., Gold-Folsom Papers, University of Michigan.

Forsythe, Robert. Foreword. *Change the World!*, by Michael Gold, International Publishers, 1936.

Freeman, Joseph. *An American Testament*. Farrar & Rinehart, 1936.

Harrington, Michael. Afterword. *Jews without Money*, by Michael Gold, Avon Books, 1965.

Hennessy, Kate. *Dorothy Day: The World Will Be Saved by Beauty*. Scribner's, 2017.

Himelstein, Morgan Yale. *Drama Was a Weapon: The Left-Wing Theatre in New York, 1929–1941*. Rutgers UP, 1963.

Kazin, Alfred. Introduction. *Jews without Money*, by Michael Gold, Carroll & Graf, 1996.

Klein, Marcus. *Foreigners: The Making of American Literature, 1900–1940*. U of Chicago P, 1981.

Lawson, John Howard. "The Stature of Mike Gold." *Political Affairs*, vol. 46, no. 6, Jun. 1967, pp. 11–14.

Lewis, Sinclair. "The American Fear of Literature." Nobel lecture, Dec. 12, 1930, http://www.nobelprize.org/ nobel_prizes/literature/laureates/1930/lewis-lecture.html.

Lhamon, W. T., Jr. "In History's Ashcan." *New Republic*, 27 May 1972.

Lieberman, Robbie. *"My Song Is My Weapon": People's Songs, American Communism, and the Politics of Culture 1930–1950*. U of Illinois P, 1989.

Madden, David, editor. *Proletarian Writers of the Thirties*. Southern Illinois UP, 1968.

Maxwell, William J. "The Proletarian as New Negro: Mike Gold's Harlem Renaissance." *Radical Revisions: Rereading 1930s Culture*, edited by Bill V. Mullen
and Sherry Linkon. U of Illinois P, 1996, pp. 91–119.

North, Joseph. "Mike Gold Won World Fame as Proletarian Writer." *The Worker*,
21 May 1967.

Pyros, John. *Mike Gold: Dean of American Proletarian Writers*. Dramatika Press,
1979.

Reuss, Richard A., with JoAnne C. Reuss. *American Folk Music and Left-Wing
Politics, 1927–1957*. Scarecrow Press, 2000.

Rideout, Walter. *The Radical Novel in the United States, 1900–1954*. Harvard UP,
1956.

Roessel, David. "Three Early Stories by Mike Gold in the New York *Call*." *Resources
for American Literary Study*, vol. 33, 2010, pp. 133–53.

———. " 'What Made You Leave the Movement?': O'Neill, Mike Gold, and the
Radicalism of the Provincetown Players." *Eugene O'Neill and His Early Contemporaries: Bohemians, Radicals, Progressives, and the Avant Garde*, edited
by Eileen J. Hermann and Robert M. Dowling, McFarland, 2011, pp. 234–49.

Roy, William G. *Reds, Whites, and Blues: Social Movements, Folk Music, and Race
in the United States*. Princeton UP, 2010.

Shields, Art. "Mike Gold, Our Joy and Pride." *Political Affairs*, vol. 51, no. 7, Jul.
1972, pp. 126–28.

———. *On the Battle Lines, 1919–1939*. New York: International Publishers, 1986.

Sillen, Samuel. Introduction. *The Mike Gold Reader*, by Michael Gold, International Publishers, 1954.

Sinclair, Upton. *Boston: A Novel*. A. & C. Boni, 1928.

Tuerk, Richard. " 'Jews without Money' as a Work of Art." *Studies in American
Jewish Literature*, vol. 7, no. 1, spring 1968, pp. 67–79.

———. "Recreating American Literary Tradition: Michael Gold on Emerson and
Thoreau." *Markham Review*, vol. 15, fall–winter 1985–86.

Wald, Alan. *Exiles from a Future Time: The Forging of the Mid-Twentieth-Century
Literary Left*. U of North Carolina P, 2002.

Wilson, Edmund. "The Economic Interpretation of Wilder." *New Republic*, 26
Nov. 1930, pp. 31–32.

———. "The Literary Class War: II." *New Republic*, 11 May 1932.

Other Sources

Anonymous "member of the collective." "Mike Gold." *The Liberated Guardian*,
Jul. 1972.

Baker, Carlos. *Ernest Hemingway: A Life Story*. Scribner's, 1969.

Boston *Journal* archive, Oct.–Nov. 1914, New York Public Library.

Breyer, Jackson, editor. *The Theatre We Worked For: The Letters of Eugene O'Neill to Kenneth McGowan.* Yale UP, 1982.

Day, Dorothy. *The Long Loneliness.* Harper & Rowe, 1952.

Dearborn, Mary V. *Queen of Bohemia: The Life of Louise Bryant.* Houghton Mifflin, 1996.

Diaz, Jose Fernandez. "Guantanamera." Arranged and adapted by Julian Orbon, Hector Angelo, and Pete Seeger, 1949, 1963, 1964.

Du Bois, W. E. B. *In Battle for Peace.* Masses & Mainstream, 1952.

Dunaway, David King. *How Can I Keep From Singing? The Ballad of Pete Seeger.* McGraw Hill, 1981.

Gold, Michael. FBI file specific to the Detroit Field Office, obtained under provisions of the Freedom of Information Act, assorted documents ranging from 1950 to 1956, internal case file no. 100-DE-18926.

Gold, Michael. FBI file obtained under provisions of the Freedom of Information Act, assorted documents ranging from 1922 to 1967, Internal case file no. 1385228-0.

Granich, Manny (Max), Oral History Interview, Transcripts, Grace and Max Granich Papers, Tamiment Library and Robert F. Wagner Labor Archives, New York University.

Hentoff, Nat. Introduction. *Frasconi against the Grain: The Woodcuts of Antonio Frasconi,* by Antonio Frasconi, Macmillan, 1972. Horne, Gerald. *Race Woman: The Lives of Shirley Graham Du Bois.* New York UP, 2000.

Hughes, Langston. *A New Song.* International Workers Order, 1938.

Kaplan, Judy, and Linn Shapiro, *Red Diapers: Growing up in the Communist Left.* U of Illinois P, 1998.

Klein, Joe. *Woody Guthrie: A Life.* New York: Knopf, 1980.

Liberator archive, 1918–1924. Marxist Internet Archive, https://www.marxists.org/history/usa/culture/pubs/ liberator/.

Maltz, Albert. "What Shall We Ask of Writers?" *New Masses,* 12 Feb. 1946, pp. 19–22.

Maxwell, William. *F.B. Eyes: How J. Edgar Hoover's Ghostreaders Framed African American Literature.* Princeton UP, 2015.

Mickenberg, Julia L. *Learning from the Left: Children's Literature, the Cold War, and Radical Politics in the United States.* Oxford UP, 2006.

Millet, Marsha. "Introduction." *The Rosenbergs,* edited by Millet, Sierra Press, 1957.

Mishler, Paul C. *Raising Reds: The Young Pioneers, Radical Summer Camps, and Communist Political Culture in the United States.* Columbia UP, 1999.

Nafisi, Azar. Letter to Michael Folsom, Jul. 28, 1979, Gold-Folsom Papers, University of Michigan, Ann Arbor.

New York Times archives, 1851–2002, https://timesmachine.nytimes.com/browser/.

O'Neill, Eugene. *Long Day's Journey into Night.* Yale UP, 1956.

Pescatello, Ann M. *Charles Seeger: A Life in American Music.* U of Pittsburgh P, 1992.

"Pete Seeger Talks about the Almanac Singers." Youtube, 2006, https://www.youtube.com/watch?v=RX3aP1DAH-c. Accessed 15 May 2019.

Richmond, Al. *A Long View From the Left: Memoirs of an American Revolutionary.* Houghton Mifflin, 1973.

Rowley, Hazel. *Christina Stead: A Biography.* Henry Holt, 1995.

———. *Richard Wright: The Life and Times.* Henry Holt, 2001.

Roy, M. N. *M. N. Roy's Memoirs.* Bombay, Allied Publishers, 1964.

Sandrow, Nahma. *Vagabond Stars: A World of Yiddish Theater.* Syracuse UP, 1996.

San Francisco *People's World* Archive, New York Public Library.

Schneider, Isidor. "Background to Error." *New Masses,* 12 Feb. 1946, pp. 23–25.

———. "Probing Writers' Problems." *New Masses,* 23 Oct. 1945, pp. 22–25.

Sullivan, William. *The Bureau.* W. W. Norton and Company, 1979.

U.S. Department of Justice. "Radicalism and Sedition among the Negroes, As Reflected in Their Publications." *New York Times,* 23 Nov. 1919.

Vapnek, Lara. *Elizabeth Gurley Flynn: Modern American Revolutionary.* Westview Press, 2015.

Wright, Richard. *Black Boy (American Hunger).* Harper & Brothers, 1945.

———. *Native Son.* Harper & Brothers, 1940.

INDEX